International
Wildlife Trade:

WHOSE
BUSINESS
IS IT?

by Sarah Fitzgerald

WWF
World Wildlife Fund

International
Wildlife Trade:

WHOSE BUSINESS IS IT?

World Wildlife Fund is the leading private organization in the United States working worldwide to protect endangered wildlife and wildlands. It is the U.S. affiliate of the international WWF family, which includes 22 other national organizations and 4 associates.

International
Wildlife Trade:

WHOSE BUSINESS IS IT?

by Sarah Fitzgerald

WWF

World Wildlife Fund
Washington, D.C.

International Wildlife Trade:
Whose Business Is It?

Quotation on p. xix by Barry Lopez, excerpted from ARCTIC DREAMS. Copyright © 1986 Barry Holstun Lopez. Reprinted with the permission of Charles Scribner's Sons, an imprint of Macmillan Publishing Company.

Design by Supon Design Group, Washington, D.C.
Typography by Rings-Leighton, Ltd., Washington, D.C.
Printed by Automated Graphic Systems, White Plains, Maryland

Book orders should be directed to World Wildlife Fund, P.O. Box 4866, Hampden Post Office, Baltimore, Maryland 21211. Telephone: (301) 338-6951.

Library of Congress Cataloging-in-Publication Data
Fitzgerald, Sarah.
    International wildlife trade: whose business is it? / by Sarah Fitzgerald.
      p.   cm.
    Includes bibliographical references.
    ISBN 0-942635-13-2
    ISBN 0-942635-10-8 (pbk.)
    1. Wild animal trade—Law and legislation.   2. Endangered species—Law and legislation.   3. Convention on International Trade in Endangered Species of Wild Fauna and Flora (1973)   4. Wild animal trade.   I. Title.
K3525.F58   1989
333.95—dc20   89-22752
                                                      CIP

CONTENTS

APPENDICES

A. How CITES Works

Figures

1. International Trade in Wildlife—What It Is, What It Means

2. CITES in Action

5. Small Cats

6. Elephants

7. Kangaroos and Other Macropods

8. Musk Deer

9. Primates

10. Rhinoceroses

13. Seals

15. Whales and Small Cetacea

16. Parrots

19. Other Birds in Trade

20. Crocodiles, Alligators, and Caimans

21. Lizards and Snakes

22. Turtles

24. Corals

28. Live Plants in Trade

29. Tropical Timber

FOREWORD

As the 1980s draw to a close, wildlife trade issues are in the news more than ever before. Elephants and rhinoceroses face likely extinction unless commerce in their tusks and horns is brought to a halt. The world's whales have declined to such perilously low numbers that almost all countries have ceased harvesting these magnificent mammals, and those few countries that continue hunting whales have faced massive international pressures, including sanctions and boycotts. Demand for tropical timber has contributed to the destruction, mostly in the last 50 years, of two-fifths of the world's original rain forest cover.

Since our founding in 1961, World Wildlife Fund (WWF) has been a leading player in international efforts to protect the world's widely varied animals and plants. Through our TRAFFIC(U.S.A.) program, we monitor trade in wildlife and wildlife products, with a special focus on endangered species. An important component of TRAFFIC's work is helping to educate both trade professionals and the general public about the many important issues related to wildlife trade: the intricacies of legal versus illegal trade; tools for discerning whether a curio seen for sale overseas can be legally brought into the United States; the ways that international wildlife trade affects the survival not just of individual species but of whole ecosystems.

I first began working to control illegal wildlife trade in 1979, when I helped to create a section in the U.S. Department of Justice aimed at improving wildlife law enforcement. Our goal was to ensure that wildlife-law violators received the same prosecution as did those who committed other profiteering crimes, such as drug smuggling. I quickly discovered that virtually no background material on wildlife trade law was then available. The major international treaty governing wildlife trade—the Convention on International Trade in Endangered Species (CITES)—had been implemented only four years earlier, and little work had been done to pull together information about CITES, other international treaties and agreements, and laws related to wildlife trade.

After a few years, I left the federal government to work for TRAFFIC, eventually becoming its director. With others at WWF, I saw an urgent need to prepare a book offering a general overview on how wildlife trade works—a book that would be invaluable to law enforcers, traders, travel agents, and the general public. The only previous publication that had tried to do this, a valuable booklet called *International Trade in Wildlife* published by the International Institute for Environment and Development, had become sadly out of date (and out of print).

And now, as we approach the 1990s, we finally have such a book: *International Wildlife Trade: Whose Business Is It?* In this book, author Sarah Fitzgerald carefully explores the general issues related to wildlife trade and also focuses species-by-species on more specific concerns. She cogently lays out the dynamics of this trade in a way that readers will find clear and readable.

International wildlife trade is *big* business, involving billions of dollars every year in legal and illegal importing and exporting. In many ways, illegal wildlife trade is strikingly similar to drug running, currency laundering, and other well-organized international crimes. The profits are huge, and the people who run the business have no concern for anyone or anything other than themselves. Most of the profits get no further then the middlemen who generally live in the capital cities and other urban areas. Certainly, very little of the money ever gets into the hands of the hunters, the poor people in developing countries who desperately need reliable and significant sources of income.

This fact helps explain why concerned leaders and citizens in developing, wildlife-producing countries are becoming increasingly committed to protecting their native wildlife. They are recognizing that well-regulated trade can provide sizable economic returns to local populations. Part of this income is through tourism, of course. But the economic benefits can be—and are—much more varied, as is evidenced by such successful ventures as crocodile and butterfly ranching in Thailand and Papua New Guinea; management of tegu lizard harvests in Argentina; and programs in Chile and Peru that allow local people to safely shear vicuñas alive, process the raw wool into woven cloth, and then sell the cloth so that they reap the financial rewards.

Such ventures are encouraging. Another hopeful sign is the recent move by for responsible members of the wildlife-trade industry to work *with* conservation organizations such as World Wildlife Fund to develop and fund projects aimed at protecting species in the wild.

One such effort, the Cooperative Working Group on Bird Trade, includes representatives of the bird industry, animal welfare groups, and the scientific community, working together to improve the welfare of birds in the wild by resolving such problems as smuggling and high mortality during shipping. Such cooperative efforts and self-regulation by the industry are essential to police the wildlife trade successfully.

Finally, it is important to remember that the wildlife-producing countries are only one part of the international wildlife trade equation. Those of us who live in wildlife-consuming countries—to a large extent, developed countries such as the United States, Japan, and Western European nations—play at least as important a role. It is our demand for fur coats, ivory carvings, spectacularly colored live birds, animals for use in laboratory research, unusual plants, and tourist trinkets that fuels the killing and capture of wildlife across the world. If wildlife trade is to be properly controlled, and if the world's endangered animals and plants are to survive, we must all be more informed and more careful about what we buy.

It is for this reason that World Wildlife Fund is pleased to publish *International Wildlife Trade: Whose Business Is It?* By better understanding the international wildlife trade, each of us can help find ways to enable people around the world to improve their standards of living while also ensuring the continued survival and health of the rest of our planet's beautifully varied species.

Kathryn S. Fuller
President
World Wildlife Fund
August 1989

ACKNOWLEDGMENTS

This book would not have been possible without the commitment of numerous people at World Wildlife Fund. Particularly deserving acknowledgment are Kathryn Fuller, president, who launched the project; Ginette Hemley, director of TRAFFIC(U.S.A.), who devoted tremendous energy to ensuring the accuracy of the text; and editor Bradley Rymph, who fashioned it into a final product. I am also indebted to Lynne Baptista, Andrea Gaski, Lili Sheeline, and Jorgen Thomsen of TRAFFIC(U.S.A.) for the hours they spent responding to queries and reviewing manuscripts and to Joel Rhymer, whose fact-checking assistance was essential.

I owe special thanks to the staff at the Wildlife Trade Monitoring Unit in Cambridge, England, for their assistance and unfailing good nature in helping with my research. Those who reviewed individual chapters and greatly strengthened the book's content included Jon Barzdo, Steve Broad, Jon Caldwell, Mark Collins, Alexandra Dixon, Brian Groombridge, Tim Inskipp, Richard Luxmoore, Sara Oldfield, and Sue Wells. Kim Lochen provided a warm welcome while I was in Cambridge.

Other members of the TRAFFIC network who kindly reviewed the manuscript and provided useful insights include Frank Antram, Tom Milliken, Manfred Niekisch, Pier-Lorenzo Florio, Daniel Slama, Cecilia Song, Minouk van der Plas-Haarsma, and Juan Villalba-Macias.

I am also grateful to experts outside the network who reviewed individual chapters and often contributed additional information, including Peter Brazaitis, Faith Campbell, C. Kenneth Dodd, Douglas Fuller, Simon Lyster, David Mack, Russell Mittermeier, Tom McShane, Dean Swanson, Michael Weber, and Rick Weyerhaeuser. Amie Brautigam was tireless in fielding questions and frequently helped clarify complicated issues. Fran Spivy-Weber provided encouragement when it counted the most.

While these reviewers were all invaluable, I, of course, bear sole responsibility for any judgments or errors in this book.

Jeanie Kim and Mary Beth Ward did a first-rate job of word processing the text and cataloging references. Jean Bernard helped with the copy editing and proofreading. Eva Eckenrode, Fannie Mae Keller, Kim Monborne, and Ruth Wieland handled numerous odd requests, and Sarah Taylor helped track down sources.

Finally, I would like to thank Rebecca Carr, Cliff Fitzgerald, and Julia Gates for their thoughtful support from beginning to end.

Sarah Fitzgerald

"The history of the intermingling of human cultures is a history of trade—in objects like the narwhal's tusk, in ideas, and in great narratives. We appropriate when possible the best we can find in all of this."

—Barry Lopez
Arctic Dreams

PART I
Overview

CHAPTER 1

International Trade in Wildlife—What It Is, What It Means

One of the most popular movie heroes of the late 1980s, "Crocodile Dundee," introduced audiences around the world to a new fashion item—the sea-snakeskin vest. In New York City and Tokyo, alligator-skin cowboy boots have been hot items, along with lots of other kinds of reptile fashions. In West Germany—the hub of the exotic fur market—bobcat coats and Argentinean fox jackets are in demand. Plant and animal parts with purported medicinal properties—such as ginseng roots, black-bear gall bladders, Asian rhinoceros horns, and fur-seal penises—remain popular ingredients in traditional Far Eastern drugs. In the Middle East, oil barons continue to hunt with rare falcons taken from the wild.

The world market for exotic wildlife is surprisingly large. Worth at least $5 billion,* one year's international trade includes some 40,000 primates, tusk ivory from at least 90,000 African elephants, at least 1 million orchids, 4 million live birds, 10 million reptile skins, 15 million pelts from wild furbearers, over 350 million tropical fish, and other items as diverse as kangaroo leather and tortoiseshell trinkets.[1] The market is growing steadily, fueled by advances in global transportation technologies, expanding economies in consumer

---

*This $5 billion figure is a conservative estimate of the minimum, wholesale value of the trade. Unless otherwise noted, all monetary references in this book are in U.S. dollars.

3

countries, and more effective wildlife hunting and exploitation techniques.

Exotic wildlife items are usually sold as luxury goods, such as fur coats, reptile-skin accessories, ivory carvings, or, in the live trade, pets. Price tags can be enormous, especially for endangered species. The glandular scent from Himalayan musk deer is worth up to four times its weight in gold in Far Eastern medicinal markets.[2] Extremely rare giant pitcher plants from Borneo can sell for $1,000 each on the black market.[3] Rare Peruvian butterflies may bring in over $3,000 apiece.[4] Horn from endangered Asian rhino species retails for upwards of $13,000 per pound in Taiwan.[5] A human-shaped wild ginseng root in especially good condition recently was advertised for $50,000 in Hong Kong.[6] And in Japan, clouded-leopard coats reportedly fetch $124,000.[7]

All of these examples involve international wildlife trade—that is, the import, export, or reexport of live animals and plants, as well as their parts and products, across national borders. When this trade is uncontrolled or mismanaged, it can seriously affect the survival of some of the Earth's most prized flora and fauna. Rhinos, sea turtles, macaws, and certain species of cacti are just some of the wildlife threatened by exploitation for international markets. Commercial hunters and collectors frequently kill or remove these and other species with little or no regard for how many individuals the population can replace through natural reproduction. Almost 40 percent of all vertebrate species that now face extinction are thought to do so largely because of hunting for trade.[8]

Granted, for most wild plants and animals, the most immediate threat to survival is habitat loss. Nevertheless, trade remains a destructive force. At least two of the three chimpanzee subspecies in Africa are threatened by dwindling natural environments and by hunting for their meat; losses to trade may tip the balance toward extinction.[9] Similarly, black market demand in some parts of the world encourages hunters to kill tigers, jaguars, grizzly bears, saltwater crocodiles, and other predators that are already pressured by "pest-control" efforts and human encroachment on their territory.

Harmful Impacts of International Wildlife Trade

Why is international wildlife trade worthy of concern? Most obviously, because it can endanger wild animal and plant species. The list of species that have disappeared as a result of human exploitation already includes the Steller's sea cow, the West Indian monk seal, the great auk, the sea mink, and the passenger pigeon, among others.[10] The Orinoco crocodile, the Spix's macaw, and the Javan and Sumatran rhinos are among the species that have been hunted to the brink of extinction. And, if current trends continue, we may soon have to add species such as the black rhino, the giant otter, and the African elephant. Such disappearances would be wasteful—and avoidable—tragedies.

Uncontrolled wildlife trade can have far-reaching ecological repercussions. Once a species is eliminated, natural food chains are upset, and delicate predator-prey relationships can be thrown out of kilter. Unwanted pests may proliferate. Some experts believe that excessive caiman hunting in Brazil may result in declining populations of invertebrates that live on caiman excrement and a consequent drop in many valuable food fishes that live on those organisms. In Bangladesh, India, and Indonesia, experts partially attribute malarial mosquito infestations to annual harvests of some 250 million Asian bullfrogs, the insect's natural predator, for the frog-leg trade. These experts also warn that the lack of wild frogs may necessitate increased reliance on DDT and other harmful pesticides.

The overexploitation of wildlife also can be economically devastating. Developing countries, which provide the bulk of the wild animals and plants in trade, depend on wildlife trade for important foreign exchange. Trade can generate income for local people involved in hunting, crafts, and manufacturing, as well as in trade, and it can add to government coffers through taxes, duties, and direct sales. If African elephants are exterminated by hunting for the ivory trade, African nations will lose income both from the animals' valuable tusks and the tourist dollars spent on guided safaris. Zimbabwe nets over $6.2 million per year on the sale of elephant ivory and other wildlife products.[11] In Asia, Indonesia receives over $8 million per year on sales of frog legs that go to French gourmet chefs and other Western customers,[12] and Sri Lanka's annual exports of tropical fish are worth over $20 million.[13] If wildlife resources are not properly managed, they simply will not be available to future consumers, hunters, fishermen, sightseers, nature lovers, and other wildlife "users" who provide important financial income to developing nations' economies.

Industrial, as well as developing, nations have a financial stake in controlling international wildlife trade (figure 1.1). The United States, Japan, and European countries import several billion dollars' worth of exotic wildlife each year. The United States alone annually imports over $15 million worth of exotic birds, $25 million to $30 million worth of tropical fish, and $200 to $250 million worth of crocodile-, snake-, and other reptile-skin products (figure 1.2).[14] Fur and skin traders, pet-shop owners, and others whose livelihoods depend on

Figure 1.1
Major Wildlife Exporters and Importers[1]

Exporters	Importers
Argentina	Canada
Bolivia[2]	China
Brazil[2]	European Economic Community
Central African Republic	Hong Kong
China	Japan
Congo	Singapore
Guyana	Taiwan
Honduras	United States
Indonesia	
Mexico[2]	
Paraguay[2]	
Peru	
Philippines	
Senegal	
South Africa	
South Korea	
Sudan	
Taiwan	
Tanzania	
Thailand	
Turkey	
United States	
U.S.S.R.	
Zaire	

1. Based on U.S. imports and export of select wildlife trade items, including primates, furskins, ivory, birds, reptile skins, coral, and cacti.
2. This country prohibits most wildlife exports. Most trade in species taken from this nation is illegal and must be "laundered" through other countries.

Source: World Wildlife Fund; U.S. Department of the Interior.

imported wildlife all stand to benefit from trade controls that help conserve these limited, but renewable, resources.

In addition, losses to our world's wildlife could deprive scientific, especially medical, research of valuable discoveries. Numerous wild animals continue to contribute to human medicine. Venom extracted from the Malayan pit viper is used to prevent the formation of blood clots, and bee venom is reputed to assuage arthritis pain. Some sea sponges produce a substance called cytrabine that helps cure leukemia and herpes. Experts believe that several other marine species as diverse as sea squirts, clams, and sharks may prove useful in producing cures for cancer.[15]

Wild animals' greatest contribution to human medicine probably lies in biomedical research. While most frogs, rats, cats, dogs, and other animals used in laboratories are captive-bred, some primates

Figure 1.2
U.S. Wildlife Imports in a Typical Year[1]

Primates	12,000 to 14,000 live (mostly for biomedical research)
	Declared value: $1.2 million
Furs	6 million raw furskins
	500,000 to 1 million manufactured products
	Declared value (estimated): $800 million
Ivory	4 to 6 million worked or carved products
	5,000 raw tusks
	Declared value: $20 to $30 million
Birds	800,000 live (including about 250,000 parrots)
	Declared value: $15 million
Reptiles	300,000 to 500,000 live
	2 to 4 million skins
	15 to 20 million manufactured products
	Declared value: $200 to $250 million
Ornamental fish	125 million
	Declared value: $25 to $30 million
Shells	12 to 15 million raw shells
	50 million manufactured products
	Declared value: $12 to $13 million
Corals	1,000 to 1,500 tons of raw corals
	2 to 3 million manufactured products
	Declared value: $5 to $6 million
Cacti	1 to 2 million whole plants
	Declared value: NA
Orchids	300,000 to 500,000 whole plants
	Declared value: NA

NA = not available.

1. Figures included are based on the average number of imports recorded from 1980 to 1985. They represent reported trade and should be considered minimum.

Source: World Wildlife Fund; U.S. Department of the Interior.

are still taken from the wild. Experiments with apes and monkeys are used to produce vaccines, test drugs, and isolate the causes of cancer, heart disease, hepatitis, and other lethal illnesses. Rhesus monkeys were vital to the development of polio vaccines, the owl monkey is the only species other than human beings that can be used to study malaria chemotherapy, and the chimpanzee is widely used in hepatitis research. Controversy swirls over the extent to which humans should be allowed to take threatened animals, such as chimpanzees, from the wild, either for biomedical research or to augment captive-breeding populations used for that purpose.* No

*Some experimental practices also raise serious questions over animal rights. The concerns of this important and continuing debate, however, fall outside the realm of wildlife trade and, therefore, beyond the scope of this book.

matter how this debate is resolved, it seems clear that overexploitation of scarce wild primates in the name of science could prove a tremendous loss to medical discoveries in the future.

In the plant kingdom, alkaloid extracts from the leaves of the rosy periwinkle, a tiny, purple, flowering plant of Madagascar, are used to treat Hodgkin's disease, leukemia, and other forms of cancer. World sales of just one of the critical alkaloids found in the periwinkle, vincristine, totaled an estimated $35 million in 1979. Bark from South American trees that belong to the genus *Cinchona* has been used for centuries to fight malaria. In the early 1800s, researchers discovered ways to extract the trees' active quinine ingredient for commercial sale. The drug became the major treatment for malaria, until medical technologists in the early 1900s uncovered ways to synthesize chemical substitutes, using the chemical structure of quinine as a model.[16] According to Mark Plotkin, director of World Wildlife Fund's (WWF's) Plant Conservation Program, "one-fourth of all prescriptions written in the United States contain an ingredient derived from plants, many from the tropics."[17]

Wild plants also make it easier to grow diverse, healthy crops by providing essential genetic variation. This variation can be used to strengthen existing crops against disease and pestilence or to develop new food varieties. For instance, by cross-breeding domestic corn, wheat, rice, and other grains with wild relatives, agricultural technologists have produced new strains more resistant to disease. Sweet potato, avocado, coffee, sweet pepper, cocoa, tobacco, and many other food crops also have been invigorated by crosses with wild relatives.

This is just a sampling of the many benefits derived from wild plants and animals found in trade and of the losses all of humanity would suffer if the flora and fauna vanished forever. It does not even begin to discuss the value of wild animals, particularly fish, as food sources the world over or the tremendous beauty and utility of teak, mahogany, and other prized tropical timbers. A full accounting would need a book of its own.*

Sustainable Use of Wildlife

If properly controlled, wildlife trade need not threaten plant and animal species. Instead, trade can be a strong force for conservation,

*Several such books have been written. A comprehensive discussion of the value of wildlife to developing countries can be found in Robert and Christine Prescott-Allen's book What's Wildlife Worth?[18] Another excellent reference, Extinction: The Causes and Consequences of the Disappearance of Species, by Paul and Anne Ehrlich, gives a careful, detailed response to the question, "Why should you care if species disappear?"[19]

providing countries with the economic incentive to protect habitat and manage wildlife in ways that allow continued harvesting while ensuring the species' long-term health and survival.

One common method for using species without threatening their survival is to breed animals in captivity and, thus, establish captive populations that can sustain commercial harvests. Ranching operations that produce mink and some foxes for the fur trade are among the most common examples of commercial use of nonthreatened species through captive breeding. Similarly, ducks and geese are raised in large numbers for their meat and for the feather trade; ostriches are bred for the skin and feather trade; some species of orchids, cacti, and other flora are commonly propagated for the plant trade; and tropical fish are bred on a massive scale to supply aquariums worldwide.

Another way to utilize wildlife without decreasing populations is to control hunting or collection so that only as many wild animals or plants are taken as their populations can replace through natural reproduction. This control requires careful monitoring of both population levels and harvests. Nonendangered animals and plants frequently collected from the wild under such "sustainable use" regimes include the American alligator, raccoon, beaver, and white-tailed deer.

In some cases, controlled removal of threatened species can actually stimulate conservation of the animals or plants and their habitats. Reptiles that reproduce rapidly and respond well to captive-breeding and ranching efforts are good examples. In the past two decades, habitat protection and strict hunting controls have helped the American alligator recover to the point where the species is no longer threatened and has been taken off the U.S. endangered species list. Spurred by lucrative markets for alligator hides and the need to control alligator population growth in some areas, some states now allow limited commercial harvests. In 1986, annual U.S. exports of American alligator had a declared value of $4.6 million.[20] Several successful ranching operations also exist for threatened Asian and African crocodile species, such as the saltwater crocodile and the Nile crocodile. In Latin America, conservationists and traders are exploring possibilities for sustainable-use management of the spectacled caiman, the most heavily hunted Latin American crocodilian; the tegu lizard, another valuable Neotropical reptile; and the green iguana.

Sensible utilization of threatened species and their products can sometimes aid wildlife conservation efforts by providing badly needed financial resources. For instance, in Zimbabwe, elephant-ivory and

-skin exports from government-controlled culling programs generate income that is used to help administer national parks where the African elephant lives.[21]

One of the most unusual methods for responsibly using an imperiled species has begun in Peru, where wildlife authorities are working on ways to use the wild vicuña without killing the animals. Under the system, vicuñas, a once-endangered relative of the llama that is prized for its velvety fleece, will be sheared, during certain seasons and under special conditions, and will remain completely protected in the wild. The vicuña wool will be spun locally into cloth, multiplying its value to the country's economy, before it is exported.

Emergence of an International Wildlife Conservation Movement

Modern efforts to control wildlife trade began to emerge during the 1870s in Europe and the United States. Much of the initial interest was in protecting birds. Wearing stylish hats made from the feathers of tropical birds was the rage at that time, and many persons became concerned over the mass killing of birds that the fashion required.[22] Some of the first wildlife trade provisions in international agreements were designed to protect birds, particularly those that were considered valuable in controlling crop pests or were hunted for food. One of the earliest European wildlife treaties, the Convention for the Protection of Birds Useful to Agriculture, signed in 1902, included a prohibition on the import of certain songbirds, owls, and other birds popular with farmers. The Convention for Protection of Migratory Birds, concluded by the United Kingdom and the United States in 1916, prohibited international trade in certain migratory birds or their eggs during closed seasons.[23]*

The first half of the 20th century brought several other multilateral wildlife protection treaties that included controls on trade in species useful to people. For instance, the Treaty for the Preservation and Protection of Fur Seals, signed by the United Kingdom, Japan, Russia, and the United States in 1911, prohibited the killing of northern fur seals on the high seas and provided that the four countries would share seal pelts from controlled harvests on the Russian and U.S. rookeries. It also prohibited the import of seal skins not taken under these controlled hunts.[25] The London Convention for Protection of African Flora and Fauna—concluded in 1932 by Belgium, Egypt,

---

*Subsequent conventions that limited or prohibited trade in migratory birds have included agreements between the United States and Mexico (1936), the United States and Japan (1972), the Soviet Union and Japan (1973), Japan and Australia (1974), and the United States and the Soviet Union (1976).[24]

France, the United Kingdom, Italy, Portugal, South Africa, and Sudan—was designed to preserve species prized by trophy hunters, ivory traders, skin dealers, and other interests. As part of its protection strategy, the "London Convention" regulated domestic and international trade in trophies of all lemurs, all pangolins, and 49 other mammal species.[26]

One of the first international agreements to go beyond the notion of protecting commercially valuable wildlife to advocate conservation of all species placed at risk by human action was the Convention on Nature Protection and Wildlife Preservation in the Western Hemisphere, or the "Western Hemisphere Convention," concluded in 1940. Simon Lyster, WWF's treaty officer and one of the world's authorities on wildlife conventions, explains:

> The Western Hemisphere Convention was a visionary instrument, well ahead of its time in terms of the concepts it espouses. The protection of species from man-induced extinction, the establishment of protected areas, the regulation of international trade in wildlife, special measures for migratory birds and the need for international cooperation are all elements of wildlife conservation which are covered by the Convention—many of them for the first time in an international treaty—and which have reappeared time and again in other conventions concluded since 1940.[27]

Among its conservation measures, the Western Hemisphere Convention required parties to the agreement to implement trade controls for "protected species" listed in an annex. Parties agreed to issue export or transit certificates for outgoing shipments of protected species and to prohibit the import of wildlife protected in its country of origin unless the shipment was accompanied by a valid export document. However, this convention, which is still in effect, has had little—if any—impact on trade. Its species list is confusing, and it contains no provisions for sharing information among parties; furthermore, no central administrative body exists to help governments uphold their responsibilities.[28]

In 1973, the Western Hemisphere Convention's trade controls were overtaken by the negotiation of a pioneering international agreement to control and monitor wildlife trade—the Convention on International Trade in Endangered Species of Wild Fauna and Flora, commonly known as CITES. Originally signed by 85 countries, CITES has 99 parties (as of May 1989) and is the only wildlife trade-control measure in the world. Nearly all of the major wildlife-importing and -exporting countries belong, and the convention receives more administrative support and enforcement attention than any other international conservation measure.[29]

About This Book

International Wildlife Trade: Whose Business Is It? provides a nontechnical overview of key issues in worldwide trade in protected species. To set the stage, chapter 2 briefly describes CITES, concentrating on results of the 1987 conference of convention parties. The chapter outlines major issues of concern, including enforcement problems, scientific questions, and the continuing tension between the need for species conservation and the economic benefits of plant and animal exploitation.

Subsequent chapters examine imports and exports of specific animal and plant groups of greatest concern to conservationists. They describe existing trade controls, legal and illegal commerce, and, where possible, the impacts of trade on particular species. Specific wildlife groups were chosen to give a representative overview of trade in species covered by CITES, as well as an understanding of commerce in nonendangered species that are of particular importance in current debate over trade policies, such as kangaroos.

The appendices supply additional references for interpretation of CITES and understanding of wildlife trade. They include detailed discussion of CITES provisions and exemptions, a complete list of animal and plant species protected under the treaty, a glossary of terms, and a bibliography of useful books and articles for further investigation of the trade.

CHAPTER 2
CITES in Action
and Citizen Action

In March 1987, Ecuadoran traders supplied over 25,000 pairs of olive ridley sea-turtle flippers to a private skin-trading enterprise in Mexico. In November 1986, port officials in Europe confiscated a shipment of 19 African rhinoceros horns purposely mislabeled as "spare parts." Earlier that year, alert Belgian customs officers uncovered an illicit cargo of nearly 1,900 African elephant tusks, disguised in containers marked "beeswax," destined for the United Arab Emirates (UAE). The tusks originated in East Africa and were probably taken from protected elephant herds. During 1985, Japan allowed enormous quantities of illegal crocodilian skins to be imported; included were over 50 tons of spectacled caiman hides from Paraguay, a notorious exit point for wildlife smuggled out of neighboring countries.[1]

These are only a few of the blatant violations of CITES, the Convention on International Trade in Endangered Species of Wild Fauna and Flora, revealed in a report on major treaty infractions presented to delegates from CITES-member countries during a meeting to update the treaty and review compliance issues. That meeting, the seventh biennial Conference of the Parties, held in Ottawa in July 1987, was marked by unprecedented frankness about the tremendous enforcement problems that continue to plague the 12-year-old wildlife treaty.

Although 99 countries are party to CITES (as of May 1989),* trade experts estimate that as much as $1.5 billion of the $5 billion in annual

*See appendix B for a complete listing of current parties to CITES.

13

M. Hutchins

M. Hutchins

M. Hutchins

WWF

world trade in wildlife is illegal, contravening CITES and/or domestic laws.[2] According to Eugene Lapointe, director of the treaty's Secretariat of permanent staff, enforcement of CITES is "maybe 60 to 65 percent effective worldwide."[3]

CITES is designed to promote conservation of endangered species while allowing commerce in species of wildlife that can withstand the pressures of trade. The convention has three categories of protection. Under its Appendix I, commercial trade in species that are threatened with extinction is generally prohibited. These species may be traded only under special conditions (usually for scientific research or display purposes). Such transactions require both an import permit from CITES authorities in the recipient country and an export permit from authorities in the country of origin (or a reexport permit if a reexporting country is involved).

Appendix I species include all the great apes, rhinos, sea turtles, great whales, the Asian elephant, the giant pitcher plant, and over 600 other animal and plant species facing extinction. Delegates to the updating session in Ottawa added 22 species to this list, including the hyacinth macaw, the world's largest parrot; the Argentine boa constrictor; the tomato frog; and the Indian pitcher plant.

CITES allows *conditional* commercial trade in species that are not yet endangered but merit monitoring. These species are listed on Appendix II and may be traded only with an export permit from their country of origin. Appendix II covers over 2,300 species of animals and more than 24,000 plants. Among the species given Appendix II status at the Ottawa meeting were several Latin American peccaries, poison arrow frogs, all hummingbirds, and the medicinal leech.

A third appendix to CITES is intended to help individual countries gain international cooperation in protecting native species. Any country may place a native plant or animal on Appendix III, making the species conditionally tradable. The species may not be traded without either an export permit from its native country (if that country listed it on Appendix III) or a certificate of origin (if it comes from a country that did not list it).

Under CITES, the burden of trade control is placed squarely on member nations. Like most international treaties, CITES has few enforcement provisions, although its administrative body, the CITES Secretariat, is responsible for monitoring its implementation and can bring international pressure to bear on violators by reviewing their infractions and highlighting other compliance problems. Individual countries are responsible for enforcing CITES within their borders. They are expected to police their own ports of entry and exit, report on trade, and punish violators. CITES does not apply to hunting, poaching, or trade that goes on within a country. National laws and enforcement activities are crucial to CITES success and to the conservation of commercially valuable rare and endangered species.*

Major Violators

The eighth biennial CITES meeting is scheduled to be held in Lausanne, Switzerland, in October 1989. What transpired at the 1987 meeting provides a good indication of the current and future agenda. In Ottawa, delegates listened to reports listing dozens of instances since 1985 in which importing nations had accepted shipments of endangered and threatened wildlife without valid documents, failed to prosecute wildlife smugglers, or weakened CITES by trading with nations that were not treaty parties. Various wildlife-exporting nations were cited for document fraud, export of protected species, and other enforcement oversights.

Burundi, which as of that time was not a party to CITES,† and the UAE, which prior to the Ottawa gathering announced plans to withdraw from the treaty in 1988, were singled out for particularly harsh criticism. Both countries are conduits of smuggled rhino horn and elephant ivory traveling from East Africa to black markets of the Middle and Far East. Burundi, a small African nation bordering Kenya and Tanzania, has long been notorious for exporting elephant

*CITES requirements and administration are discussed in greater detail in appendix A.

†Burundi became a party to CITES in November 1988.

ivory marked as native, even though the country has no wild elephant population of its own. Tusks are brought in from neighboring countries and given false permits, a practice known as "laundering." This practice disguises the origin of the contraband and enables it to enter international trade channels. Experts believe that, in 1986, some 50,000 elephant tusks were exported via Burundi.[4]

According to the CITES Secretariat, the UAE is "one of the most important havens" for illicit wildlife trade in the world.[5] In May 1986, for example, smugglers flew over 18 tons of illicit elephant ivory from Mogadishu, Somalia, to Abu Dhabi, UAE. Despite the Secretariat's official queries to UAE diplomats, the tusks apparently entered the country without hazard.[6] At the Ottawa conference, CITES parties voted to send a diplomatic mission to both Burundi and the UAE in an effort to bring them into line with the treaty. The parties also urged individual countries to use unilateral diplomatic, political, and economic sanctions to encourage Burundi's and the UAE's participation.*

Delegates criticized three major wildlife-consuming countries— Japan, France, and Austria—for ineffective import controls. Latin American nations and nongovernmental conservation organizations argued that poor compliance with CITES in these three countries undermines exporting nations' efforts to protect native plants and animals. To promote international cooperation and goodwill, delegates turned down a proposal to censure the three, instead passing a resolution calling for stricter enforcement of import controls in general.

"Japan has the largest illegal wildlife trade in the world," according to Tom Milliken, director of the Tokyo office of TRAFFIC†, an international network that tracks wildlife trade around the world. For example, Japanese demand for reptile skins has soared in recent years, sparking voluminous imports without appropriate permits of crocodilian skins. A large part of the problem stems from the government's reluctance to investigate the veracity of export permits, says Milliken. "By failing to look behind CITES permits to ensure that trade is legal, Japan undermines the effectiveness of the treaty."[7] When questioned about the lack of permit investigations, an official in Japan's ministry of trade and industry claimed that it is "the

---

*A few months after the CITES conference, Burundi banned all ivory imports effective November 5, 1987. On April 29, 1988, the U.S. Fish and Wildlife Service banned the importation of any ivory from Burundi that was not registered with the CITES Secretariat as of December 1, 1986.

†TRAFFIC stands for Trade Records Analysis of Flora and Fauna in Commerce.

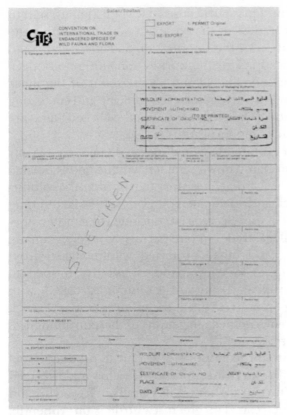

CITES export permit

responsibility of the exporting countries" to ensure proper documentation.[8]

Japan also was criticized in Ottawa for massive imports of endangered species that enter the country under the treaty's special exemption provisions. CITES allows parties to claim a "reservation" to the listing of a species and thus continue trade, although strict permit requirements still apply. Prior to the conference, Japan had reservations on 14 endangered species, including six whale species, three sea turtles, four reptiles, and the Himalayan musk deer. Startled by a report from TRAFFIC(Japan) that documented Japanese imports of over 2 million sea turtles—including thousands of kilograms of illegal shells and skins—in the past 17 years, conservation groups urged Japan to drop key reservations and improve import controls.

Japanese representatives to the conference responded by abolishing reservations on the green sea turtle and the desert monitor lizard, effective immediately, and the musk deer, as of 1989. Conservationists greeted this action with cautious optimism. At the time of the conference, Japan's 1987 imports of musk were proceeding at a rate

CITES in Action and Citizen Action   17 triple the annual norm. This spurt caused TRAFFIC(Japan) staff to suspect strongly that traders in that country were stockpiling the substance in anticipation of the import ban, an action that could have disastrous implications for the world's remaining musk deer. (Musk—an expensive, aromatic, glandular secretion of the musk deer—is sold in Japan as a purported heart medicine and energizing drug. Most of the products labeled as musk in the United States are scented with synthetic compounds.)

Another market for exotic endangered species, France, was harshly criticized for failing to clamp down on illicit wildlife goods flowing through French Guiana, a French territory that borders the wildlife-rich countries of Brazil and Suriname. Following a 1986 fact-finding mission to French Guiana, the Secretariat concluded that the territory was "a turntable for illegal trade" in rare parrots, monkeys, caimans, peccaries, small cats, and other protected wildlife taken from neighboring countries. The contraband is usually shipped to members of the European Economic Community (EEC), with documents declaring French Guiana as the point of origin.[9] French officials at the conference denied allegations of their unwillingness to enforce trade controls.

France also drew fire for its imports of sea turtle products. Conference delegates voted down France's proposal to allow trade in green sea turtles raised on turtle ranches on its islands of Tromelin and Europa in the Indian Ocean. The green sea turtle is on Appendix I, but parties may vote to transfer populations to Appendix II when certain "ranching" criteria are met (see chapter 22). The Ottawa action marked the third time since 1979 that CITES parties failed to accept French efforts to trade in sea turtles. In the past, the opposition argued successfully that biological evidence showed that the turtle populations involved did not yet meet treaty criteria for ranching. This time, the French plan was voted down because of the country's poor enforcement record; other nations doubted France's ability to differentiate between legal trade in ranched turtles and illegal trade in wild turtles.

Policies on trade in endangered species raised in captivity, particularly sea turtles and crocodiles, have caused continual, divisive debate among parties for the past decade. While trade in captive-bred animals provides financial incentives to manage breeding colonies for long-term, sustainable harvests—thus providing conservation benefits—it also can harm the species by encouraging demand for animals taken from the wild. The same holds true for artificially propagated plants. CITES parties have set up strict criteria for trading of Appendix I flora and fauna to avoid such problems. These measures can only be successful, however, if traders, enforcement officers, and consumers can differentiate wild (and illegal) animals and plants from those that are captive-bred or artificially propagated.

Several conference participants criticized Austria for allowing an Austrian pharmaceutical firm to import 20 African chimpanzees in 1986 for use in research. Austrian authorities contended that the chimps were imported for medical purposes and thus did not violate CITES prohibitions. The Secretariat and others argued that this import contravened treaty rules by being, in reality, part of a profit-making transaction for the private company.

Among the wildlife-exporting nations identified by the CITES Secretariat as having the most dismal record in regulating exports of protected flora and fauna, Bolivia and Paraguay were most severely criticized.[10] Both countries are perennial targets of criticism for lax

---

LINKS TO THE DRUG TRADE

Rumors that wildlife smugglers are also in the narcotics business are sometimes true. In June 1985, for instance, Miami drug investigators arrested a local couple after finding over $70 million worth of cocaine and "coke"-producing paraphernalia on their property; only two years earlier, the pair had been caught smuggling 100 Indonesian palm cockatoos. Alert Miami agents also found $33 million in cocaine wafers tucked inside tropical fish containers from Colombia in 1985. A group of Latin American drug dealers reportedly laced caiman skins en route to Europe with cocaine, passed the goods through customs, and then vacuumed up the pricey "skin preservative." There are also isolated reports of dead Bolivian parrots arriving in the Netherlands stuffed with pure cocaine.

The fact that some drug dealers are also bird bandits or involved in other wildlife trafficking should not be surprising, considering that both feature huge profit margins and that the products involved are often shipped from the same regions (for example, Bolivia, Colombia, and Paraguay). John Nichols, author of *The Animal Smugglers*, recounts an Argentine informant's report that heroin is sometimes smuggled into the United States in shipments of live parrots or snakes. A few of the animals are killed before export and stuffed with the drug, then dispatched along with live specimens, disguised as transit mortalities.[1] Donald Carr, former chief of the Wildlife and Marine Resources Section of the U.S. Department of Justice, suggests that "the interface between drugs and wildlife is more common than we know."[2]

There is also at least one known instance of wildlife smuggling occurring in concert with gunrunning. California wildlife authorities reportedly found a father-and-son team involved in the pet trade who were illegally importing parrots from Mexico in exchange, it later turned out, for U.S. firearms.[3]

enforcement, particularly for acting as entrepôts for caiman skins, rare macaws, and other threatened species smuggled out of Brazil, where wildlife exports are banned. For example, some 40,000 caiman hides are reportedly smuggled out of the Brazilian Pantanal region to Bolivia and Paraguay every month.[11] From there, the hides are tanned and shipped to luxury leather markets in the EEC and Japan.

In Bolivia, a Secretariat report said, the use of forged or stolen permits is widespread, and genuine permits are often given to illegal shipments. The country has no management program to regulate the caiman-skin trade and ensure that local supplies are not wiped out by profit-seeking hunters. Despite domestic measures to ban live wildlife exports and regulate the reptile-skin trade; an embargo among CITES parties on all wildlife imports from the country; and numerous efforts on the part of CITES staff, conservation organizations, the U.S. government, and others to improve trade controls during the 1980s, Bolivia remains one of the weakest links in the CITES system, according to the report. Until recently, the Bolivian government paid little heed to CITES and "seemed to strongly promote" illegal trade in wildlife taken from other countries.[12] One trade official was even caught selling export permits to an unscrupulous hide trader, for a personal profit of some $100,000.[13]

The Secretariat expressed optimism, however, about a new agreement between the Secretariat and Bolivia's president, Victor Paz Estenssoro, to improve wildlife trade matters. In April 1987, Paz Estenssoro agreed to a two-part program to oversee and regulate the caiman- and peccary-skin industries and to establish a completely new federal system for CITES compliance, including new laws and training programs for enforcement personnel. The first phase of the program is under way, with experts inventorying legal stocks of caiman and peccary skins in preparation for their export. Funds for the second phase are being sought from the U.S. Agency for International Development.[14]

In Paraguay, too, traders regularly export thousands of skins from protected snakes, caimans, small cats, and other wildlife without CITES permits. This is in clear violation of an existing ban on nearly all wildlife exports. A common ruse is to mark such shipments as "cow and sheep skins" or use other false declarations.[15] In one of the most blatant examples, in 1983 traders exported 2,000 reptile skins labeled as American alligator.[16] Traffic in rare parrots, too, is a perpetual problem. In 1985, for instance, 49 hyacinth macaws, of which there are only 2,500 to 5,000 left in the wild, were exported from Paraguay to Austria without proper documents.[17] Conference participants called on Paraguay to work harder to establish effective controls and asked importing countries to step up efforts to ensure the legality of all imports from the country.

Notably absent from the list of offenders were Belgium and Singapore, two countries once renowned for their role in laundering illegal wildlife from developing countries to the major markets of the world. Although Belgium—with its strong economic ties to the African states of Brunei, Cameroon, and Zaire—long has been a hub of the illicit elephant ivory trade, controls have improved recently. This has been partly the result of Belgium and these African countries participating in a worldwide quota-and-marking system for elephant tusks adopted by CITES parties in 1985 to clamp down on illegal ivory trade. Singapore, which ratified CITES in 1986 in response to international conservation pressure, also is now tightening trade controls. Unfortunately, as one "black hole" closes up, another usually emerges. In Asia, Taiwan has become a large-scale laundering point for scores of rare parrots, South American reptile skins, and African elephant tusks.[18]

The United States, the largest consumer of wildlife in the world, was not singled out for trade infractions. Although the United States has serious problems controlling illegal wildlife trade—particularly involving live birds and fashion items made from protected snakes and crocodilians—U.S. wildlife trade law is more extensive than that found in most other countries, and enforcement efforts have brought

Storage room at the U.S. Fish and Wildlife Service for confiscated illegal wildlife products.
Steve Hillebrand / U.S. Fish and Wildlife Service

Figure 2.1
How the U.S. Wildlife Trade System Works

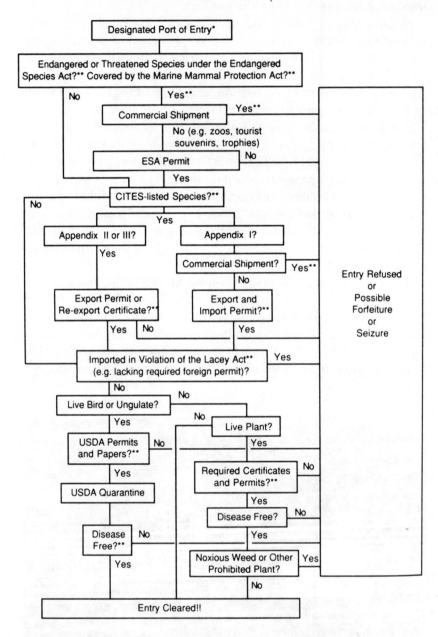

* All commercial shipments must enter through one of the designated ports of entry.
**Special exemption or procedures may govern these steps.

Source: World Wildlife Fund

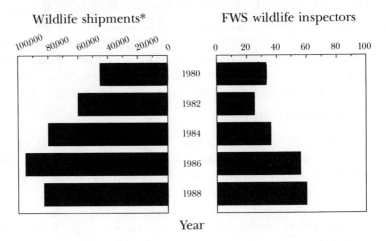

Figure 2.2
Volume of U.S. Wildlife Imports and Exports
Compared with Number of Inspectors, 1980–1988

Wildlife shipments*   FWS wildlife inspectors

*Combines imports and exports; does not include all non-CITES shipments.

Source: U.S. Department of the Interior.

some noteworthy successes (figure 2.1). The Endangered Species Act sets out domestic requirements to implement CITES, and the Lacey Act makes it a crime to import any animal taken in violation of foreign law. The Lacey Act is often cited by wildlife lawyers as an exemplary, much needed measure to uphold other countries' efforts to protect their wildlife. The U.S. Fish and Wildlife Service (FWS), the nation's lead agency in CITES implementation, has used undercover operations to crack down on international smuggling, resulting recently in major "busts" of illicit parrot- and cacti-trading rings along the Mexican border.

It may be only a matter of time, however, before the United States comes in for increased scrutiny from CITES parties. TRAFFIC(U.S.A.), the Washington-based trade-monitoring arm of World Wildlife Fund (WWF), estimates that as much as $300 million worth of illegal wildlife imports enter the United States each year.[19] "United States trade controls haven't improved since the last CITES meeting in 1985," Ginette Hemley, director of TRAFFIC(U.S.A.), told reporters before the Ottawa conference. Hemley noted that there are only 60 specially trained port inspectors to check the 90,000-plus shipments of wildlife and wildlife products that enter and leave the country annually, an overload that enables many illicit items to slip through (figure 2.2).[20]

Mexico is the major source of rare and endangered species smuggled into the United States, according to Jerome Smith, deputy chief of the FWS Division of Law Enforcement. Smith told one reporter, "With a border that is extremely long, basically unprotected, and easy to cross, it's like a funnel pouring wildlife skins and other animal products into the United States." For instance, as many as 50,000 parrots may be brought in illegally from Mexico each year. Because Mexico has never joined CITES, trade monitoring and controls on both sides of the border are particularly complicated.[21]

Bad News/Good News

In a desperate move to curtail the dramatic decline in world rhino populations, CITES parties in Ottawa voted to ban domestic commerce in rhino horn and other rhino products—the first time members have sought to control internal trade in any species. All rhino species are in imminent danger of extinction. Two species have suffered particularly heavy losses to poachers in the past decade. Only 17 northern white rhinos remain in the wild, down from several thousand in the 1960s, and black rhinos have plummeted from 65,000 in 1970 to fewer than 4,000 today. Demand for rhino horn is centered in North Yemen, where ornate daggers with handles made of rhino horn are fashionable, and in traditional Chinese medicinal markets of the Far East, where horn extracts are believed to cure all manner of ailments. As WWF staff told Ottawa delegates, "Every effort to shut down the trade in rhino products completely must be made if rhinos are to be saved."[22]

Looking forward to an update on the new African elephant tusk-marking and export-quota system, delegates were stunned to learn that African elephant populations had fallen by 36 percent since 1981 and that more than 100,000 elephants are being killed each year, the majority by poachers. A report issued by the African Elephant and Rhino Specialist Group (AERSG) called for improved controls on the ivory trade, rather than an outright ban on it. This advisory group of the International Union for Conservation of Nature and Natural Resources felt that such a ban would wipe out African countries' incentives to protect their elephant populations.[23] Delegates agreed to follow the AERSG's recommendations and strengthen the system's provisions, rather than adopt a ban, apparently feeling that the system needs more time to prove itself. However, if the battle against ivory smuggling does not have more to show for itself when CITES parties reconvene in 1989, WWF sources predict, serious efforts to outlaw all trade in elephants and elephant products are likely.[24]

The Ottawa conference did contain some good news. Wild herds of Chilean and Peruvian vicuña, which had been near extinction, are recovering, thanks to legal protection and prohibitions on trade in vicuña cloth. Announcing plans to manage vicuña-shearing operations in the Andes, Chile and Peru successfully petitioned to reopen trade in cloth taken from live animals. Observers were quick to laud the balance struck between conservation and trade. As one reporter wrote, "The vicuña decision exemplifies the treaty's philosophy: managing, not prohibiting, trade in wildlife products and striving to create financial incentives for saving species."[25]

What Can Be Done: The Importance of Citizen Action

It is clear from the revelations in Ottawa that individual governments have much to do to improve international compliance with CITES. Tough domestic legislation, including Lacey Act-like measures to enforce other nations' trade laws and stricter penalties for smugglers, is crucial. Governments also need to give enforcement efforts greater attention—beefing up port-inspection capabilities, educating customs officials to the peculiarities of wildlife trade restrictions, providing secure permitting systems, and taking offenders to court. Better communication with the CITES Secretariat and trade authorities in foreign countries would also help bolster the treaty system.

Major wildlife-consuming countries—the United States, Japan, and members of the EEC—must bear the greatest responsibility for upholding CITES and policing international trade in wildlife and wildlife products. Not only are these countries' markets the driving force behind much of the lucrative international wildlife business, but their governments are generally better equipped with the enforcement personnel, communications systems, domestic laws, and other tools needed to control wildlife imports and exports than are governments in wildlife-rich developing countries. In many cases, the consumer countries also have a significant base of popular support for species conservation, which can encourage governments to carry out their CITES mandate.

Unfortunately, many of these consumer countries are not yet upholding wildlife trade controls as uniformly or as stringently as is needed to give species adequate protection. Market forces in these countries continue to encourage unsustainable use of rare or endangered species. Japan's large-scale trade in products from sea turtles, musk deer, and certain crocodilians is one of the most compelling examples.

The general public in countries can be invaluable in stopping illegal wildlife trade. By refusing to purchase rare parrots for pets, elephant ivory carvings, spotted cat fur coats, sea turtle or tortoiseshell jewelry, endangered wild cacti, or any other items made from threatened species, individuals can greatly curb the market for CITES-listed species. As Manfred Niekisch, director of the TRAFFIC office in West Germany, tells constituents, "CITES is one of the treaties all citizens can help carry out. Everyone can contribute to the treaty's success by refusing to buy goods made from endangered species."[26]

Expression of public concern is also extremely powerful in influencing wildlife industry officials and trade-policy makers at all levels. Citizens interested in helping stop illegal trade in endangered species can write to their national and state representatives urging greater support for wildlife-trade law enforcement programs. Letters to the editors of newspapers and magazines are tremendously useful in promoting illegal trade issues as well. Direct communication with companies that advertise products made from protected species and local stores that carry such products also can make an important difference.

In taking action, it is important to communicate an understanding of the issues and to know which species are in jeopardy. The following chapters summarize key issues involving groups of wildlife, ranging from marsupials to mollusks to plants, that play a major role in international wildlife trade. For more information on wildlife trade issues, readers are encouraged to contact their nearest TRAFFIC office or their national wildlife law enforcement agency. In the United States, write to:

TRAFFIC(U.S.A.)
World Wildlife Fund
1250 Twenty-Fourth Street, N.W.
Washington, DC 20037
Or contact the U.S. Fish and Wildlife Service by calling its Office of Public Affairs at (202) 343-5634 or writing to its:
Office of Management Authority
P.O. Box 3507
Arlington, VA 22203

PART II
Land
Mammals

CHAPTER 3
Bears

Bears are persecuted for their predatory habits, not the least of which is their legendary appetite for human flesh. This reputation is usually undeserved. The average bear is more interested in roots, tubers, or squirrels. Even the most carnivorous of the lot—the polar bear—is not blatantly antagonistic toward people. According to Steve Amstrup, polar bear project leader for the U.S. Fish and Wildlife Service, these bears are mostly curious, though he adds, "It must be remembered that the things polar bears eat are about the size of people."[1] Chance human encounters with polar bears, brown bears, black bears, or other members of the bear (Ursidae) family are clearly dangerous.

Bear populations have declined markedly in many places. Two major factors lie behind this—hunting and habitat loss. At least one subspecies probably has been driven to extinction by hunting in recent years; no one has seen a Mexican grizzly (*Ursus arctos nelsoni*) since the early 1960s. Habitat loss, though beyond the range of this book, is a particular threat since bears need relatively large territories. South America's only ursid native, the spectacled bear (*Tremarctos ornatus*), reportedly is being pushed into increasingly remote regions of the Andes as farmers clear more of its prime foraging lands.[2]

Trade Control

Several species of bear are traded on international markets. Because many of these species are listed on CITES appendices, much of this trade is either illegal or strictly controlled. Three brown bear (*Ursus arctos*) subspecies are on Appendix I, the remainder are on Appendix II, and many are partially protected by national laws. Asiatic black bears (*Selenarctos thibetanus*) are on Appendix I. American black bears

(*Ursus americanus*) are not listed under CITES, though hunting is regulated in the United States and Canada, and some states and provinces ban commercial trade. Polar bears (*U. maritimus*) are listed on Appendix II and are also protected from being hunted by nonnative peoples in most polar nations. At least one other species—the Malayan sun bear (*Helarctos malayanus*), which is listed on Appendix I—is also traded internationally.

Trade Volume and Routes

International demand for bear products has propelled hunting for centuries. Since the days of the Roman Empire, foreigners have coveted the polar bear's glossy, cream-colored fur. Demand for this fur led whaling and sealing expeditions to wipe out entire polar bear populations during the late 19th and early 20th centuries[3] Potentially ruinous commercial polar bear hunting continued through the mid-1970s.

In 1976, Canada, Denmark, Norway, the Soviet Union, and the United States signed an agreement to regulate the take of adult males and to protect females and cubs throughout the species' range. Today, all these nations restrict commercial polar bear hunting, though some are more successful than others. The Soviet Union and Norway prohibit all hunting[4] Canada protects females and cubs, and controls hunting of males with a quota system that allocates the total take among native villages[5] Denmark allows hunting of polar bears only by Greenland natives; they must kill the bears for subsistence purposes and use dog sleds, kayaks, and other traditional means in their hunting. The United States restricts hunting to Alaskan natives living

Polar bear (*Ursus maritimus*).
Colin Wyatt

International Wildlife Trade: Whose Business Is It?

Japanese advertisement for a stuffed
polar bear.
TRAFFIC(Japan)

within polar bear ranges but does not limit the number, age, or sex of animals killed.[6] Many polar bear experts are concerned that the U.S. harvest is mismanaged and fails to protect female bears, which are the key to a healthy wild bear population.[7] Canada, Denmark, and the United States allow exports of legally killed bears,* and the United States bans polar bear imports under the Marine Mammal Protection Act.

The current worldwide polar bear population is estimated at 40,000.[8] Native hunts kill approximately 1,000 per year, mostly in Canada and the United States.[9] The majority of the skins from these bears probably do not reach international markets. According to CITES data, a total of 2,671 polar bear skins were in international trade in the decade from 1975 to 1985, with most of these exported from Canada. Roughly 60 percent went to Japan, where polar bear rugs and stuffed specimens with ferocious, frozen snarls are popular.[10] A Japanese mail-order company recently advertised Canadian polar bear skins for over $10,000 apiece. The skins sell for up to $3,000 each in Europe[11] and as much as $5,000 in the U.S. black market.[12]

CITES data also show that at least 268 live polar bears reached world markets between 1975 and 1985, largely from Canada, the United States, and the Soviet Union.[13] Japan and Western European countries were the major customers for these Arctic specimens.

*In Denmark, subsistence hunters are allowed to sell the skins and other products of bears they kill. The Danish government regulates the number of exports that are allowed.

U.S. federal law prohibits selling polar bears or their products unless they are used for native subsistence purposes or for traditional handicrafts and clothing. In January 1987, undercover investigators for the U.S. Fish and Wildlife Service exposed a broad-reaching wildlife-poaching and ·smuggling operation centered in Anchorage, Alaska, that allegedly involved the illicit purchase and sale of polar bear hides, as well as grizzly and black bear parts.[14] Similar investigations in the recent past suggest that abuse of restrictions on polar bear hunting and sales is a recurrent problem in the United States.

The most damaging market for bear products today appears to be in gall bladders from the endangered Asiatic black bear. These gall bladders are sold in traditional Far Eastern markets, where they are often dried and ground into powder for use in hot tea or other concoctions as "internal cure-alls."[15] This market is particularly driven by growing demand in South Korea. Asiatic black bears inhabit South Korea, but they were so endangered by 1982—only 57 bears were reported in the wild—that they were given complete legal protection. Koreans apparently responded to the ban by increasing their imports from Japan, and Japanese who owned bears as pets began receiving calls from traders eager to ship their animals to South Korean "zoos."

Black bear (*Ursus americanus*) gall bladders such as these can fetch $30 and $300 each on the black market, depending on the size and condition.
U.S. Fish and Wildlife Service

In fact, TRAFFIC(Japan) reports, most of the animals would have been slaughtered.[16]

South Korea is not a CITES party, but Japan is and thus should not allow commercial exports of the species. TRAFFIC(Japan) estimates that South Korea imported more than 280 live Asiatic black bears from Japan between 1980 and 1983, mostly in violation of CITES. Japanese exporters frequently declared their shipments as "captive-bred," but an investigation by TRAFFIC(Japan) found no evidence to support those claims, particularly since there were no registered captive-breeding operations in the country. The three wild Asiatic black bear populations known in Japan are not faring well. Bears in Honshu are under considerable pressure from habitat loss; those in Shikoku are critically endangered; and the Kyushu population may have disappeared altogether.[17] Complicating the situation is the fact that Japan has an active medicinal market for imported bear gall bladders of its own, with supplies probably coming from bears killed in China, Nepal, and India.

The high price that gall bladders can bring undoubtedly encourages the killing of Asiatic black bears. In 1983, a bidder reportedly paid $55,000 for an especially prized specimen auctioned off in South Korea. In Japan, the organs retail for $2,000 or so each.[18]

Exclusive restaurants in China, Japan, Hong Kong, Taiwan, and Singapore offer entrees made from bear paws. Japanese restaurateurs pay about $188 per paw—of various species—then turn the fleshy pads into soups and meat that fetch $400 to $800 per plate (and take three days to prepare). Most of the Japanese bear paw supply comes from China, which is home to the brown bear and the endangered Malayan sun bear, as well as the Asiatic black bear.[19]

Products from American black bears also are sold in trade. Gall bladders from the species are exported to traditional medicinal markets in the Far East and sold in ethnic markets in Los Angeles, San Francisco, New York, and other U.S. cities. In California, they sell for as much as $330 an ounce[20] and, when exported, can bring upwards of $2,000 apiece in the Far East. In addition, the animals' paws are used like other species' paws in soups and meat dishes, their claws are sold for use in necklaces and other jewelry, and their canine teeth are sometimes found in trade.[21]

Fortunately, the American black bear is not endangered in the United States. There are an estimated 200,000 or more black bears in the continental United States and perhaps another 50,000 in Alaska.[22] The species occurs in 23 states, and, although populations in the Southeast are severely pressured by habitat fragmentation, they are stable or increasing in many other parts of their range. Alaska

American black bear (*Ursus americanus*).
T. Hall

and many other states ban the sale of bear parts. Hunting is regulated, and some 25,000 to 30,000 bears are killed annually in the United States and Canada.[23] However, spurred by the high market value of black bear organs and other parts, illegal hunting has become a serious problem in some areas of the species' range.[24]

California wildlife officers are trying to keep up with black bear poachers and smugglers. In 1985, law enforcement agents arrested a Los Angeles businessman for possession of 19 gall bladders worth an estimated $16,000, as well as 20 bear paws. The man was sentenced to six months in jail and fined $7,800 for violating state laws against selling bear parts.[25] There have since been several black-bear-trade "busts," aided in part by anonymous tips phoned in to the state's 24-hour poaching hotline* Despite such efforts, a recent exposé on illicit black bear hunting concluded that only a tiny fraction of California's poachers are arrested, and many of those get off with light sentences.[26]

Little is known about the volume of trade in American black bears. One California newspaper reported that black bear poachers work year-round in the state's northern forests to supply domestic and foreign markets.[27] There are an estimated 12,000 to 15,000 black bears in California, but as many as 20 percent may fall prey to hunters and poachers each year.[28]

Brown bears in the United States also are not safe from the ravages

The state Department of Fish and Game maintains the CALTIP line, 1-800-952-5400, to collect information on wildlife poaching and smuggling. Callers can remain anonymous.

of illegal trade. The brown bear is listed as threatened in the continental United States, and on the endangered species control list in Canada. It is legal to hunt brown bears for sport in Alaska and Canada with a permit. Guided hunts can cost upwards of $5,000.

Brown bears are highly prized among big-game hunters, and brown bear rugs and wall mounts are considered status symbols in some circles. Selling brown bear parts of any sort in the United States is illegal. In Canada, trade restrictions vary from province to province. In British Columbia, for instance, hunters can sell all but the meat of legally killed bears, while in Alberta one can trade the organs but not the skin.[29] According to an Alaskan state wildlife investigator, a large black-market demand from outside the state exists for brown bear trophies, even at a cost of $8,000 to $12,000 apiece. Some underground trade also occurs in brown-bear gall bladders, paws, claws, and teeth bound for California and other western states.[30]

Recent U.S. customs data show that 66 brown bear pelts were exported in 1985.[31] There are an estimated 1,000 brown bears in the continental United States, another 30,000 or so in western Canada and Alaska, and perhaps 100,000 in Eurasia (over two-thirds of which are in the Soviet Union).[32]

What Can Be Done

Several steps can be taken to help curtail illegal trade in wild bear parts. It is essential that traditional medicinal suppliers in the Far East stop any further use of endangered species, such as the Asiatic black bear, in their wares. TRAFFIC(Japan) has made important prog-

---

KEEP IN MIND . . .

■ You can directly help wildlife officials curb poaching by being alert to incidents of bear poaching. These incidents are on the rise in the United States, even in national parks. If you witness acts of poaching or come across any evidence of illicit sales of gall bladders, feet, or other bear parts, notify the fish and game department in your state.

■ Do not buy any product containing bear parts. You may encounter jewelry or other trinkets made of bear claws or teeth, especially in the western United States.

■ Some suggested readings:

Domico, Terry. *Bears of the World*. New York: Facts on File, 1988.
Pelton, Michael. "The Black Bear." In DiSilvestro, Roger L., ed. *Audubon Wildlife Report 1987*. Orlando, Fla.: Academic Press, 1987. Pp. 520-29.

---

ress by exposing and monitoring the trade, and now additional public pressure and educational efforts are needed.

In the United States and Canada, where many bear populations are not yet endangered, citizens can alert wildlife authorities to any evidence of bear poaching or illicit sales of feet, gall bladders, or other items. In states or provinces that do not outlaw such sales, they can encourage their representatives to adopt trade bans and penalities. This will make it more difficult for crooked traders to claim that their goods come from a state or province where such sales are legal. The public can also voice strong support for regional and national wildlife law-enforcement programs.

Finally, it is critically important that wildlife agencies monitor both black and brown bear populations to determine the long-term effects of increased market demand for these species and adjust hunting regulations accordingly.

CHAPTER 4
Big Cats

B ig cats have long been hunted for their fur, fangs, claws, and other parts. During the first half of this century, world demand for fur coats, rugs, and other luxury items was very strong; hunting took a serious toll on "classic" cat species such as the tiger (*Panthera tigris*), snow leopard (*P. uncia*), and cheetah (*Acinonyx jubatus*), bringing them close to extinction. After World War II, these cats became even more heavily exploited, as the availability of jeeps and new weapons put them at an even greater disadvantage.

The United States was a major cat-skin consumer during much of this time. As recently as 1968, the United States imported over 10,000 skins from big cats, including 1,300 cheetah and 9,600 leopard (*Panthera pardus*) skins.[1] European trade was also sizable through the 1960s.

The tide turned dramatically in the 1970s. As the conservation movement gained momentum in the United States and elsewhere, people increasingly paid attention to the plight of endangered species. Conservation protests and consumer-awareness campaigns discouraged affluent shoppers from purchasing luxurious garments made from leopards, cheetahs, jaguars (*P. onca*), and other large cats. In 1971, the International Fur Trade Federation (IFTF) called for a voluntary halt to further trade in snow leopard, clouded leopard (*Neofelis nebulosa*), and tiger skins.[2] However, it was not until the implementation of CITES in 1975 that the big cats received strong, legal protection.

Trade Controls

In 1975, the jaguar, leopard, snow leopard, cheetah, clouded leopard, and all but one subspecies of tiger were listed on Appendix I, and the lion (*Panthera leo*) was in Appendix II. Two years later, the very rare Asiatic lion (*P. leo persica*) was uplisted to Appendix I status. The Siberian tiger (*P. tigris altaica*), the tiger subspecies on Appendix II, was uplisted to Appendix I in 1987.

Trade Volume and Routes

In the aftermath of the IFTF action and the CITES listings for big cats, most professional cat-fur merchants turned away from the rare and well-protected big cats and focused on the small, spotted cats, such as the ocelot and lynx (see chapter 5). Hunters and pelt smugglers, however, continue to threaten big cats in some parts of the world. For instance, the beautiful and elusive snow leopard of the high Himalayas is still hunted for its luxurious ashen pelt, which can sell for thousands of dollars on the black market. In the early 1980s, consumers with the right amount of cash could pick up an endangered-cat-skin coat in Japan, where a clouded-leopard coat fetched $124,270 and tiger-skin jackets were advertised for over $90,000. Snow leopard fashions were a comparative bargain at $33,000 per wrap.[3]

Major Species in Trade

TIGERS

One of the largest of all cats, the tiger once ranged from the shores of the Sea of Okhotsk in Siberia, through China to Sumatra, southern Java, and Bali, and westward through India to the Caspian Sea and eastern Turkey. Centuries of heavy hunting pressure and spreading human encroachment on traditional tiger habitat have reduced that range significantly and have endangered or killed off all eight tiger subspecies. The Bali, Java, and Caspian subspecies are now considered extinct, and the South China tiger (*P. tigris amoyensis*) could soon follow.[4] Although about 4,000 South China tigers roamed the wild as recently as 1949, today experts believe that fewer than 50 remain outside of zoos and other artificial habitats.[5] The Siberian tiger is down to 350 or fewer, Sumatran tiger (*P. t. sumatrae*) numbers have probably dropped below 1,000, and just 1,100 to 1,500 Indochinese tigers (*P. t. corbetti*) are thought to be scattered across Malaysia, Thailand, Burma, Vietnam, Kampuchea, and Laos.[6]

Only the Bengal tiger (*P. t. tigris*) is holding its own, thanks to efforts of the Indian and Nepalese governments, World Wildlife Fund, and other contributors to an international conservation program known as Operation Tiger. Bengal tigers numbered an estimated 40,000 near the turn of the century but were facing extinction by 1970 because of zealous hunters and human encroachment on their native habitat. (One Indian maharaja reported killing 1,500 tigers in his lifetime.) In 1972, Indian foresters counted only 1,800 or so tigers in the wild.[7] Today, there are an estimated 3,500 to 4,500 tigers in India and another 200 to 300 in Nepal. When Bengal tiger populations in Bangladesh and Burma are also considered, the estimated noncaptive population of this subspecies totals between 4,300 and 5,700—more than half of the world's 6,000 to 8,000 wild tigers.[8]

Wild tigers continue to be threatened by poachers and smugglers in many parts of their range. For instance, tigers are still poached in Sumatra and their skins smuggled to Singapore.[9] Tigers are also hunted in Burma, one of the few countries where the species is not legally protected, and smuggled across the border for sale in Thailand.

Tigers and their parts are sold openly in markets through much of Southeast Asia. In 1984, the *Los Angeles Times* reported a thriving market for Burmese tiger parts and products in Bangkok: tiger teeth sold for $100 to $300 each, claws for $50 to $150, and skins for $1,000 or more. Targeting tourist dollars, some 300 Thai shops sold tiger body parts, including teeth and claw pendants said to bring good luck and "create a macho image."[10] In Taiwan, a controversial tiger-killing incident erupted in 1985 when 12 live tigers were put up for sale. Eight were butchered, and their meat was sold "before a protest by animal lovers and newspapers saved the remaining four," according to a report in a major Singapore newspaper.[11] Tiger skins and products reportedly are available in the People's Republic of China as well. In Shanghai, an inquisitive German tourist not long ago discovered tiger pelts on sale for $2,700 each.[12] In 1986, a top Chinese environmental official reported an upsurge in the price of tiger meat taken from animals killed along the Burmese border; tiger meat was said to be selling for roughly $45 per pound.[13]

The greatest demand for dead tigers probably stems from the Far Eastern medicinal trade. From tail (ground and mixed with soap for skin disease ointment) to whiskers (a charm for protection and courage) and from penis (an aphrodisiac) to brain (a body rub to cure acne), the tiger has long been a staple of traditional Oriental medicines.[14] Ground tiger tails and other illegal products, which can be difficult for port inspectors to spot, often find their way into international commerce. In 1983, U.S. officials seized more than 72,000 "tiger derivatives," mostly crushed tiger bone, that entered the country from Hong Kong. Another 3,000 were confiscated in 1984.[15]

Commerce in live tigers bound for zoos and circuses is mostly legal, comprising captive-bred animals. According to the International Species Information System, 1,021 Siberian tigers, 275 Bengal tigers, and 50 Sumatran tigers now exist in captivity in zoos around the world.[16]

CHEETAHS

The lithe, fleet-footed cheetah is considered vulnerable throughout its African range and nearly extinct in most of its former Asian and Middle Eastern range.[17] Only about 200 to 300 Asiatic cheetahs (*Acinonyx jubatus venaticus*) are believed to remain in Iran and the region bordering Afghanistan, Pakistan, and the Soviet Union.[18] In 1984, it was estimated that cheetahs in East Africa were down to 3,000, and dropping, but were "holding their own" in southern Africa.[19]

The fur trade has been a major factor in the cheetah's decline, along with habitat loss and its persecution as a pest. During the "cat fur boom" of the late 1960s, sleek, spotted cheetah skins were made into shoes, handbags, wallets, and coats, as 3,000 to 5,000 cheetah skins reached the United States and Europe from abroad each year.[20] Large-cat furs were also popular in Japanese fashion from the mid-1970s through 1981.[21]

In 1970, public protests prompted the major U.S. fur dealers to agree not to handle skins from cheetah or some of the other big spotted cats. While this helped curtail U.S. consumer demand, European and Japanese sales did not slow until several years later, when the big cats received trade protection under CITES.

Though greatly reduced, some international commerce in cheetah skin still occurs. CITES data for 1984 show over 230 skins, trophies, or "products" in trade, most originating in Namibia, with many traveling through South Africa. All of these transactions reportedly occurred for personal, rather than commercial, purposes. Only 11 of the skins or trophies in trade that year were imported into the United States, according to CITES records, and 5 of those were seized.[22]

Cheetah (*Acinonyx jubatus*) and cub.
Norman Myers / WWF

CLOUDED LEOPARDS

The clouded leopard is considered vulnerable throughout its Asian range. Conservationists are especially concerned about clouded-leopard populations in areas such as Sumatra, where extensive clearing of the species' lowland forest for farming and some hunting for illegal pelt trade occur.[23]

The habits of this elusive cat are little known. Its beautifully mottled pelt makes it a target for fur fanciers; a clouded-leopard coat was advertised for as much as $124,000 in Japan in the early 1980s.[24] Although no trade in clouded-leopard skins has been reported by CITES parties in recent years, there may be significant illegal or underground markets. For instance, according to one cat specialist with the International Union for Conservation of Nature and Natural Resources, clouded-leopard skins were readily available in Bangladesh in 1984.[25]

SNOW LEOPARDS

The cream-and-gray-coated snow leopard, also known as the ounce, is endangered throughout its high alpine range in the Altai, Hindu Kush, and Himalayan mountains of Asia. Prized for its thick, softly shaded winter pelt, the snow leopard has long been hunted for the international fur trade.

Clouded leopard (*Neofelis nebulosa*).
Bruce Bunting / WWF

The snow leopard's Appendix I listing has helped curb hunting and discouraged Indian traders from buying snow leopard pelts.[26] However, it has not shut down all trade. According to Indian cat specialist Hemendra Panwar, snow leopard sales continue in parts of India.[27] In Srinagar, the capital of Kashmir, a journalist spoke with local furriers willing to sell her snow leopard coats for $1,300 to $2,300*; one merchant offered to mail her a coat to help her avoid customs delays, showing off a packet of letters from other satisfied foreign customers.[28]

JAGUARS

Known as "el tigre" in local circles, the jaguar is the largest, strongest, and most highly prized cat species in the Western Hemisphere. Its powerful jaws are legendary, allowing it to prey on capybara, deer, or peccary with crushing bites to the head.

Once found in relative profusion as far north as California and as far south as Argentina, this little known, secretive cat is greatly reduced in number throughout much of its former range because of hunting and the destruction of its forest habitat—though it still has a relatively wide distribution. In addition to its Appendix I listing, the jaguar is protected by national legislation in most of the places where it is found.

*Exporting and importing can add significantly to the price of furs. Snow leopard coats were advertised for $33,000 in Japanese fur salons in the early 1980s.[29]

Jaguar (*Panthera onca*).
Russell A. Mittermeier / WWF

Poacher skinning jaguar, interior
of Suriname.
Russell A. Mittermeier / WWF

In 1986, a group of leading jaguar experts estimated that only 150 to 200 jaguars remained in Costa Rica, 2,500 to 3,600 in Venezuela, and 1,800 to 3,500 in the Brazilian Pantanal of Matto Grosso.[30] These scientists, who were meeting in Brazil to discuss the jaguar's status, agreed that poaching is still a serious threat to the species' survival.

A 1986 CITES-sponsored study of cat species in Bolivia found that jaguars were considered common and even locally abundant in some parts of the country, but rare or severely declining near towns and larger villages. Perhaps as many as 300 to 400 jaguar are killed annually in Bolivia, usually to protect livestock or for sport. There is reportedly no professional jaguar hunting for the skin trade: the price of jaguar skins in rural areas was only $5 to $10 in 1986, while farmers would pay about $250 as a bounty for jaguars shot on their lands.[31]

Jaguar pelts were in great demand in the mid-1960s, when hunters and trappers brought more than 15,000 skins out of the Brazilian Amazon each year.[32] In the latter part of the decade, jaguar-skin coats could command $20,000 in New York. Today, however, although there are many reports of illegal trade, documented trade in jaguars and their parts is minimal. CITES data for 1984 show only 25 skins and

3 garments in world trade; most of these were shipped from Latin America to the United States and Canada, where they were seized upon arrival. According to Pier-Lorenzo Florio, director of TRAF-FIC (Italy), jaguar pelts and other spotted-cat skins are no longer in demand in Italy, and furriers have a difficult time selling such wares. The price of a jaguar-fur coat in Italy may be as low as $1,000 to $1,500. Lorenzo adds, however, that a limited market for the endangered cats remains in southern Italy and in small cities where spotted-cat coats are still considered status symbols.[33]

A SPECIAL CASE: LEOPARDS

The leopard* is the most widespread of all big cats. It ranges through most of Africa and the Middle East and across the Indian subcontinent to Siberia. It inhabits widely varied ecosystems, from the dry savannas of Kenya to moist, steamy tropical forests of the Zaire basin and even the frigid Siberian taiga.

The leopard seems to be a survivor, better able to adapt to changing conditions than other big cats. The main threat to the species appears

*The leopard, clouded leopard, and snow leopard are three distinct species. As indicated above, the leopard and snow leopard are members of the genus Panthera, while the clouded leopard belongs to the genus Neofelis.

Leopard (*Panthera pardus*).
Norman Myers / WWF

to be large-scale habitat destruction, although leopards manage to live even in densely populated areas, such as the Kenyan and Ethiopian highlands. Although the species is officially considered threatened, its population status is hotly debated, as is its inclusion on Appendix I. According to a ground-breaking report on the status of leopards in sub-Saharan Africa, the leopard is not actually threatened with extinction and should be downlisted to Appendix II. This report contends that over 70,000 leopards may roam in sub-Saharan Africa, with nearly one-third of those found in Zaire. Leopard populations in the region could safely withstand an annual harvest of 32,000 or so animals, the report predicts.[34]

Leopards are hunted, legally and illegally, in several African countries. Because leopards kill cattle and other livestock, farmers often trap or poison them; big-game hunters stalk the leopard for sport and pleasure; and others seek to profit from its luxurious pelt. Some 6,000 of the cats may be killed each year. Of these, 2,500 are taken in pest-control actions, another 2,500 are killed for trade, and some 1,000 are shot by sport hunters.[35]

Some trade in leopard parts and products is legal. Since 1983, a

---

KEEP IN MIND . . .

■ Travelers beware! Exercise caution when making purchases of products made of certain small cat species. A few of these are legal to buy and bring into the United States. If you are planning a trip, check with TRAF-FIC(U.S.A.) (World Wildlife Fund, 1250 Twenty-Fourth Street, N.W., Washington, DC 20037) or the U.S. Fish and Wildlife Service (Office of Public Affairs, (202) 343-5634; or the Wildlife Permit Office, 1000 N. Glebe Road, Room 601, Arlington, VA 22201) for the fur products that are legal to bring home.

■ Think conservation and make the connection. Remember that although trade in certain species is legal, the fur trade has had a history of decimating the striped and spotted cats. It can take 20 to 30 pelts of a smaller species to make one full-length fur coat.

■ Some suggested readings:

Miller, S. Douglas, and Everett, Daniel D. *Cats of the World: Biology, Conservation, and Management*. Washington, D.C.: National Wildlife Federation, 1986.

Young, Stanley P. *The Bobcat of North America*. Lincoln, Nebr.: University of Nebraska Press, 1978.

special quota system has allowed the export of legally obtained leopard-hunting trophies, individual skins, or other items not intended for resale. Exporting countries each set their own quotas, based on the status of their particular leopard populations. Each skin must be tagged and numbered, and annual exports must be reported at biannual CITES conferences. Individual importers can bring in no more than one skin per year, thus keeping them from trading skins in commercially profitable numbers.

This quota system is a compromise designed to satisfy both those countries that view the leopard as a valuable, exploitable resource, a competitor, or a nonthreatened species and those that believe the species' questionable status in many areas merits strict conservation measures and a ban on commercial trade. In practice, the system largely covers present world demand[36] and is relatively easy to police.

Leopards are a profitable and potentially renewable resource for African nations. Local hunters, safari companies, and others involved in skin sales to hunters or trophy hunting currently net about $6 million per year. Tanned leopard skins sold on an individual basis can bring $500 to $1,000, and each leopard killed by trophy hunters can generate total revenue as high as $10,000, when permit fees, accommodations, and other hunting costs are included.

LIONS

Still stalked by big-game hunters, the lion is most seriously pressured both by habitat loss and persecution by farmers protecting their livestock. There may be only 200,000 or fewer lions left in Africa. Experts believe the day may soon come when wild lions occur only in parks and reserves.[37]

Trade in the African lion is minimal and generally involves either animals destined for zoos or hunting trophies such as heads and skins. The Asiatic lion is completely protected from commercial trade under CITES. It is found only in western India, where it probably numbers only 180 or so individuals.[38] There are approximately 430 lions, including 74 Asiatic lions, in captivity in zoos around the world.[39]

CHAPTER 5
Small Cats

D uring the 1970s, CITES and national controls—combined with public protests—stopped most furriers in the United States and Europe from selling products made from tiger, snow leopard, jaguar, and other "big cats." Demand for cat fur did not die out, however. World tastes simply turned to the big cats' smaller cousins—the cats of the genus *Felis*. With their thick, tawny brown pelts, often dappled with elegant black spots and face stripes for camouflage in shadowy underbrush, these cats were used for elegant coats, stoles, and other luxury items.

Scientists differ over the exact number of species of felid cats, but most agree that all 30 or so share at least one common trait: they are physically unable to roar and instead meow, hiss, or growl. Felids range in size from the 2-pound black-footed cat (*F. nigripes*) to the 200-pound puma (*F. concolor*), and in number from the rare Iriomote cat (*F. iriomotensis*), which only occurs on the single Pacific island for which it is named, to the ubiquitous house cat (*F. catus*).

A few species are especially popular as furs and therefore vulnerable to hunting. In North America, the bobcat (*F. rufa*) and lynx (*F. lynx canadensis*) are hunted heavily; roughly half of all small-cat skins in world markets are one of these two species, exported from the United States or Canada. In Latin America, most trade has revolved around four species—the ocelot (*F. pardalis*), Geoffroy's cat (*F. geoffroy*), little spotted cat (*F. tigrina*), and margay (*F. wiedii*); these species make up one-third of the felid skins in trade. The remainder generally come from Asia and include the leopard cat (*F. bengalensis*), Eurasian lynx (*F. lynx lynx*), wildcat (*F. silvestris*), and, to a lesser extent, Pallas's cat (*F. manul*).[1]

This lynx coat (left) required 25 pelts to produce. The ocelot coat (right) was made entirely from the tails of this rare cat.
Cleveland Museum of Natural History

The intricacy of felids' pelt markings further contributes to their peril. Furriers need great numbers of pelts to match patterns for each new garment.

Trade Controls

All felid species are listed on either Appendix I or II of CITES. Some species, such as the margay, ocelot, and little spotted cat, are divided between the two, with some subspecies listed on Appendix I and the remainder on Appendix II. In 1977, any felid species that were not already included on Appendix I or II were added to Appendix II for "look-alike" reasons. Because skins of many cat species and subspecies are almost identical, distinguishing skins of some Appendix I cats from pelts of other cats can be nearly impossible. Thus, if trade in nonthreatened felids were unrestricted, underhanded traders could subvert trade controls by mislabeling skins from protected species. CITES parties felt that authorities would have an easier time controlling trade if *all* cat trade had to meet at least Appendix II permit requirements.*

Wild felids' secretive habits and propensity for remote regions make them notoriously difficult to count. However, reports from South

*The look-alike listing method is not foolproof, since smugglers sometimes get around Appendix I prohibitions by shipping skins with falsified Appendix II declarations or by using other mis-representations. At the very least, however, this method increases the likelihood that shipments of cat skins and skin products will receive some official scrutiny before reaching consumers.

American observers suggest that some heavily traded species may be dying out in parts of their range (for example, in Bolivia and Venezuela) because of the combined pressures of habitat loss and hunting.[2] Several Latin American countries have instituted export controls or bans on native felid species, but in many instances the bans have not been enforced. Paraguay, for example, outlawed cat-skin exports in 1975[3] but remained a major supplier to world markets through the early 1980s, exporting over 123,000 ocelot skins from 1980 to 1985.[4]

Many fur-importing countries have stringent restrictions of their own. The U.S. Endangered Species Act (ESA) categorizes several small cats as endangered, thereby prohibiting the importation of any of these cats' skins. They include three Latin American species—the ocelot, margay, and little spotted cat—as well as some non-American felids—the leopard cat, Pakistan sand cat (*F. margarita scheffeli*), Iriomote cat, and Spanish lynx (*F. pardina*). In addition, the Lacey Act prohibits all imports into the United States of wild animals taken or traded in violation of another country's laws.*

The European Economic Community (EEC) also strictly regulates trade in small-cat species. Among the EEC's regulations is a ban, since 1986, on all imports involving the Geoffroy's cat, ocelot, margay, and little spotted cat, the four species that comprised the bulk of European felid imports through 1985.

Trade Volume and Routes

The market for small-cat furs boomed throughout the late 1960s and 1970s. From 1968 through 1970, an estimated 1.4 million small-cat skins reached world fur markets, an average of nearly half-a-million skins per year. In 1980, European nations alone imported over 430,000 skins.[5] Then, in the early 1980s, worldwide demand for small cat skins dropped sharply. By 1984, total reported world trade had fallen to about 250,000 skins.[6] According to TRAFFIC(U.S.A.) director Ginette Hemley, this decline suggests that prized species are now harder to find and that new trade controls in consumer countries have discouraged imports of key commercial species. Hemley believes the trend also may reflect waning fashion demand for spotted cat fur.[7]

Approximately four out of every five small-cat pelts known to reach international markets go to Western Europe, particularly West Germany and France. West Germany is the world's largest importer of small cat skins (figure 5.1). In the late 1970s, West German furriers and others in that country's import business purchased between

---

See appendix A for a more detailed discussion of these two laws and CITES requirements.

220,000 and 370,000 felid skins a year, though by 1984 West German imports had dropped to about 90,000 skins.[8] As importing of Latin American cat skins becomes increasingly difficult, some of the European market for cat furs may shift to the leopard cat, a spotted Asian native. This species is listed on Appendix II, except for one subspecies that is on Appendix I.[9] The shift would appear to be under way in Italy, where some 10,000 leopard cat skins from China were

Figure 5.1
West German Imports of Small Cat Skins,
1978–1986

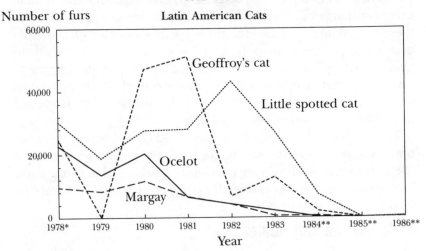

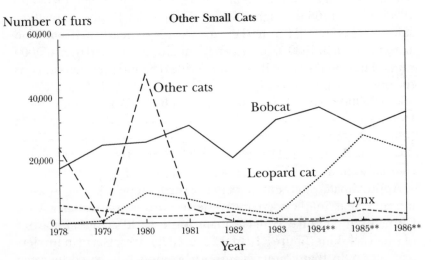

*"Other cats" total does not include 157,400 skins of unspecified species.
**Imports from other EEC countries not included.

Source: West German CITES annual reports.

International Wildlife Trade: Whose Business Is It?

imported in 1985—double the number of *all* Appendix II cat skins Italy imported in 1984.[10] Similarly, European demand for bobcat and lynx skins from North America may increase.

Japan and Hong Kong are also important markets for exotic felid fur. The United States and Canada are heavily involved in domestic trade and exports of bobcat and lynx furs but no longer are large-scale consumers of nonnative cat furs. Because of prohibitions in the Endangered Species and Lacey acts, the United States imports very few Latin American cat skins.

Latin American Species in Trade

OCELOTS

With its sleek striped and spotted coat, the ocelot was a prized fashion item during the 1960s and 1970s. Once the most heavily exploited small cat species in Latin America, it has declined so much in many parts of its range that it is considered vulnerable.[11] Although the ocelot is primarily a South American cat, its full range extends from northern Argentina to southwest Texas. (In Texas, it numbers only 100 to 130 individuals.) Preferring to travel alone within large territories, the ocelot preys on small mammals, fish, lizards, and even rattlesnakes.[12]

International trade in ocelot skins is now rare. Business boomed in the late 1960s and early 1970s. Then, it turned sharply downward, falling from 35,000 ocelot skins in 1978 to fewer than 1,000 in 1985

Ocelot (*Felis pardalis*).
F. Vollmar

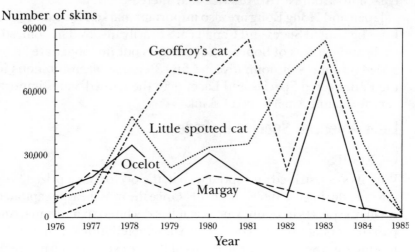

Figure 5.2
Net Trade in Skins of Latin American Small Cats,
1976–1985

Number of skins

Source: CITES annual reports.

(figure 5.2).[13] CITES prohibits commercial trade in two subspecies of ocelot (*F. pardalis mearnsi* and *F. p. mitis*); all other ocelot subspecies are regulated by Appendix II.

The United States imported over 100,000 ocelot skins a year in the late 1960s, mostly from Brazil and Colombia. These imports occurred even though Brazil outlawed ocelot and most other wildlife exports in 1967[14] and, under the Lacey Act, the United States was legally compelled to uphold the ban. Not until 1972, after the species was listed as endangered in the United States, did U.S. imports drop dramatically.[15]

The European market for ocelot continued strong in the 1970s. In 1975, the United Kingdom alone imported over 76,000 ocelot skins.[16] Between 1978 and 1985, West Germany, France, Italy, and Spain were the most important consumers in a rapidly diminishing market.[17] Consumer demand for ocelot fur had virtually collapsed by 1985 in West Germany and other European countries. The public recognized the ocelot and other "classic cats" as protected and thus refused to buy their fur. In 1984, an ocelot coat sold for $10,000 or so in Munich; by the end of 1986, furriers were practically giving the garments away, at $1,000 each. Fur fanciers in West Germany apparently are not yet aware of the potential trade peril to lesser known species, such as Geoffroy's cat, as these markets continue to thrive.[18]

From 1980 through 1984, Paraguay was far and away the single greatest supplier of ocelot skins, shipping over 120,000 skins abroad. The Paraguayan shipments were clearly illegal, because Paraguay banned exports of wildlife products in 1975, and the ocelot subspecies found in Paraguay is listed on Appendix I. Moreover, the country is known to reexport wildlife skins smuggled out of Brazil.[19] Although the Paraguayan management authority has not issued export permits in recent years,[20] the political and financial power of local traders makes halting exports extremely difficult. Skins simply are smuggled out without legal papers.

GEOFFROY'S CATS

During the early 1980s, one of the most heavily traded Latin American small cats was the Geoffroy's cat. An average of 55,000 Geoffroy's cat skins reportedly reached world markets each year from 1980 through 1984 (figure 5.2).[21] Most were exported by Paraguay or, to a lesser degree, Argentina or Bolivia and went to West Germany, France, Italy, and other EEC nations. A Geoffroy's cat fur coat sells in West Germany today for about $4,000.[22]

Much of the Geoffroy's cat trade in the early 1980s would appear to be illegal because of Paraguay's 1975 ban on wildlife-product exports and Argentina's 1980 ban on trade in this species. Argentina later reopened exports on a limited basis; in 1986 and again in 1987, authorities permitted some exporters to clear out skin stockpiles held in the country.

LITTLE SPOTTED CATS

An excellent tree climber, the little spotted cat lives on a diet of birds, squirrels, monkeys, and other arboreal fare. It is threatened not only by hunting but also by deforestation. Known in some countries as the "oncilla," this species is listed on Appendix II, except for a Costa Rican subspecies (*F. tigrina oncilla*) that is on Appendix I.

On average, over 50,000 little spotted cat skins entered world trade annually between 1980 and 1984 (figure 5.2). Most were officially listed as coming from Paraguay, where the species is legally protected, or Bolivia, where its existence has not been confirmed.[23] The supposed "Bolivian" pelts may have been smuggled out of Brazil. Fur lovers can purchase garments made from this species' skins for about $7,500 from German furriers.[24]

MARGAYS

About the size of a healthy house cat, the margay is another species popular among cat-skin dealers. Its tawny brown coat looks much like that of the little spotted cat and the ocelot, and the three species often are confused in trade. CITES records show over 12,000 margay

Margay (*Felis wiedii*).
Russell A. Mittermeier / WWF

skins in annual markets between 1980 and 1984 (figure 5.2), down from some 20,000 skins in 1977 and 1978. Paraguay was the major source for margay skins during those years, despite its ban on such trade. As with other Latin American cats, most of the margay skins shipped abroad were imported into West Germany, France, Italy, and other EEC countries.[25]

North American Species in Trade

BOBCATS

The bobcat is currently one of the world's most heavily traded small cat. Its pelts are fashioned into coats, trim, and accessories and are sometimes used as rugs or wall decorations. Its spotted belly fur is particularly sought after. In addition, in some regions, bobcat meat is considered a culinary delicacy.[26] The bobcat's range extends from Canada to Mexico, with most of the population in the United States.

World demand for bobcat fur rose sharply in the mid-1970s, after CITES and national controls afforded complete protection to the large-cat species. During that period, the price for bobcat fur jumped from $10 or less to $300 per pelt.[27] By 1984, over 84,000 skins of the species reportedly were reaching world markets each year. Seventy-five percent of these came from the United States (figure 5.3), and the remainder from Canada.[28] In 1987, the U.S. Fish and Wildlife Service's Scientific Authority reported that the U.S. bobcat harvest totaled approximately 60,000 skins per year.[29]

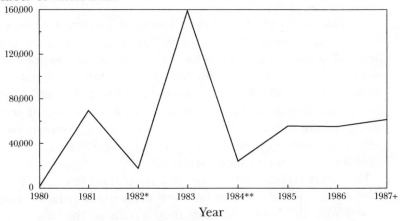

Figure 5.3
U.S. Exports of Bobcat Skins, 1980–1987

Number of whole skins

*Plus whole skins reported to weigh 535 pounds.
**Plus whole skins reported to weigh 450 pounds.
+ Plus whole skins reported to weigh 9,638 pounds.
Source: U.S. CITES annual reports.

Evaluating the impact of trade on the bobcat is problematic because, like other small cats, its secretive nature and remote habitats make it very difficult to count.[30] Populations also undergo annual fluctuations in response to changes in the availability of the species it depends on for food—for example, the cottontail rabbit.

The bobcat's wide distribution and high reproductive potential enables it to sustain fairly significant levels of hunting and trapping.[31] If it is protected by sound management programs, the likelihood of its long-term health as a species is good despite its popularity in trade.

In 1983 at the biennial conference of CITES parties, the United States attempted to have the bobcat removed from Appendix II, but strenuous opposition from other countries led the delegation to drop this proposition. The delegation then announced that the United States would treat the bobcat as a "look-alike" Appendix II species, and not a species truly threatened by trade. This new position effectively removed tight U.S. trade restrictions on the bobcat, and the Fish and Wildlife Service soon began issuing multiyear export findings.

LYNXES

Although about the same size and shape as its relative the bobcat, the lynx has noticeable differences. Its legs are longer, and it has furred footpads to help with travel in deep northern snows. The lynx's pelt is plainer and grayish to blend in with the northern tundra, and its ear tufts are longer than the bobcat's. Some biologists, believing that ear tufts help animals to hear, conjecture that the lynx needs longer tufts to detect sound over farther distances, while the bobcat relies more on its eyesight.[32]

As is the case with the bobcat, there are no accurate estimates of the lynx population. Like its cousin, the lynx is difficult to count, lives in low densities, and is subject to dramatic natural population swings.[33] The North American subspecies occurs in 14 states and throughout Canada, with the exception of Prince Edward Island.[34] The population appears stable in much of its range, but abnormal declines have occurred in some regions, raising concern among conservationists and others. Heavy trapping often is cited as a contributing factor in these declines.[35]

Many experts believe that the lynx population fluctuates in 8- to 11-year cycles, possibly in response to shifts in the availability of snowshoe hares, the lynx's primary prey.[36] Because this could make populations especially vulnerable to trapping during natural periods of decline,[37] trapping controls need to be flexible enough to avoid overexploiting the lynx at all times, and particularly when breeders are in naturally short supply.

The lynx is listed on Appendix II. In Canada and the United States, lynx trapping and hunting are either regulated or prohibited in all areas where the species occurs.[38] The combined annual harvest for lynx pelts in these two countries averages over 20,000 pelts.[39] In 1984, Canada reportedly exported 18,000 lynx skins, and the United States exported another 6,000 or so.[40]

Like bobcat, lynx pelts are used for coats, trim, and fashion accessories. Although not central to the market, other parts of the animal also are used: teeth and claws are made into jewelry, and lynx meat is commonly consumed by hunters and trappers.[41] Demand for lynx pelts remains strong. In 1985, a prime pelt could fetch more than $1,000; the average price that year was $650.[42] In West Germany, lynx and bobcat garments seem to be gaining popularity. Manfred Niekisch, director of TRAFFIC(Germany), predicts that lynx and bobcat (as well as various fox species) will continue to gain favor and eventually take over the German fur market.[43]

Asian Species in Trade

LEOPARD CATS

Perhaps because of its striking dark spots, the leopard cat is the most heavily traded Asian small cat. It may also be one of the easiest Asian cats to obtain, as it occurs in many forest habitats throughout southeast Siberia, China, and Southeast Asia. It is even found on many

Eurasian lynx (*Felis lynx lynx*).
Strumbelj

offshore islands, such as the Philippines.[44]

Trade in leopard cats is difficult to control, since some populations of one subspecies (*F. bengalensis bengalensis*), which occurs in peninsular India and Southeast Asia, are on Appendix I, while other populations and subspecies are on Appendix II. Over 45,000 leopard cat skins reached world markets in 1984, mostly from the Soviet Union, North Korea, and China. The bulk reportedly went to furriers in Western Europe,[45] although Japan was an important market as well. According to a study by TRAFFIC(Japan), Japan is the only major cat-fur consumer in Asia, and leopard cat fur is the industry's primary staple. In the early 1980s, a soft, comfortable leopard-cat jacket sold for about $3,300 in Munich and approximately $3,700 in Tokyo.[46]

EURASIAN LYNXES

Long considered a separate species from the North American lynx, the Eurasian lynx (*F. lynx lynx*) is now classified by many authorities as one of three lynx subspecies.* This forest-dwelling native of western mainland Europe, mountainous central Asia, and the Soviet Union is prized for its yellowish brown pelt. Hunting and trapping

*The third lynx subspecies, the Spanish lynx (F. lynx pardina) of central and southern Spain and Portugal, numbers only 1,000 to 1,500 or so individuals and is not pressured by commercial trade.[47]

are regulated in Europe and the Soviet Union.[48] CITES reports show approximately 7,500 Eurasian lynx skins from the Soviet Union and China in trade in 1984.[49]

OTHER ASIAN CATS

Thought to be the closest relative of the domestic cat, the wildcat is found throughout Eurasia and the woodland and savannas of Africa. The species is generally about one-third larger in size than the average house cat. Its members are not considered threatened. CITES records from 1984 show 3,600 wildcat skins in international trade.[50] Most skins were shipped from various Asian sources to East Germany, West Germany, and Italy.

The Pallas's cat is unusually fluffy looking due to its short legs, rounded body, and dense, long fur. The species needs the added insulation of its thick coat to survive in the rugged, often snow-covered terrain of southeastern Siberia and Tibet. It also occurs as far west as the Caspian Sea.[51] CITES reported in 1984 that some 3,500 Pallas's cat skins reached world markets, primarily from Mongolia. Major importing countries included Austria, East Germany, the United Kingdom, and Italy.[52]

KEEP IN MIND . . .

■ Travelers beware! Exercise caution when making purchases of products made of certain small cat species. A few of these are legal to buy and bring into the United States. If you are planning a trip, check with TRAFFIC(U.S.A.) (World Wildlife Fund, 1250 Twenty-Fourth Street, N.W., Washington, DC 20037) or the U.S. Fish and Wildlife Service (Office of Public Affairs, (202) 343-5634; or the Office of Management Authority, P.O. Box 3507, Arlington, VA 22203) for the fur products that are legal to bring home.

■ Think conservation and make the connection. Remember that although trade in certain species is legal, the fur trade has had a history of decimating the striped and spotted cats. It can take 20 to 30 pelts of a smaller species to make one full-length fur coat.

■ Some suggested readings:

Miller, S. Douglas, and Everett, Daniel D. *Cats of the World: Biology, Conservation, and Management*. Washington, D.C.: National Wildlife Federation, 1986.

Young, Stanley P. *The Bobcat of North America*. Lincoln, Nebr.: University of Nebraska Press, 1978.

Continuing Problems

The market for small-cat pelts has been marked by rampant poaching and smuggling, especially pelts from Latin America. As many as half of all Latin American small-cat skins reported in trade in the early 1980s may have been illegal, either because they were Appendix I animals (such as the south Brazilian ocelot) or because they were Appendix II cats that were legally protected in their native countries (for example, the Geoffroy's cat and little spotted cat).[53] The "look-alike" problem further complicates enforcement efforts.

Clearly, existing controls on trade in Latin American small-cat skins have not worked well, suggesting that new approaches are needed. Until studies prove that Latin American small cats can withstand commercial pressures, and until wildlife managers develop regulatory schemes that control trapping and hunting in a reliable way, it seems prudent for exporting countries to step up their efforts to prohibit trade. It also makes sense for consumer countries to uphold more vigorously Latin American countries' efforts to protect their resources. Because so much remains unknown about both Latin American and Asian felid populations, species research should be a top priority, followed by the development of sound management plans.

International trade in bobcat and lynx seems to be reasonably well-regulated, but management programs in these North American species are less than optimal. Species research and population monitoring, improved regulatory mechanisms, and increased habitat protection are crucial to the continuing health of both species. Citizens can play an important role by expressing their views on the issue and by encouraging U.S. and Canadian public officials to strengthen bobcat and lynx research and management programs.

Trade controls can only succeed with consumer support. Tourists and cat-fur fanciers should be aware of the many trade bans and other restrictions on the felid market and should not purchase protected species, either in domestic markets or during travels abroad. Port inspectors are likely to be on the lookout for illicit cat skins; cat furs and products now make up one-third of all wildlife seized from tourists returning to the United States.[54] If caught with such goods, travelers must forfeit them, even if the items were purchased in ignorance of foreign legal restrictions. Fur buyers should always check labels, ask vendors about the type and source of furs in garments, and buy only from reputable dealers.

CHAPTER 6
Elephants

The largest living land mammal on Earth, the elephant, has long earned human respect, as a trustworthy mode of transportation in Asia and as a symbol of strength and wildness in Africa. But elephants are perhaps most prized for their oversized incisors—smooth, cream-colored tusks that are carved into piano keys, earrings, billiard balls, scrimshaw, mythical figurines, Japanese name seals, chess pieces, chopsticks, and other ivory items sold around the world.

There are two elephant species: the Asian elephant (*Elephas maximus*) and the African elephant (*Loxodonta africana*). The Asian elephant differs from its African relative in physique and temperament; the former is smaller and has a more modest pair of ears, only one lip on the end of its trunk, a different number of toes, and much smaller—or often nonexistent—tusks. The Asian species has been a reliable beast of burden for centuries; the African elephant seldom takes to such tasks.

Trade Controls

The Asian elephant is considered endangered and is listed on Appendix I of CITES. The species suffered overhunting for the Far Eastern ivory trade before the African species became the primary source for ivory. Today, the Asian elephant is seldom hunted for its ivory. Although most male Asian elephants still have tusks, in several restricted populations (most especially in Sri Lanka) they do not. Female Asian elephants lack visible tusks. Nevertheless, some poaching of Asian elephants for ivory and meat still occurs. This poached ivory is used primarily locally and seldom reaches the world market.[1] Inbreeding of certain populations (caused by excessive poaching of males resulting in a disproportionate number of females) and habitat loss caused by human encroachment are now the greatest dangers to the long-term conservation of the Asian elephant. Only an estimated 29,000 to 44,000 remain in the wild, scattered in isolated pockets of India, Nepal, Sri Lanka, Sumatra, Thailand, and other Southeast Asian countries.[2] The Asian elephant's survival depends foremost on protection of its dwindling habitat (figure 6.1), though strict enforcement of trade controls remains essential.

In just one decade, the African elephant population dropped by nearly 50 percent, from an estimated 1.3 million in 1979 to 625,000 or so in 1989 (figure 6.2).[3] Some of the most drastic reductions have occurred in Sudan (30 percent decline per year), Tanzania (16 percent decline per year), and Kenya (13 percent decline per year). The ivory trade is the major cause of this, although in some regions habitat pressure, drought, and disease have also played a part. The African elephant is presently considered threatened, but experts believe it may soon become endangered if illegal ivory trade is not brought under control.[4]

The African elephant has been listed on Appendix II of CITES since 1977, and hunting and ivory collection are regulated or prohibited in most African nations. In late 1985, CITES parties imposed international controls on the tusk trade through a system of export quotas and special tusk-marking procedures by which exporting countries identify and stamp each legally exported tusk with its own serial number, exporting country code, weight, and export year (figure 6.3).* The parties also set up an ivory-control unit in the CITES Secretariat's office in Switzerland to monitor the tusk trade. In addition, ivory-importing countries agreed not to accept shipments that lacked valid serial numbers and export permits or that came from countries without export quotas, such as Burundi.

Trade Volume and Routes

Elephant hunting has been going on for millennia, but it began a steady increase after World War II, when the price and demand for ivory surged upward. International ivory trade—and elephant killing—skyrocketed in the 1970s as ivory prices quadrupled and inves-

---

*Under the plan, which was drawn up and agreed to by the CITES parties during their 1985 conference in Buenos Aires, the major African ivory-exporting countries established quotas ranging from 0 to 20,000 tusks for annual shipments of raw ivory. All CITES parties agreed to mark and register their stockpiles of ivory tusks by December 1986 to ensure that smugglers could not add their new tusks to existing stockpiles for trade as "old" tusks. CITES officials later found that nearly 100,000 tusks, probably worth over $50 million, were being held as stockpiles in 1986. Three countries held most of the store: just over half were in Singapore, another quarter were in Hong Kong, and one-fifth were in Burundi.[5]

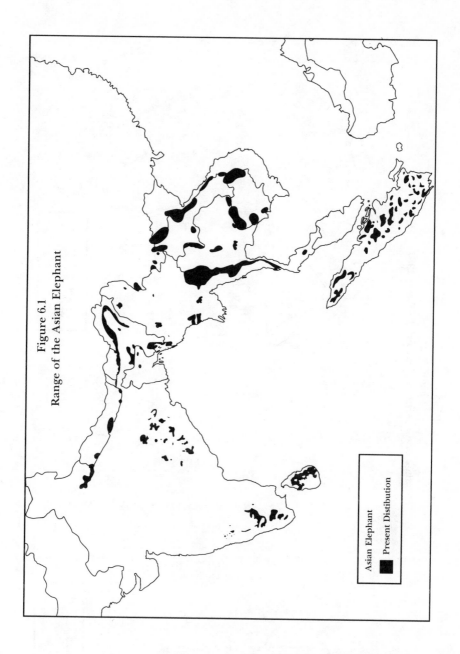

Figure 6.1
Range of the Asian Elephant

Asian Elephant

■ Present Distibution

Figure 6.2
Range of the African Elephant, 1979 and 1987

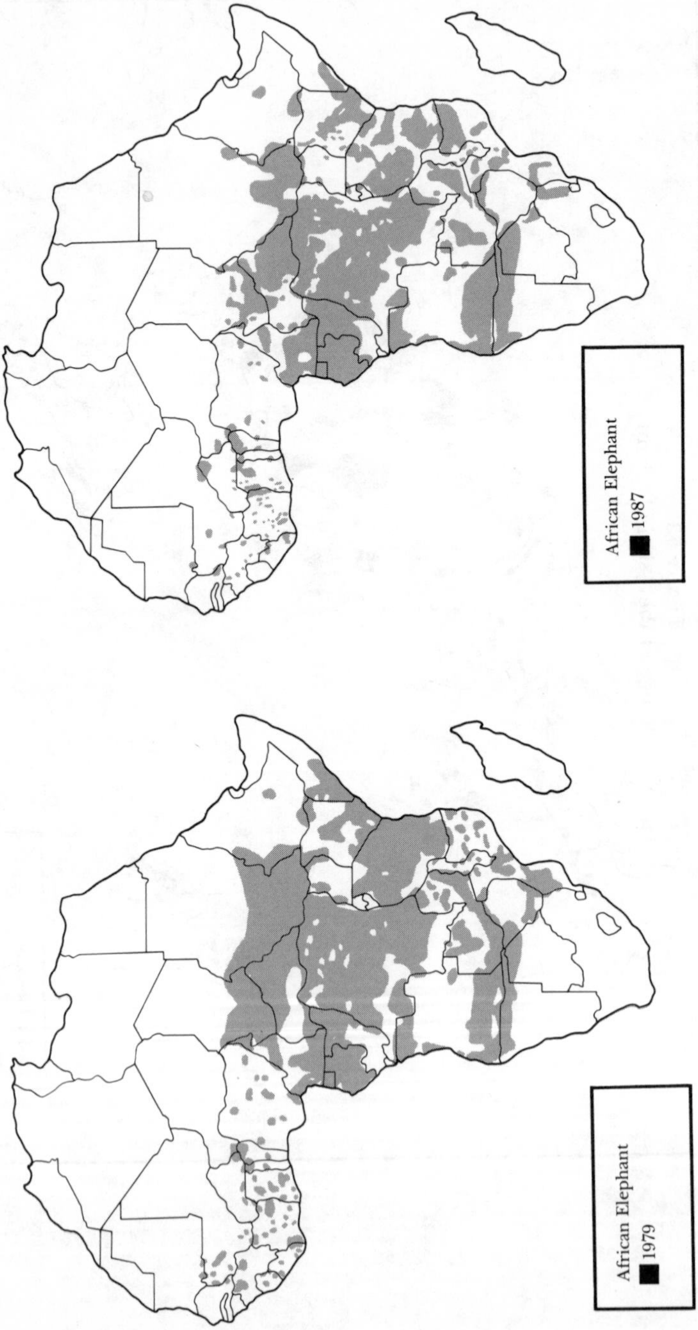

African Elephant
■ 1987

African Elephant
■ 1979

International Wildlife Trade: Whose Business Is It?

JUST HOW MANY TONS OF IVORY ARE IN TRADE?

Figures used in reference to the amount of tons of ivory in international trade can seem to vary widely. Part of this confusion is due to the distinction between metric tons versus U.S. tons. All official national and international documents on ivory trade (and other wildlife trade) are filed in metric measurements. Hence, government and press reports commonly will use the metric figures—often referring to them as "metric tons" or "tonnes" but sometimes saying simply "tons."

In this chapter, as throughout the rest of *International Wildlife Trade: Whose Business Is It?*, measurements are in *U.S.* tons. Anyone interested in converting these figures back to metric measurements should remember that 1 U.S. ton equals 0.907 metric tons.

tors turned to ivory as a hedge against worldwide inflation. The upswing was also fueled by tremendous growth in Hong Kong's ability to mass produce ivory carvings. Prices for raw ivory in the major ivory-consuming markets of Japan, Hong Kong, and Europe rose from between $3 and $10 a pound in the 1960s to $50 a pound in the mid-1970s. By 1987, the price was as high as $125 a pound, creating a powerful incentive to hunters and poachers.[6]

During the 1970s and 1980s, growing political turbulence in some countries and increased availability of automatic weapons greatly

Figure 6.3
African Exports of Ivory, 1987*
(by country)

	Tusks exported	Tusk quota
Botswana	20	520
Cameroon	18	300
Central African Republic	123	800
Chad	305	320
Congo	3,587	3,784
Ethiopia	81	530
Gabon	350	2,600
Kenya	0	2,000
Malawi	279	420
Mozambique	1,735	19,700
Somalia	0	0
South Africa	2,226	14,000
Sudan	20,614	21,500
Tanzania	334	18,150
Uganda	37	156
Zaire	932	15,000
Zambia	543	8,500
Zimbabwe	413	9,000

*Includes both raw and polished ivory.
Source: CITES Secretariat.

Elephants

Elephant poachers in Africa
Alan Root

accelerated poaching. Governments found it more difficult to patrol elephant lands and enforce game laws, as illicit hunters slaughtered thousands of animals with automatic rifles. Some countries suffered heavy losses. Kenya and Uganda, for example, lost 85 percent of their native elephant population between 1973 and 1987. Tens of thousands of illegal tusks were being smuggled out of such countries as Zaire, Tanzania, Zambia, the Central African Republic, Sudan, Congo, Somalia, and Angola.[8]

Despite the African elephant's listing on Appendix II of CITES and many nations' restrictions on ivory exports, efforts to control trade and protect dwindling herds often met with little success. As soon as one country banned ivory exports, smugglers sneaked their cargoes across a border into a more lenient country for shipment overseas. Many African governments lacked adequate resources to combat powerful poaching forces, and, in some cases, widespread political corruption also undermined antipoaching efforts.

Poaching and illicit trade continued in full force during the early 1980s. In Sudan, dangerous, organized poaching teams armed with automatic rifles killed hundreds of elephants and even turned their sights on humans when surprised by game wardens.[9] In the Central

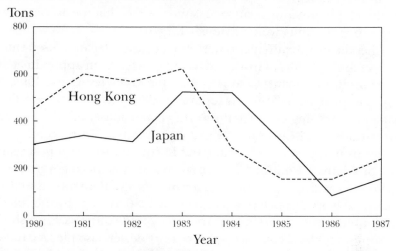

Figure 6.4
Imports of Raw Ivory by Hong Kong and Japan,
1980–1987

Tons

Year

Source: Japanese Customs data; *Traffic Bulletin.*

African Republic, Chadian and Sudanese poachers on horseback reportedly chased elephants with spears, slowing them down for the kill by slashing or "hamstringing" their back legs.[10] Poaching also persisted in other nations with large elephant populations, particularly Tanzania and parts of Zaire.

Poached ivory was usually laundered through neighboring countries on the continent, such as Sudan and Burundi, to foreign entrepôts, including Belgium, the United Arab Emirates, Macao, and Singapore. From these staging posts, tusks often were shipped to Hong Kong and Japan, the major ivory-consuming countries in the world (figure 6.4).

In recent years, the ivory trade has been forced to find new routes as some of the more notorious smuggling ports have been closed off. Largely as a result of international conservation pressure, Sudan banned all raw ivory exports in 1983, and the flow of illegal tusks through that country slowed considerably. Belgium, previously one of the key ivory-smuggling entrepôts in the world, acceded to CITES in 1984.[11] And in 1985 international protest against Japan's illicit ivory trade helped convince Japanese ivory importers and officials to toughen their stance toward smugglers by requiring export permits for all incoming tusk shipments.

Japan had imported some $30 million worth of ivory from Africa in 1984, an estimated 80 percent of it illegal.[12] While Hong Kong had maintained strict import controls on raw ivory since 1978, Japan had done little to confirm the legality of incoming shipments. Accord-

Elephants   67

ing to Tom Milliken, director of TRAFFIC(Japan), in 1984 Japanese authorities accepted shipments from Zaire, Sudan, and the Congo, countries where ivory exports were banned; Burundi, which had no native elephants; and Uganda, despite the fact that the accompanying export permits were obviously forged.[13]

After the new requirements were implemented, Japan refused entry to several shipments of ivory, and its imports fell from approximately 524 tons in 1984 to just 87 tons in 1986, the lowest level since 1965.[14]* More important, as Milliken reported, 1986 "was the first year that Japan was not singled out as the world's major abuser of the elephant ivory trade . . . . I can't say now that every gram [of ivory] coming in is not from a poached elephant, but in comparison with past years the problems are minor." The progress stemmed from government action to require export permits for incoming shipments, as well as Japanese ivory importers' agreement in 1986 to "play by the rules" and submit ivory to preimport reviews by trade officials.[15] In a show of support for legal controls, Japanese ivory dealers also pledged more than $100,000 in 1986 to help CITES establish its ivory-control unit. Macao and Singapore, previously considered key Asian entrepots for African elephant ivory, also took steps in 1986 to control the trade. Macao, an overseas territory of Portugal, enacted CITES legislation, and Singapore acceded to the treaty late in the year.

Japan's imports increased again in 1987, rising to almost 158 tons.

Old elephants with huge, curving tusks like these are rarely seen in Africa today. Most were killed for their ivory years ago.
Norman Myers / WWF

Some experts believe seizures of large shipments of illegal tusks in 1986 suggest that smugglers were forced by these countries' crackdowns and CITES' new system of export quotas and tusk-marking procedures to find riskier routes and more unusual techniques to ship their ivory contraband. In January 1986, officials in Antwerp, Belgium, seized 11 tons of tusks, valued at over $1 million, from a boat arriving from Tanzania. Shipped in containers marked "beeswax," the cargo of over 1,800 tusks from at least 900 recently killed elephants comprised the largest illegal shipment ever discovered outside Africa.[16] Not long after, authorities in Lisbon, Portugal, seized another 1.65 tons of African tusks from an illicit shipment labeled "malachite." That June, Zambian authorities seized a massive, 6.6-ton load of 564 tusks concealed in a truck heading for Burundi. In the last several years, other elephant tusk seizures have occurred in Tanzania and Kenya.[17]

CONTINUING PROBLEMS WITH ILLEGAL TRADE

Nearly 102,000 African elephants were killed in 1986, according to one estimate, producing some 193,000 tusks for the trade.[18] While not all of those tusks entered world markets that year, the harvest would be worth an estimated $100 million on the wholesale ivory market. The actual total international ivory trade was worth approximately $70 million in 1986, down from about $90 million in 1983.[19]

Tusks from about 21,000 elephants entered world trade "legally" under quota in 1986. The two leading source countries were Somalia and Sudan, but most of their tusks were "confiscated" and undoubtedly came from neighboring countries. Tanzania, Zaire, and Zambia exported significant amounts of "legal" ivory as well. Also important were South Africa* and Zimbabwe, where elephant herds are carefully monitored and selectively culled to ensure that they do not outgrow their ranges.

Apparently three-fourths of the 1986 raw ivory trade came from an estimated 89,000 poached elephants. A substantial portion of this illicit ivory was processed through the central African nation of Burundi, which in the past has been a major entrepôt for poached ivory taken in surrounding African countries—particularly Tanzania, Zaire, and Zambia. Although this small country did not belong to CITES until November 1988, some 23,000 tusks that were registered with CITES in 1986 left the country in early 1987, according to CITES records. Inside sources estimate that perhaps another 27,000 or so

---

*However, a considerable amount of ivory poached in neighboring countries is believed to emanate from South Africa.

Raw ivory in an ivory room in Mombassa, Kenya.
P.R.O. Bally/WWF

tusks were shipped out unrecorded. From Burundi, illicit tusk shipments often have gone to the United Arab Emirates, or by other routes,
eventually reaching the Far East. Fortunately, a new government in
Burundi imposed a ban on all ivory imports in November 1987.*
Immediately after the ban, the government confiscated 23.9 tons of
ivory that apparently entered the country illegally.[21]

Large quantities of illicit ivory are believed to have exited Africa
through Sudan and the Ivory Coast. Some ivory also is smuggled
directly from the East Coast of Africa. And a great number of poached
tusks never appear at all in trade statistics, as they are used in ivory-
carving industries within Africa.[22]

In the mid-1980s, roughly 70 percent of all ivory shipments from
Africa eventually went to Japan or Hong Kong. Together, Japan and
Hong Kong imported about 215 tons of raw ivory in 1986, down from
292 tons in 1985. (One expert noted that traders' fears of export restrictions caused unusually high volumes of ivory exports in 1985.[23])

---

*The Burundian government, however, believes that it has no authority to confiscate ivory that
entered the country prior to the ban. To deter trade in that ivory, which almost certainly was
poached, the U.S. Fish and Wildlife Service (FWS) announced in April 1988 a ban on all imports
of Burundian ivory that was not registered with the CITES Secretariat as of December 1, 1986.
The FWS also declared that it will prohibit from import into the United States ivory from any
country that allows the illegal Burundi ivory to be imported into or pass through its borders.[20]

African elephant tusks sell for upwards of $100 per pound on the wholesale market.[24] At just over 10 pounds, the average tusk is worth more than $450; an old bull elephant may have a prize pair worth several thousand dollars each.[25] As ivory trade expert John Caldwell explains, "You can name your price for big tusks because they are so rare."[26] Tusks coming out of Africa are smaller than in the past, a trend of great concern to conservationists because it suggests that more young elephants are being killed to supply world markets.[27]

WORKED IVORY

Most of the raw tusks in world trade end up as "worked ivory," carved into bangles, bracelets, small animals, "netsuke" figurines, Japanese name seals, and other ornamental items. All tusks or ivory products that are carved are considered worked ivory.

According to John Caldwell, "It is impossible to monitor the worked-ivory trade in a way that is meaningful to elephant conservation." Ivory carvings are often small, and their total weight in a shipment does not necessarily correspond to the number of tusks used to produce them. Raw ivory, in contrast, is usually shipped by the tusk (because it is most valuable that way), so it is easily recognizable and provides a realistic basis for figuring out how many elephants were killed to collect it.

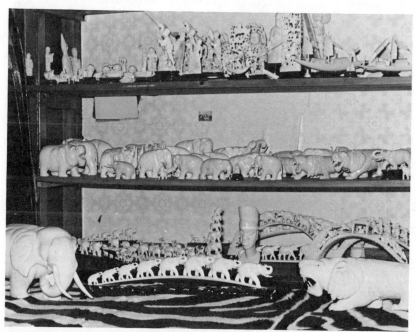

Worked ivory for sale in a Nairobi shop in 1973. Such sales are now illegal in Kenya.
M. Boultin

Hong Kong is a major world center for ivory carving, with Japan and India also producing worked ivory in quantity. Some traders in Hong Kong, which produces most of its worked ivory for reexport, have contended that local ivory carvers have lost foreign customers to Japan because Hong Kong authorities enforce CITES controls more strictly than do the Japanese. Japanese progress in tightening trade controls—combined with the fact that most ivory carving in Japan is for the home market only—may remove the basis for such claims. Hong Kong ivory merchants may have been more concerned about carving businesses cropping up in Taiwan and Dubai, one of the United Arab Emirates, places where no trade controls on raw ivory existed. Relying on illicit sources of ivory, these operations were able to ship carvings to Hong Kong, where they were laundered to compete with locally produced items. Often, the carving done in Taiwan or Dubai was the bare minimum necessary to qualify the ivory as worked and thus able to be traded outside the controls for raw ivory. After Hong Kong carvers received the ivory, they then carved it into finished products.[28]

A new policy announced by the Hong Kong government in July 1988, should make it much more difficult to import worked ivory of any sort into that jurisdiction. As has already been the case with imported raw ivory, traders will have to demonstrate that worked ivory is from legal sources (that is, not poached) before it can enter Hong Kong.[29]

An *Asian Business* article stated in 1986 that Hong Kong carvers are "bloodied by the conservation movement," losing 3,000 jobs in eight years. The chairman of a major Hong Kong ivory manufacturers' association explained, "Tusk suppliers now prefer to sell to our competitors in Japan and China, where documentation procedures are more streamlined." Another trade spokesman added that he supported elephant protection and trade regulations, but that the new tusk-marking system "will break most of us," although this has not proved to be true.[30]

The domestic carving industry within African countries is of growing interest—and concern—to conservationists. While several operations are legitimate, using ivory taken from carefully managed elephant populations, a study released in 1986 pointed out that "domestic carving industries in many [African] countries are major users of illegal ivory and governments need to figure out how to stem this flow."[31]

U.S. TRADE IN ELEPHANT IVORY

Trade in African elephant ivory was legal in the United States before June 1989, provided that the ivory came from a CITES party, reached

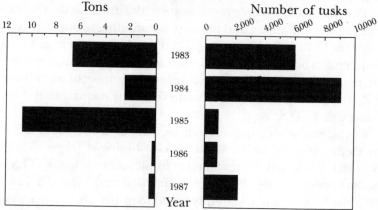

Figure 6.5
U.S. Imports of Raw Ivory, 1983–1987*

*Trade in raw ivory is reported either by number of tusks or by weight. Records for the two categories shown here are mutually exclusive.
Source: U.S. CITES annual reports.

the nation via legal trade routes, and was accompanied by valid permits. The U.S. Endangered Species Act (ESA) lists the African elephant as "threatened," while the Lacey Act governs ivory imports by prohibiting the import of wildlife products taken or traded illegally from their source country. The United States also has banned all commercial trade in Asian elephant ivory, since the species is listed on Appendix I and as endangered under the ESA.

Until the late 1980s, U.S. controls on ivory imports were poorly enforced. For instance, in 1984, the United States imported approximately 8.3 tons of raw ivory, three-quarters of which reportedly came from Zaire, at a time when all commercial ivory exports from that country were banned.[32]

The United States is not a major importer of raw ivory. In 1986, the nation imported 855 or more raw tusks, down from about 9,000 tusks in 1984 (figure 6.5). The total declared value of all tusks and other raw ivory shipments entering the country in 1986 was just under $200,000, although industry sources suggest the true value was probably higher, $430,000 or so.[33]

Most of the ivory entering the United States arrives in the form of worked, rather than raw, ivory. The United States is considered the second largest consumer of worked ivory in the world, after Japan.[34] In 1986, the nation imported 5 million piano keys, carvings, scrimshaw, and other elephant ivory products worth more than $17 million at the ports, down slightly from $24 million in 1985.[35] Annual U.S. trade in all types of elephant products, including tusks, worked ivory, and elephant skin, is probably worth at least $29 million whole-sale, with a retail value reaching $100 million or more.[36]

The public has become more aware of the dramatic decline in African elephant numbers, and pressure is mounting to stop the elephant ivory trade. In 1988, Congress passed the African Elephant Conservation Act, a bill that had been introduced by Representative Anthony Beilenson (D.-Calif.). This act prohibits the import of ivory from any country dealing in illegal ivory and from any country that does not adhere to CITES.[37]

Despite somewhat limited volume, a detailed analysis of U.S. trade in elephant ivory by TRAFFIC(U.S.A.) biologist Jorgen Thomsen found that U.S. authorities failed to implement the new CITES ivory quota system in 1986. Thomsen concluded that "The U.S. Fish and Wildlife Service has apparently failed to notify port inspectors that an ivory quota system has been established, that individual quotas and marking schemes have been set up for African countries, and that numerous changes have taken place in the national legislation of many African countries." Thomsen found that U.S. imports from the Central African Republic, Liberia, Sudan, and Zaire took place outside the quota system; he also turned up evidence of problems with imports from South Africa, Tanzania, and Zimbabwe. As recently as July 1987, the United States accepted a shipment of 140 tusks from Zaire that probably had forged permits, as Zaire had not authorized commercial shipments to the United States at that time. The United States later launched an investigation of its ivory trade with Zaire.[38]

In June 1989, President Bush imposed a moratorium on all ivory imports into the United States following the disclosure by World Wildlife Fund (WWF) of new data showing the drastic effect that ivory trade was having on elephant populations.

OTHER ELEPHANT PRODUCTS

Wrinkled, gray elephant skin often is used to make leather wallets, briefcases, and boots. This market reportedly is expanding as a result of new technology that allows artisans to use the whole elephant hide, rather than just the thin ear-skin pieces used in the past.[39] There is also a small market for curio items such as unmistakable elephant-foot umbrella stands.

The prevailing structure of the elephant-skin trade is much different from that of the ivory trade, most notably because the trade is usually legal and there is no evidence of poaching for skins.[40] Elephant hides generally come from government-controlled culling programs in Botswana, South Africa, and Zimbabwe, where they are important to local economies.[41] In Zimbabwe, for instance, elephant-skin sales net the local government about $2 million per year, an income par-

Wastebaskets made from elephant feet sold as souvenirs in East Africa.
WWF / OKAPIA

tially invested in elephant management and conservation. Key consumers are the United States and the European Economic Community. In the mid-1980s, the United States imported skins from an estimated 11,000 elephants annually. Most of the skins were fashioned into cowboy boots in Texas, although some were shipped across the border to Mexico for manufacture into boots that were then reimported to U.S. markets.[42]

The Long-Term Outlook

In 1987, an international group of African elephant experts determined that the entire species would take a rapid turn for the worse if present hunting levels continued. The downturn would not affect all populations equally; a few in southern Africa are secure and well-protected, while most others are not. WWF's highly respected elephant expert, Iain Douglas-Hamilton, believes the situation is more perilous. He has pointed out that elephants are doing well in Botswana, Malawi, South Africa, and Zimbabwe but are severely stressed throughout much of East, Central, and West Africa, where an estimated 80 percent of the African elephant population occurs. Douglas-Hamilton added that elephants have been virtually eliminated in certain areas within Sudan, Chad, the Central African Republic, and Zaire.[43]

A startling 1987 report underscored Douglas-Hamilton's concerns. The African Elephant and Rhino Specialist Group of the International Union for Conservation of Nature and Natural Resources concluded that the species "is not yet endangered, but will become so if the illegal trade continues at present levels." Terming the current situation in Africa one of "appalling conservation and mis-

Elephants

management," the group called for more effective management of existing populations and continued adherence to the quota system, rather than a ban on the trade.[44]

If elephant populations continue their precipitous decline, pressure for a complete ban on the ivory trade is likely to increase. Proponents of a ban argue that it is the only way to ensure that elephants are not killed to satisfy foreign demand. They contend that the battle against severe, entrenched poaching demands such drastic measures. But some in the conservation community disagree, arguing that a ban would penalize those few African countries that are managing and conserving their elephants adequately and would take away incentives to protect the species. Some opponents of a ban believe that the ivory trade is so well entrenched that it would not disappear and would instead go underground, circumventing all monitoring and controls.

Some countries, such as South Africa and Zimbabwe, have developed successful elephant management programs that protect the herds while allowing selective harvests to make sure that elephant numbers do not outpace existing food sources or encroach on surrounding settlements. Others, such as the Central African Republic and Tanzania, face tremendous obstacles in their efforts to suppress powerful, well-armed poachers and to stamp out corrupt trade practices. Personnel shortages and limited resources greatly increase the challenge of their law enforcement task, which is ultimately critical to the African elephant's survival.

Importing countries are responsible for creating market incentives to poach elephants. Because they often have far greater resources to devote to the problem, their efforts to halt illegal trade are particularly crucial. Hong Kong, Japan, India, China, the United Kingdom, the United States, and Belgium—the world's major ivory importers—must support the new CITES ivory-control system, seize illegal ivory shipments, and carefully report all ivory trade. Countries that are not doing their share will continue to face increasing pressure to do so—from CITES parties, from conservation organizations, and from a growing number of outraged citizens around the world.

CHAPTER 7
Kangaroos and Other Macropods

Most celebrated for their jumping prowess and ability to nurture their young in pouches, kangaroos, wallabies, and other macropods (marsupials that belong to the family Macropodidae) are often depicted as eccentric, fascinating, and harmless creatures. In their native Australia, however, these marsupials are legally shot as pests; they compete with sheep and cattle for forage, destroy farmers' grain crops, and knock down fences. Kangaroos and wallabies are also killed to fuel a multimillion dollar leather, fur, and meat industry. Annual exports of unfinished skins and meat are worth approximately $10 million to Australian traders. Domestic sales probably raise the industry's total value to $20 million or so, although the actual totals fluctuate greatly from year to year.

Each of Australia's six states regulates its own harvest and trade by running quota and licensing systems based on estimates of the macropod populations within its jurisdiction.[1] The federal government approves each state's quotas, which specify the maximum number of animals that may be killed, and administers all export licensing.

Australia's massive macropod harvest has been the source of ecological and ethical debate for years. Some opponents of culling question the accuracy of official macropod head counts and argue that the quotas are too high, pushed up by increasingly powerful commercial forces and strong local politicians. Some suggest that red (*Macropus rufus*), eastern grey (*M. giganteous*), and western grey (*M. fuliginosus*) kangaroos, the most hunted species, will die out in 20 years. The governments of most Australian states, however, claim that the

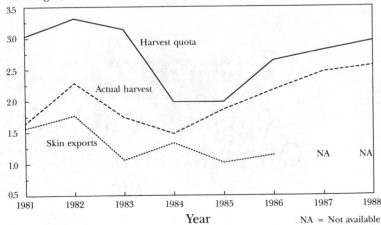

Figure 7.1
Australian Kangaroo Harvests and Exports,
1981–1988

Million kangaroos

Harvest quota

Actual harvest

Skin exports

NA   NA

Year   NA = Not available

Source: *Traffic Bulletin*, TRAFFIC(Japan).

cull is a necessary management tool to control pest populations. They also maintain that the market for macropods and their products is merely a useful way to deal with the dead animals, rather than an industry in its own right.

Supporters of culling further argue that kangaroos and related species reproduce more quickly when conditions are favorable and are thus able to withstand controlled hunting pressures. They point out that large fluctuations in kangaroo populations are natural. Rainfall is highly variable in Australia, especially in the drier interior, and, if a drought lasts long enough, substantial declines in the kangaroo populations are likely. But, because kangaroo populations have great powers of recovery, they reproduce rapidly in good seasons.[2] According to Frank Antram, director of TRAFFIC(Oceania), "provided that harvests are properly managed, macropod populations should be well able to withstand the additional pressure."[3]

Experts generally agree that Australia has more kangaroos today than it had in 1770 when Captain James Cook made his first landfall on the shore of Botany Bay. By clearing brush for crops and livestock, European settlers inadvertently opened prime feeding grounds for their pouched neighbors, and kangaroos flourished.[4]

The yearly macropod harvest has experienced some management difficulties; in 1985, for instance, the government of the state of Queensland reportedly gave out tags to kill 1.4 million animals, rather than the 1.08 million allowed by quota, and failed to keep track of

Red kangaroos (*Macropus rufus*).
John Houldsworth / Australian Information Service

the kill for different species.[5] Some biologists argued that the harvest would severely reduce the population of whiptail wallabies (*M. paryii*) in Queensland. Responding to a legal challenge to Queensland's 1985 management program, Australia briefly suspended exports of all native fauna, subject to management programs, including all macropod products.[6]

But, despite such problems, Antram says, there is no evidence that any kangaroo species currently is being endangered by the cull. He points out that, if the industry were to be closed down, indiscriminate killing likely would rise, causing increased cruelty and the destruction of nontarget species.[7] Animals shot by professional hunters for the commercial trade are usually killed quickly and relatively humanely, but those that fall prey to inexperienced amateurs may suffer unnecessarily.

Species in Trade

The three largest species—the red, eastern grey, and western grey kangaroos—make up most of the commercial trade in macropods. These species' large and often scarred hides are virtually indistinguishable after tanning. Some trade also occurs in the wallaroo (*M. robustus*), whiptail wallaby, Bennett's wallaby (*M. rufogriseus*), and rufus wallaby (*Thylogale billardierii*). None of these species is listed on the CITES appendices.

Kangaroos and Other Macropods

A female eastern grey kangaroo (*Macropus giganteus*) with its young in its pouch. The little "joey" is about nine months old and is ready to leave the doe's pouch permanently.
W. Brindle / Australian Information Service

Trade Volume and Routes

Australia exported roughly 1 million to 1.7 million skins per year from 1981 through 1986. Many of the kangaroos and wallabies harvested under the quota system are used to make leather, especially for shoes. Shoe manufacturers say kangaroo leather "breathes" better than other hides, an important asset for sportswear. Macropod leather is also fashioned into golf bags, bicycle seats, belts, and other leather products that require soft but durable material. Because goods made from kangaroo and wallaby leather usually are not labeled as such, they may be difficult for consumers to recognize.[8] Smaller markets for macropod fur and meat also exist.

According to one study, over three-quarters of the macropod skins exported from Australia between 1980 and 1984 went to shoemakers and other leather-goods manufacturers in Italy, West Germany, France, the United Kingdom, and other European countries. Italy alone accounted for close to 60 percent of the trade. Only 3 percent went to the United States.[9]

In September 1987, the European Economic Community took a major step toward curtailing imports of wallaby leather. The European Parliament adopted a resolution calling on the European Economic Commission and Council of Ministers to ban commercial trade in all macropods, except red and grey kangaroos; however, the resolution also called for careful monitoring of trade in red kangaroo and grey kangaroo products.[10]

In the 1960s and early 1970s, the United States was the world's major importer of kangaroo products. Then, in 1973, Australia temporarily banned exports. The following year, in response to reports from conservationists that the kangaroo harvest was unmanaged and population estimates were unreliable, the United States listed the red, western grey, and eastern grey species as threatened under the U.S. Endangered Species Act and imposed a moratorium on all kangaroo imports. To avoid losing the U.S. market, the Australian government forced the states to establish management programs and quotas. In 1981, the United States lifted the moratorium, but the trade, which had been diverted to Europe, never regained its former levels.[11] In 1987, the United States imported approximately 34,000 kangaroo skins, compared with nearly 160,000 in 1981. In a 12-month period in 1972-73, the United States imported close to 270,000 skins.[12]

Australians rarely eat kangaroo meat but do feed it to their dogs and cats. This is partly a matter of taste but mostly a health concern. Kangaroo meat is sometimes contaminated by bacteria, parasites, or dirt, and kangaroos are often killed and stored in ways that do not meet public health standards.[13]

In the early 1980s, however, much of the over 1,000 tons of kangaroo meat being shipped annually from Australia to Europe was sold as sausage or other edibles seldom marked as "kangaroo." In 1983, undercover imports and sales of kangaroo meat labeled as beef, pork, or venison touched off scandals in West Germany and other European countries. Consumers were angry about being duped, and officials were concerned that the meat probably failed to meet public health standards. Once the news broke, European imports dropped—to fewer than 50 tons in 1984—and customs officers tightened controls on the trade.[14]

Today, Australia continues to export kangaroo meat, much of it marked as "unfit for human consumption." Most of these shipments go to Hong Kong, Japan, and other Far Eastern countries, where they presumably are processed into pet food.

CHAPTER 8
Musk Deer

One of the most valuable wildlife products in the world comes from a small, primitive, rabbit-like deer found in the high Himalayas and remote alpine regions of China and the Soviet Union. Known as "musk," the strongly aromatic glandular secretion produced by male musk deer (*Moschus* spp.) is worth over $32,000 per pound in some markets.[1] A powerful perfume ingredient and purported energizing drug, musk has been used to tantalize humans for over 5,000 years. Musk deer usually are killed for this product, even though it is possible to collect it in nonlethal ways, such as by capturing live animals and "milking" their glands.

Trade Controls

The Himalayan population of musk deer in Afghanistan, Bhutan, Burma, India, Nepal, and Pakistan is listed on CITES Appendix I; all other populations are covered by Appendix II. According to Michael Green, a musk deer researcher associated with the International Union for Conservation of Nature and Natural Resources, intensive hunting combined with habitat loss—due to fuelwood collecting and livestock grazing—threatens the Himalayan population. Hunters and trappers in the Himalayas may annually harvest one-fifth to one-half of those mountains' musk deer population, crudely estimated at 30,000 animals.

While less is known about musk deer in China, these populations probably are severely stressed as well. The Chinese have attempted to farm musk deer but apparently with little economic success. Musk from captive-bred animals is reportedly inferior to that from wild animals, and captive musk deer are difficult to breed and manage. Musk deer are probably holding their own in the Soviet Union, where

Musk deer (*Moschus* spp.).
Pralad Yonzon

the government-controlled harvest accounts for the death of only 5 percent of the population per year.[2]

Trade Volume and Routes

Over 700 pounds of musk reach world markets in an average year, largely from the Himalayan and Chinese deer populations.[3] Since one male deer produces less than one ounce of musk, this annual toll represents the death of as many as 12,800 males—and an estimated two to three times as many females and fawns, which are mistakenly shot or inadvertently caught in snares.[4]

Scientists believe that much of the world's musk may be smuggled out of China to Hong Kong, the international center for the trade. Eighty-five percent of the world supply of musk eventually finds its way to Japan, where it is used principally in medicines for heart patients and young children.[5] Japan has had a reservation on the CITES listing of all musk deer species, though in July 1987 Japanese diplomats announced that the country would drop its reservation in 1989.* This change became effective April 1, 1989.

Between 1974 and 1983, Japan imported over $4.2 million worth of musk per year.[6] In 1985, after pressure from TRAFFIC(Japan), Japan stopped the practice of mixing musk into energy drinks and launched a review of its use in medicines. The country's medicinal industry

See appendix A, "How CITES Works," for an explanation of CITES reservations.

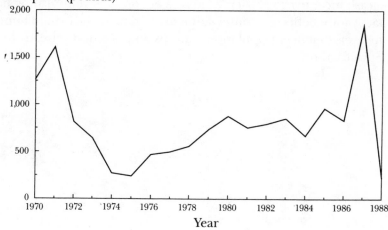

**Figure 8.1
Japanese Musk Imports,
1970–1988**

Musk imports (pounds)

Year

Source: TRAFFIC(Japan).

is now working to reduce the practice of using musk in drugs and should soon reregister its patents for these medicines.[7] However, Japan's musk trade surged in 1985 and then shot off the charts in 1987, when musk imports totaled over 1,800 pounds (figure 8.1). That activity surpassed the previous record for a year—about 1,600 pounds in 1971. Japan's 1987 musk imports retailed for up to 10 million yen per kilo, equal to an astounding $32,468 per pound.[8]

Tom Milliken, director of TRAFFIC(Japan), believes the run on imported musk indicates that Japanese dealers stockpiled the product in anticipation of the government's action to drop its reservation on musk deer.[9]

Not surprisingly, most of the remaining musk on the international market goes to the well-established perfume industry in France. Pricey French perfumes such as Chanel No. 5 and Madame Rochas still use natural musk in their formulas. However, the real thing is seldom used anymore in common perfumes because it is expensive, hard to find in unadulterated form, and often illegal. Instead, most fragrances labeled as "musk" actually contain substitute synthetic musk compounds.[10]

What Can Be Done

According to Dr. Green, one way to protect musk deer in the wild may be to allow controlled collection of their musk. Local people would be encouraged to catch the deer, extract their musk, and then release the animals, rather than snaring or shooting them in greater numbers than their populations can sustain. If managed effectively, this approach could support rural economies and give local people a cash incentive to conserve musk deer and their diminishing habitat. Another effective conservation method might be to limit hunting to levels that deer populations can sustain, as is done already in the Soviet Union.[11]

CHAPTER 9
Primates

The primate order includes over 200 species of "higher primates"—monkeys and apes, as well as humans—and "lower primates"—such as the tarsiers and lemurs of Madagascar. Humans aside, 90 percent of these species live in the tropical rain forests of Africa, Asia, and Latin America. As human activities destroy these forests, they also decimate native primate populations. One in three primate species is now considered endangered, vulnerable, or rare.[1]

Many species have been pushed to the brink of extinction by widespread habitat loss, the single greatest cause for the worldwide decline in primate populations. The mountain gorilla (*Gorilla gorilla beringei*) of Africa, the golden-headed lion tamarin (*Leontopithecus chrysomelas*) of Brazil, and the orangutan (*Pongo pygmaeus*), a shaggy orange inhabitant of Borneo and Sumatra, are a few of the primates endangered by human encroachment on their native territories.

Hunting pressures are also responsible for the demise of wild primates in several parts of the tropics. According to World Wildlife Fund Primate Program Director Russell Mittermeier, the main reason primates are hunted is as a source of food for humans.[2] For example, native people kill thousands of primates for "bushmeat" in the Peruvian and Brazilian Amazon, causing local extinctions of woolly monkeys (*Lagothrix* spp.) and spider monkeys (*Ateles* spp.). In the dense interior forests of Suriname, monkey meat can account for as much as one-quarter of all meat eaten by the forest tribes.[3]

Some species of monkeys and apes also are persecuted as pests in some regions, particularly in Africa and Asia. West African villagers, for instance, shoot interloping baboons (*Papio* spp.), mangabeys

(*Cercocebus* spp.), and vervet monkeys (*Cercopithecus pygerythrus* sspp.) because they are known to ransack local gardens and rob farmers' fields. The major crop raiders in Asia are probably the pig-tailed macaque (*Macaca nemestrina*), the crab-eating macaque (*M. fascicularis*), and the rhesus monkey (*M. mulatta*). Interestingly, Central and South American primates are seldom implicated as agricultural nuisances, possibly because they are primarily tree dwellers, living on a diet of fruits and leaves found in the upper canopy of Neotropical forests.[4]

Trade Controls

All nonhuman primates are listed by CITES. Appendix I primates include the aye-aye (*Daubentonia madagascariensis*), all lemurs and indrids (Lemuridae and Indridae), all dwarf lemurs (Cheirogaleidae), all gibbons (Hylobatidae), and all of the great apes—chimpanzees (*Pan troglodytes*), gorillas (*Gorilla gorilla*), and orangutans. Appendix I also includes numerous marmosets and tamarins (Callithricidae), spider monkeys (Cebidae); guenons, macaques, and baboons (Cercopithecidae); and other species. All remaining primates are on Appendix II.

In addition, most endangered or rare primates have some legal protection at the national level. In an effort to conserve native species,

Ring-tailed lemur (*Lemur catta*).
Russell A. Mittermeier / WWF

Brazil banned all wildlife exports in 1967. Since 1973, Bangladesh, Bolivia, Colombia, India, Malaysia, Peru, and Thailand also have imposed export bans, cutting off major primate supply lines.[5]* Almost all countries with indigenous primate populations now control export in some way.[7] The United States includes over 30 primate species on its national list of endangered and threatened species. It is also obligated under the Lacey Act to refuse entry to any primates exported from another country in violation of that country's domestic law.

Trade Volume and Routes

Apes and monkeys have been traded for thousands of years, from the days of ancient Egypt when guenons (*Cercopithecus* spp.) were prized possessions and baboons were used to harvest figs. Today, most imported, live primates are shipped to research laboratories in the United States, Japan, the European Economic Community, Taiwan, Canada, or the Soviet Union.[8] Valued in medical circles for their close biological resemblance to people, such primates as crab-eating macaques, rhesus monkeys, squirrel monkeys (*Saimiri sciureus*), and chimpanzees are used primarily to test vaccines and cures for all kinds of human diseases—among them, leprosy, malaria, polio, hepatitis (non-A, non-B), and, most recently, acquired immune deficiency syndrome (AIDS).[9]

Although 80 to 90 percent of primates used in medical research come from the wild,[10] the primate trade has decreased significantly over the past 30 years. In the 1950s, researchers imported over 1.5 million monkeys per year in their race to develop a polio vaccine, and the United States alone imported 200,000 primates annually.[11] By 1979, world primate trade had dropped to approximately 65,000 animals.[12] Experts estimate that international trade in monkeys and apes has remained steady during the 1980s.

One major cause of the reduction is the tightening of trade controls by key countries in which primates are native. In addition, during the 1960s and 1970s, new CITES controls on all primate trade, advances in primate breeding programs, more frequent reuse of animals in laboratories, escalating prices for primates caught in the wild, and the high cost of caring for live primates during biomedical research contributed to the slowdown.

The pet trade remains the second major market for wild primates, especially monkeys from Latin America. However, the pet monkey

*India established export quotas for rhesus monkeys during the 1960s and early 1970s, then levied an outright ban in December 1977 in protest against the use of rhesus monkeys in U.S. nuclear research.†

and ape business has been outlawed in several importing countries. Based on evidence that monkey bites could spread rabies and other diseases, health officials in the United States banned all primate imports for the pet trade in 1975.[13] Denmark moved a decade earlier, banning primate imports out of concern for public health in 1965.[14] Other European countries that restricted primate trade for health reasons during the 1960s and 1970s included Finland, West Germany, Italy, and Switzerland. But some major markets, such as Japan and Taiwan, have not taken similar actions.[15] In Japan, for instance, squirrel monkeys and gibbons are still popular pets.[16]

Zoos, circuses, and other animal exhibits also contribute to world demand for primates. Most primates held in zoos around the world were probably caught in the wild.[17] Although the exhibition market is a relatively small part of the trade in wild primates, it can have important repercussions when it involves threatened species, such as the great apes.[18]

Because many primates (among them, gorillas and chimpanzees) are so rare, they are expensive. Zoos will pay $75,000 or so for a lowland gorilla, and researchers can expect to pay $25,000 or more for a young chimp.[19]

Fewer than one-third of the world's primate species have been recorded in trade, but international markets have contributed to some local extinctions. For instance, Thailand's peninsular population of

White-handed gibbon (*Hylobates lar*).
Russell A. Mittermeier / WWF

Stump-tailed macaque (*Macaca arctoides*).
Russell A. Mittermeier / WWF

stump-tailed macaques (*Macaca arctoides*) was seriously depleted by foreign trade until the government levied a primate export ban in 1976. The species is now uncommon in international trade. Rhesus monkeys, too, were trapped in great numbers for overseas research markets and are now gone from much of their former range in northern India.[20] Today, the species is protected in its native countries, and successful captive-breeding programs supply the great majority of rhesus monkeys used in research. The United States, for example, became "self-sufficient" in rhesus monkeys in the early 1980s, breeding enough animals to supply its research needs.[21]

Experts are still worried about some species for which either good population data do not exist or adequate management programs have not been developed. Chief among these are the pig-tailed macaque, which is exported in particularly large numbers; the crab-eating macaque, mostly from Indonesia and the Philippines; the hamadryas baboon (*Papio hamadryas*), exported from Ethiopia and Somalia; and the patas monkey (*Erythrocebus patas*), from Chad and Nigeria.[22]

Trade figures underestimate the number of animals actually "taken" from the wild, partly because estimates fail to count those that die during capture and shipping. Hunters frequently capture a baby ape by first killing the animal's mother and other adults in the family group. As many as 5 to 10 animals may perish for every live chimpanzee infant secured for an international buyer.[23] Infant chimpanzees and other apes, who are often completely dependent on their mothers for the first several years of their lives, may die before exportation because of the trauma of capture, infection by human-transmitted disease, or improper feeding.

Once in transit, primates are placed under further stress. A mid-1980s study of primate mortality in trade found that one wild crab-eating macaque dies in transit for every one that is successfully delivered to a research facility in the United States,[24] and other evidence suggests that chimpanzees may also suffer as high as 50 percent mortality during shipping.[25]

Stress and improper care—a particular hazard of illegal trade—can cause irreversible damages that do not become apparent until after importation. In 1982, for instance, all nine chimpanzees in a shipment imported illegally into Austria died within weeks of their arrival, despite rehabilitative efforts by the Vienna Zoo.[26]

While the downturn in international commerce in primates taken from the wild is promising, it does not mean that trade is no longer a concern. Some species are so threatened by other forces, such as destruction of their habitat, that they can ill afford any losses to trade. West African chimpanzees are a noteworthy example;[27] conservationists are also worried about such species as the white-cheeked gibbon (*Hylobates concolor*), the white-handed gibbon (*H. lar*), and the highly endangered golden-headed lion tamarin.

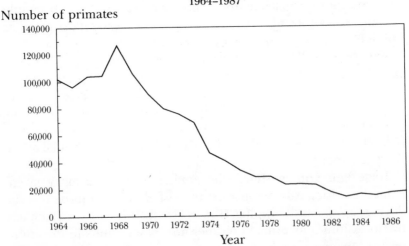

Figure 9.1
U.S. Live Primate Imports,
1964–1987

Number of primates

Year

Source: U.S. Customs data.

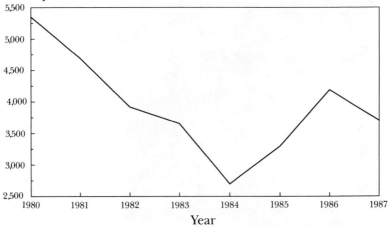

Figure 9.2
Japanese Live Primate Imports,
1980–1987

Number of primates

Year

Source: Japanese Customs data.

The United States, the largest primate market in the world, imports 13,000 to 17,000 primates per year (figure 9.1).[28] The second-ranking United Kingdom imports about 6,000 primates annually, down from about 8,000 in the mid-1970s.[29] Japan, in third place, saw primate imports decline from more than 22,000 in 1972 to about 2,700 in 1984 (figure 9.2).[30]* Taiwan, Canada, the Soviet Union, France, and the Netherlands are also important consumers.[31]

These importing countries receive most of their macaques from the Philippines and Indonesia, while wild-caught green monkeys and baboons generally come from Kenya, Somalia, Ethiopia, and Tanzania. Malaysia, once an important Asian source of primates, banned such exports in 1984, and Kenya, which once was a top African supplier, banned primate exports in 1981.[32] Most New World species probably are exported from Guyana and Peru; the Peruvian government has a special program to facilitate and oversee the primate export trade.[33]

Species in Trade

Nearly 80 percent of all primates in trade belong to the Old World monkey family (Cercopithecidae).[34] Considered the most "typical" or monkeylike of all primates, Old World monkeys commonly found in international trade include the macaques, guenons, and baboons.

After 1984, Japanese live primate imports increased somewhat, to almost 4,200 in 1986 and about 3,700 in 1987.

Rhesus monkey (*Macaca
mulatta*).
Russell A. Mittermeier / WWF

The crab-eating macaque, the most widely used species in
biomedical research, comprises roughly half of the entire world
trade.[35] Also known as the long-tailed macaque, this species is an "all-
purpose" research animal frequently used in drug safety testing and
other experiments. Primate suppliers have established a few small
captive-breeding colonies for the species in the United States, the
United Kingdom, and the Philippines, but most of the animals still
come from wild populations.[36] Another Old World standby, the rhesus
monkey, is no longer available in large numbers from the wild. The
species now is bred in quantity in the United States and used to test
vaccines and other biological products.[37] Biomedical researchers also
rely heavily on other members of the family, primarily the green
monkey (*Cercopithecus aethiops*), used in toxicology testing; various
baboons, particularly the olive baboon (*Papio anubis*) and yellow
baboon (*P. cynocephalus*), which are used for experimental surgery and
reproductive research, and the hamadryas baboon, which is used for
hepatitis research; and the patas monkey, most heavily used for polio
vaccine production in France. All of these species are taken almost
exclusively from the wild.[38]

Another 10 percent of all primates in trade belong to the family

Cebidae.[39] Denizens of the Latin American tropical forest, the most widely used Cebidae include the night monkeys (*Aotus* spp.), nocturnal animals with the owllike habit of hooting on clear, moonlit nights, and the inquisitive and social squirrel monkey. Not surprisingly, night monkeys are used for vision experiments. They also feature prominently in malarial research because they are apparently the only nonhuman species able to contract the disease.[40] Squirrel monkeys are also used in a wide range of research efforts, including vision and cardiovascular experiments, drug testing, and general disease inquiries. Night monkeys and squirrel monkeys used for experimentation mostly come from the wild.[41]

Most of the remaining primates in trade belong to the Callitrichidae family, which includes Neotropical marmosets and tamarins.[42] The common marmoset (*Callithrix jacchus*) is often found in trade; most of the animals involved, however, are captive bred. The tamarin trade is largely made up of the red-chested tamarin (*Saguinus labiatus*), saddleback tamarin (*S. fuscicollis*), and moustached tamarin (*S. mystax*). According to primate trade experts Michael Kavanagh, Ardith Eudey, and David Mack, the market for the cotton-top tamarin (*S. oedipus*) used to be "the symbol of the worst side of the primate trade." Found only in northwestern Colombia, the species was seriously threatened by local and international pet markets as well as the research trade

Young chimpanzees (*Pan troglodytes*) illegally shipped from Sierra Leone to zoos and laboratories in Europe.
D. Van den Hoorn

during the 1970s. Colombia gave this primate complete legal protection in 1970, but to no avail. Animals frequently were laundered into foreign trade via Panama, Bolivia, and Paraguay. Some of the smuggling problems were finally abated when the United States listed the species as endangered in 1976, cutting off much demand, and Panama and Paraguay improved their export controls in 1979 and 1980.[43]

CHIMPANZEES

A 1987 report of the Committee for the Conservation and Care of Chimpanzees claimed that only 150,000 to 230,000 chimpanzees were left in Africa. The report's authors believe that two subspecies, the western (*Pan troglodytes verus*) and eastern (*P. t. schweinfurthii*) are in danger of extinction, while a third subspecies (*P. t. troglodytes*) of Central Africa is not faring much better.[44] All chimpanzees are listed on Appendix I of CITES. Twelve out of the 21 countries with native chimpanzee populations belong to CITES, and some of these countries also have domestic legislation to protect the species. In 1989, the United States listed the chimpanzee as "endangered" under the Endangered Species Act. With endangered status, all U.S. chimpanzee trade is to receive more thorough government review and public scrutiny.

As of mid-1989, there were some 3,000 captive chimpanzees in the United States, including 1,400 to 1,600 in research facilities. Some 350 of those were in breeding programs.[45] Most wild chimpanzees held in captivity probably came from Guinea, Sierra Leone, and Liberia.[46]

Continuing demand for chimpanzees, particularly for research on hepatitis and AIDS (and, especially for testing commercial vaccine batches if an AIDS vaccine is discovered), presents serious moral, ethical, and conservation concerns. Highly sensitive to being wrenched from their family groups and left without comforting role models, whether in the wild or in captive-breeding facilities, young chimpanzees are difficult to breed and expensive to maintain properly.[47] And, as world-famous primatologist Jane Goodall points out, there are serious concerns about how chimpanzees are actually treated in laboratories. She reports that chimpanzees are by nature very social, active, and highly intelligent but "chimpanzee facilities in most biomedical research laboratories allow for the expression of none of these activities and behaviors. They provide little—if anything—more than the warmth, food and water, and veterinary care required to sustain life."[48]

Demand for chimpanzees is fueled by biomedical laboratories that are racing to develop a vaccine against AIDS. Goodall asserts, "Chimpanzees are not good models for AIDS research; although the AIDS virus stays alive and replicates within the chimpanzee's bloodstream, no chimp has yet come down with the disease itself."[49] Agreement on this point is not unanimous. Some scientists agree with Goodall; others claim that using chimpanzees is essential for safely testing potential vaccines. Once a workable vaccine is created, U.S. demand for "test" chimpanzees could range into the thousands.[50]

Chimpanzees are held in captivity in zoos as well as in research facilities. There are around 2,000 chimps in zoos registered with the International Species Information System (ISIS), a global information and breeding network.* Just over half of these animals are known to have been captive-born, one-fifth are known to have come from the wild, and the origins of the remainder are unknown.[51]

Often, trade in chimpanzees involves illegal activity. Infant chimps taken in Liberia and Guinea are known to be smuggled into Sierra Leone for shipment overseas, though Sierra Leone has officially prohibited exports of the species since 1978. Evidence also points to increasing illegal exports from Uganda, from Zaire by way of Zambia and Burundi, and from Tanzania via Burundi.[52] Young chimps sometimes are taken from the wild and exported to Spain, the Canary Islands, and Israel, where local photographers at beach resorts use them to lure tourist business, in violation of CITES' prohibition of commercial trade in Appendix I species.

Efforts by some research organizations to use chimpanzees caught in the wild for profit-making ventures have touched off protests. In 1982, a private Austrian pharmaceutical company, Immuno AG, came up with a plan to circumvent trade barriers by doing its hepatitis work in Sierra Leone using native chimps and, eventually, to develop a breeding center there for future supplies. The company chairman maintained that the only chimps that would be used were those that otherwise would lose their lives to the forces of deforestation or local pest control.[53] Concerned about the project's impact on local ape populations, conservationists in the United States and Europe strongly opposed some of Immuno's plans. The firm struck back with multiple multimillion-dollar libel suits against several detractors.[54]

In 1986, however, Immuno leapt into controversy again, when it received a shipment of 20 chimpanzees from Sierra Leone for hepatitis and AIDS research. This move prompted protests from

---

*There are perhaps 600 to 800 legitimate zoos in the world and countless numbers of roadside displays, manageries, and informal animal exhibits. Some 340 zoos participate in ISIS, including most of North America's licensed zoos.

Mountain gorilla (*Gorilla gorilla*) family.
A. Veddar

TRAFFIC(Austria) and other conservation groups because of Sierra Leone's ban on chimpanzee exports and because Immuno's imports were viewed as contraventions to CITES' prohibition on using Appendix I species for commercial purposes. Nevertheless, the Austrian Ministry of Trade evidently granted an exception to normal CITES restrictions.[55]

GORILLAS

Trade in gorillas from the wild also raises important conservation dilemmas. Although gorillas apparently are not traded in large numbers, even a few exports may be harmful. This is particularly true since poachers often capture young gorillas—as they capture chimpanzees—by first killing mothers and other adult group members. Some experts believe the number of gorillas traded in the late 1970s and early 1980s could have had a significant impact on local populations.[56]

Gorillas from the wild seldom show up in trade reports, and those that do occur are usually for zoos. There were reports of regular Belgian trade in smuggled western lowland gorillas (*Gorilla gorilla gorilla*) before that country joined CITES in 1984.[57] The same year, the Netherlands office of the International Union for Conservation of Nature and Natural Resources (IUCN) paid the import expenses for seven wild lowland gorillas from Cameroon in what proved to be a highly controversial gesture. The animals were placed in a Dutch zoo, with IUCN-Netherlands arguing that the apes had been captured already and would die otherwise. But some conservationists countered that the action only encouraged more poaching.[58] Because the countries involved had not yet ratified CITES, they were exempt from CITES controls.

In 1987, the United Kingdom's minister of state decided to authorize the importation by a British zoo of three western lowland gorillas from the People's Republic of the Congo, against the advice of a national panel of noted primatologists and other scientists inside and outside the U.K. government. The animals reportedly were orphan gorillas, their parents having been killed by hunters, and were being held in very poor facilities in the Congo.[59] U.K. officials contended that the import was a justifiable one-time exception, and the zoo director argued that, if he could not take them in, the animals would perish or be sold to institutions that could not care for them. Opponents of the transaction said that it would perpetuate trade in the Appendix I species and that the animals were not needed for breeding purposes because the United Kingdom had a sufficient captive population on hand, provided that the country's zoos cooperated in sharing breeding animals and offspring.

The American Association of Zoological Parks and Aquariums (AAZPA) had offered earlier to place the Congolese orphan animals in U.S. zoos and include them in a comprehensive species survival plan for gorillas. In addition, the AAZPA had proposed supporting gorilla conservation measures in the Congo, including gorilla population surveys and training for local conservation personnel. The offer presented a compromise: the animals would still be imported and cared for by zoos, but they would become part of an overall survival strategy; wild populations would receive additional conservation attention. The Congo government apparently ignored the offer.[60] Later in 1987, the three gorillas were imported into the United Kingdom, in spite of protests from many conservationists and scientists.

The International Primate Protection League reported two other 1987 incidents of baby gorillas being taken from the wild. In January 1987, three gorillas were exported from Cameroon via Zaire to Taiwan, with permits describing them as "monkeys." Two died en route, and the sole survivor was sent to the Taipei Zoo. Following the incident, which stirred considerable protest from private conservationists, Taiwan banned the importation of Appendix I species. Later in the year, four more gorillas were shipped from Equatorial Guinea to Spain.[61]

As of late 1987, there were about 400 gorillas in ISIS-listed zoos around the world. All but 14 of these belonged to the western lowland subspecies. Fifty-three percent of these gorillas were known to have been born in captivity, 43 percent were known to have been born in the wild, and the remaining 4 percent were of unknown origin. In 1987, these zoo-housed gorillas produced 18 western lowland gorilla offspring.[62]

Captive Breeding

As several species of wild primates have become more difficult—in some cases, impossible—to obtain, researchers have begun to "recycle" laboratory stock, using the same animals for more than one project. They also have turned to less expensive lab animals, such as dogs or rats, in experiments where primate models are not essential.[63] The

Fur coat made from the skin of a
colobus monkey (*Colobus guereza*).
A. Brash

need for "fresh," affordable primates continues, however, leading
countries with long-term interests in biomedical research and the
necessary financial resources to support costly captive-breeding
facilities to improve their primate-producing capabilities. The United
Kingdom and West Germany now breed large numbers of common
marmosets, which are no longer legally available from the wild.[64]
Primate breeding facilities are also active in the United States. In 1981,
for example, 8,645 primates were born in U.S. facilities; over two-thirds
of these were rhesus monkeys, but baboons, squirrel monkeys, long-
tailed macaques, and small numbers of other primates were also
produced.[65] In 1983, the World Health Organization adopted a policy
statement strongly recommending that endangered, vulnerable, or
rare primates not be used in biomedical research unless they come
from existing, self-sustaining captive-bred populations, but
compliance is voluntary.

Although such breeding programs take some trade pressure off
wild populations, they do not yet fill world demand for most species.
In Japan, researchers reportedly are making increased use of the
native Japanese macaque or snow monkey (*Macaca fuscus*), prompting
concern from local conservationists as entire troops just "disappear"
from the wild.[66] In the United States, where primate use is guided

by a National Primate Plan developed by the National Institutes of Health's Interagency Primate Steering Committee, reliance on wild animals is lower than the world average. In 1981, for example, U.S. breeding programs supplied 28 percent of the primates used in research; another 16 percent were taken for use from other programs. As a result, 56 percent came from either the wild or foreign breeding programs.[67]

Trade in Parts and Skins

Although primates are most sought-after in foreign markets when alive, there is some international commerce in monkey skins, whole stuffed animals, and baboon trophies.

The black and white colobus monkey (*Colobus guereza*) of East Africa, whose glossy, jet black and white coat is sewn into exotic wall-hangings and throw rugs, has been exploited for the skin trade for years. Over 200,000 skins from this Appendix II species were on sale in tourist shops around Nairobi and Mombasa, Kenya, and Addis Ababa, Ethiopia, during the early 1970s.[68] (Kenya and Ethiopia now prohibit such trade.[69]) Although CITES data show only 125 or so colobus skins in annual international trade from 1980 to 1984, little is known about illegal trade volumes, and some experts believe that the species may not be able to sustain current commercial pressure.[70]

Other species prized for their skins include the blue monkey (*Cercopithecus mitis*), an Appendix II species whose hide is sometimes made into handbags for sale in Uganda, and *C. m. kandti*, a rare golden subspecies of the blue monkey whose skins are featured by shopkeepers in Rwanda and Zaire.[71] Stuffed specimens of China's golden monkey (*Rhinopithecus roxellanae*), a large, blue-faced endangered species, are showing up in Japanese markets, despite Chinese claims that such items have not been exported since the 1930s.[72] There are also reports of some internal African trade in chimpanzee skins and dried parts for purported "magic" and medicinal uses.[73]

CHAPTER 10
Rhinoceroses

All five of the world's rhinoceros species have sharply pointed, gray horns on their foreheads—some have one, some two. Composed of the same keratin protein fibers that make up horses' hooves and human fingernails, rhino horn can be carved, slivered, shaved, or ground into dust. Traditional Eastern cultures prize rhino horn in all of these forms. It is fashioned into valuable "jambia" dagger handles in North Yemen, while in South Korea it is pulverized and rolled into honey-coated medicine balls—along with crushed donkey hide and antelope horn.

Fewer than 11,000 rhinos are left in the world today, down from 73,000 as late as 1970. No other animal family has been as devastated by trade. During the 1970s, the growing popularity and high price of rhino horn encouraged heavy hunting, bringing all rhino species close to extinction. In the 1980s, trade has slowed but remains the single greatest threat to surviving rhino populations. A full 85 percent of the world's rhino population is estimated to have been lost between 1970 and 1987.[1] Although conservationists have made progress in convincing government leaders in some consumer countries, most notably North Yemen, to control the trade, markets remain open in some parts of the Far East, and the deadly, illicit trade continues.

Rhino Uses

Rhino experts Esmond and Chryssee Bradley Martin term the rhino a "mobile pharmacy" to the peoples of East Asia (figure 10.1). Not only are rhino horn and horn powders used for everything from high blood pressure to impotence, there are traditional Oriental recipes for cures made of rhino hide, bones, meat, penis, blood, and even urine.[2] In India, Esmond Martin found zoos selling rhino urine for

44 cents a liter; sufferers would drink the frothy liquid to cure asthma or a sore throat. In Nepal, he discovered the unusual practice of tying rhino umbilical chords around babies' waists to stop the infants from crying.[3] In Thailand, some merchants sell not only rhino horn but also hide, nails, penises, blood, and dung. A whole, fresh Sumatran rhino carcass commands $3,800 to $7,600 in Bangkok. The animal's penis alone can fetch $600 and is used, not surprisingly, as an aphrodisiac.[4]

Rhino Species and Population Status

Various species of rhinoceros are native to Africa and Asia (figure 10.2). Africa has two species—the black (or hook-lipped) rhino (*Diceros bicornis*) and the white (or square-lipped) rhino (*Ceratotherium simum*) (figures 10.3 and 10.4). Once the most numerous of all rhinos, the black rhino has been the target of the greatest hunting pressure. In 1970, the world population of black rhinos was 65,000; by 1980, the count had dropped to 15,000; today, fewer than 4,000 remain.[6] The white rhino is almost equally scarce. One subspecies, the southern white rhino, was nearly extinct by the 1920s, when only 20 or 30 animals could be found in the wild.[7] Today, this subspecies is reasonably well-protected in parks of southern Africa, and its population has actually grown over the past 15 years to over 4,000 animals.[8] Some southern white rhinos, mainly older nonbreeding males, are hunted legally. The northern white rhino subspecies is verging on extinction, with only a remnant population of 17 or so well-guarded survivors left in a Zairian park and perhaps a few others in southern Sudan.[9]

Figure 10.1
Uses of Rhino Horn, by Country

China	Patented traditional medicines for export
Japan	Traditional medicines
Singapore	Primarily an entrepot and trading center; horn is presumably used for medicinal purposes
South Korea	Traditional medicines, including edible Chyng Sim Hwan ball (used for "high blood pressure, nose bleeds, paralysis, body pains, and 'contaminated blood' ")
Thailand	Trades large quantities of horn, as well as hide, nails, dried blood, and other body parts
North Yemen	jambias (horn used to carve handles for knives, which have been a sign of status for Yemeni men)

Presumably, all other Asian nations importing rhino horn use it for medicinal purposes.

Source: *TRAFFIC(U.S.A.)*

Figure 10.2
Rhino Populations, by Species and Over Time

	Black	Northern white	Southern white	Indian	Javan	Sumatran	Total
1922			20–30				
1970	65,000	Several thousand					app. 70,000
1979	15,000	650					
1984	8,800						
1986	4,500						
1987	3,800	20	approx. 4,000	1,700	55	fewer than 700	11,000– 11,500

Source: See References.

There are three Asian species—the Indian (or great one-horned) rhino (*Rhinoceros unicornis*), the Sumatran (or hairy) rhino (*Dicerorhinus sumatrensis*), and the Javan rhino (*Rhinoceros sondaicus*) (figures 10.5 and 10.6). Possibly as few as 1,700 Indian rhinos exist today, all in protected wildlife reserves of India and Nepal. Noted for its armor-plated appearance, the Indian rhino has been poached heavily in its Indian habitat: since 1982, at least 223 have been killed in the state of Assam. The Sumatran species also is faring poorly. Down from 1,500 animals in 1980 to a mere 400 to 800 today, Sumatran rhinos have almost completely disappeared from Burma, Thailand, Vietnam, Kampuchea, and Laos. So far, the species is managing to hang on in remote parts of Malaysia and Indonesia, although in Malaysia rhinos are still killed to supply Asian medicinal markets. The Javan rhino is probably the most highly endangered Asian rhino. Only 55 individuals are left, all in a small reserve on the island of Java in Indonesia.[10]

Trade Controls

All five rhino species are endangered and are listed on Appendix I of CITES. They are also protected by national law throughout their range, with the possible exception of animals found in Kampuchea and Vietnam. Under the Endangered Species Act, the United States generally prohibits all trade in wild rhinos and rhino products, with the single exception of the southern white rhino; this subspecies can

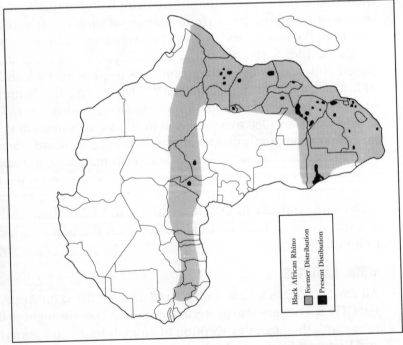

Figure 10.4
Ranges of the White Rhinos, Past and Present

Northern White Rhino
Former Distribution
Present Distribution
Southern White Rhino
Former Distibution
Present Distibution

Figure 10.3
Range of the Black Rhino, Past and Present

Black African Rhino
Former Distribution
Present Distibution

Skins of polar bears (*Ursus maritimus*) have been sought in world trade since the days of the Roman Empire because of their glossy texture and cream color. E. Flipse

Cheetahs (*Acinonyx jubatus*) are endangered throughout their African range and are nearly extinct in Asia. Nevertheless, some international commerce in cheetah skins and trophies continues.
M. Boulton

The jaguar (*Panthera onca*) is the largest, strongest, and most highly prized trophy cat in the Western Hemisphere. It is still relatively common in a few portions of its original range, but hunting and habitat destruction have combined to make it quite rare in many other areas where it once was common.
Y. J. Rey-Millet

The Bengal tiger (*Panthera tigris tigris*) is the only subspecies of tiger currently holding its own in the wild, thanks largely to efforts by the Indian and Nepalese governments. Three subspecies are considered extinct, and all others are seriously threatened.
E. P. Gee

The bobcat (*Felis rufus*) is legally trapped in the United States and Canada. Together with the lynx, it accounts for nearly one-half of all small-cat skins recorded in world markets today.
Conrad Fjetland/U.S. Fish and Wildlife Service

Imports of skins of the leopard cat (*Felis bengalensis*) into the United States are illegal. However, Far East markets for this Asian cat are still active, particularly in Japan.
E. P. Gee

Ocelot (*Felis pardalis*) skins were a prized fashion item from the 1960s to the early 1980s, with over 68,000 skins recorded on the international market in 1983 alone. Trade has declined dramatically, however; fewer than 1,000 skins of this endangered species were reportedly traded in 1985.
Andrew Young

Poaching for its ivory tusks has caused the population of the African elephant
(*Loxodonta africana*) to decline precipitously. Kenya and Uganda, for example,
have lost 85 percent of their elephants since 1973.
Rick Weyerhaueser / WWF

The endangered Asian elephant (*Elephas maximus*) is seldom hunted for the
international ivory market now, though a small amount of poaching for locally
used ivory and meat remains. The greatest threat to this species, which
numbers only between 29,000 and 44,000 in the wild, is habitat loss.
Alain Comfort

The highly endangered golden-headed lion tamarin (*Leontopithecus rosalia chrysomelas*) was nearly wiped out when about 50 individuals were taken from the wild in Brazil and smuggled into Europe and Japan in the early 1980s.
Russell A. Mittermeier/WWF

The crab-eating macaque (*Macaca fascicularis*) is the most widely used primate species in medical research, with most coming from the wild in Indonesia and the Philippines.
Russell A. Mittermeier/WWF

Trade in gorillas (*Gorilla gorilla*) from the wild is relatively uncommon and mostly to zoos. However, even a small amount of trade may be more than this rare African ape can safely absorb.
Rick Weyerhaueser/WWF

Only an estimated 150,000 to 230,000 chimpanzees (*Pan troglodytes*) are left in Africa, as demand from medical researchers and other live animal markets continues to propel hunting of this ape. Between 5 and 10 chimpanzees in the wild may die for each infant captured by hunters.
Geza Teleki

Severe hunting pressure has caused Africa's black rhinoceros (*Diceros bicornis*), once the most numerous of the world's five rhino species, to decline from about 65,000 in 1970 to fewer than 4,000 in the late 1980s.
Rick Weyerhaeuser / WWF

The 1,700 or so remaining Indian rhinoceroses (*Rhinoceros unicornis*) in the wild are all legally protected in wildlife reserves in India and Nepal. Nevertheless, poaching continues to be a serious threat to this and other rhino species.
M. Boulton

Large-scale hunting wiped out so many Antarctic fur seals (*Arctocephalus gazella*) that only a few dozen were left in the early 1900s. Today, they have recovered somewhat, so that about 400,000 live in the wild.
F. O'Gorman

Crabeater seals (*Lobodon carcinophagus*) are probably the world's most abundant large mammal, with a total population broadly estimated at between 8 and 50 million.
F. O'Gorman

Hunting has decimated the giant otter (*Pteronura brasiliensis*), which survives only in parts of South America.
N. Duplaix

The International Whaling Commission agreed to a voluntary moratorium on all commercial whaling, including in humpback whales (*Megaptera novaengliae*), beginning in 1986. However, a few countries have skirted this moratorium by claiming that their whaling is for "scientific" purposes.
Ocean Films, Ltd.

From the 17th through the early 20th centuries, ivory hunters and opportunistic whalers killed massive numbers of the Atlantic walrus (*Odobenus rosmarus rosmarus*) in quest of its long, sharp tusks.
R. Hernandez

be imported legally in the form of noncommercial hunting trophies under certain conditions.[11]

Rhino-horn Exports

Since most rhino-horn trade is illegal, tracking market routes is difficult. Experts believe, however, that over 95 percent of all commercial horn comes from African—rather than Asian—rhinos. Angola, Chad, Kenya, Mozambique, Somalia, Sudan, Tanzania, and Uganda are known to have lost thousands of rhinos during the 1970s. During the early 1980s, poachers turned their sights on the Central African Republic, Zaire, and Zambia and were extremely active in Zimbabwe in 1984 and 1985. Today, the heaviest poaching probably occurs in the east African nations of Tanzania, Zambia, and Mozambique. Smugglers frequently ship horn from these countries to Burundi, Djibouti, Sudan, or the United Arab Emirates (UAE) for eventual transport to black marketeers in North Yemen. Another common

Figure 10.5
Ranges of the Indian and Javan Rhinos, Past and Present

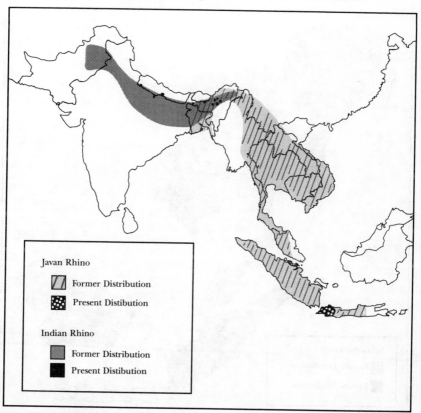

Javan Rhino

    Former Distribution

    Present Distibution

Indian Rhino

    Former Distribution

    Present Distibution

smuggling route leads to eastern Asia by way of Burundi, the Central African Republic, Namibia, Portugal, Tanzania, or the UAE.[12]

Rhino poaching is serious business in Africa. In Zimbabwe, Africa's largest remaining population of black rhino is under siege, and, in Zambia, poaching of black rhino is virtually out of control. Between July 1984 and June 1988, gangs armed with high-powered rifles targeted black rhinos in the remote Zambezi Valley of Zimbabwe, killing 423 of the rhinos in the area.[13] By early June 1988, guards in the valley had shot and killed 39 poachers and sent at least 30 others to prison.[14] A team of 70 armed scouts now guards the 150-mile border along the Zambezi River to keep Zambian poachers at bay. Park staff also have moved 110 rhinos to safer sanctuaries.[15]

Figure 10.6
Ranges of the Sumatran Rhino, Past and Present

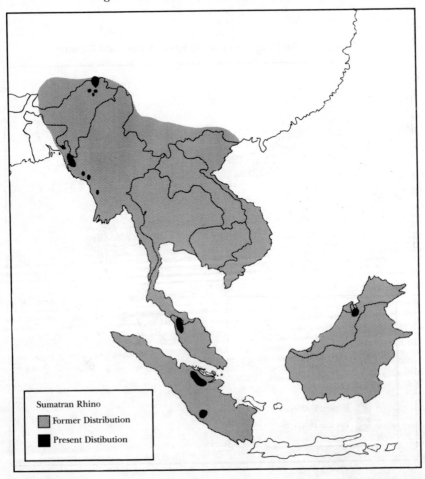

International Wildlife Trade: Whose Business Is It?

Black rhinoceros (*Diceros bicornis*).
M. Amin

Sumatran rhinoceros (*Dicerorhinus sumatrensis*).
Hakon Skafte / WWF

The Consumer Market

In recent years, North Yemen has been the world's largest consumer of rhino horn, importing over half of all commercial horn on the world market in the early 1980s.[16] Daggers adorned with finely carved rhino-horn handles are in great demand among traditionally oriented—and wealthy—North Yemeni men, selling for $300 to $13,000 each.[17] Although the North Yemeni government banned rhino-horn imports in 1982, for years the law was not strictly enforced and smugglers reportedly had little trouble greasing palms to bring rhino horn into the country.[18] From 1982 through 1984, about 3,700 pounds of horn entered North Yemen each year.[19] The trade began to decline, however, as falling oil revenues discouraged indulgence in high-priced weapons. In 1986 the government finally toughened up on local horn smuggling operations,[20] and, in that year, imports fell to fewer than 1,100 pounds. In December 1986, the government adopted a six-point action plan to halt further trade. Today, only 1 out of 20 dagger handles sold in North Yemen comes from rhino; water buffalo is an increasingly widespread substitute.[21]

Most of the commercial horn other than what is shipped to North Yemen finds its way to traditional medicinal markets in the Far East, where it is chopped into slivers, steamed, and mixed into various fever-reducing potions. Black markets continue in China, Hong Kong, South Korea, Taiwan, Thailand, Macao, and possibly Singapore.[22] The

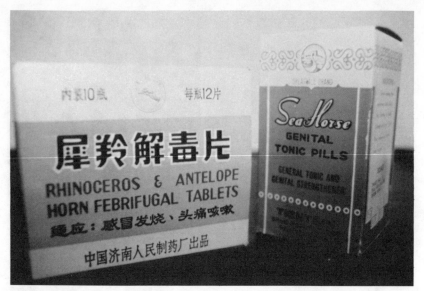

Some practitioners of traditional Asian medicine still use rhino horn in their ingredients.
Ginette Hemley / WWF

Chinese produce large quantities of patented medicines purportedly containing rhino horn, which are marketed worldwide.[23] (In November 1986, European officials seized a shipment of 19 rhino horns marked "spare parts" en route from Africa to China.[24]) In Brunei, which does not belong to CITES, Sumatran rhino-horn imports and sales are still perfectly legal, and the species' horn and skin are imported openly. Fortunately, Brunei does ban trade in African horn.[25]

In the Far East, African rhino horn sells wholesale for about $1,000 per kilogram or $450 per pound, which comes to approximately $1,500 per horn.[26] Asian horn wholesales for the startling sum of $4,090 per pound in some places.[27] Worldwide, the rhino horn trade may be worth $3 million per year.[28]

At the urging of conservationists, several major rhino-consuming countries have outlawed the trade. Japan, among the largest rhino-horn consumers in the 1970s, banned all rhino-horn use in 1980 and forced manufacturers of patented medicines containing rhino horn to rework their mixtures so that horn powders and other products were no longer used. Since then, little rhino horn has entered the country.[29] South Korea banned the medicinal use of rhino horn in 1983 and prohibited imports in 1985. A 1986 survey of horn trade in the country found significantly fewer clinics selling rhino-horn products and little evidence of smuggling. The study also discovered that druggists increasingly were using water buffalo horn in place of rhino.[30]

International pressure motivated Taiwan to ban imports in 1985, and the country's trade records show a marked drop in rhino-horn imports following the ban. Imports fell from about 264 pounds in 1984 to 95 pounds in the first nine months of 1985.[31] Hong Kong outlawed exports of legitimate stockpiled horn in 1986, having banned all imports in 1979.[32] Also in response to international pressure, Macao, another key market for African horn, promised in 1986 to abide by CITES and to control horn imports. However, some trade in Macao continues, mostly for reexport to China and Hong Kong. Over three-quarters of the Chinese medicine shops in this Portuguese colony still sell rhino products. Singapore, which had been a leading entrepôt for Asian horn, prohibited imports and exports of rhino products in October 1986 and joined CITES the following month.[33]

In July 1987, CITES parties convening in Ottawa, Canada, approved a resolution calling for the destruction of all confiscated rhino-horn stocks, which are attractive targets for thieves (see chapter 2). The resolution also called for domestic bans on trade in rhino horn and other products. The parties agreed to use political and economic leverage to discourage Burundi and the United Arab Emirates from further involvement in the trade and to send a special diplomatic mission to visit the countries and address rhino-horn and elephant-ivory trade concerns.[34]

The Long-term Outlook

International pressure and national actions to stop the flow of rhino horn in world markets are showing promising results, as evidenced by curbs on the rhino-horn trade in South Korea and elsewhere. Nevertheless, most rhino populations are now so endangered that they cannot withstand *any* trade pressure. To stamp out the market, conservationists must continue to urge all consumer countries to use rhino-horn substitutes—such as antelope, cow, and water buffalo—in traditional medicines and water buffalo as an alternative for dagger handles.

CITES parties must enforce strict bans on the trade. Special attention needs to be paid to the problem in Burundi, which apparently allows imports and exports of rhino horn and is a major transit point for horn exiting Zambia, Mozambique, Tanzania, and Kenya.[35] Countries that do not belong to CITES—notably, Brunei and North Yemen—must be recruited to join the convention and halt the horn trade. It is equally important for African and Asian nations with rhino populations to maintain strong antipoaching efforts, protect dwindling rhino habitat, and expand breeding programs.

Finally, conservation groups must continue working hard to promote rhino conservation on both continents, 'providing equipment to park guards, helping relocate rhinos to protected reserves, and funding studies on the legal and illegal markets for rhino products.

CHAPTER 11
Vicuñas

Asoft-fleeced member of the camel family, the vicuña (*Vicugna vicugna*) survives on the sparse grass and thin air found up to the 12,000-foot mark in the central Andes. The vicuña's unique wool coat, which protects it from cold winds, has been a prime target for profit-seeking hunters, who have killed vicuñas to obtain the wool. It takes the fleece of one animal to make a scarf, three for a sweater, and as many as 250 for a full-sized blanket.[1]

Vicuñas once were abundant in the highlands of what are now Argentina, Bolivia, Chile, and Peru. The Incas were the first to use vicuña wool, rounding up the animals every three to five years to clip their fleece—a time-consuming and laborious practice. When the Spanish reached vicuña territory during the 15th and 16th centuries, they used quicker methods, killing and skinning upwards of 80,000 animals each year.[2] Vicuñas continued to be slaughtered en masse until the mid-1960s, when the entire species faced almost certain extinction. Modern hunts primarily supplied wool to chic fabric shops in the United Kingdom, the United States, West Germany, and Japan.[3] The vicuña population in Argentina, Bolivia, Chile, and Peru plummeted from over two million in the 15th century, to about 400,000 in 1957, to a mere 6,000 by 1965.[4]

Trade Controls

The first significant international move to save the vicuña came in 1969, when Argentina, Bolivia, Chile, and Peru signed a treaty protecting the animal and outlawing wool exports. That accord was replaced by a second agreement in 1979 that included Ecuador but not Argentina.[5] All of these countries also passed national laws to prohibit hunting and established national reserves for remaining populations. CITES parties listed the vicuña on Appendix I in 1973.

During the last dozen years, several vicuña populations have recovered to healthy levels, a conservation success story. By 1981, the total population had reached 85,000 or so,[6] and today there are almost 130,000 vicuñas. These include 13,000 in Argentina, 11,500 in Bolivia, 22,000 in Chile, and 90,000 in Peru. The Pampas Galeras National Vicuña Reserve in Peru has the largest concentration of the species, with 59,500.

Peru allowed some vicuña culling between 1977 and 1979 to keep the animals from outgrowing their feeding grounds, with hides, meat, and wool from the cull going to local villagers.[7] This drew critical fire from some quarters. The International Union for Conservation of Nature and Natural Resources and World Wildlife Fund in 1980 hired consultants to do a vicuña head count and evaluate the range. Those researchers concluded that the population was healthy enough to sustain a carefully controlled harvest.

Peru has tried for some years to reopen commercial exports of vicuña wool by convincing CITES parties to lessen trade restrictions. The initial failure of those efforts—primarily due to opposition lobbying by wildlife-protection groups and wary enforcement

Vicuñas (*Vicugna vicugna*).
William Franklin

officials—angered those who considered Appendix I protection unreasonable for a species of tremendous local value that might withstand limited trade. At the 1987 biennial conference of CITES parties in Ottawa, Canada, Peru and Chile persuaded delegates to reopen commercial trade in vicuña cloth and to downlist Peruvian and Chilean populations of vicuña to Appendix II.

The proposals to reopen trade were passed on several conditions designed to minimize potentially harmful impacts on the vicuña population and to maximize trade benefits accruing to local people. The vicuñas must be sheared alive, and shearing cannot take place during certain times when the animals are more vulnerable to stress. The months of September through November are considered the best time for shearing because the temperature is relatively warm, and the females are not so far along in the 11½-month gestation period that they are likely to suffer stress-induced abortions.[8] There are restrictions on trade as well. CITES allows trade in woven cloth— but not raw wool—which promotes local weaving industries and simplifies enforcement. There are requirements for marking wool and cloth, as well as other special trade conditions.

The Peruvians and Chileans are now working on programs that will follow in the tradition of the Incas by collecting vicuña wool without killing the animals. The wool will be spun locally into cloth for export to London, Paris, New York, Tokyo, and other foreign trade centers.

Before CITES parties agreed to reopen trade in vicuña cloth, enforcement of the ban was inconsistent, and vicuña cloth was advertised openly in major clothing markets around the world. Some countries contended that their supplies were legal "preconvention" goods. CITES parties are still working to refine the new system. If successful, the new option means that Peru and Chile can use native vicuñas without diminishing their numbers. It is hoped that the new restrictions and vicuña management programs will help iron out problems in controlling the trade.

PART III
Aquatic Mammals

CHAPTER 12
Otters

O tter fur—like mink, sable, or fox—is warm, dense, and luxurious. One characteristic in particular, however, distinguishes otter fur from most other furs: it comes strictly from wild animals that live either in river basins or along ocean coasts rather than from farm-raised stock. This fact has proved devastating to several of the world's 12 otter species, as hunters have slaughtered them, sometimes at random, over the last few centuries. Especially hard hit have been the giant otter (*Pteronura brasiliensis*), a native of South American creeks and rivers, and the sea otter (*Enhydra lutris*), an inhabitant of the Pacific Rim of North America and Asia. Since the turn of the 20th century, the sea otter has bounced back from near-extinction, becoming something of a conservation success story. The giant otter, however, is still struggling to survive, and several other species are also endangered at present.

Trade is not the only threat facing the world's otters. Both marine and river otters often are hunted for sport and pest control, since they sometimes are considered competitors for fish and mollusks. In both industrial and developing countries, river otters also are affected increasingly by water-borne pollutants—industrial effluents, pesticides washed from farmlands, and eroded soils that cloud freshwater streams. Deforestation and building construction, too, are destroying more of their habitat every year.

Trade Controls

All otters are afforded some trade protection by CITES. The giant otter and the southern subspecies of the sea otter (*E. l. nereis*) are on Appendix I, along with three South American species—the marine otter (*Lutra felina*), South American river otter (*L. longicaudis*), and southern river otter (*L. provocax*)—the Eurasian river otter (*L. lutra*), and Cameroon clawless otter (*Aonyx congica*) populations in Cameroon and Nigeria. All remaining species, including other sea otter subspecies, are on Appendix II for "look-alike" reasons. The skins of various species are difficult to tell apart, particularly when traders cut off the animals' nose pads and feet before shipping.

Major Species in Trade

SEA OTTERS

The sea otter was the first species of otter to be seriously depleted by trade pressures. Sea otters originally ranged from Japanese waters across the northern Pacific through Alaska and as far south as Mexico. Then, during the 18th and 19th centuries, fur traders nearly exterminated the entire species in a clamor for its sleek, brown pelt. By 1900, commercial hunters had taken nearly 1 million animals from Alaskan waters alone.[1]

Sea-otter pelts were among the most prized furs on the market. In the early 19th century, a sea-otter pelt could bring North American hunters $60, while grizzly-bear skins fetched $10, river otters brought in $5, and mink pelts sold for just 40 cents each. During the 40 years after the United States purchased Alaska from Russia, the cash returns from the Alaskan sea-otter harvest topped the $7.2 million paid for

Southern sea otter (*Enhydra lutris nereis*).
C. Linet

the territory in 1867.[2] In the 1880s, sea-otter pelts reportedly sold for $105 to $165 each in London. As the species became scarce, pelt prices skyrocketed, reaching $1,125 for top-quality furs by 1903.[3]

Commercial sea-otter hunting slowed after the turn of the century as populations declined and, in 1911, finally stopped altogether by international agreement. Scientists believe that only 1,000 to 2,000 animals survived at that time, scattered across the Pacific in isolated populations. The commercial sea-otter market reopened briefly in the late 1960s, and pelts sold for approximately $280 each.[4]

The sea otter's recovery in northern regions is remarkable. At least 100,000 animals now live in major populations off the coasts of Alaska and the Soviet Union. Small, reintroduced groups also occur off Vancouver Island, Canada, and the Washington and Oregon coasts. The southern sea-otter subspecies, once considered extinct, is now found along the California coast and numbers approximately 1,800.[5] This small population, however, is still extremely vulnerable to human disturbance, particularly oil pollution and antagonistic fishermen who view otters as unwelcome competitors for abalone and other shellfish. As a result, the U.S. Department of the Interior continues to consider the southern sea otter threatened, and it remains listed on Appendix I.

At present, there is very little trade in any subspecies of sea otter. According to CITES data, only 33 pelts were in international commerce between 1977 and 1983; most of that trade was from Canada to Italy. During that period, the United States and Canada together exported just 24 live animals, primarily to Japan.[6] Most of these live trades were for zoos, aquariums, and other public displays.[7]

GIANT OTTERS

During the mid-20th century, uncontrolled hunting, often to supply U.S. and European furriers, decimated the giant otter. Today, this species survives only in pockets of the greater Amazon Basin.[8] It is extinct in Uruguay and faces severe hunting pressure in Brazil, Bolivia, and Argentina.[9] A few giant otters are also known to live in Colombia, Ecuador, French Guiana, Guyana, Paraguay, Peru, Suriname, and Venezuela.[10]

In addition to being listed on Appendix I, the giant otter is protected by national laws throughout most of its range. Nevertheless, it is still hunted by poachers seeking quick profits.[11] By far the largest otter species, growing to over one yard long, the giant otter is simple quarry for prowling hunters. Hunters also can lure giant otters within easy shooting range by mimicking a few otterish snorts.

Giant-otter fur traditionally has been the most valuable of all river-

Giant otter (*Pteronura brasiliensis*).
F. White

otter pelts in trade. In 1981, hunters in the Amazon Basin could net about $50 a pelt (roughly equal to 10 days' pay for cutting trees) and five times that much for pelt sales to foreign furriers.[12] In Bolivia, giant-otter skins and Neotropical river-otter skins were at one time more valuable than jaguar skins, and a single otter skin could bring in more than a *vaquero* (cowboy) typically earned in three months.[13]

According to Juan Villalba-Macias, director of TRAFFIC(South America), the domestic market in Latin America for giant-otter skins is limited, although he did find some skins on sale in a tourist shop for $57 during a fact-finding tour of French Guiana in October 1986.[14] Villalba-Macias believes that the greatest demand for skins is from abroad, particularly West Germany.[15] The bulk of this trade is apparently through illicit channels, since CITES records indicate that legal commercial trade in the species is low. The only recorded large-scale trade between 1980 and 1984 occurred in 1981, when West Germany imported 1,007 giant-otter skins from Italy, with Paraguay as the reported country of origin.[16]

OTHER APPENDIX I SPECIES

The other three Latin American species of otter listed on Appendix I also have been devastated by hunting. Populations of the southern river otter, found in Argentina and Chile, are still drastically low, despite its legal protection.[17] The marine otter, which is extinct in Argentina and down to only 1,000 or so animals along the Peruvian and Chilean coasts, continues to fall prey to pelt hunters and disgruntled fishermen, who view marine otters as competitors.[18] And the South American river otter is becoming increasingly rare, though it has fared slightly better than the other two species and continues to inhabit remote tropical waterways and other sparsely settled regions throughout Latin America. In the 1960s and early 1970s, South American river otters were heavily hunted; Peru alone exported over 117,000 pelts from 1960 through 1973.[19] In the early 1980s, South American river otters were traded more frequently than any other Latin American otter species, with over 63,000 skins reaching world markets from 1980 through 1984; as with the giant otter, most of these were exported from Paraguay and imported by West Germany.

There may still be some illegal trade in these three species. However, they seldom appear in international trade records—that is, in legal trade. CITES records show fewer than 1,000 southern river-otter skins in world trade during the 1980s and only one marine-otter transaction between 1976 and 1985. Trade in South American river otters declined drastically between 1980 and 1984, to only 157 skins in 1984, and no exports or imports appeared in CITES reports for 1985.[20]

In addition to being listed on Appendix I, the Eurasian otter is protected by hunting regulations in many European nations. It is seldom trapped for trade, except in the Soviet Union. Soviet trappers took an estimated 7,800 animals per year in the 1960s, and 4,500 per year in the 1970s.[21] CITES records for 1984 show only 20 Eurasian otter skins, 4 garments, and 9 live animals in international trade.[22]

The Cameroon clawless otter, which has no claws except for a pair of rudimentary nails on two toes of its hind feet, survives only along mountain streams in rain forests of Cameroon and Nigeria. Although the species' fur generally is considered inferior to its South American and Eurasian relatives, the Cameroon clawless otter population has been reduced drastically by commercial hunting.[23] However, Cameroon clawless otter skins are now seldom found in international trade.[24]

APPENDIX II SPECIES

Only one otter species—the North American river otter (*Lutra canadensis*)—is trapped in high volume for *legal* international commerce. Its pelt, prized for coat collars and other trimmings, is considered one of the more durable, high-quality furs. North American river otters still occur in the Southeast, Northeast, Pacific Northwest, and Great Lakes regions of the United States, as well as in Alaska and Canada. Trapping and/or hunting of North American river otters occurs legally in 26 of the 43 states, and 11 of the 12 Canadian provinces, in which the species can be found today. The remaining 17 U.S. states and 1 Canadian province in which the species occurs all protect it completely.[25]

It should not be assumed, however, that the future of the North American river otter is assured. Once ranging from southern Texas all the way to the Alaskan arctic, this species was "trapped out" through much of its central and southern territory by 1935. Today, it faces major threats from pesticide pollution, loss of wetland habitats, and the effects of acid rain on its food supply.

Approximately 50,000 North American river-otter pelts, worth $1.5 to $3 million, are marketed each year in the United States and Canada. The number of otters being killed each year and the prices their pelts bring have remained relatively stable in recent years.[26] In 1984, Canada reportedly exported over 9,000 pelts, mostly to the United States, while the United States shipped some 5,000 skins abroad, primarily to Canada, China, West Germany, and other European nations.[27] This U.S.-Canadian exchange reflects close commercial ties between furriers and large auction houses in both countries.

Except for the Cameroon clawless otter, Asian and African otters have so far largely escaped the fate of their South American relatives. Otters in these two continents are killed for their meat and fur and to protect local fish populations from alleged competition, but they are not endangered by high volume trade. A more serious threat to these otters is habitat loss through soil erosion and pesticide pollution of waterways, two by-products of spreading agricultural development.[28] Hunting may heat up, however, if other commercial otter species are trapped out. Some illegal trafficking in Asian otters apparently does occur. For example, according to CITES, three-quarters of the over 1,000 Asian smooth-coated-otter (*L. perspicillata*) skins in trade from 1980 to 1983 were exported from Bangladesh, a country that officially bans trade in this species. West Germany, once again, was the primary market for these skins.[29]

CHAPTER 13
Seals

In the past decade or so, seal hunting has become a highly charged emotional issue. Harp (*Phoca groenlandica*) and hooded (*Cystophora cristata*) seal harvests have sparked outrage among animal welfare groups because the hunts traditionally involve clubbing baby seals to death for their soft fur. The commercial killing of young male northern fur seals (*Callorhinus ursinus*), which took place annually on the Pribilof Islands off the coast of Alaska until 1985, was similarly criticized. In the past, the hooded seal and northern fur seal hunts have also drawn fire from researchers who argue that the harvests are harmful to the health of the populations involved. The net result of the public outcry against seal hunting has been a dramatic drop in world demand for all sealskin products.

One of the oldest types of commercial wildlife exploitation, seal hunting, or sealing, began in earnest in the late 18th century.[1] During the 18th and 19th centuries, large-scale commercial expeditions killed millions of fur seals, with little restraint, primarily to obtain seal oil. Hunters wiped out whole populations of southern fur seals, including the Juan Fernandez fur seal (*Arctocephalus philippii*), Guadalupe fur seal (*A. townsendi*) and Antarctic fur seal (*A. gazella*). As early as the 1820s, the Juan Fernandez and Antarctic fur seals had become commercially extinct, that is, they were so depleted that they could no longer be harvested and processed in profitable numbers.[2]

As southern fur seal stocks declined, hunters turned their sights on the two elephant seal species (*Mirounga spp.*). By the end of the 19th century, elephant seals, too, were no longer plentiful enough to be worth the hunt, and the northern species (*M. angustirostris*) was nearly extinct. Off the Alaskan coast, commercial hunters took an equally heavy toll of northern fur seal populations, reducing the estimated 2.5 million population to a mere 300,000 in the short time between 1889 and 1909.[3]

With the imposition of some international controls on seal hunting, the 20th century has seen the recovery of several seal populations. Antarctic fur seals, reduced to a few dozen individuals in the early 1900s, now number upwards of 400,000. The northern elephant seal grew from 100 or fewer survivors in 1890 to an estimated 48,000 by 1976.[4] And there are now 1 million or so northern fur seals.[5]

For some species, however, protection and declining commercial pressures may be too late. For example, the Guadalupe fur seal now numbers only 500 to 1,000 individuals off the coast of Baja California and northern Mexico. Though it is protected by U.S. and Mexican law, its long-term survival is far from certain.[6]

Today, most commercial seal harvests are controlled so that they do not deplete wild stocks. The only two species that probably occur in large volumes in international trade—the ringed seal (*Phoca hispida*) and Cape fur seal (*Arctocephalus pusillus pusillus*)—are generally not considered threatened by annual hunts. These seals are killed for their meat, oil, skins, and reproductive organs. At present, meat and oil are usually consumed locally; sealskins are traded in the dwindling

Guadeloupe fur seal (*Arctocephalus philippii*).
California Academy of Sciences

international market; and seal penis bones, known as seal sticks, are sometimes shipped to Far Eastern medicinal markets, where they are considered aphrodisiacs.

Though hunting and trading have declined significantly, other human activities present continuing threats to many of the world's seals. Biotoxic pollutants such as DDT as well as beachfront development probably have contributed to the decline of ringed seals in the Baltic Sea. Power boating and other activities endanger the highly sensitive monk seals that inhabit tropical and subtropical waters. The Caribbean monk seal (*Monachus tropicalis*) is almost certainly extinct, the Mediterranean monk seal (*M. monachus*) is down to 500 to 1,000 individuals, and the Hawaiian monk seal (*M. schauinslandi*) probably numbers fewer than 700.[7] Recent studies suggest that discarded nets, plastic packing straps, and other debris also kill large numbers of seals and other marine mammals.[8] Each year an estimated 15,000 to 40,000 northern fur seals drown after becoming entangled in discarded fishing gear, especially trawling nets, off the Alaskan coast.[9]

Trade Controls

In the late 1800s, countries that had been major sealers began to protect dwindling seal stocks through international agreements. The first formal sealing treaty, which did not even last a full year, was concluded in 1891 between the United States and the United Kingdom (on behalf of Canada).[10] In 1911, the United Kingdom (for Canada), the United States, Russia, and Japan adopted the Treaty for the Preservation and Protection of Fur Seals, an international treaty that prohibited the killing of northern fur seals on the high seas and remained in effect until 1941, when Japan withdrew. In 1957, these countries drew up the Interim Convention on Conservation of North Pacific Fur Seals. This agreement again prohibited the killing of northern fur seals at sea. It also established a regulated annual harvest of seals from U.S. and Soviet rookeries and allocated the pelts among the four nations.

The Convention for the Conservation of Antarctic Seals, which took effect in 1978, has been ratified by Argentina, Belgium, Chile, France, Japan, Norway, Poland, South Africa, the United Kingdom, the United States, and the Soviet Union.[11] This treaty prohibits sealing on the open sea in the region and requires parties to report any seals they catch along coastlines. However, it puts few real controls on potential harvests and carries no enforcement power.[12] The treaty sets catch limits of 175,000 crabeater seals (*Lobodon carcinophagus*), 1,200 leopard seals (*Hydrurga leptonyx*), and 5,000 Weddell seals (*Leptonychotes*

Elephant seals (*Mirounga* spp.).
N. Moore-Craig

veddelli) in any one year.[13] It completely protects Ross seals (*Ommatophoca rossi*), southern elephant seals (*Mirouga leonina*), all southern fur seals, and adult Weddell seals when they are on land or ice attached to land, although it allows limited taking of any species for scientific research, display in educational or cultural institutions, or "to provide indispensable food for men or dogs." This "Antarctic Seals Convention" also establishes seal reserves where all species are strictly protected.[14]

CITES protects 13 seal species, though only one, the Cape fur seal (on Appendix II), is still found in commercial trade to any significant degree.[15] Appendix I species include the Guadalupe fur seal and the three monk seal species. Appendix II species include all other southern fur seals and the elephant seals.

Trade Volume and Routes

The international sealskin trade has declined sharply in recent years due to public outrage over the inhumane killing of baby harp and hooded seals. In 1983, citizen protests prompted the European Economic Community (EEC) to ban all imports of skins from hooded seal pups and newborn harp seal pups. Prior to that ban, EEC countries—especially Denmark, France, West Germany, and Italy—probably had been the world's largest market for sealskin. The campaign to stop killing baby seals caused many European consumers to stop buying products made from adult seals of all species, though

International Wildlife Trade: Whose Business Is It?

fashion trends may have influenced the market drop to some degree as well. "Light" furs such as fox and lynx came into vogue, and seal furs may have been considered too heavy for current tastes. By 1984, European fur industry representatives reported that the seal import trade had slowed to a trickle, so that few furriers considered sealskin financially worthwhile.[16]

The United States has not been an important market for seals since it adopted the Marine Mammal Protection Act of 1972. This act placed a moratorium on the importation of all marine mammals, except in cases where the government finds that a proposed harvest will not reduce a population below the maximum level that a particular habitat or ecosystem can sustain naturally. The act further prohibits importation of any marine mammal that has been taken inhumanely, is less than eight months old, is nursing at the time of the taking, or is pregnant.[17]

In the early 1980s, the European sealskin trade was comprised primarily of five species: the harp seal, hooded seal, ringed seal, Cape fur seal, and northern fur seal. The South American fur seal (*Arctocephalus australis*) and common seal (*Phoca vitulina*) also were traded in smaller numbers.[18]

Harp seals were once the mainstay of the modern sealskin trade.

Seal skins after stretching.
K. Blanchard, Harrington Harbor, P.Q.

Harp seal (*Phoca groenlandica*).
B. Davies

In recent times, however, they have been harvested principally for their fur, with only a small number of skins used in the leather trade. In addition, harp-seal meat is still eaten by native peoples. Historically, the harp-seal pelt market has centered on skins from newborn white pups, known as whitecoats, and spotted pups under one year old, called beaters. There has also been a small market for bedlamers, older pups that do not yet have the traditional harp markings, and for adult harp seals. With the 1983 EEC prohibitions, the European market for whitecoats has virtually disappeared. Although the EEC ban only covers whitecoats' skins, by 1984 only a handful of leather processors in the United Kingdom and West Germany were still importing and tanning older harp-seal skins.[19]

Canada and Norway traditionally have been the largest suppliers of harp-seal skins to European markets, followed by the Soviet Union. Canadian and Norwegian harp-seal exports plummeted after 1981, mostly in response to reduced consumer demand resulting from antisealing publicity. The total harvest of whitecoats in Canada dropped from over 150,000 animals in 1981 to roughly 10,000 in 1983, and Canadian sealskin exports (mostly harp seals) declined from 224,000 in 1981 to 65,000 in 1983. Also between 1981 and 1983, Norway's harp-seal kill tumbled from 50,000 to 20,000.[20] In 1984, Norway's only sealskin trading company closed one of its major processing plants for lack of business.[21]

Hooded seals from Canada and Norway were also important to the skin trade until the early 1980s, although they were never traded in as large numbers as harp seals were.[22] Pelts from pups, or bluebacks, were the most prized hooded-seal commodity and fetched as much as $35 apiece in 1979.[23] By 1984, there was virtually no European demand for hooded seals.[24]

Ringed seals, traditionally hunted by native peoples in the Arctic, are exploited for their bristly pelts, blubber, meat, and other products. Greenland Eskimos annually kill some 40,000 to 50,000, and Canadian natives take another 75,000 or so each year, mostly to meet their local needs.[25] Most of the skins in international trade come from Greenland and are auctioned in Denmark. In 1983, the average Danish price for ringed seal fell from $38 to $5 per pelt, and the second of two yearly auctions had to be canceled due to the low price of sealskin.[26] In 1984, the Royal Greenland Trade Department, which controls the Danish colony's sealskin trade, was believed to have some 200,000 excess skins in stock, the majority of them ringed seal.

There may, however, still be a moderate market for ringed-seal skin coats, shoes, and other products in some European countries. In 1984, Danish companies were continuing to sell ringed-seal skins and products to German retailers, though the market had declined steeply. One trader reported that he used to sell 50,000 to 60,000 ringed-seal skins in Germany each year but that he could sell only 4,000 or so in 1984. Norway imported at least 2,000 ringed-seal skins from Greenland in 1984, mostly for reexport to the West German shoe industry. (Before the sealskin market plummeted, West German boot manufacturers imported large quantities of ringed-seal skin.)[27]

World demand for the only other seal still traded in commercially significant numbers, the Cape fur seal, also has diminished since 1980. This Appendix II species is harvested under a culling program regulated by the South African government.[28] Skins also are harvested in Namibia, often for export to South Africa. In the late 1970s, 70,000 to 80,000 Cape fur seals were harvested each year in South Africa, mostly for export to West Germany and Norway. A small number of Cape fur seal penis bones were shipped to the Far East at that time as well.[29] After the European market collapsed in 1983, South Africa stopped harvesting seals and tried to get rid of old skin stocks.[30] In 1985, South Africa exported fewer than 20,000 Cape fur-seal skins to the EEC, mostly to West Germany and Norway. Of the skins Norway still imports, it reexports significant numbers to Denmark.[31]

Until 1985, northern fur seals were harvested for commercial purposes under the 1911 and 1957 conventions signed by Canada, Japan, the United States, and the Soviet Union. Under the 1957 convention, Alaskan natives on St. Paul and St. George islands were paid by the U.S. government to harvest roughly 22,000 fur seals each year to fulfill the quota. These skins were then processed for the federal government, and many were exported to Canada, probably for sale at international fur auctions. Other skins were exported directly to furriers overseas, primarily in Switzerland, Italy, France, and West Germany.[32]

This system worked reasonably well until the sealskin market crashed in the early 1980s. The price of a northern fur-seal pelt plunged from $110 in 1980 to $65 in 1982,[33] and federal budget balancers began to wonder about the financial wisdom of the hunt. Animal welfare groups also protested the hunt because it involved clubbing seals to death. The Alaskan harvest came under further scrutiny when researchers discovered that the northern fur-seal population had dropped from over 1 million in the mid-1970s to 800,000 or so in the mid-1980s,[34] even though the hunt was not considered a cause of the decline.

Faced with an increasingly expensive and controversial convention-mandated harvest and evidence that the seal population was declining, the U.S. Senate chose not to ratify the agreement when it came up for renewal in 1984. As a result, the nation's commercial harvest ended that year. Aleut residents of the Pribilof Islands are now allowed to harvest northern fur seals for subsistence purposes only. In 1985, Pribilof Islanders harvested some 3,700 animals, and in 1986 they took another 1,400. The 1987 subsistence harvest brought in 1,802 seals, and the 1988 harvest totaled 1,262.[35]

The only skins that can be exported legally from the United States are those taken prior to 1985 (figure 13.1). U.S. exports of sealskins dropped markedly in 1983, and no further drop occurred after the commercial harvest ended in 1984. Nearly 24,000 skins were exported in 1985 and 1986, all of which were probably old stocks.

Only one country, Uruguay, continues to exploit the South American fur (or lobo) seal. Thus, it is the country of origin for the few skins that reach world markets.[36] To maintain healthy populations, the Uruguayan government manages the annual kill of this seal. Between 1959 and 1986, Uruguay harvested an average of 8,750 seals per year, out of a total world population of approximately 320,000 animals.[37] Uruguayan officials predicted that 7,000 animals would be killed in 1987. Most skins are traded domestically due to the lack of foreign demand. In 1982, Uruguay exported approximately 500 skins to West Germany and other European ports, but in 1985 the EEC report showed no imports of the species.[38] In addition, Uruguay exports some seal penis bones to the Far East.[39]

Figure 13.1
U.S. Sealskin Exports, by Importing Country,*
1979–1986

	Canada	France	United Kingdom	West Germany	Italy	Japan	Switzerland	Other countries
1979	10,691	1,435	949	965	3,226	1,745	3,478	933
1980	4,484	801	1,420	4,455	3,105	33	6,028	1,266
1981	6,121	950	703	676	1,635	1,164	2,786	799
1982	28,592	53	403	430	807	15	84	739
1983	5,530	756	181	0	193	88	717	395
1984	10,182	2,736	644	70	229	309	124	295
1985	12,468	108	0	20	0	422	0	11
1986	10,807	30	0	0	0	0	0	0

*Dressed sealskins only.

Source: Steve Koplin, Fisheries Statistics.

There are apparently no commercial sealing operations in the Antarctic at present. The Soviet Union hunted seals in the region in 1987,
purportedly for "scientific purposes." (The environmental group
Greenpeace challenged the Soviets' scientific-research claim, asserting
that the seals were being sold for meat, fur, and leather.[40]) Some 4,804
seals reportedly were taken, including 4,000 crabeater seals, 30 Ross
seals, and 2 southern elephant seals. Crabeater seals, probably the
most abundant large mammals in the world, are estimated to number
between 8 and 50 million. The other two species, however, are far
less numerous. The Ross seal, which is not listed on Appendix I or
II, may have a population totaling 100,000 to 150,000; and the southern elephant seal, which is listed on Appendix II, is estimated at
600,000 to 700,000 individuals.[41]

CHAPTER 14
Walruses

To a two-ton walrus, a pair of long, sharply-pointed tusks may be one of life's small treasures: they can be used to get a grip on slippery ice before hauling out to bask, to prop up one's tired muzzle, to scrape the ocean bottom for food, or, most important, to establish dominance in a herd.[1] But a pair of treasured tusks is also a deadly encumbrance—the target for gun-toting ivory hunters and poachers in northern polar regions.

For thousands of years, Arctic natives have hunted the rotund, cinnamon-colored walrus for its leathery skin, meat, blubber, and tusks. These traditional harvests had little impact on either the Atlantic walrus (*Odobenus rosmarus rosmarus*) or the Pacific walrus (*O. r. divergens*).[2]* From the 17th through the early 20th centuries, however, European and North American ivory hunters and opportunistic whalers caused the decline first of Atlantic walrus and then of Pacific walrus populations in the Bering and Chukchi seas, killing the beasts primarily for their ivory but also for their blubber, which was melted into oil.[3]

In 1941, the United States outlawed exports of raw walrus ivory from Alaska. Subsequent federal legislation extended the ban and now allows only Alaskan natives to take walruses to meet their subsistence needs for food, clothing, and traditional carving materials. Canada, the Soviet Union, and Greenland also established policies to protect walruses, while allowing subsistence hunts. Free from the pressure of commercial hunts, the Pacific walrus population rebounded, from about 100,000 in the mid-1950s to approximately

*Odobenus rosmarus *stems from the Greek words meaning "tusk walk," reflecting one British zoologist's view of walrus behavior.*

Walrus (*Odobenus rosmarus*).
E. Flipse

250,000 by 1980.[4] By the 1970s, the walrus population was considered to have reached its carrying capacity, and the annual harvest was allowed to increase. Since 1981, the total kill of Pacific walrus, including Soviet and Alaskan catches, is estimated at a minimum of 10,000 per year.[5] The Pacific walrus population is believed to have declined to 233,000 or so during this decade.[6]

The Atlantic walrus, which has not recovered as successfully, probably numbers about 25,000.[7] There is also a small population of some 4,000 to 5,000 animals in the Laptev Sea, north of Siberia. This walrus population is considered by some Soviet experts to be a third subspecies (*O. r. laptevi*).[8]

Like modern seal hunting, walrus harvest policies are highly controversial. The debate centers on excessive take by Alaska natives for ivory, however, rather than on international trade. World trade has had little, if any, impact on walrus populations in recent times. Canada has listed the species on Appendix III, so all CITES parties must issue documents for export of walrus, including parts or products. In the United States, the Marine Mammal Protection Act prohibits imports and any domestic sale of walrus, except for traditional native carvings obtained as a by-product of the subsistence hunt. Some illegal trade is known to occur,[9] and additional monitoring would be useful.

CHAPTER 15
Whales and Small Cetacea

The world seems to be moving toward an end to commercial whaling. Whaling vessels no longer patrol the polar seas as they once did in search of gray whales (*Eschrichtius robustus*), bowhead whales (*Balaena mysticetus*), right whales (*B. glacialis*), humpbacks (*Megaptera novaengliae*), or the giant blue whales (*Balaenoptera musculus*). Hunting missions for smaller species have declined dramatically in the past decade. In 1982, the International Whaling Commission (IWC), which is authorized by the International Convention for the Regulation of Whaling to set world whale-catch limits, agreed to a moratorium on all commercial harvests, beginning in 1986. All but a handful of whaling nations have since hung up their harpoons and pulled in their fleets.

But whaling is not yet over. To begin with, the International Convention for the Regulation of Whaling is a voluntary agreement. The IWC, like other international bodies, does not have the ability to enforce its rulings, so violators are able to proceed at will. It is up to individual nations, conservation advocacy groups, and others to dissuade them.

In addition, member countries can sidestep IWC rulings by lodging formal objections to them. Japan, the Soviet Union, and Norway—the countries responsible for over 80 percent of all whaling in the 1970s and early 1980s—formally objected to the moratorium. Thus, they continued to hunt certain whale species without violating the convention. In 1986, Japan reportedly took 2,769 whales, the Soviet Union took a similar number, and Norway took 380.[1] In July 1985, the Soviet Union announced its intention to halt further commercial whaling two years hence. In 1987, Japan killed 877 whales for commercial use, and Norway harvested 400.[2]

For centuries, whale oil was a common ingredient in such products as soap, margarine, and candles.
Kendall Whaling Museum

Iceland and South Korea were the first to exploit a loophole in the moratorium by permitting their fleets to engage in "scientific" harvests of whales. The convention allows countries to grant themselves special permits to harvest whales for scientific research. In 1986, Iceland took 76 fin whales (*B. physalus*) and 40 sei whales (*B. borealis*) under this provision, and South Korea took 69 minke whales (*B. acutorostrata*).

In 1987, Japan and Norway also said that they would abandon commercial whaling and conduct "scientific whaling" instead. Japanese "research" whalers took 273 minke whales during the 1987-88 season[3] and 241 during the 1988-89 season.[4]

Conservationists strongly question the true scientific nature and value of such efforts. They are concerned that these operations are merely a front for continued commercial whaling. They believe that the whale data needed to develop sound conservation and management programs can be gathered without killing the animals, such as by surveying populations from the air and sea. In June 1987, the IWC voted to tighten the loophole for research whaling and condemned Iceland, Japan, and South Korea for their inadequate scientific whaling plans.

Iceland announced that it would continue to kill about the same number of whales for scientific purposes in 1988 as it had killed in 1987. A portion of the Icelandic catch was expected to be exported to Japan.[5] Iceland's decision and the resulting protests from conservationists prompted U.S. officials to threaten sanctions, since the Icelandic research-whaling program had not been endorsed by the IWC. In September 1987, U.S. and Icelandic diplomats struck a deal that allowed Iceland to take 80 fin whales and 20 sei whales in 1987 without the threat of U.S. sanctions. In exchange, the Icelandic government agreed to submit its 1988 research program to the IWC Scientific Committee for review and then to uphold whatever scientific recommendations the committee made.[6] South Korea has not done any whaling since 1986.[7]

Under the Packwood-Magnuson Amendment to the U.S. Fishery Conservation and Management Act of 1976, the United States has given itself the power to invoke sanctions against countries that violate IWC rulings by cutting their fishing quotas in U.S. waters by 50 percent or more. Under the Pelly Amendment of 1967, the United States also has the discretionary power to prohibit importation of fishery products from any country that "diminishes the effectiveness" of the IWC.

In 1985, the United States used its power under the Packwood-Magnuson Amendment to penalize the Soviet Union for taking more than its quota of minke whales. The government did not, however, invoke sanctions against Japan after the Japanese ignored the IWC's directive that no sperm whales be taken in 1984. The U.S. secretary of commerce at that time, Malcolm Baldrige, instead entered into an agreement with the Japanese government that allowed Japanese sperm, Bryde's (*Balaenoptera edeni*), and minke whaling to continue at specific reduced levels until 1988. Several U.S. conservation groups sued the federal government to invalidate this agreement. In 1986, the U.S. Supreme Court determined that the secretaries of commerce and state were not required to penalize Japan and that the secretary of commerce could use his discretion in invoking sanctions.

In January 1988, U.S. conservation groups again filed suit against the federal government, this time under the Pelly Amendment,

Minke whale (*Balaenoptera acutorostrata*).
A. Rus Hoelzel

arguing that Japan's so-called scientific minke whaling in the Antarctic violated the IWC moratorium on commercial whaling. A month later, the new commerce secretary, C. William Verity, Jr., declared that Japan was indeed "diminishing the effectiveness" of the IWC. His ruling triggered a Pelly requirement that the president decide within 60 days whether to embargo fish imports from Japan.

In response, President Reagan eliminated all Japanese-directed fishing privileges in U.S. waters but chose not to impose any sanctions against Japanese fish products for 1988. Instead, he instructed Secretary Verity to file another report by December 1, 1988, informing him about Japanese "scientific research" and what the IWC has concluded about the research. When Verity filed that report, he concluded that there had been no significant changes in circumstances and promised that the future secretary of commerce would make recommendations to the president for further action.[8]

If Pelly sanctions eventually are imposed against Japan, that country will have a great deal to lose. The estimated value of Japanese fisheries products exported to the United States in 1986 was $565 million.[9] However, the United States has an even higher stake in the possible consequences of sanctions, having sold more than $1 billion of fish products to Japan in 1986 alone. Thus, U.S. officials are understandably wary of touching off a trade war.

Secretary Verity's February 1988 decision also invoked the Packwood-Magnuson Amendment. Restricting Japan's right to fish in U.S. waters would have little practical effect, however, since Japan already has no fishing quota in U.S. waters.

As of mid-1988, the Japanese government was contending that it was unsure how much whaling it would do in Antarctic waters in the coming year. The Japanese say that they are analyzing data collected during the previous whaling season and that, when that analysis is completed, they will assess their needs for further research.[10]

The IWC moratorium is to be reviewed in 1990. At that time, IWC members will review the population status of whale stocks and consider whether to renew the moratorium on whaling. However, many observers believe that the 1990 decision will have little to do with actual numbers of whales but will be based on lobbying, special interest politics, and international clout instead.

Overview of World Trade in Whales

Unlike exotic birds, crocodile skins, elephant ivory, and other wildlife items collected in developing countries and sold to consumers in industrial nations, whales are primarily caught by hunters from a few industrial nations, and most whales are killed for those countries'

Japan has historically dominated the world market for whale meat, but it's trade in this product has declined dramatically in the 1980s.
Kendall Whaling Museum

internal markets. So whale products rarely enter international trade. In the past two decades, several factors—the expense of finding and catching such scarce species on the open ocean, IWC controls on whaling, CITES controls on trade, and widespread public sentiment against whale killing—have helped close nearly all markets for imported whale meat and oil.

There is one noteworthy exception. World commerce in whale meat has been dominated by a single nation, Japan. In the early 1980s, over 90 percent of whale meat reaching the world market went to Japan.[11] Japan's trade in whale meat has declined dramatically in the past decade, from a peak of 39,600 tons in 1977 to 3,960 tons in 1986 (figure 15.1).[12]

In the early 1980s, the Soviet Union was consistently the major foreign supplier of whale meat to Japan. Between 1981 and 1985, the Soviets shipped 7,700 to 11,000 tons of meat to Japan each year. In 1986, however, this trade dropped to 504 tons, and the Soviets pledged to stop all whaling after the 1986-87 season.

In 1986, Iceland and Brazil became Japan's most important foreign sources of whale meat, followed by the Soviet Union, Spain, the Philippines, and Norway.[13]* U.S. officials estimate that up to half the meat from Iceland's 1986 catch of minkes, fins, and seis may have been exported to Japan.[16] By 1987, Iceland was the sole supplier of whale meat to Japan.[17]

Smuggling of whale meat may be increasing, motivated by a recent upsurge in the price of whale meat in Japan. Japanese customs officials

---

Norway has apparently dropped out of this trade, partly because the northeast Atlantic minke population upon which the country relies is seriously depleted.[14] As mentioned earlier, the Soviet Union has promised to stop all whaling. Spain stopped taking whales in 1985 and has halted further exports.[15] In December 1987, Brazil banned killing of whales in territorial waters.

Whales and Small Cetacea

Figure 15.1
Japanese Whale Imports, 1970–1987

Whale Meat Imports

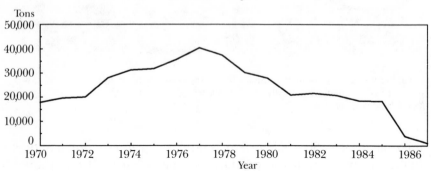

Whale Oil Imports

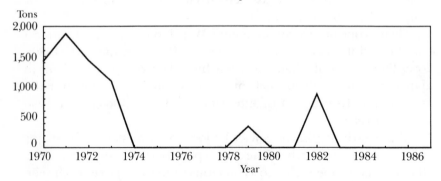

Whale Spermaceti Imports

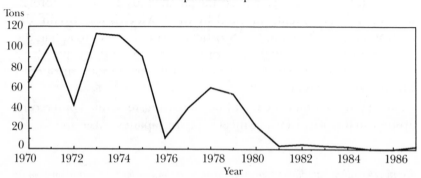

Source: Japanese Customs data.

arrested two men in June 1987 for smuggling 215 tons of whale meat, valued at $8.9 million, from Taiwan.[18]

On average, the price of whale meat in Japan has more than doubled over the past five years.[19] In 1988, meat from the minke whale sold for approximately $9.80 per pound in Tokyo, where choice parts such as tail meat fetched as much as $140 per pound.[20] Japan's imports of whale products probably are limited to meat. During the early 1970s, the country was an important market for whale oil, which often came from the United States.[21] Japanese customs statistics indicate that Japan has not imported whale oil since 1979.*

Members of the European Economic Community (EEC)—particularly West Germany, the United Kingdom, and Norway—were major consumers of oil from sperm whales until the late 1970s, when protests from conservationists and declining sperm-whale stocks encouraged leather tanners and other whale oil users to find substitutes. The European market for whale oil all but vanished after sperm whales were listed on Appendix I of CITES in 1981 and the EEC instituted its own strict regulations on whale product imports in 1982.[22]

Trade Controls

All whales (order Cetacea) are listed on either Appendix I or II of CITES. The principal commercial species—sperm, minke, sei, and Bryde's whales—are on Appendix I. The only exception is the western Greenland population of minke whales, which is on Appendix II.

CITES has not been very effective in regulating trade in whale meat. Japan, the market leader, has entered reservations for six species—the sperm, Baird's beaked (*Berardius bairdii*), minke, sei, Bryde's, and fin whales—and arguably pays little heed to the convention. The major Japanese whale meat supplier, Iceland, is not a CITES party; nor is South Korea, which also has exported whale meat to Japan during past years. Other important whale meat sources in the early 1980s—Norway, the Soviet Union, Brazil, and Peru—also held reservations on species that they traditionally traded. Moreover, Japan's 1986 whale-meat imports from the Philippines and Spain probably violated CITES, as these exporting countries did not hold reservations on any whale species at the time.

Countries that belong to the EEC are subject to regulations on whales that are even more strict than CITES requires. Since 1982, the EEC has treated all cetaceans, with the exception of the Greenland

---

Japan's statistics for trade in another category, imports of "oil and fats of marine mammals," show continued imports from many of the same countries that have traded in whales. The composition of this general category is not known.

population of minke whales, as Appendix I species. All commercial whale-product imports and exports are banned.

Hunting and Trade Patterns

Whaling has long followed a species "boom-and-bust" cycle, exploiting the slower large species to the point of commercial extinction, then moving on to the more fast-moving large species, and finally to the smaller species. Whales are especially vulnerable to hunting pressures because they mature slowly and have low reproductive rates. It takes from 4 to 26 years for whales to reach breeding age, and then they only give birth every 2 to 5 years (depending on the species), usually to one calf per pregnancy. The larger whales may live for 50 to 100 years.

The first whale species to suffer from overhunting were the right, bowhead, and gray whales, which proved prime targets for European and American whaling fleets during the 18th and 19th centuries. As North Atlantic and North Pacific stocks of these species disappeared, whalers ranged farther afield or turned their sights on sperm and humpback whales. A valuable source for oil, sperm whales were widely depleted by the late 19th century. During the same period, invention of the exploding harpoon and use of steam-powered whaling vessels contributed to the decline of humpback whale populations. Unable

Female humpback whale (*Megaptera novaengliae*) after slaughter, Akutan, Alaska, 1938.
V. B. Scheffer/NOAA

to recover, right whales, bowheads, humpbacks, and one of the two gray whale populations (the western Pacific) are still endangered today.

In the early 20th century, whalers began to exploit species that feed in the Antarctic, harvesting blue whales until that population declined precipitously in the 1940s, then fin whales until the 1960s, when they, too, became rare. Both species are now considered endangered.

For the past 15 years, whalers have relied primarily on the smallest commercially valuable species—the sei, Bryde's, and minke whales—and on dwindling northern Pacific supplies of the oil-rich sperm whale. With the exception of the minke, all of the species are considered endangered under the U.S. Endangered Species Act.

Species in Trade

Smallest of all "baleen" whales, which feed by straining plankton-rich water through baleen fibers in their mouths, the minke whale is now the mainstay of the world's whaling industry. Minkes usually are harvested for their meat, which is often sold in thin, purple-rimmed slivers in Japanese fish markets. Fresh flukes and tail meat are considered particular delicacies in Japan.[23] Minke intestines and other organs are manufactured into vitamins and insulin, and the whale's oil is used in margarine, cosmetics, and detergent. In 1986, a nine-ton minke whale was estimated to be worth about $16,000 to Japanese wholesalers.[24]

Despite the IWC moratorium, two countries hunted minkes in 1987. Japan and Norway took a combined total of just under 1,000 minke

Blue whale (*Balaenoptera musculus*) and calf.
General Whale

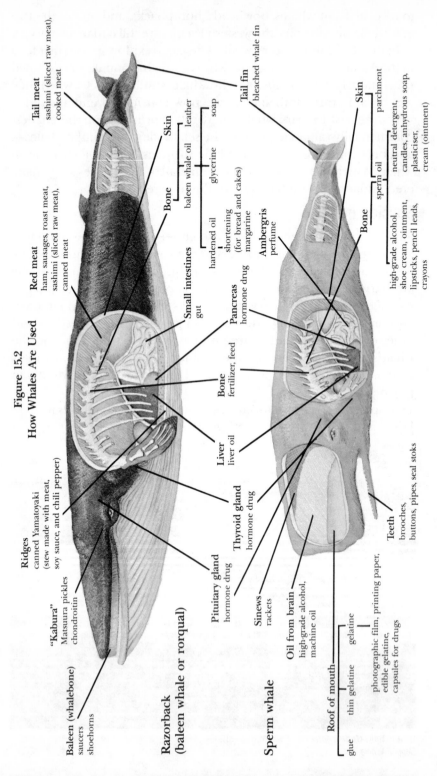

Figure 15.2
How Whales Are Used

Tail meat sashimi (sliced raw meat), cooked meat

Tail fin bleached whale fin

Red meat ham, sausages, roast meat, sashimi (sliced raw meat), canned meat

Skin — leather

baleen whale oil — glycerine — soap

— hardened oil — shortening (for bread and cakes) margarine

Skin

parchment

sperm oil — neutral detergent, candles, anhydrous soap, plasticiser, cream (ointment)

Bone

Ambergris perfume

high-grade alcohol, shoe cream, ointment, lipsticks, pencil leads, crayons

Small intestines gut

Pancreas hormone drug

Bone fertilizer, feed

Bone

Ridges canned Yamatoyaki (stew made with meat, soy sauce, and chili pepper)

Liver liver oil

Thyroid gland hormone drug

Teeth brooches, buttons, pipes, seal stoks

"Kabura" Matsuura pickles chondroitin

Pituitary gland hormone drug

Sinews rackets

Baleen (whalebone) saucers shoehorns

Oil from brain high-grade alcohol, machine oil

Razorback (baleen whale or rorqual)

Sperm whale

Roof of mouth — thin gelatine — gelatine — photographic film, printing paper, edible gelatine, capsules for drugs

glue

whales during their 1987 whaling seasons.* Japan reportedly killed 576, including 276 for "scientific research," and Norway harpooned 400.[25]

Until recently, the sperm whale was the second most widely hunted of the great whales,[26] and the Soviet Union and Japan were the world's major sperm-whaling nations. In the early 1980s, however, the Soviets closed down their sperm-whaling operations. Under a bilateral agreement with the United States, concluded in 1984, the Japanese agreed to limit their harvest of sperms to 400 whales during each of the 1984-85 and 1985-86 seasons and to 200 sperm whales during each of the 1986-87 and 1987-88 seasons, after which the Japanese promised to stop the commercial taking of sperm whales. Japan reportedly completed its sperm whaling in April 1988.

Sperm whales have been hunted primarily for their oil, which is used for high-grade industrial lubricants (figure 15.2). It is also used to tan leather and to manufacture shaving cream, detergents, and ink. Ambergris, a lumpy intestinal mixture, is used as a scent fixative in perfume, soaps, and cosmetics. The massive sperm-whale head yields spermaceti oil and a row of sharply pointed teeth, which are carved into piano keys or scrimshaw.

International trade in sperm whale oil now appears to be quite rare. Japan generally keeps its supply at home. Although Japan has entered a reservation on the species to allow imports from other countries, Japanese customs data show no whale-oil imports since 1979.

Bryde's whale—a relatively small rorqual† native to warm, tropical waters of the Pacific, Atlantic, and Indian oceans—was hunted as recently as 1986 by whalers in a vessel carrying the Filipino flag.‡ This operation, which began in 1983, was extremely controversial because it openly defied the IWC moratorium since the Philippines had never filed an objection to the moratorium with the IWC. These whalers reportedly captured 34 Bryde's whales in 1986 and used a factory ship to process the whale meat at sea, a practice that is also considered illegal by the IWC. Greenpeace reports that the catch was

---

*These figures apply to seasons that began during 1987. The Japanese and Soviets generally hunt minke whales in the southern hemisphere from November of one year to March or April of the next.

†The rorquals, which means "tube whale" in Norwegian, have long furrows under their mouths and throats that enable them to take in large quantities of tiny crustaceans and other organisms at one time. Other species include minke, fin, sei, blue, and humpback whales.

‡According to Greenpeace, this vessel was actually a pirate whaling boat, owned and controlled not by Filipinos but by Japanese nationals.

Humpback whale (*Megaptera novangliae*).
Ken Balcomb / WWF

then exported to Japan in violation of CITES.[27] In 1987, Japanese whalers reportedly took 357 Bryde's whales,[28] though they have since ceased this practice.[29]

The fin whale was exploited most heavily during the 1950s and 1960s, when annual harvests ranged from 20,000 to 32,000 animals.[30] Today, it is still a target for Icelandic whalers, who (as noted earlier) harvested 80 fin whales during the 1987 season. Spain, the only other country with a commercial fin-whale harvest in recent years, stopped whaling in 1985 in accordance with the moratorium.

In 1987, Icelandic whalers harvested some 20 sei whales (as has also been noted). Iceland claimed that these whales were needed for "research purposes."[31] The Icelandic government has announced plans to bring in another 20 for "research whaling" in 1988. One of the swiftest swimmers among the cetaceans, the sei whale became a prime target for whalers only in the 1960s, after blue, fin, and other species had become scarce.

Whaling by Native Peoples

Under the International Convention for the Regulation of Whaling, native peoples who have traditionally killed whales may continue to do so. They must comply with quotas set by the IWC, however, unless their governments submit formal objections to those quotas. Today, these quotas exist for gray whales taken in the northern Pacific by Soviet and Alaskan Eskimos; bowheads caught in the Bering Sea by

Alaskan Eskimos; and humpback, fin, and minke whales killed by the native peoples of Greenland. The Alaskan-bowhead quota, for instance, limits hunters to 44 "strikes" (which includes animals hit but not brought in) or 41 "landings" per year. Unused strikes from one year (up to a maximum of 3) can carry over into the next year. Native hunters in the United States (Alaska), Greenland, and the Soviet Union took a total of 211 whales in 1987.[32]*

Several local whaling operations continue without IWC quotas. For example, pilot whales (*Globicephala melaena*) have been harvested annually in Denmark's Faeroe Islands. The 1986 harvest took approximately 1,700 of these small whales.[34] (Some countries deny that the IWC has any jurisdiction over pilot whales. These and other small cetaceans have ranges that fall entirely within national jurisdictions, making their harvest a domestic, rather than international, concern.)

Since whaling by native peoples is allowed by the IWC only for cultural and subsistence purposes, the resulting whale products usually are consumed locally. Oil from the Bequia catch, for example, is used by islanders for cooking, in lamps, and as a lubricant. The meat sometimes is sold on the larger island of St. Vincent and other nearby markets, although much of it is given away, eaten, or distributed locally.[35]

Whaling by native peoples has been the focus of considerable debate in the United States and other IWC member countries. The controversy centers on conservation needs for whales vis-à-vis the cultural merits of native hunts—particularly those that involve endangered species such as the bowhead whale—and has little to do with commercial whaling. Commercial whaling and trade is now becoming part of the debate, however, since Japan is seeking IWC permission to keep alive a part of its domestic whaling industry, which it claims has both cultural and commercial traits. Japan has requested a new "small-type whaling" classification for its Hokkaido-based whaling industry, which takes hundreds of minke whales each year from the north Pacific. The IWC has not yet decided whether to approve Japan's proposal.

Small Cetaceans in Trade

Most of the smaller members of the Cetacean order—dolphins, porpoises, white whales, and beaked whales—are not hunted for

---

*There is also a small catch of humpbacks by a whaler living on the island of Bequia in St. Vincent and the Grenadines. Equipped with two double-ended wooden boats and hand-thrown harpoons, this whaler reportedly killed two humpback whales in 1986 and three humpbacks in 1987.[33] In 1987, the IWC approved for the first time a whaling quota of three whales per year through 1990 for the Bequia operation.

commercial markets. There are, however, several noteworthy exceptions.

A free-swimming aquatic unicorn of sorts, the narwhal (*Monodon monoceros*) is actually a small Arctic whale that has a sharply pointed, twisting tooth protruding from its snout. In males, these elongated teeth, known as tusks, grow 3 to 10 feet long. Tusks on females are rare. Until the mid-1980s, the tusks were valuable collectors' items and sold for $1,500 to $2,000 in urban markets, making the narwhal tempting bait for whale hunters and poachers. Today, the price has dropped to $500 to $700 for an average 3- to 4-foot tusk and about $150 for smaller or chipped specimens. This dramatic decline is believed to be the result of stricter trade controls.[36]

To protect narwhal stocks, Canada and Greenland—the two jurisdictions in whose waters narwhals are killed—allow only restricted native subsistence hunts. Each year, native whalers in the seas off western Greenland and in the Canadian Arctic harpoon 1,000 or so of the estimated 29,000 narwhals in the region. Little is known about other narwhal populations east of Greenland.[37]

The narwhal is listed on Appendix II of CITES. Since 1984, the EEC, which had been a major market, has banned imports of narwhals from any place except Greenland. The United States bans all narwhal imports under the Marine Mammal Protection Act. The tusk trade does not appear to be a threat to narwhal populations. From 1980 through 1985, CITES annual reports show an average of 113 tusks in international markets annually, with two-thirds of these coming from Canada. However, the world trade is probably somewhat larger, totaling 150 to 300 tusks. Canadian exports are now estimated at 50 to 200 tusks per year, with another 100 or so sold to domestic collectors.[38] There is no evidence of significant illegal trade in narwhal tusks.[39] Greenland probably exports 100 or so tusks per year and uses the remaining tusks domestically.[40]

A close relative of the narwhal, the beluga whale (*Delphinapterus leucas*) inhabits cold northern waters, where it is hunted for its meat, oil, and skin. In past centuries, U.S. and European whalers butchered these bulbous, white animals by the hundreds when they could not kill enough bowheads to fill their oil vats.[41] Today, belugas are primarily hunted by Arctic natives, but a small quantity of beluga skin reportedly enters world leather markets, where it is fashioned into bicycle seats, shoes, and handbags.[42]

Much of the trade in river dolphins (family Platanistidae), dolphins, porpoises, and small whales (family Delphinidae) is made up of live animals bound for aquariums and zoos. This market is limited and is usually not considered a threat, but trade in endangered, rare species, such as the 1987 export of 17 Commerson's dolphins (*Cephalorynchus commersoni*) from Chile to Japan, is cause for concern.[43]

In 1986, the United Kingdom imposed a five-year ban on dolphin and orca (*Orcinus orca*) imports. The move came in response to a Cambridge University study that uncovered major flaws in the operation of Britain's six dolphin exhibits, as well as concern about the high incidence of mortality among the animals held in captivity.[44]

PART IV
Birds

CHAPTER 16
Parrots

People have been teaching parrots to "talk" for over 2,000 years. The first documented effort took place in 400 B.C., when a Greek physician successfully convinced a plum-headed parrot (*Psittacula cyanocephala*) to switch from speaking an Indian language to squawking in Greek. Parrots' ability to mimic human words and phrases, combined with their colorful plumage and longevity, have kept them in vogue for centuries.[1]

Members of the parrot family (Psittacidae) are among the most popular pets in the world, perhaps second only to dogs and cats.[2] As many as 500,000 live parrots enter international trade each year.[3]

Psittacines are an amazingly varied family, with 330-odd species. Though often simply called parrots, they include parakeets, macaws, cockatoos, rosellas, amazons, lorikeets, conures, lovebirds, and others. They vary greatly in size and plumage, from the largest, the brilliantly blue-feathered hyacinth macaw (*Anodorhynchus hyacinthinnus*), to the sparrow-sized and rather drab green-rumped parrotlet (*Forpus passerinus*). All sport a downward-curving beak, which is often used as a third "foot" to maneuver from branch to branch. Most parrots are tropical, with nearly half of all species native to Latin America and the Caribbean and the rest from Africa, Asia, and Australia.

Hazards of the Parrot Trade

Trade can be devastating to parrots. This is particularly true for larger birds that reproduce slowly—such as the hyacinth macaw of South America—and those already depleted by habitat loss—such as the blue-streaked lory (*Eos reticulata*) of Indonesia.[4] More than 30 species and subspecies of parrots are considered endangered and are listed on CITES Appendix I, and all except three of the others are listed

Military macaw (*Ara militaris*).
Ginette Hemley / WWF

on Appendix II. Many are also protected by national legislation in their native countries. Despite all of these measures, there is a thriving global black market for the more exotic, colorful, expensive—and endangered—specimens.

Trapping for the commercial market is considered to be a major reason that the Spix's macaw (*Cyanopsitta spixi*) has almost died out in the wild. This Appendix I-listed species is thought to be the most endangered parrot in the world. Experts estimate that fewer than 10—and possibly only 3 or 4—of the grayish-blue, medium-sized birds are left in the wilds of northeastern Brazil.[5]

Trade is also thought to have been a major cause in the decline of the hyacinth macaw. Prized for its striking plumage, this endangered Neotropical parrot was listed on Appendix I in 1987. Two other parrots were given Appendix I protection that year: the military macaw (*Ara militaris*), because at least one subspecies, *A. m. boliviana*, is threatened with extinction and subject to trade pressures;[6] and the palm cockatoo (*Probosciger aterrimus*), which is nearing extinction in part of its range— the Aru Islands—but is still trapped illegally.[7]

Wildlife trade experts have singled out several Indonesian species, including the salmon-crested cockatoo (*Cacatua moluccensis*) and the blue-streaked lory, as worthy of concern. These birds can sell for hundreds of dollars in the United States, Europe, and the Far East. Indonesia has an export quota system for trade in these species, and thousands of the birds are trapped for shipment overseas each year.[8]

Scientists are equally concerned about another Indonesian parrot popular among pet owners, the chattering lory (*Lorius garrulus*), named for its speaking ability.[9] Indonesia is a major Asian supply point for the trade in wild parrots, and its commerce is on the rise. Indonesian parrot exports nearly doubled between 1981 and 1984, from 26,000 birds to 50,000.[10]

The African gray parrot (*Psittacus erithacus*) may suffer in some areas from excessive capture, though the species is still quite common in other parts of its range.[11] Gray-cheeked parakeets (*Brotogeris pyrrhopterus*) and blue-fronted amazons (*Amazona aestiva*) are two additional examples of wild parrots threatened by trade.[12]

Wild parrots also are threatened because traders often feel that they must capture large numbers of birds to compensate for those that will die before they are sold. Birds are among the most fragile animals taken from the wild for commercial markets, and many do not reach their final destinations. A study of U.S. bird imports from 1980 to 1984 found that 23 wild parrot species suffered losses of 40 percent or more during shipping and quarantine alone.[13]

Finally, wild birds in trade may carry diseases that can be fatal to domestic chickens and other birds. Parrots, in particular, are notorious carriers of psittacosis and exotic Newcastle disease,* which are especially virulent and contagious. After outbreaks of exotic Newcastle disease killed millions of domestic chickens in the early 1970s, the United States developed a quarantine system to weed out wild birds with potentially harmful infections. According to the U.S. Department of Agriculture, a serious epidemic of exotic Newcastle disease could cost as much as $250 million to bring under control.[14]

Quarantine programs are far from infallible, however, and even the best cannot reach smuggled birds. In 1987, nearly 1,750 birds in 10 U.S. states had to be killed following an outbreak of exotic Newcastle disease traced to infected yellow-naped amazons (*A. ochrocephala auropalliata*) believed to have been smuggled into the country from Mexico.[15]

Trade Volume and Routes

Most parrots in international trade are exported from Asia, Africa, and Latin America for sale in the United States, the European Economic Community (EEC), and Japan. The United States is the largest market for parrots, importing over one-quarter million each year (figure 16.1).[16] In 1984, U.S. gross imports totaled approximately 293,000 parrots; in 1985, another 312,000 entered the country.[17] These

---

Also known as viscerotropic velogenic Newcastle disease.

Parrots

Figure 16.1
Major Parrot Importers,
1984 and 1985

	1984	1985
Belgium*	12,439	21,078
Denmark*	4,384	5,877
France*	7,774	17,059
West Germany*	52,513	54,627
Greece*	3	1,310
Italy*	8,529	7,771
Japan	38,961	23,022
Netherlands*	16,173	28,775
Portugal*	989	1,198
Spain*	5,145	13,100
United Kingdom*	11,934	21,336
United States	292,607	312,467

*Member of the European Economic Community.
Source: CITES annual reports.

imports have a declared value of $10 million annually, with domestic parrot sales totaling $300 million in the retail market.[18] The EEC imported approximately 114,000 parrots in 1984 and roughly 158,000 in 1985, while Japan imported nearly 38,000 in 1984 and 23,000 in 1985. An increasingly important player is the Middle East. Countries in that region imported nearly 27,000 parrots in 1985.[19]

More than half of U.S. parrot imports come from Latin America, particularly Argentina, Guyana, Honduras, and Peru. Bolivia, once the largest exporter of macaws and other psittacines destined for U.S. markets, banned exports of all live wildlife in 1984, and its parrots have virtually disappeared from U.S. records of legal parrot trade.[20]

The EEC draws much of its parrot supply from Africa. In 1984, EEC member states imported roughly 50,000 African psittacines— 40 percent of that continent's total reported parrot exports.[21] A study of the United Kingdom's trade showed that two-thirds of all reported Appendix I and II parrots imported between 1980 and 1984 came from Africa. Chief among these imports were the African gray parrot, the Senegal parrot (*Poicephalus senegalus*), and peach-faced and Fischer's lovebirds (*Agapornis roseicollis* and *A. fischeri*).[22] Australasia and Latin America also supplied a wide variety of species sold in EEC parrot markets.

Not surprisingly, over half of Japan's parrot imports in the early 1980s came from Taiwan, Thailand, India, Indonesia, and other Asian nations, according to one study.[23] Japan is also an important market for African parrots.[24]

Some birds in trade—for example, the monk parakeet (*Myiopsitta monachus*)—not only are not threatened in their native countries; they are considered agricultural pests. Those countries may view exporting these "crop robbers" as the preferred method of population control. However, this may merely spread the scourge to importing countries. When these birds escape from captivity and establish successful breeding populations, they can end up competing with birds native to their new locales for limited food and nest sites.

Probably fewer than 5 percent of all parrots in the world market come from captive-breeding centers.[25] Popular pets such as the peach-faced lovebird come primarily from bird-breeding centers in Belgium, the Netherlands, South Africa, and (probably) Taiwan.[26] As trade controls get tighter, aviculturists are increasing their efforts at captive breeding. Captive-bred birds often make better pets because they are generally healthier (with lower mortality rates) and tamer than wild birds, although they tend to be more expensive.

Captive breeding of parrots and other birds can take pressure off— and, in some instances, actually help rebuild—wild populations. However, when threatened species are involved, sale of captive-bred birds may complicate efforts to control trade in their wild counterparts since it can be difficult to tell them apart. In many instances, captive breeders are required to band their birds to help distinguish them from wild stock. Still, some conservationists argue against keeping *any* market open for a bird species when the wild population is in trouble.

Illegal Trade

Illegal trade is a serious problem in world parrot markets. Though legally protected, many rare parrots can sell for thousands of dollars on the black market, providing an irresistible temptation to poachers and smugglers. In the United States, up to one-third of all imported wild parrots may be illegal, either under the Lacey Act, because they were taken from countries where they are protected by national laws, or under the Endangered Species Act, because they were traded in contravention of CITES.[27]

Some parrot smuggling takes a direct route—with birds being transported from their country of origin to their final destination with no intermediary countries. For instance, U.S. officials estimate that 150,000 birds, mostly parrots, are smuggled across the border from Mexico every year.[28]

Much illegal trade in parrots, however, is more indirect. Birds are smuggled out of one country in which they are legally protected into

Palm cockatoo (*Probosciger aterrimus*).
Jorgen B. Thomsen / WWF

another where they are not. They are then shipped with falsified permits to markets in a third or even fourth country. For instance, parrots are sneaked past customs checkpoints in Brazil, Australia, and other parrot-rich nations to countries where export controls are poorly enforced. Paraguay, Indonesia, Bolivia, and Singapore have been common laundering points in recent years.[29] Honduras and El Salvador, too, have been known entrepôts for smuggled Latin American parrots.[30] In Africa, Senegal appears to be a laundering point for African gray parrots captured in other countries.[31]

The palm cockatoo, which is legally protected throughout its Indonesian, Papua New Guinean, and Australian range as well as listed on Appendix I, has been particularly hard hit by illegal trade paired with loss of its natural habitat to human encroachment. In 1983, officials in Singapore raided one bird trader's house and found 100 palm cockatoos that had been smuggled in from Indonesia.[32] That same year, two U.S. bird importers were caught smuggling 100 of the parrots, worth an estimated $700,000, into Miami. The birds were brought in with Malaysian papers declaring that they had come from

Salmon-crested cockatoos (*Cacatua moluccensis*) packed in shipping boxes arriving in Europe from Indonesia.
Jorgen B. Thomsen/WWF

Indonesia even though Indonesian law prohibits their export. Indonesian authorities later confirmed that the cargo was illicit.[33]* Illicit trade has been a problem for other cockatoos from Australia as well. Although Australia protects most of its parrot species, poachers are known to sneak the Major Mitchell's cockatoo (*Cacatua leadbeateri*), sulphur-crested cockatoo (*C. galerita*), and other parrots by private plane through illegal channels to the markets of Asia and on to the United States and Europe.[34] This trade differs from trade in Indonesian species, however, in that several of the Australian birds are not rare or endangered. Major Mitchell's cockatoo and the sulphur-crested cockatoo are numerous in Australia and are even considered pests in some areas.[35]

Macaw snatchers are responsible for decimating some of Latin America's most unique and colorful species, including the Spix's macaw, hyacinth macaw, and red-fronted macaw (*Ara unbrogenys*). In 1980, a notorious British bird smuggler was caught importing a pair of the highly endangered Spix's macaw. The birds entered the country under permits authorized for relatively common blue-crowned conures (*Aratinga acuticaudata*). At the time, a Spix's macaw could sell for about $9,000, while a conure was worth only a few hundred dollars.[36] Today, smuggled Spix's macaws command $10,000 to $20,000 each.

In 1987, alert wildlife-trade investigators operating undercover in

*In an interesting twist, the same U.S. couple was arrested in 1985 on charges of producing over $70 million worth of cocaine at their home in southern Florida (see box in chapter 2 on "Links to the Drug Trade"). U.S. agents also seized toucans, macaws, and other birds believed to be illegal imports.

Brazil and Paraguay exposed another smuggling caper involving the Spix's macaw. A trapper dispatched by a Brazilian bird dealer filched two fledglings from the only known Spix's nest in the world. The valuable birds were sold to another dealer for approximately $18,000 total and then were resold to a Paraguayan dealer in Asunción. After forging trade documents for the birds, the dealer prepared to sell the young parrots to a dealer in Europe for $40,000. But, before putting down such a hefty sum, the prospective purchaser contacted wildlife officials to confirm that the birds' documents were in order. At that point, the scheme began to unravel. The CITES Secretariat concluded that the documents were fakes and notified Paraguayan CITES officials of the problem. TRAFFIC then sent undercover investigators posing as bird buyers to visit the smuggler and locate the birds. Once the macaws' whereabouts were established, TRAFFIC tipped off Paraguayan officials, who raided the smuggling operation in Asunción and returned the birds to Brazil. The young Spix's macaws now live in the São Paulo Zoo with three adults of the species.[37] They could not be returned to the wild because they had been held in captivity too long and had become accustomed to humans.

Black marketeers also target the coveted hyacinth macaw, which can be purchased from poachers for $40 to $60 but fetches as much

Spix's macaw (*Cyanopsitta spixi*).
Russell A. Mittermeier / WWF

as $5,000 to $10,000 in the United States and other foreign markets.[38] Pressured also by habitat loss and hunting for its meat and feathers, this striking blue macaw now numbers only 2,500 to 5,000 birds in the wild. It has an extremely low reproductive rate, which only adds to its peril. There are just 2 known survivors in Paraguay and a mere 100 to 300 birds in Bolivia. The remainder are found in Brazil.[39]

Although all three countries outlaw export of the bird, hundreds of hyacinths have reached world markets in the past five years, often through Bolivian, Paraguayan, or Argentinean trade routes. Most of the supply is believed to originate in Brazil, where well-organized, professional bird catchers and traders prey on at least two of the three remaining populations.[40] As an indication of the probable supply line from Brazil, traders in Bolivia, which had only a few hundred native hyacinth macaws in the early 1980s, exported close to 1,400 to the United States alone between 1980 and 1983.[41]

Many dedicated Brazilian, Bolivian, and Paraguayan wildlife officials and private conservationists are fighting to stop illegal trade and to protect the hyacinth macaw's future in the wild.[42] In 1984, Bolivia banned all exports of live wildlife in response to international pressure to combat such problems, but enforcement of the ban remains a problem. Paraguay, too, is a trouble spot for the hyacinth macaw trade. In late 1985, a shipment of 49 hyacinths arrived in Austria from Paraguay without legal CITES permits. Despite repeated requests from the CITES Secretariat, Austrian officials apparently did not confiscate the birds or penalize the smugglers involved.[43] In 1986, TRAFFIC(South America) turned up evidence that illicit trade channels for Brazilian hyacinth macaws ran through French Guiana as well.[44] The species has been advertised for sale in Antigua and Guyana and as far away as Indonesia, the Philippines, Singapore, and Thailand. There is also considerable internal trade in hyacinth macaws; some Brazilian bird dealers contend that in-country sales account for half of their transactions.[45]

The scarlet macaw (*Ara macao*), a large, rainbow-colored parrot that retails for $2,000 to $3,000 in the United States, is another victim of widespread illegal trade in Latin America.[46] Although the bird is protected throughout most of its range, over 2,500 birds were exported from the region in 1982 and 1983.[47] Some exited via El Salvador, where scarlet macaws have been extinct for many years; these birds were no doubt smuggled from neighboring countries. Although the species is reportedly still common in some parts of Amazonia and the Guianas, it is seriously threatened elsewhere, especially in Central America.[48] CITES parties listed the scarlet macaw on Appendix I in 1985 because of its declining numbers in the wild.

The African gray parrot, one of the most widely traded parrots in the world, is another species that may be plagued by black marketeers. Upwards of 40,000 birds reached world markets in 1984, including almost 7,000 from Senegal, where the species is not known to occur, and another 1,200 from Zaire, despite a national ban on its export imposed in February of that year.[49]

Developing countries that supply wild parrots to foreign markets often lack adequate border controls and other resources to keep legally protected species out of the trade. But importing countries must share at least as much blame for their failure to uncover, identify, and confiscate bird contraband. In the United States, for example,

KEEP IN MIND . . .

If you want to buy a parrot, be an educated consumer. With two exceptions, all parrot species are protected under CITES, and wild imported specimens, therefore, are subject to trade controls. Illegal trade, which includes smuggling and document tampering, continues to plague the parrot trade and contributes significantly to bird mortality.

■ Ensure that the parrot you are thinking of buying came from a legitimate source. If the pet shop owner or bird dealer does not know the origin of his or her stock, make another choice.

■ Look for captive-bred birds. You can be sure these have entered trade legally and in general are healthier and tamer than their wild counterparts.

■ If you are inexperienced in keeping parrots, select species whose captive living requirements are well known, such as budgerigars (budgies) and certain cockatiels and lovebirds. Larger species require specialized care and can die in inexperienced hands.

■ Learn all you can on parrot conservation and their care in captivity. Join a bird society such as the American Federation of Aviculturists (P.O. Box 1568, Redondo Beach, CA 90278), which publishes *Watchbird*, the Amazonas Society (P.O. Box 73547, Puyallup, WA 98373), and the International Loriidae Society (832 S.W. 137th Street, Seattle, WA 98166).

■ *Some suggested readings:*
American Cage-Bird Magazine. Published monthly. 1 Glamore Ct., Smithtown, NY 11787.
Bird Talk magazine. Published monthly. Fancy Publications, 3 Burroughs, Irvine, CA 92718.
Forshaw, Joseph M. *Parrots of the World.* Neptune, N.J.: T.F.H., 1977.

a TRAFFIC(U.S.A.) study found that customs officers know little about bird identification or trade regulations and that many bird shipments slip in while wildlife inspectors are off duty.[50] Even during working hours, port authorities simply cannot keep up with the overwhelming flow of bird shipments crossing their borders each year. In addition, it is often very hard to find housing facilities and appropriate care for live birds once they have been seized. Importing countries are also known to ignore export bans levied by other countries. Clearly, illegal trade in wild parrots remains a lucrative and deadly business.

CHAPTER 17
Raptors

"**R**aptor" means plunderer in Latin, stemming from the verb *rapere*: to seize or snatch. In the bird world, raptors (order Falconiformes) are accomplished snatchers, often swooping out of the sky with outstretched talons to whisk away live rodents or fish. Also known as birds of prey, the group is composed of five families: New World vultures (Cathartidae); kites, eagles, and hawks (Accipitridae); falcons (Falconidae); the osprey (Pandionidae); and the secretary bird (Sagittariidae). Though their hunting habits and food preferences vary, all are well adapted to finding and eating meat—with keen eyesight, sharply hooked beaks, and agile legs and claws.

Raptors are both prized and persecuted for their hunting acumen. Some falcon species fetch sums of up to several thousand dollars among European, U.S., and Middle Eastern falconers, while golden eagles, goshawks, and other birds of prey frequently are shot or poisoned because they feed on game birds and young livestock. Most countries now outlaw killing threatened raptor species, but some illicit hunting continues.

International trade in raptors is tightly regulated. All species except the New World vultures are listed on either Appendix I or II, and many are given added protection by their native countries.

Raptor trade restrictions are controversial because some of the species most favored in falconry, including the gyrfalcon (*Falco rusticolus*) and the peregrine falcon (*F. peregrinus*), are also considered endangered.[1] Black-market demand for some protected species provides great incentives to capture wild birds. Sophisticated smuggling operations for live birds and eggs have been uncovered recently in the United States, Canada, West Germany, and Japan. Captive-breeding programs for some endangered raptors have been successful, but problems in identifying whether a bird is captive-bred or caught in the wild make trade difficult to police.

The greatest threats to the world's raptor populations are habitat loss and contamination by toxic chemicals. The California condor (*Gymnogyps californianus*), which no longer occurs in the wild, is perhaps the best-known example. Predators such as the peregrine falcon, sparrow hawk (*Accipiter nisus*), sharp-shinned hawk (*A. striatus*), Cooper's hawk (*A. cooperii*), and osprey (*Pandion haliaetus*) have all been hard hit by pesticides in the past three decades. Chemicals present in the bodies of animals they kill for food accumulate in their own bodies. DDT (dichloro-diphenyl-trichloro-ethane) and other organochlorides cause the birds to lay eggs with shells that are too thin. Lead poisoning also kills adult birds. Use of DDT and other harmful chemicals is largely outlawed in Europe and North America, but it is actually on the rise in some developing countries.[2]

Species in Trade

Birds destined for falconry make up much of the international trade in live raptors. World demand for new birds in the sport is estimated at over 4,000 a year.[3] Most of the birds come from the United States, Canada, northern Europe, or China. Saudi Arabia, the United Arab Emirates, and other Middle Eastern countries are major consumers,

Peregrine falcon (*Falco peregrinis*).
P. McLain / VIREO

International Wildlife Trade: Whose Business Is It?

as are West Germany, the United States, and Japan.

The peregrine falcon is one of the most popular species in falconry—and in world trade—because it is a superb hunter and flier. Peregrines can dive or "stoop" at speeds of 100 or more miles per hour to attack other birds, killing them with sharp claws. Found in varied habitats around the world, from tundra to tropical rain forest, peregrines are endangered throughout much of their range and are listed on Appendix I of CITES.[4] CITES data for 1980 to 1983 show at least 150 peregrines in international trade per year. Most of these were from West Germany and Canada, and approximately half were listed as captive-bred. These numbers probably do not reflect the total volume of trade, however. Falconers and breeders often exchange— rather than sell—birds, making the exact market difficult to determine.

In a Middle Eastern market fueled by petrodollars, peregrines reportedly once sold for $7,000 to $10,000,[5] but their price has since fallen. According to the president of the North American Raptor Breeder's Association, $2,000 was the median asking price for a peregrine in 1984, and prices are expected to fall to $500 to $1,000 by 1990.[6]

Another popular Appendix I species, the gyrfalcon, can bring particularly high prices in world markets, although the bird's popularity among falconers is debatable. Price estimates range from an average of $6,000 to a top price of $25,000 or so for high-quality, large, female birds offered to wealthy Arab falconers.[7]

U.S. agents turned up a lucrative international black market for gyrfalcons in 1984, but some experts doubt that the world market is substantial. One expert believes that only 20 or so of the birds are traded in the Middle East each year, and that the rest are bought by European falconers and "optimistic breeders."[8]

West Germany is the major gyrfalcon exporter. Birds shipped from that country are commonly listed as captive-bred and sent to Pakistan and Saudi Arabia.[9] West German wildlife-trade experts, however, doubt that most gyrfalcons exported from their country are captive-bred. They claim that many of the prized birds are actually raised from eggs taken from the wild and are then given inaccurate trade papers. With permits marked "captive-bred," gyrfalcons are illegally treated as Appendix II rather than Appendix I birds.[10]

Several other birds are frequently found in international commerce. One bird that is popular among falconers is the northern goshawk (*Accipter gentilis*). This large predator, listed on Appendix II, is known for its audacious hunting behavior, frequently targeting wild rabbits and grouse and even raiding local hen houses from time to time. The saker falcon (*Falco cherrug*) of eastern Europe, Asia, and North Africa

Raptor feathers and claws are popular not only in trade in such countries as Japan and China. They have also been used in some traditional Native American crafts, such as these peyote fans confiscated by the U.S. Fish and Wildlife Service for violation of the Lacey Act and other U.S. wildlife protection laws.
U.S. Fish and Wildlife Service

is a favorite hunting bird of Arab falconers. It closely resembles its larger cousin, the gyrfalcon.

Apart from the falconry market, live raptors in trade are usually headed for breeding programs. In addition, the bateleur (*Terathopius ecaudatus*), white-tailed eagle (*Haliaeetus albicilla*), and other birds of prey are traded in small numbers to private collectors and zoos.[11]

Finally, a large international demand for stuffed raptor bodies, feathers, talons, and other body parts concerns some raptor specialists. Much of the this trade involves specimens used for research or museum displays or stuffed birds for commercial sale. The Japanese are among the main raptor-feather consumers, reportedly importing over 30,000 golden-eagle (*Aquila chrysaetos*) feathers from China in one recent year alone.[12] In Japan, these rather drab feathers are used to fletch bamboo arrows for traditional Japanese archery or "kyudo."

Captive Breeding

About half the peregrine falcons reported in trade during the early 1980s were listed as captive bred, as were most of the gyrfalcons and almost one-quarter of the saker falcons. In contrast, most of the northern goshawks came from the wild.[13]

In 1981, captive-breeding programs in the United States produced over 450 young raptors.[14] Many of these programs, such as the publicly supported Peregrine Fund, Santa Cruz Predatory Bird Research

Group, and the United Peregrine Society, breed peregrines to help rebuild populations threatened by past exposure to toxic chemicals. Other programs breed the Harris' hawk (*Parabuteo unicinctus*) and other large hawks for falconry. The American kestrel (*Falco sparverius*) is sometimes bred for laboratory use. In addition, peregrine falcons are captive bred in Austria, Canada, Denmark, and West Germany. Saudi Arabians breed saker falcons for sport hunting, and operations in Bahrain raise peregrine falcons, gyrfalcons, and hybrids for falconry.[15]

Illegal Trade

In 1984, U.S. agents exposed an international raptor-smuggling operation that shocked both conservationists and falconers around the world. With evidence collected during a three-year undercover investigation dubbed "Operation Falcon," the federal government has since convicted over 60 people in the United States, Canada, West Germany, the Middle East, and other countries with criminal activities related to taking as many as 400 young falcons from the wild for commercial sale.[16] The biggest raptor bust in history, Operation Falcon netted 102 live raptors, including gyrfalcons, peregrine falcons, prairie falcons (*Falco mexicanus*), and northern goshawks. Wild birds that had been smuggled through captive-breeding operations and sometimes given false papers or leg bands from dead captive-bred birds were sold to falconers in the United States, Europe, and the Middle East.[17]

In 1986, a Saudi prince implicated in the smuggling racket settled

Sparrow hawk (*Accipiter nisus*).
Tom Smylie / WWF

with the U.S. government by donating $150,000 to federal law-enforcement efforts. According to Justice Department lawyer Donald Carr, "The Saudis understand this illegal trade is a problem and they are willing to try to stop it in their kingdom."[18]

An investigation in Canada related to Operation Falcon discovered 60 gyrfalcons and 40 peregrine falcons taken illegally from the wild and laundered through captive-breeding programs before shipment abroad.[19] In response to these problems, as well as evidence of declining gyrfalcon populations, the North American population of the gyrfalcon was uplisted from Appendix II to Appendix I in 1985.

On a smaller scale, falcon smuggling has been a problem in other countries. In the United Kingdom, a falconer was fined $895 in 1985 for taking four northern goshawks from the wild and selling two of them on the black market.[20] Game wardens and trade officials must also keep on the lookout for raptor thieves in Belgium, France, Finland, and Japan; in Japan, collectors often target the common kestrel (*Falco tinnunculus*) and northern goshawk.[21]

Egg smuggling is also a continuing concern. Operation Falcon uncovered illicit raptor-egg stealing involving fertile northern goshawk eggs from the United Kingdom and other parts of Western Europe.[22] In 1986, a West German breeder was arrested by U.K. officials when he attempted to smuggle peregrine eggs, purportedly given to him by a Yorkshire gamekeeper, out of the United Kingdom. He was fined $840 for his efforts. Calling the bust "the tip of the iceberg," the Royal Society for the Protection of Birds (RSPB) estimated that egg thieves were robbing 50 raptor nests in the United Kingdom every year. Incoming illicit egg shipments are also a problem for U.K. customs officials. In 1986, for instance, three people were arrested for bringing 26 eggs, valued at over $26,000, from the Appendix II lanner falcon (*Falco biarmicus*) into the Manchester airport from Morocco.[23]

One of the most notorious egg-stealing scandals to date broke in 1984, when a top Zimbabwean ornithologist and his son were convicted of robbing hundreds of raptor nests while participating in a 21-year survey of black eagles (*Aquila verreauxi*) and other rare raptors in Zimbabwe's Matopos National Park. According to the RSPB, black eagle eggs are worth an estimated $600 each among some ornamental egg collectors. The collection of 900 blown eggs found in the thieves' possession was valued at over one-half-million dollars. A Zimbabwean court fined the erstwhile ornithologist and his son approximately $2,800 and gave them four-month suspended sentences. The father was later charged with smuggling live eggs abroad.[24]

CHAPTER 18
Songbirds

O ver half of all living bird species are songbirds, known technically as passerines (that is, members of the Passeriformes order). Adapted for perching on all manner of reeds, branches, and telephone wires, passerines include larks, swallows, magpies, blackbirds, and other familiar families. The order also encompasses perennial cage-bird favorites such as the canary (*Serinus canaria*), the blue-capped cordon bleu (*Uraeginthus cyanocephalus*), and the hill myna (*Gracula religiosa*).

Passerines are the most frequently traded cage birds in the world. Each year, at least two million live finches (Fringillidae), waxbills (Estrildidae), weavers (Ploceidae), and mynas (Sturnidae) are shipped to global markets. Most of these come from Senegal, the world's largest exporter of wild birds, and other African countries.[1]

Most of the passerines in trade are not considered threatened, and a few, such as the canary and zebra finch (*Poephila guttata*), are usually captive bred. The zebra finch is so easy to breed and maintain that it often is used for experiments in U.S. and European laboratories, prompting one ornithologist to predict that it may become "the mouse of the avian world."[2]

Species of Concern

Some songbirds, however, are less secure, and a handful of passerine species are listed on the CITES appendices. One such bird is the red siskin (*Carduelis cucullata*), the only finch on CITES Appendix I. This bird was nearly trapped to extinction in Venezuela in the early 20th century after aviculturists discovered that it could breed with domestic canaries to produce fertile copper-feathered offspring. It has

Waxbills (Estrildidae, left and center) and red-cheeked Cordon-blue (*Estrilada bengala*, right) in a Senegalese bird exporter's premises.
Dave Currey / E.I.A.

completely disappeared from its former range in Colombia and Trinidad. Today, the species is bred successfully in captivity, with average birds selling for $100 to $200 each.[3] Only 600 to 800 birds are thought to survive in the wild, nearly all in pockets of northern Venezuela. A small local population also has been introduced in Puerto Rico. Although the red siskin is completely protected by CITES and Venezuelan law, trapping continues, and the species may soon die out. Wild red siskins are commonly smuggled offshore to Curaçao, then laundered into trade, reportedly selling for nearly $1,000 apiece.[4] They are then bred with domestic birds to reinvigorate the captive gene pool, particularly to pass on their impressive coloring.

In addition to CITES controls, some major exporting countries, such as Senegal and Tanzania, are working to regulate the trade through national laws. Such trade restrictions, however, can be unpopular and difficult to uphold in exporting countries where the trade provides a livelihood to local trappers and the species involved are known crop robbers, which is the case with several weavers.[6]

Although the impact of trade on songbirds is usually not nearly so drastic, there is some concern that certain other finches, waxbills, weavers, and mynas also may not be able to sustain heavy collecting pressure. Conservationists are especially concerned that passerines may be being depleted by overtrapping in Senegal.[5]

As with parrots, much of the trade in wild passerines involves species that are not well suited to the rigors of capture and shipping. According to one report, fire finches and some other waxbill species suffer particularly high mortality during shipment. From 1980 to 1984, 40 percent or more of the red-billed fire finches (*Lagonosticta senegala*), blue-capped cordon bleus, violet-eared waxbills (*Uraeginthus granatina*), and lavender waxbills (*Estrilda caerulescens*) imported to the United States from Africa reportedly did not survive either the trip or the 30-day quarantine period. Feeding problems may explain some of the loss, since finches in transit are often fed seeds that differ radically from their native diets.[7]

Trade Volume and Routes

Today, Senegal is considered the world's largest supplier of wild passerines, shipping approximately 1 million of the birds each year. These exports include hundreds of thousands of yellow-fronted canaries (*Serinus mozambicus*) and cut-throats (*Amadina fasciata*).[8] India was once a leading world supplier of passerines, shipping over 14 million birds to international markets in the 1970s. Its exports dropped sharply after 1977, however, partly because the country banned the export of many species.[9]

The United States, Europe, and Japan are major markets for imported songbirds. The United States alone reportedly imported more than 1.4 million passerines from 1980 to 1984. More than 50,000 cordon bleus, 75,000 waxbills, and 40,000 yellow-fronted canaries entered the United States during those five years.[10]

CHAPTER 19
Other Birds in Trade

International trade in birds is a widely varied industry. As discussed in the preceding chapters, parrots, raptors, and songbirds make up the bulk of the trade—but not the totality. For example, the world's largest bird, the ostrich, and the smallest, the hummingbird,

Figure 19.1
Bird Trade in an Average Year

World Trade

Minimum in birds (estimate)	3,500,000
Minumum declared value of world trade in birds	$44,000,000

U.S. Trade

Import of birds	800,000
Import of parrots	250,000
Declared value of birds imported into the United States	$15,000,000
Declared value of parrots imported into the United States	$10,000,000
Retail turnover in parrots	$300,000,000
Current aviary and cage bird population	45,000,000 to 70,000,000

U.S. Quarantine Stations

U.S. Department of Agriculture	3
Private	83

U.S. Ports of Entry

U.S. Department of Agriculture (USDA)-approved ports of entry for commercial bird shipments	15
U.S. Department of the Interior (DOI)-designated ports of entry for commercial wildlife shipments	9*
Ports of entry approved or designated by both USDA and DOI	11

*Plus three U.S.-Mexican and six U.S.-Canadian border ports for trade between the two border countries only.

are both sought across national boundaries.

Each year, the world bird trade totals an estimated $44 million. At least 4 million live birds enter international trade every year.[1] In addition, an indeterminate number of birds are killed each year, and their feathers, skins, and other body parts are marketed. Eggs of some birds are also put into trade.

Most wild birds in trade come from developing countries in the tropics, where bird life is the most diverse and exotic. Senegal is believed to be the world's biggest bird exporter, shipping over 1 million finches, waxbills, parrots, and other birds per year.[2]

The United States is the single largest consumer of wild birds and bird products, cornering as much as one-quarter of the market. In a single year, the United States imports about 800,000 wild birds, valued at $10 to $15 million.[3] These birds join 45 to 70 million birds kept in aviaries and cages around the country.[4] Japan and the European countries, particularly West Germany, the Netherlands, and Belgium, are also large-scale wild bird importers.

Hummingbird

Known for their dazzling flying feats, such as scooting backward or hovering feverishly in place, and their often equally stunning coloration, hummingbirds (family Trochilidae) occur throughout the Americas, but most typically in the tropics. The same threats that endanger other wild birds apparently are affecting hummingbirds. In 1987, all hummingbirds were added to CITES' Appendix II. Many of the 320 to 350 species appear to be suffering the effects of habitat loss, although not enough population data are available to be sure.[5] Commercial trade also may threaten some species.[6] In addition, experts are concerned that these birds are ill-suited to the rigors of

Ruby-throated hummingbird
(*Archilochus colubris*).
K. L. Coogle

International Wildlife Trade: Whose Business Is It?

capture and shipping and may suffer higher mortality than less delicate species popular in the world bird market.[7]

During the mid-1800s, hummingbirds reportedly were imported by the thousands for European collections. Today, the tiny birds are sometimes exploited for their feathers, which are fashioned into jewelry, but are increasingly popular in the live bird trade, particularly in Europe and the United States. While the total volume of hummingbird imports is hard to gauge, observers estimate that West Germany may import some 10,000 hummingbirds a year, and the Netherlands may take in another 1,000 or so. The United Kingdom's imports averaged about 180 birds from 1980 through 1986. U.S. trade data for 1980-84 show an average of 150 or so hummingbird imports per year.

During the 1980s, most hummingbirds imported by these countries have come from Peru, Ecuador, Chile, or French Guiana. Much of the Ecuadorean trade probably has been illegal, since Ecuador outlawed all commercial wildlife exports in 1983.[8]

Ostrich and Rhea

Modern-day ostriches are multipurpose birds, raised like cattle on South African and Zimbabwean ranches. The gangly, flightless species (*Struthio camelus*) originally was farmed in the 1850s to provide plumage for the millinery trade. The hat feather market is now minimal, but 25,000 or so captive-bred South African ostriches are raised annually for leather.[9] Tough, feather-pocked ostrich skin is made into Italian billfolds, Texas cowboy boots, and other exotic leather goods. The United States alone imported some $4 million worth of raw

Ostrich (*Struthio camelus*).
Rick Weyerhaeuser / WWF

ostrich skin and products in 1982, mostly for boots.[10] In 1987, U.S. ostrich skin and product imports were worth more than $8.2 million. The mainstay of the bird-leather trade, ostrich comprised 80 percent of U.S. bird-skin imports in the early 1980s.[11]

The market for ostrich products is not limited to leather. Ostrich eggshells, roughly the size of American softballs, are fashioned into jewelry and ornaments for sale to tourists. Ostrich meat is sometimes sold as steaks or dried jerky, and ostrich-leg curios such as standing ashtrays or lamps go to the highest bidder. In the United States, there is reportedly a small market for live ostrich "watchdogs," which are let loose in fenced work sites to fend off intruders.

A New World version of the ostrich, the greater rhea (*Rhea americana*) of central and southern South America, is also killed for trade in its leather and plumage. The United States imported roughly $1 million worth of skin and products of this South American native in 1981.[12] Italy is also an important market for rhea skin.[13] Like ostrich leather, rhea often is used in cowboy boots, which sell for up to $600 a pair in New York City, as well as in gloves and handbags.

In 1983, Argentina, formerly the largest source of rhea products, legally protected the species.[14] Rhea feathers, however, continue to be smuggled from Argentina to Brazil, where the plumage is used to adorn carnival headdresses and costumes.[15] In Argentina, bones from the birds' feet are fashioned into flatware handles and rhea eggs are sometimes consumed by the *campesinos*.

Some, but not all, ostriches and rheas are protected under CITES. Wild ostriches in 12 African countries are listed on Appendix I; those in other countries are not covered by the treaty. One subspecies of greater rhea (*Rhea americana albescens*) is listed on Appendix II. The other rhea species, the lesser rhea (*Pterocnemia pennata*), is listed on Appendix I and seldom enters trade.

The Feather Trade

The wild-bird feather market hit an all-time high during the Victorian era, when stylish European and American hats were adorned with plumage from birds of paradise (family Paradisaeidae), egrets (*Egretha* spp.), scarlet ibis (*Eudocimus ruber*), crowned pigeons (*Columba leucocephala*), kingfishers (family Alcedinidae), tanagers (family Thraupidae), and parrots (family Psittacidae) from tropical colonies. From 1890 to 1929, France alone consumed an estimated 50,000 tons of foreign bird feathers.[16]

The days of the high-volume trade in feathers from wild birds are over, though demand for some of the most exotic and beautiful species such as the bird of paradise and scarlet ibis continues. All birds of

Scarlet ibis (*Eudocimus ruber*).
T. Pyle

paradise are listed on Appendix II, and most are protected in their native countries, Indonesia and Papua New Guinea. Nevertheless, poachers and smugglers still supply feathers and stuffed birds through illicit channels to Japan and other parts of the Far East.[17]

In French Guiana, the scarlet ibis is legally protected, but exploitation continues, for both the bird's feathers and its meat. Rustlers reportedly dynamite entire rookeries of this bird to collect feathers for flower-shaped ornaments sold to tourists.[18] A 1987 survey found that more than half the country's tourist shops offer ibis "flowers."[19] An art center in French Guiana sells about 20,000 of the flowers each year, including 1,000 or so of one type of ornament that is composed of the birds' primary feathers. Each scarlet ibis has 8 of these feathers, and it takes 10 to 12 primary feathers to craft one ornament. Thus, it could take as many as 1,500 ibises just to supply that single variety of ornament!

In all, an estimated 70,000 to 100,000 breeding pairs of ibis remain throughout the species' entire Latin American range. Breeding by the birds has declined drastically in French Guiana, probably in response to hunting pressures.[20] In 1987, at the request of Suriname and France, the species was added to Appendix II.

Feathers also have been used for centuries to stuff pillows, outfit fly fishers, and supply other needs. Today, most feathers used in large quantities for these purposes come from domesticated fowl such as chickens, geese, ducks, and turkeys.

PART V
Reptiles

CHAPTER 20

Crocodiles, Alligators, and Caimans

C rocodilians thrived on much of this planet alongside the dinosaurs 150 million years ago. Few other animals today can claim this distinction. Yet, for many crocodilian species, time may be running out. Fully two-thirds of the 21 crocodilian species* alive today are considered endangered, mostly because of the combined effects of trade and habitat loss.

Thirty years ago, rising world demand for alligator skin shoes and crocodile leather purses wiped out many wild populations of the American alligator (*Alligator mississippiensis*), Nile crocodile (*Crocodylus niloticus*), and other species of crocodilians. In the 1950s and early 1960s, trade in these wetland inhabitants accounted for some 5 to 10 million skins per year.[1] More than 750,000 hides were processed in one year by a single tanner in the New York City area.[2]

By the 1960s, the American alligator and many crocodiles were so depleted that hunters had trouble finding them, and some were so scarce that it was no longer possible to kill and process them in profitable numbers. As these species became endangered and more extensively protected, exotic leather markets shifted to more abundant relatives with less valuable skins.

Crocodilians are divided into three families: Crocodylidae (crocodiles), Alligatoridae (alligators and caimans), and Gavialidae (gavials). Gavials are not discussed in this chapter because they have never been heavily traded.

When the Nile crocodile, the most popular African species among hide importers, was added to the U.S. endangered species list, traders began focusing on another species from that continent—the slender-snouted crocodile (*C. cataphractus*). In South America, as the most sought-after species—American (*C. acutus*) and Orinoco (*C. intermedius*) crocodiles—declined, the reptile leather industry turned to the slightly bonier black (*Melanosuchus niger*) and broad-nosed (*Caiman latirostris*) caimans. Then, as those species became too scarce to allow the industry adequate profits, hunters began killing more and more spectacled (*C. crocodilus*) caiman, which is smaller and substantially bonier than the black and broad-nosed species and thus less desirable.[3]

Today, an estimated 1.5 to 2 million crocodilian skins reach world markets each year.[4] As many as three-quarters come from spectacled caiman, virtually all of which are taken from the wild. The remainder are "classic" skins, primarily from the highly coveted saltwater or estuarine crocodile (*Crocodylus porosus*), New Guinea crocodile (*C. novaeguineae novaeguineae*), Nile crocodile, and American alligator. In 1986, the United States alone imported about $15 million worth of crocodilian skins and manufactured products, the bulk of which were spectacled caiman.[5]

While effective conservation measures have allowed some previously endangered species to recover, wildlife experts are worried that this trade continues to pose serious threats to the survival of several crocodilian species. However, concern over overexploitation

Figure 20.1
U.S. Imports of Skins and Manufactured Products
from Selected Crocodilian Species, 1988
(with dollar values)

	Skins	Manufactured products
American alligator*	12,634 ($ 3,205,141)	25,781 ($ 3,423,638)
New Guinea crocodile	1,764 ($ 309,802)	17,233 ($ 3,980,550)
Saltwater crocodile	805 ($ 149,516)	300 ($ 73,165)
Spectacled caiman	104,719 ($13,437,478)	595,711 ($21,479,345)

*Skins often exported to Europe for tanning and then reimported into the United States.
Source: U.S. Fish and Wildlife Service.

arises not only on this ground. Overhunting of some species may cause serious ecological repercussions as well. For example, extermination of caiman populations may change the ecology of swamps and river systems. In some parts of the Pantanal, the world's largest swampland, which stretches over 76,000 square miles through southwestern Brazil across the border into Bolivia and Paraguay, the disappearance of fish-eating caimans is believed responsible for surges in piranha populations.[6] In lakes in the central Amazon, the caiman decline may lead to shortages of some fish species that are valuable sources of food for people in the region. Two separate processes may cause these shortages: (*a*) with caimans no longer numerous enough to keep the piranhas in check, the piranhas may outcompete food fish for invertebrates that they eat, and (*b*) those invertebrates may themselves decline as the caiman excrement on which they feed vanishes.

Species in Trade

CROCODILES

The most important of the crocodile species in trade today are the New Guinea crocodile, Nile crocodile, African slender-snouted crocodile, and saltwater crocodile.

All crocodiles receive some protection under CITES. During the 1970s, all species were listed in Appendix I, with the exception of the Papua New Guinea populations of the saltwater crocodile and the New Guinea crocodile. In the first half of the 1980s, however, CITES trade regulations began to loosen significantly, allowing trade in

Nile crocodile (*Crocodylus niloticus*).
Jorgen B. Thomsen / WWF

numerous crocodiles that previously had been completely protected by the treaty. For instance, some populations of saltwater and Nile crocodiles have been downlisted to Appendix II. The changes arose in response to crocodile-ranching programs that had been highly successful in some countries, recovering populations of some species, and strong market pressures for continuing supplies of valuable crocodile skins.

Most trade in crocodiles today involves Appendix II species. Some Appendix I species, however, are also traded under CITES' "reservation" exemption.* Austria, an important crocodile consumer, holds reservations on ·saltwater and African slender-snouted crocodiles. Singapore also maintains a reservation on the saltwater crocodile, as does Japan (which is thereby able to remain the world's largest consumer of "salty" skins). (See appendix D for a complete list of countries with reservations on crocodile species.)

Certain crocodiles can also be traded from captive-breeding "farms" approved by the CITES Secretariat. For CITES purposes, captive-bred Appendix I animals are treated as Appendix II species. As of 1985, there were at least 10 such operations in the world: the largest, in Thailand, for several species; 5 in South Africa for the Nile crocodile; 1 in Australia and 1 in Malaysia for the saltwater crocodile; and 1 in Madagascar and another in Kenya for the Nile crocodile.[7] The number of farms breeding crocodiles is growing annually.

Trade in "ranched" animals is also increasing. Ranched crocodiles are similar to farm-raised animals in that they are also raised in

*CITES reservations procedures are explained in detail in appendix A, "How CITES Works."

Certain Appendix I crocodiles bred in captivity at a "farm" such as this one in Bangkok, Thailand, can be traded legally in international markets.
Al Larson

captivity. But they differ in that ranched animals are taken from wild nesting areas—as eggs or as hatchlings—while farm-raised animals are actually bred in captivity. Successful ranches can raise hundreds of wild-born crocodiles under optimum conditions, increasing their chances of survival above those of wild animals left to fend for themselves in predator-infested swamps and rivers.

Crocodile ranching was pioneered in the southwest Pacific island nation of Papua New Guinea in the 1970s. With assistance from the Food and Agriculture Organization of the United Nations, local people began capturing and raising wild saltwater crocodile hatchlings as well as New Guinea crocodiles. The policy successfully produced a sustainable supply of wild animals, and, as a result, the Papua New Guinea population of saltwater crocodiles was kept on Appendix II when all other saltwater crocodile populations were transferred to Appendix I in 1979.

Under new criteria for ranching operations adopted by CITES parties in 1981, countries can petition to have wild populations of native Appendix I crocodiles transferred to Appendix II. Those countries must be able to demonstrate both that their ranched crocodiles can withstand managed harvests and that their ranches help wild populations, possibly through the release of some young back to the wild. The countries must also ensure that ranched skins will be marked to avoid confusion with other skins from wild crocodiles. Another rule, adopted in 1985, stipulates that countries with approved ranching programs cannot ship skins to countries that do not belong to CITES or that still hold reservations on Appendix I crocodile species.

In addition to Papua New Guinea, ranching seems to be working particularly well in Zimbabwe, where Nile crocodile eggs and hatchlings are collected from the wild and reared on private ranches. Australia also has crocodile ranching operations. In 1985, the Australian saltwater crocodile population was moved to Appendix II to accommodate ranching programs, though this action was somewhat controversial because of disagreement over the population's size and its ability to withstand trade pressure.

Finally, certain species can be traded under a special quota system. Selective transfer from Appendix I to Appendix II of certain wild Nile and saltwater crocodile populations took place in 1985; skins from these populations can now be exported under quotas. Ten African countries and Indonesia are now able to export wild crocodiles under this system.

The quota system accommodates countries wishing to manage and profit from native crocodile populations that are deemed stable enough to exploit. Each country must propose to CITES parties a national crocodile management scheme and an annual export quota. Skins taken from wild-caught animals in these countries must be marked to ensure that they are recognizable in trade. Otherwise, for example, skins from Indonesian saltwater crocodiles, traded legally under the quota system, would likely be indistinguishable from those of another country's more endangered animals. Foreign traders could easily mix illicit skins in with legal ones, and port officials would find it impossible to enforce trade regulations. Conservation-minded leather brokers would find it equally difficult to identify and refuse skins from illegal sources.

Since its inception, this quota system has been one of the most hotly contested issues related to CITES. It was created largely in response to arguments by Indonesia and several African CITES parties that certain crocodile species were not endangered within their borders and that the animals were dangerous pests in some areas. The quotas remain a sore point for some trade experts and advocates of crocodile preservation because of the paucity of data; they argue that too little is known about certain crocodiles' population status and "health" to allow commercial trade. But others consider the quota system to be an important success for CITES, pointing out that it is designed to assure that quotas are demonstrably sustainable.

Approval of specific quota petitions has also proved controversial at times. When CITES members agreed in 1985 to allow Indonesia's request for a quota for its saltwater crocodile population, many conservationists opposed the move, arguing that that population was still considered scarce throughout its range and that there was no evidence that it could survive significant trade.[8] In addition, the country's ability to control the trade was also cause for concern: Indonesia reportedly supports a large illegal trade, shipping thousands of skins to Japan and Singapore each year.

Unfortunately, despite these various options, many countries exporting crocodile skins apparently do not yet have trade controls in place, nor do they know how many crocodiles live in their country. And illegal imports remain a serious problem, particularly in Japan.[9] It is clear that CITES parties must continue to hammer out regulations for crocodile management programs and to reevaluate their efforts to allow trade without compromising fragile populations. Moreover, it is absolutely essential that importing countries, especially Japan and EEC members, cooperate fully if conservation efforts are to be a success.

U.S. markets are not affected by many of these new CITES regulations because, under the Endangered Species Act (ESA), federal

Crocodile luggage for sale in Japan.
TRAFFIC(Japan)

law is more restrictive than CITES regulations. The ESA prohibits imports of most classic crocodile skins, including all key commercial species except the New Guinea crocodile, saltwater crocodile from Papua New Guinea, and ranched Nile crocodile from Zimbabwe. The United States, however, is still an important consumer of other crocodilian skins, primarily spectacled caiman (see below).

ALLIGATORS

Ravaged by the skin trade in the early 20th century, the American alligator was endangered by the late 1950s. The species was protected by state and U.S. law in the 1960s and was listed on Appendix I of CITES in 1973. Strict enforcement of these measures coupled with careful management and habitat protection enabled the species to recover quickly. Today, alligators are again thriving in many of the southern states.*

In 1987, the American alligator's recovery was considered complete by the removal of the species from the U.S. endangered species list. All alligator populations are now classified as "threatened due to similarity of appearance" under the Endangered Species Act. As a result, states may now hold regulated annual harvests. Louisiana, the most prolific supplier of alligator skins, has developed an alligator conservation program that combines captive breeding, farming, and hunting of wild populations. By 1986, it had produced a robust 25,000 to 26,000 skins in one year for commercial sale. The second largest alligator-producing state, Florida, is experimenting with private alligator farming, ranching, and regulated trapping to manage

---

Alligators differ visibly from crocodiles in that the latter have (a) a fourth bottom tooth that sticks out when their mouths are closed and (b) a generally longer, more pointed snout.

Crocodiles, Alligators, and Caimans

American alligator *(Alligator mississippiensis)*.
Luther C. Goldman/U.S. Fish and Wildlife Service

alligator populations for sustainable use. This state's harvest had produced 8,000 or so skins in 1986, and the Floridian harvest is expected to raise about $500,000 in annual sales by 1990. A third state, Texas, had contributed several hundred skins by 1986, for a national total of more than 33,000 skins in that year.[10] Alligator skin production is expected to climb even higher in the coming years. The dramatic success of the American alligator's recovery indicates that crocodilian populations, if given the chance, have a remarkable ability to rebuild themselves.

The American alligator was transferred from Appendix I to Appendix II in 1979, making commercial exports possible under CITES. The United States exports most of its skins to leather tanners and manufacturers in France, Italy, and Japan. In 1986, U.S. exports had a total declared value of $4.6 million.[11]

American alligator skin sold for an average of $23 per foot in 1986. In 1987, some skins sold for more than $45 per foot. Alligator meat has become fashionable in restaurants in the United States. At $4 to $6 per pound, raw, deboned alligator meat makes a reasonably priced, exotic southern stew.[12]

The only other true alligator species in the world, the Chinese alligator *(Alligator sinensis)*, has been seriously threatened with extinction due to human encroachment on its habitat. Fortunately, it is not a player in international trade, since it is not valued for either its hide or meat. However, the species is listed in Appendix I.

Figure 20.2
U.S. Exports of American Alligator Skins,*
by Importing Country, 1980–1988

	France	Italy	Japan	Other countries	Total
1980	8,990	0	0	4	8,994
1981	18,180	8,037	1,976	105	28,298
1982	14,016	6,056	5,355	408	25,835
1983	10,676	3,981	4,660	752	20,069
1984	9,236	5,393	6,542	348	21,519
1985	9,051	5,590	5,718	180	20,539
1986	10,931	12,708	7,242	354	31,235
1987	28,611	9,455	6,173	938	45,177
1988**	23,154	20,179	5,845	2,343	57,521

*Whole skins only.
**Preliminary data.
Source: CITES annual reports.

LATIN AMERICAN CAIMANS

Of the five species of caiman that exist in Latin America, three—the black, broad-nosed, and spectacled—have been severely affected by international trade. The remaining two—the dwarf (*Paleosuchus palpebrosus*) and smooth-fronted (*P. trigonatus*)—are not valued by the industry, because of their particularly bony skins.

Although they are rarely traded today, the most valuable caiman skins traditionally came from the endangered black caiman, a larger species once common in quiet Amazonian backwaters but now nearly extinct due to exploitation. The black caiman was the original target for most caiman hunters. In 1950 alone, hunters collected an estimated 12 million black caiman skins from the Amazon basin.[13] Today, the species is listed on Appendix I and protected throughout its range, but some poaching continues. In Bolivia, officials recently confiscated 972 black caiman skins from one poacher operating along the Apere River.[14]

In past decades, leather brokers also favored the soft skin of the broad-nosed caiman, making it a prime target for South American hunters. This species is now endangered throughout its range and listed on Appendix I. In the early 1980s, noted crocodilian specialist Federico Medem uncovered a thriving black market for broad-nosed caiman skins in Europe, primarily West Germany, supplied by yearly

Spectacled caiman (*Caiman crocodilus*).
National Museum of Natural History

shipments of some 20,000 skins from Brazil.[15]

The most common Latin American caiman in trade, the spectacled caiman, has been killed by the millions and shipped to U.S. and European ports for manufacture into "caiman" handbags and shoes. Despite its inferior quality and relatively rough texture, caiman skin has replaced much of the classic crocodilian leather in U.S. markets.

Widespread trade-reporting gaps, document fraud, and other problems have made it difficult to track and measure the caiman trade. It appears that at least 1 million skins from the spectacled caiman, worth an estimated $120 million, reach world markets each year.[16] The caiman trade is driven primarily by demand from leather product manufacturers in the United States, Italy, West Germany, France, Spain, Austria, Switzerland, Hong Kong, Japan, and Taiwan.

In the 1980s, demand for caiman skin seems to be on the upswing. Trade figures show a remarkable increase in U.S. imports of caiman skin shoes, handbags, watchbands, and other leather products. In 1982, traders imported about 113,000 manufactured caiman products. By 1986, imports had more than quadrupled, to 537,000 items.[17] The bulk of these imports came from Italy, a key manufacturing center for caiman skin shoes and handbags. Other significant suppliers included France and West Germany. Caiman skin products sell for enormous prices: $595 for a belt, up to $800 for a pair of shoes, and upwards of $3,000 for the finest caiman skin handbag.[18]

The bulk of the spectacled caiman trade is probably in the yacare subspecies (*Caiman crocodilus yacare*) of central South America, prized for its wide flanks and finely graded scaling. This subspecies is listed in Appendix II but is prohibited by U.S. law from import into the

Caiman hunter
in the Brazilian Amazon.
Norman Myers / WWF

United States. Authorities generally agree that there are three other subspecies of spectacled caiman: the brown caiman (*C. c. fuscus*), common caiman (*C. c. crocodilus*), and Rio Apaporis caiman (*C. c. apaporiensis*). The brown caiman and common caiman, listed in Appendix II, are also important commercial targets. Comparing the volume of trade in yacare, brown, and common caiman subspecies is difficult. Skins and products are often identified only to the species level and sometimes are misidentified at the subspecies level to avoid legal controls.* For instance, U.S. restrictions provide an incentive to mislabel yacare skins. Authorities speculate that most of the caiman in trade is yacare, whether labeled as such or not.[19] The Rio Apaporis caiman, listed in Appendix I, may actually be extinct.[20]

As the prohibition on yacare imports indicate, U.S. law imposes stricter standards than CITES does for the spectacled caiman trade. Under the ESA, both the yacare and Rio Apaporis subspecies are

---

Distinguishing subspecies' skins, especially after processing, is very difficult—a fact that frustrates efforts by officials to enforce trade laws.

considered endangered and thus prohibited from import.* Under the Lacey Act, the import of any wildlife protected in its country of origin is prohibited. Since many Latin American countries restrict or completely prohibit the export of caiman skins, the Lacey Act also applies to much of the U.S. trade, although it is not well enforced.

Complications in the Spectacled Caiman Skin Trade

Despite export restrictions, import controls, and CITES coverage, a large portion of world trade in spectacled caiman is illegal. Although most of the major caiman-consuming countries belong to CITES, their efforts to control the trade have been notably unsuccessful. For instance, a 1986 study of trade records by World Wildlife Fund uncovered the illegal import of tens of thousands of caiman hides and products from Paraguay, where wildlife exports are banned, into the EEC, and particularly into France. In 1984, the study found, France imported some 200,000 highly questionable and probably illegal caiman skins from Paraguay. Italy, too, imported over 100,000 caiman skins with questionable origins, including 40,000 yacare skins shipped from Paraguay via Panama.[21] Trade experts in Japan have documented large-scale illegal caiman imports into that country, as well as Singapore.[22]

The United States, too, has severe problems in stopping the influx of illegal caiman skins and products. The U.S. trade primarily involves finished products from the EEC, rather than skins from Latin America, so illegalities are doubly difficult to monitor and control. In 1986 alone, the United States imported over 65,000 spectacled caiman skins and over 530,000 caiman handbags, shoes, and other leather products.[23]

From the importing countries' perspective, part of the problem arises from the high volume of incoming shipments and the dearth of trained inspectors qualified to check and verify trade documents. In the United States, for instance, 57 wildlife inspectors are charged with checking all wildlife shipments arriving at designated ports across the country. These few experts cannot possibly monitor each individual shipment.

The inspectors' task is made even tougher by the nature of the animals themselves: it is very difficult to distinguish skins from the various caiman subspecies. Even seasoned experts can have trouble telling yacare skin from common caiman, for instance. But it is essential to make these distinctions because exports of one subspecies

*Some experts dispute the "endangered" status of yacare, claiming the original ESA listing was inappropriate. Biological surveys now under way in Bolivia, Brazil, and Paraguay should help clarify the status of the various spectacled caiman subspecies.

from a particular country may be legal while others are not.

Further complications arise when the trade involves products, rather than skins. Since it is difficult to tell skins apart, one can imagine the problems in identifying watchbands and other small items down to the subspecies level. Unlike certain crocodiles and American alligators, caiman skins are not required to be tagged, which makes it even more challenging to differentiate skins. In addition, the product trade commonly involves several countries, making the "paper trail" complex and time consuming to follow. Caiman products reaching the United States from manufacturing centers in Europe usually arrive with CITES reexport certificates indicating the Latin American country-of-origin of the skins involved. U.S. port authorities generally accept these declarations and do not investigate whether the skins were exported legally from the originating country. Unfortunately, trade data show that many skins do not enter trade through legal channels. Valuable caiman contraband is frequently shipped from countries where such exports are prohibited or laundered through intermediary countries where exports are still allowed.

Although Latin American caiman-producing countries have steadily tightened export restrictions over the past decade, unscrupulous traders continue to find and exploit the weakest links in the system. In recent years, illicit skins have continued to flow out of Brazil, Paraguay, and Bolivia, despite these countries' legal constraints on wildlife exports. Brazil banned commercial hunting of all wildlife in 1967, Paraguay banned virtually all wildlife exports in 1975, and Bolivia banned the export of most wildlife in 1985 and the next year attempted to institute an export quota system of 50,000 caiman skins per year. Nonetheless, experts believe that smugglers take an estimated 1 million caiman skins annually from the region.[24]

Caiman smuggling is a dangerous but well-established industry in the region. Bands of backcountry Amazonian cowboys moonlighting as poachers kill thousands of caimans each month and have also killed several wildlife law officers in recent years. In 1983, Brazil mounted a major dragnet, run by armed military police and wildlife agents, to round up poachers, but caught few of the culprits. Most of those arrested were soon released.[25] According to Peter Brazaitis, assistant curator of animals for the New York Zoological Society, who is surveying yacare caiman populations in the Brazilian Pantanal, poachers in this prime caiman habitat are well equipped and well organized. "Even when apprehended, they often escape imprisonment and have fines and the value of confiscated skins reimbursed by the hide buyers," Brazaitis explains. He notes that Brazilian wildlife authorities are making an outstanding effort to stop illegal caiman skin trade but are hindered by financial constraints, equipment shortages, and lack of support from the courts.[26]

Caiman smugglers frequently take the skins to Paraguay and Bolivia, where they may be processed by politically powerful tannery operations. The hides are often misidentified or given falsified papers to mask their origin for shipment abroad. A common ruse has been to give illicit skins Bolivian export papers and then smuggle them out of Brazilian ports where the landlocked country has export privileges. In 1985, officials found 44,000 smuggled "Bolivian" caiman skins aboard a Greek ship docked in the port of Manaus, Brazil. That same year, customs officials in Rio de Janeiro seized over nine tons of caiman skins—worth more than $4.5 million—from a vessel bound for Spain; experts believed the illicit shipment to be the work of smugglers in Bolivia.[27]

In a similar gambit, smugglers in the Pantanal region ship raw or processed hides to other countries, where the items are given falsified documents to mask their origins; Venezuela, Colombia, El Salvador, Guyana, and French Guiana are among the known laundering points for caiman skin exports.[28] These countries generally have inadequate resources to police the trade or combat powerful smuggling operations.

In desperation, Latin American countries unable to regulate caiman exports are turning increasingly to outright trade bans or very restrictive quotas. In fact, the only countries from which caiman exports are generally legal today are Guyana and Venezuela. But enforcement of these tactics has proved difficult. In Colombia, caiman skin traders negotiated a limited exemption to the country's 1974

Curios such as these stuffed caimans, for sale in a Latin American tourist market, are subject to seizure if brought into the United States.
WWF International

International Wildlife Trade: Whose Business Is It?

ban on virtually all wildlife exports. Under the exemption, caiman skin stocks held by certain companies were exported through 1984, when legitimate stocks were reportedly cleaned out. Even though authorities authorized only about 25,000 caiman skin exports from 1984 through 1986, an odd thing happened: trade records show U.S. imports of over 650,000 "Colombian" caiman products between 1984 and 1986. Ginette Hemley, director of TRAFFIC(U.S.A.), found that so-called Colombian products comprised 50 percent of the U.S. caiman market from 1984 through 1986. She surmised that the Colombian tag was merely a label of convenience. The skins' origins are virtually impossible to trace, although most experts believe the bulk of the skins originated in the Brazilian Panatal.[29]

The most notorious example of what can go wrong in enforcing tough trade controls occurred in Bolivia in 1986, when a top official in the Bolivian CITES management authority sold the entire year's quota of caiman export permits to a black market dealer for personal profit. Fortunately, the ploy was exposed, and the official subsequently lost his job.

Clearly, tough trade laws alone cannot successfully combat illicit and ecologically unsound exploitation of caiman populations. The best conservation scenario may include a combination of harvest limits, trade controls, and management schemes. Several experts believe the spectacled caiman may be able to withstand limited harvests because of its great ability to adapt to habitat changes and its strong reproductive potential. They advocate management regimes providing a sustainable cash crop of caimans that will benefit the people who live in caiman territory and create adequate incentives to conserve the species.

As a step toward better management, in 1986 a team of scientists launched a study of caiman populations in Bolivia, Paraguay, and Brazil. Their effort will help clarify questions over the proper classification of spectacled caiman subspecies and provide good data on their ranges and numbers. The group's work should provide a scientific basis for building caiman conservation and management plans satisfactory to exporting and importing countries, traders, and conservationists.

Venezuela is currently experimenting with controlled spectacled caiman harvests. So far, reports of management and hunting abuses have made trade control difficult, but observers remain optimistic that Venezuela can establish a viable sustainable-use system. Brazilian landowners and government agencies have also begun to develop experimental yacare caiman ranching operations. According to Peter Brazaitis, the Brazilian efforts hold real promise and may best be pursued in complement with other local industries.[30] Brazil's efforts face tremendous challenge, however. As one of the largest and most remote wetlands in the world, the Pantanal will undoubtedly continue to be extremely difficult to police.

Despite tougher export laws and an emerging interest of producer countries in sustainable-use regimes, the 1980s have seen little progress in bringing the high-volume caiman trade under control. Persistent problems in the market point to the need for greater involvement and leadership from importing countries. The EEC, Japan, and the United States could all upgrade their capabilities to monitor the trade and investigate possible infractions and could give higher priority to catching and prosecuting violators. More important, they could play a greater role in helping producer countries develop sound management models. Conservation concerns aside, it is clearly in these developed countries' own economic interest to do so; without forward-looking, wisely controlled methods for managing caiman stocks, this valuable fashion staple is unlikely to survive.

CHAPTER 21
Lizards and Snakes

Crocodile, alligator, and caiman skins may be the most costly reptile products in trade, but lizard and snake skins are the most numerous. A casual glance through a fashion magazine or upscale clothing catalog will likely fall on several advertisements for Swiss watches with genuine lizard bands or Italian shoes made from lizard or snake skins. Particularly popular with leather brokers are monitor and tegu lizards, with their smooth, durable, and fine-grained hides. Over 1 million tegu skins, worth some $15 to $20 million, reach world markets every year from Argentina alone. Another million or so monitor lizard skins come from African and Asian ports. And hundreds of thousands of snake skins are exported annually, primarily from Asia and Africa.[1]

Trade in lizards and snakes is not limited to skins. Thriving markets also exist for live snakes and lizards in the United States and elsewhere, although there have been few studies of either legal or illegal trade. According to TRAFFIC(U.S.A.), at least 1 million live snakes and lizards enter international commerce each year, with an average of 300,000 to 500,000 entering the United States.

Species in Trade

LIZARDS

Little reliable information exists on the number of monitor and tegu lizards remaining in the wild, but several species are considered threatened and declining. Trade, of course, is a major problem. However, they also are being pressured by habitat loss, hunting for local meat markets, and, in some instances, pest extermination.

Four monitor lizard species are on Appendix I of CITES: the Bengal monitor (*Varanus bengalensis*), yellow monitor (*V. flavescens*), desert monitor (*V. griseus*), and the giant of all lizards, the Komodo dragon (*V. komodoensis*). The remainder are on Appendix II, including the three most heavily traded species—the African savannah monitor (*V. exanthematicus*), Nile monitor (*V. niloticus*), and water monitor (*V. salvator*). Both known species of tegu lizard, the common or banded tegu (*Tupinambis teguixin*) and the Argentine or red tegu (*T. rufescens*), are on Appendix II. A third type of lizard in the international skin trade, the common iguana (*Iguana iguana*), is also listed on Appendix II.

Some lizards popular in the live trade, mostly as pets, are also protected by CITES. For example, the tuatara (*Sphenodon punctatus*), a native to New Zealand, is listed on Appendix I. The Gila monster (*Heloderma* spp.), found in Mexico and the U.S. Southwest, and the Gould's goanna or sand monitor (*Varanus gouldii*) of Australia are on Appendix II.

Many of these valuable lizards are protected by national laws, as well as by CITES. Australia and Mexico, for example, ban virtually all animal exports, including reptile. (Australia makes exceptions for those species covered by management programs.) Officials in Papua New Guinea have a long-standing policy of not allowing exports of live reptiles or other vertebrates except by approved scientific institutions.

Tuatara (*Sphenodon punctatus*).
W. Strangenberg / WWF

These measures often fail markedly in their efforts to control lizard trade, however. Enforcement is problematic, and financial incentives to exploit valuable reptiles remain high. In Latin America, for instance, tegu-hunting restrictions are often violated, and skin smuggling still occurs in some areas.[2]

Tegu Lizards

Rugged denizens of tropical and subtropical South America, tegu lizards are probably the most heavily hunted reptiles on that continent.[3] Some are taken alive to foreign pet shops, where they sell for $15 to $30, and others go no farther than local soup pots. Most, however, are destined for the international exotic leather trade. Both tegu species, the common or banded tegu and the Argentine or red tegu, are traded heavily. The former is found throughout South America, except in Chile and possibly Ecuador, and in Trinidad and Tobago.[4] The latter species is a native of Argentina, Bolivia, Brazil, Paraguay, and Uruguay. While no one is really sure how tegu lizard populations are faring, evidence suggests a slow overall decline.[5]

Argentina is the principal legal source for tegu hides. Paraguay is a major supplier of apparently illegal hides. Smaller volumes also are exported largely illegally from Colombia, Peru, Uruguay, Brazil, and Panama.[6]

In 1985, over $24 million worth of tegu skins and products were imported by the United States, the leading tegu skin customer and the primary importer of skins from Argentina. West Germany, France,

Figure 21.1
Major Importers of Tegu Skins,
1980 and 1985*

	1980	1985
Canada	25,712	40,481
Colombia	14,000	0
France	0	115,179
West Germany	22,747	0
Italy	202,402	113,439
Mexico	12,515	47,428
South Korea	0	21,950
Spain	0	96,515
Switzerland	27,856	37,154
United Kingdom	76,160	16,074
United States	1,454,299	918,468
Other countries	32,714	74,554
Total	1,868,405	1,481,242

*Minimum net skin imports as reported to CITES. Excludes Japan and other countries that report imports by weight or meters.
Source: International Union for Conservation of Nature and Natural Resources.

Tegu lizard (*Tupinambis rufescens*).
Ginette Hemley / WWF

Italy, Japan, and Hong Kong are also significant importers of tegu skins and products. (figure 21.1)[7]

International smuggling schemes hinder efforts to monitor the tegu trade. Brazil, Paraguay, and Bolivia ban most wildlife exports, but skin shipments sometimes slip over their borders into Argentinean markets. According to one source, as many as 300,000 illicit Bolivian tegu skins may cross into Argentina each year. To make matters worse, 1 to 2 million Paraguayan skins registered as "legal stockpiles" may be sitting in Argentinean warehouses ready for export. Because the stockpiled skins supposedly arrived in Argentina before 1981, when Paraguay stepped up enforcement of its 1975 export ban, Argentina considers them legal for trade. But they have never been counted, and experts believe that the whole scheme could well be a fraud. Some believe that few skins were actually stockpiled before Paraguay's ban, and the skins passing through the system are from newly killed animals.[8]

The tegu skin industry is an important income producer in Argentina. Campesino hunters make $2 to $3 per raw skin, brokers who take the skins to tanneries get $4 each, and processing companies sell semifinished hides for $5 to $6. A tanned and finished skin can fetch $9 to $10 from foreign manufacturers, who might use it to make lizard shoes priced at $200 to $300 a pair.[9] Exporters are now multiplying their profits by offering precut tegu boot pieces ready for stitching.[10]

Argentine officials, skin exporters, the CITES Secretariat, and World Wildlife Fund are working in alliance with Argentine scientists in

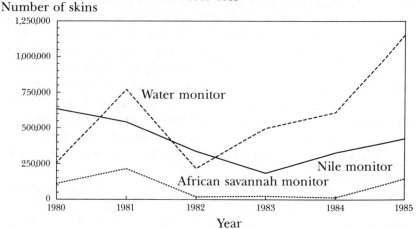

Figure 21.2
Net Imports of Monitor Lizard Skins,
1980–1985*

Number of skins

*Minimum net skin imports as reported to CITES.
Source: International Union for Conservation of Nature and Natural Resources.

a unique effort to improve management of Argentina's tegu population. Their efforts will provide tegu population data and establish a plan for controlling the annual lizard harvest, which could become a model for other, similarly exploited reptiles around the world. Some Argentine traders are also experimenting with captive breeding, which ultimately could take pressure off wild tegu populations.

Monitor Lizards

Two of the four species of monitor lizard found on Appendix I—the Bengal and yellow monitors—were popular in the skin trade during the 1970s. By 1980, however, exports had dropped to a trickle.[11] Nevertheless, these threatened lizards are still hunted in their native countries, and some continue to appear in international markets. On a trip to study monitors in Pakistan, lizard expert Walter Auffenberg, of the Florida State Museum, uncovered a thriving illegal market for Bengal monitor skins, culled from local populations and smuggled in from India.[12] There is also some international trade in live specimens. One pet dealer in the United Kingdom advertised live Bengal monitors for $112 each in 1984.[13]

Altogether, 1 million or more hides of the three most heavily traded monitor species—the water, African savannah, and Nile monitors—reportedly enter world commerce each year (figure 21.1), with approximately one-quarter of these going to the United States.[14] As with much of the world market for reptile skin, the exact volume of trade is very difficult to assess for a variety of reasons: shipments often go unrecorded; the unit used to measure skins varies from one country to the next; data sometimes are based on the number of skins listed in issued permits, which may vary from the actual number of skins shipped; and species often are misidentified in trade documents.[15]

Nearly half a million water monitor hides may be exported from Indonesia, Thailand, and, to a lesser degree, Malaysia and the Philippines every year. These hides go to leather manufacturers in Hong Kong, Japan, Singapore, the United States, and members of the European Economic Community, particularly Italy and France.[16] In 1985, U.S. imports of some 70,000 water monitor skins and over 1 million purses, shoes, and other goods made from the species topped $36 million.[17]

Heavy trade pressure may be taking a toll on some populations of this Asian lizard, but too little population data are available to be certain. Experts do believe, however, that the species is still common in most of its range.[18] Indonesia and Malaysia give water monitors partial legal protection. India and Sri Lanka afford the species full protection, but poaching and smuggling continue.[19]

Most African savannah monitor skins in trade come from Nigeria and Sudan and eventually are imported by the United States, France, West Germany, Italy, and other European countries.[20] Nile monitor skins follow similar routes. These lizards' small-grained hides often are manufactured into purses, shoes, or other finished goods in Europe and then reexported to the United States. In 1985, the United States imported some $6 million worth of Nile monitor skins and such skin products as Swiss watch bands and Italian purses.[21]

Although the greatest commercial use of Appendix II monitors is for the skin trade, they are also hunted locally for their meat and exterminated for eating chickens, getting into garbage, and even— in the case of the water monitor—foraging on graveyard corpses. In parts of Southeast Asia, "water monitors are being eaten to oblivion," according to Auffenberg. Called lizard dragons or land crocodiles by the locals, Asian water monitors are used for everything from soup bones to "tea bags"—the animal's dried gall bladder being steeped in water for use as a tonic. Whole baby lizards are bottled in spiced alcoholic concoctions that are served by the jigger-full.[22]

Iguanas and Other Lizards

Notorious for its role in horror films, the common iguana has been popular in the pet trade for years. In 1984, the United States imported about 34,000 of these green, dragon-like creatures, mostly from El Salvador, Guatemala, Guyana, and Suriname. (Faced with massive illegal trade problems, El Salvador and Guatemala have since banned all wildlife exports.[23]) The market has declined since 1980, when U.S. live iguana imports topped 50,000 animals in a year.[24] West Germany also imports thousands of live iguanas from Central and South America each year. Common iguanas sell for $12 to $35 each in U.S. pet shops and for similar prices in West Germany.[25]

Trade in iguana skins is apparently minimal. This skin is reportedly too delicate to compete in the purse or shoe industries, and some experts believe that basketball shoes and other footwear sewn with "iguana" panels are actually made from tegu lizard.[26] This may reflect the fact that the tegu lizard is often known as "iguana" in South America, or it may be a marketing ploy to suggest more exotic origins.

Whether perched in the upper reaches of a palm tree or basking on a warm rock, the common iguana is a favorite target for hunters looking to fill a stewpot. The lizard is considered an important protein source in Central America. Unfortunately, in the last 20 years, iguana populations in some countries have plummeted, mainly as a result of growing human populations and loss of habitat in Central America.[27]

In the United States, the legal market for live lizards centers not just on the iguana but also on more common species such as the Haitian curlytail lizards (*Leiocephalus* spp.), American chameleons (*Anolis* spp.), Nile and other monitors, tegus, and African chameleons (*Chameleon* spp.).[28] Retail prices for some common lizards can be downright cheap. American chameleons sell for $1 to $3 each, while Haitian curlytail lizards also go for about $3 each. Tegus average $35 apiece, monitors range in price from $30 to $2,000, and African chameleons sell for $25 to $100 (and sometimes more). Some of the rarer protected species that are traded illegally can cost significantly more, as discussed below in the section on smuggling.

SNAKES

The world's demand for snakes is enormous. Every year, customs officials must oversee international trade in hundreds of thousands of live snakes, millions of snake skins, and tens of millions of shoes, belts, and purses fashioned from all manner of snake hides.[29] Yet, despite this massive market, very little information exists on how wild, commercially valuable snake populations are faring, according to Kenneth Dodd, a U.S. Fish and Wildlife Service expert on the snake trade. Dodd says that current assessments show very little evidence that snake species are declining, but he stresses that this may well reflect a lack of good information rather than a true picture of the situation.[30]

Habitat loss is undoubtedly the single greatest threat to wild snakes.

Other threats include use of chemical herbicides, introduction of exotic species—such as toads that are poisonous to snakes—malicious snake killing, and trade. Although trade is generally less threatening than habitat pressure for most species of snake, Dodd believes that collection for trade is "the major suspected cause of the decline in larger species inhabiting developing countries." Some European vipers (*Vipera* spp.) and rat snakes (*Elaphe* spp.) may also be at risk due to their popularity in the live trade.[31] In 1987 CITES parties listed on Appendix I most European populations of the meadow viper (*Vipera ursinii*), a small, harmless snake preferred by European vivarium keepers and reptile collectors. This was done in response to French and Italian reports that the species faced heavy collecting pressures and other threats such as habitat destruction for resort development.[32]

The volume of snake trade is difficult to gauge. Trade data are few and often are inaccurate or difficult to interpret. Nevertheless, CITES reports and other trade records that do exist outline some general patterns in the flow of snakes and snake skin to world markets. Raw or tanned snake skin is commonly exported from Africa, Asia, and South America to leather manufacturers in the Far East, the United States, or Western European countries. In those importing countries, it is fashioned into purses, shoes, wallets, and other products. These finished goods are often shipped overseas to foreign consumer markets, sending the durable hides across international boundaries two, three, or more times. In 1985, the United States alone imported over $105 million worth of snake skin products.[33] The live-snake trade is smaller and involves less transshipping, though trade routes are similar. The United States imported over 160,000 live snakes in 1985.[34]

The boas and pythons (family Boidae), Indian rat snake or whip snake (*Ptyas mucosus*), and Oriental water snakes (family Acrochordidae) are among the most heavily traded snakes in the world. In the United States, three snake species—the Taiwan stink snake (*Elaphe carinata*), the dog-faced water snake (*Cerberus rhynchops*), and the Indian rat snake—dominated the trade in 1985, comprising nearly three-quarters of snake skin imports.[35]

Some exporting countries are taking steps to control commercial snake exports. India, the source of over 3 million snake skins from 1976 through 1979, has banned most commercial exports of snake skin and allows only government-controlled export of snake skin products. Sri Lanka, too, has legally halted the trade.[36] Other countries control exports of species destined for the live trade. The United States, known in collecting circles for its rattlesnakes and other prized native species, has placed 8 snake species that are native to the 50 states

PROBLEMS IN THE INDIAN SNAKE TRADE

According to Romulus Whitaker, director of India's Madras Snake Park, a conservation and education refuge, "a quiet but steady stream of smuggled skins" leaves India every year.[1] This contraband may be worth as much as $60 million annually.[2] Once Asia's leading exporter of snake skins[3], India has a long history of legal snake catching and trade, but the government banned almost all commercial snake skin exports in 1976 and reinforced this with added controls in 1977. In 1984, India also listed the Indian rat snake or whip snake and six other species on Appendix III of CITES. Indian regulations now allow only a single government agency, the Bharat Leather Corporation (BLC), to export snake skin products. Following the export ban, private companies reportedly held approximately 5.7 million snake skins.[4] The BLC was supposed to purchase these skins from private traders and export them in a controlled way, eventually ridding the country of its pre-1977 skins and halting illegal trade.

Under the Indian system, some of the snakes leaving the country are thus legal: the BLC purchases snake skins held in domestic stockpiles for manufacture into products that can be exported legally.[5] It also exports items fashioned out of snake skins seized from private traders.[6] In all, the BLC exported an average of 60,500 snake skin products per year from 1984 through 1986, with well over half going to the United States.[7]

But smugglers apparently have well-established avenues for bringing thousands of Indian snake skins to world markets. Gold smugglers sailing

Part of an illegal shipment of 150,000 snake skins seized at the Calcutta airport and destined for Hamburg, West Germany.
A. Wright / WWF

to India from the Middle East reportedly take shipments of illicit snake skins (and narcotics) home on their return voyages.[8] snake skins are slipped across the border to Nepal, Bangladesh, Sri Lanka, and Pakistan for easier export.[9] Singapore is probably another intermediate stop for illicit Indian snake skins.[10] In 1985, an Indian longshoreman accidentally broke open part of a cashew kernel shipment bound for Singapore and discovered that it contained whip snake skin instead. Customs officers seized the cargo, worth $1.6 million, and arrested six smugglers.[11]

The presence of large, privately held skin stockpiles complicates efforts to control India's snake trade. These stocks are supposed to be registered with the government. It is legal to sell old skins within the country, and India does, in fact, have a thriving internal market, aimed almost entirely at foreign tourists, for wallets, handbags, vests, and other products made of cobra, checkered keelback watersnake (*Xenochrophis piscater*), and other native species. Interestingly, though, while India has granted no licenses to catch snakes for commercial trade since 1979, the stockpiles of "old" skins, most of which should be at least 10 years old, have actually increased since 1979 to an estimated 6 million skins. British researchers Josephine Andrews and Chris Birkinshaw, who investigated the Indian snake skin industry in 1986, explained that some of the increase could be attributed to reporting errors, the seizure and legal registration of illicit skins, or other legitimate means. But they also found that many dealers may have given high reports of the number of skins on hand and then added fresh skins to their stores, or used other ruses to add illicit new skins to their "old stocks."[12]

In 1986, India imposed stricter measures that would outlaw snake skin stockpiles held by anyone other than the BLC, prohibit non-BLC sales of snake skin goods to tourists, and require more stringent penalties for smugglers. The 1986 law encourages the BLC to buy up the massive snake skin stocks currently held by private companies.[13] Indian officials hope that these actions will discourage large-scale skin smuggling and put an end to Indians "revolving" stockpiles.

---

or Puerto Rico on its endangered list, thus banning commercial exports and domestic trade. A few western states, including California, Arizona, and Utah, also prohibit commercial snake collecting.[37]

The world market for snake skin demonstrates nearly everything that can go wrong in the wildlife trade. The snake trade is plagued by smuggling, species and subspecies mix-ups, and other enforcement problems. (See box, "Problems in the Indian Snake Trade.") Consumer countries readily accept imports of several Appendix II snake species that are completely protected by their native countries. Smugglers have been known to find ingenious ways to slip illicit skins from one country into another, sometimes falsifying trade papers along the way. Some snake species, such as the Indian python (*Python molurus*),

Indian rat snake or whip snake
(*Ptyas mucosus*).
WWF India

have subspecies that look very much alike when alive and become virtually identical once skinned, tanned, and fashioned into belts or shoes; these subspecies are treated differently under CITES and national laws, making even the best efforts to uphold the law difficult. Like other facets of the wildlife trade, heavy traffic in snakes can raise wide-ranging ecological concerns. Rat snakes, for instance, often live on a diet of mice and other rodents, and excessive harvest apparently contributes to increased rodent damage to crops. Finally, there are very few complete population data on many heavily exploited species, which makes it impossible to know how they are faring in the wild.

Boas and Pythons

All boas and pythons are listed under CITES. The Indian rock python (*Python molurus molurus*) is listed on Appendix I, along with the Argentine boa constrictor (*Boa constrictor occidentalis*), all Madagascar boas (*Acrantophis* spp.), and seven other boa species endemic to specific islands. All other boas and pythons are listed on Appendix II.

Latin American hunters harvest thousands of boa constrictors every year for the skin trade. They may be depleting breeding stocks by taking older and larger snakes. Moreover, much of this trade appears to be illegal. The species is protected in Paraguay, Argentina,

Indian rock python (*Python molurus molurus*).
U. Woy

Colombia, Peru, and Panama, the major countries to which it is native, and the Appendix I listing of the Argentine boa constrictor makes all commercial trade in that subspecies illegal. Yet, consumer countries have imported an average of 100,000 skins annually in recent years. Obviously, these importing countries have ignored many of the controls, simply taking permit declarations at face value in many cases rather than investigating permit claims. The United States, Italy, Mexico, West Germany, Spain, France, and the United Kingdom all imported significant quantities of boa constrictor skins between 1980 and 1984.[38] (Italian officials claim that their country has implemented proper trade controls since 1984.[39])

Two other Appendix II South American boas—the giant or green anaconda (*Eunectes murinus*) and its smaller relative, the yellow anaconda (*E. notaeus*)—are also subject to large-scale skin trade. Anacondas are reportedly the "best wearing" of all snake skins. The snakes are also popular in the pet trade, with dealers in the United States selling four- to six-foot anacondas for about $100 each.[40]

Most—if not all—of the anaconda trade is illegal. There are currently few other sources for yellow anaconda skin because the species is prohibited from commercial export throughout its South American range, with the exceptions of Guyana and Suriname.[41] Nonetheless, in 1985 over 14,000 yellow anaconda skins reportedly entered the United States, exported from Argentina, Bolivia, Panama, and Peru.[42] Most giant anaconda skins on the market are also suspect.

Boa constrictor (*Boa constrictor*).
National Museum of Natural History

The majority supposedly come from Paraguay, but there are few records of giant anacondas existing in that country and Paraguay prohibits the export of anaconda skins as part of its ban on most wildlife exports. According to trade records, Bolivia and Colombia also contributed large numbers of anaconda skins to world markets in 1983 and 1984, despite national export bans there. And Panama, which has no giant anaconda population of its own, somehow supplied one-quarter of all skins reaching world markets in 1983. Experts believe that much of the anaconda supply actually is smuggled out of Brazil.[43]

Across the world in Southeast Asia, trade in pythons (*Python* spp.) is equally troublesome. Herpetologists are concerned about the impact of trade on some members of this heavily exploited group of snakes, although there is little information on population trends. For instance, from 1980 to 1984, an estimated 300,000 reticulated python (*P. reticulatus*) skins were exported annually, mostly from Indonesia and, to a lesser degree, Thailand.[44] The skins often passed through Singapore on their way to leather traders in the United States and Western Europe.[45] The United States also imports reticulated python skins directly, taking in over 50,000 skins in 1983 alone.[46] Some populations of this Appendix II species may be suffering from such large-scale trade.[47] An unusually long snake—adults can grow to 25

Figure 21.3
Indonesian and Thai Exports of Selected Snake
Species in an Average Year*

	Indonesia	Thailand
Indian cobra		88,570
Burmese python	183	98,771
Reticulated python	237,306	85,787
Indian rat snake (or whip snake)	873,771	232,143
Dog-faced water snake	82,815	123,163

*Annual average, 1984-1986.
Source: CITES annual reports.

feet, although the average specimen is about 9 to 12 feet long—the reticulated python is also hunted for local markets, for its meat, blood, and internal organs. It is also captured for the pet trade. In 1985, the United States imported over 2,600 live reticulated pythons.[48]

Reticulated python skins sometimes are shipped through illegal channels, though officials in some countries have toughened up on such imports. In 1981, for instance, U.S. Fish and Wildlife Service agents charged a Massachusetts shoe company with illegally importing 1,325 pairs of reticulated python skin shoes without proper permits. The firm forfeited the shoes, worth more than $100,000, and paid a $15,000 fine.[49]

Trade in another popular species, the Indian python, is also creating problems. One of the two subspecies of this large, seemingly lethargic serpent—the Indian rock python, found on the Indian subcontinent—is listed on Appendix I. The other—the Burmese python (*P. molurus bivittatus*), found in Southeast Asia—is listed on Appendix II. Pressured by habitat loss, both subspecies also are attacked as pests and hunted for trade. The Indian subspecies is thought to be depleted or locally extinct throughout most of its range.[50] It seldom appears in the skin trade today, but U.S. federal agents found live Indian pythons available on the black market during an undercover investigation of wildlife traffic in the early 1980s. (See below under "Smuggling of Live Lizards and Snakes—A Continuing Problem.")

In the snake skin trade, as with many other wildlife groups, larger and/or more valuable species are targeted first, but, as these animals are protected or killed off, the market shifts to their less valuable relatives. As a result, several small-sized pythons and boas, such as the Asian blood python (*P. curtus*), may now be facing stronger trade pressures. In 1985, the United States imported at least 7,000 skins and 3,000 products made of Asian blood python.[51]

Very little is known about trade in African snakes. African pythons are apparently popular as pets and in the skin trade, but information on their volume of commerce is scarce, as is documentation of their status in the wild. U.S. trade figures for 1985 show a total of approximately 42,300 snake skin products imported from Africa. All were made from African rock python (*P. sebae*).

Water and Sea Snakes

The world leather industry also snaps up millions of mottled Oriental water snakes or "wart snakes" every year. In 1984, Indonesia alone exported skins from over 2 million of these completely aquatic, prolific snakes. In 1985, the United States reported imports of over $1.4 million worth of the largest species, the karung or elephant trunk snake (*Acrochordus javanicus*), named for its close resemblance to a thick, five-foot-long elephant snout.[52] Karung snakes are particularly popular in the leather trade because of the uniformly diamond-shaped scales on most of the snakes' bodies. Unlike land snakes, these snakes' leather is strong and durable because of the nonoverlapping scales.

Another Oriental water snake, the Indian wart snake or calacab (*Chersydrus granulatus*), is a smaller, less fecund marine species. About 250,000 calacab products entered the United States in 1985.[53]

There is also some trade in tropical sea snakes (Hydrophiidae) and sea kraits (Laticaudidae). About three to four feet long, with unmistakably flattened tails and usually with striking black and white bands, sea snakes are collected in mass quantities in the Philippines for manufacture into shoes, belts, handbags, and other leather items that are often exported to the United States or Europe.[54] In 1974, Filipino divers took some 450,000 sea snakes per month from the waters of Gato Island, causing local populations to decline.[55] Today, sea snake divers concentrate on more abundant populations around the island of Cebu.[56] The divers catch these highly poisonous snakes by hand,* then bring them ashore, where they are skinned and sold to local tanneries for about two cents apiece.

These snakes rarely attack unless provoked; the hundreds of people who succumb to sea snake bites annually in Southeast Asia are usually bitten after stepping on the snakes in shallow waters or trying to untangle them from fishing nets.

In Australia, the government of the state of Queensland allows fishermen to sell sea snakes that accidentally get tangled in their prawn fishing nets, as a "sensible use of an otherwise wasted resource."[57] The national government, however, does not allow the export of sea-snake skin or products, unless there is a management plan for the species involved.

Little information is available about the impact of trade on sea-snake populations. In the Philippines, according to one observer's report, "None of the species are thought to be endangered, but little is known."[58] An Australian study is now assessing the effects in that country's waters, where sea-snake diversity is purportedly greater than anywhere else in the world. One Australian company currently uses 3,000 to 4,000 sea-snake skins per year for production of wallets, purses, and other leather items. These exotic leather items are sold domestically, but pressure to open a sea-snake skin export trade is mounting, particularly following the release of the popular film *Crocodile Dundee*, in which the Australian star sported a sea-snake skin jacket.[59]

Live Snakes

Although some people regard live boa constrictors with little enthusiasm, the familiar reptile is far and away the most popular pet snake in the United States and possibly the world. Of the 246,000 live CITES-listed snakes that the United States imported between 1977 and 1983, nearly half (113,000 +) were boa constrictors, approximately one-fifth were reticulated pythons, and another one-fifth were Indian pythons.[60] There is also an extensive U.S. market for domestic species. While some snakes sold in the United States are captive bred, the bulk are taken from the wild.[61] Since young snakes make up most of the pet trade and volumes are relatively low, many experts believe that wild boa constrictor populations can withstand collecting for the pet trade.

Oddly enough, the most common subspecies reported in the live trade, the Central American boa constrictor (*Boa constrictor imperator*) may be temperamentally less suited to pet life than its relative, *B. c. constrictor*, sometimes called the red-tailed boa.[62] Most live boa constrictors in trade come from the forests of Central America, Colombia, and Suriname. (Many of the boa constrictors of Central America are being traded illegally, since countries in that region now ban their export, although individual countries sometimes open the trade for limited periods. In addition, the Colombian trade is illegal, as that country also protects the species.) Upwards of 80 percent of boa constrictors reported in international trade are imported into the United States,[63] but the level of trade fluctuates widely. Recorded world commerce in live boa constrictors dropped from 20,000 in 1980 to 4,700 in 1984, probably because of export bans.[64] However, in 1985 the United States alone imported over 16,000 live boa constrictors.[65]

It is difficult to measure other aspects of world trade in live snakes because—with the exception of boas and pythons— much of the trade falls outside CITES restrictions, and collectors are generally cautious about discussing their operations. As one researcher concluded after trying unsuccessfully to gauge the nature of poisonous snake collections in the United States, "a quite active but secretive marketing and exchange mechanism exists in the collector communities."[66] Collectors may be tight-lipped because several states and countries prohibit keeping venomous snakes without a permit, and some protect both poisonous and harmless snakes that are considered rare. Moreover, under U.S. federal law, it is illegal to import or export live snakes or any other reptiles through the mail, out of concern for unsuspecting postal workers and package recipients, as well as animal welfare.

For the most part, U.S. trade in live snakes is legal.[67] However, there is some concern over illicit traffic in protected foreign species, such as the Appendix I-listed Indian rock python. Concern also exists over black market sales of domestic snakes facing extinction, such as the eastern indigo snake (*Drymarchon corais couperi*), which is protected under the U.S. Endangered Species Act.

European countries and Japan, as well as the United States, are important importers of live snakes, while African, South American, and Asian countries are the main exporters. Although trade statistics for these countries are difficult to come by, Kenneth Dodd reviewed the situation and termed their volume of live-snake transactions "extremely high."[68] As an example, he noted one report indicating that Italy imported over 14,000 live colubrids and over 50,000 vipers between 1968 and 1970.[69] A study of snake preferences in the United Kingdom found that the imported venomous snakes most popular among reptile collectors there were the western diamondback rattlesnake (*Crotalus atrox*), puff adder (*Bitis arietans*), Gaboon viper (*B. gabonica*), and Indian cobra (*Naja naja*).[70]

Smuggling of Live Lizards and Snakes— A Continuing Problem

Unfortunately, information on illegal trade in lizards and snakes is largely anecdotal, based on stories of dramatic arrests of smugglers by government inspectors. Nevertheless, a clear picture can be painted of a problem that is widespread, highly profitable, and potentially disastrous to the world's endangered and threatened lizards and snakes.

Traders say that U.S. reptile smugglers concentrated on Mexican snakes and lizards during the late 1970s and early 1980s, but that many Mexican species are now captive-bred and thus more commonly available through legal channels. There is still a high-priced U.S. market for certain rare Mexican imports—for example, the Mexican rosy boa (*Lichanura trivirgata roseofusca*)—and illicit traffic continues.[71] However, Mexican authorities have instituted tougher trade controls to thwart smuggling attempts.[72]

Australian species are now extremely popular. They are often endemic, easy to collect, and valuable in world markets because of Australia's ban on most commercial wildlife exports.[73] A 1987 wildlife investigation in California netted two reptile smugglers who imported numerous Mexican reptiles, including the Gila monster and beaded lizards (*Heloderma horridum*), as well as Australian lizards, such as Gould's goanna or sand monitors, western bearded dragons (*Amphibolurus minimus*), and blotched blue-tongued skinks (*Tiliqua nigrolutea*). Wildlife officials believe that these smugglers illegally shipped between 100 and 150 reptiles over a three-year period. To escape detection, the collectors brought many of the lizards into the country through the U.S. mail. The pair pleaded guilty and received three-year suspended sentences and total fines of nearly $15,000.[74]

At roughly the same time, an American in Australia was convicted of attempting to export four desert death adders (*Acanthopis pyrrhus*), in contravention of the Australian ban. The death adders could have

Komodo dragon monitor (*Varanus komodoensis*).
E. Schuhmacher/WWF

fetched between $400 and $600 each in U.S. black markets.[75]

Smuggling is not limited to Mexican and Australian species. The Indian rock python and eastern indigo snake were among the rare reptiles favored by customers of the Atlanta Wildlife Exchange, a front for a federal investigation of U.S. wildlife smuggling in the early 1980s. Law enforcement agents posing as traders in the undercover investigation, dubbed "Snakescam," seized over 10,000 illicit reptiles and arrested 27 people, including amateur and professional biologists. The "sting" exposed widespread illegal traffic in protected snakes native to the United States such as the eastern indigo snake, the New Mexico ridge-nose rattlesnake (*Crotalus willardi obscurus*), and the San Francisco garter snake (*Thamnophis sirtalis tetrataenia*). At the time, the U.S. Fish and Wildlife Service estimated that as many as 100,000 reptiles were being bought and sold illegally through the mail each year.[76]

In early 1987, alert officials in Los Angeles confiscated an incoming shipment of live reptiles without proper permits that included 18 Boelen's pythons (*Python boeleni*), a rare species from Papua New Guinea only discovered in 1956. The snakes were being sent to an importer claiming to have a reptile research facility.[77]

With the huge profit that rare lizards and snakes can yield, all this smuggling is hardly surprising. The Indian pythons captured in Snakescam, for example, could have brought dealers $500 or so each on the U.S. black market at the time and as much as $2,000 from collectors in Japan and Europe.[78] Live tuatara can command $6,800 per specimen in world markets.[79] (New Zealand authorities have voiced concern that some drug traffickers may be swapping narcotics for this endangered reptile.[80]) In Japan, a television commercial in the early 1980s starring the fascinating frilled lizard (*Chlamydosaurus kingii*) sparked a jump in demand for the dinosaur-like reptile. In 1984, a pair of frilled lizards smuggled into Japan from Papua New Guinea commanded the staggering sum of $683,500. In response to the frilled lizard incident and other reports of illegalities, often involving deceitful claims of "scientific purposes," Papua New Guinea authorities decided in June 1987 to stop issuing any export permits for live vertebrates, with the exception of fish.[81]

What Can Be Done

Clearly, closer attention must be paid to the enormous global snake and lizard markets, particularly to assess the combined impacts of collecting, habitat destruction, and other pressures on wild populations of the boa constrictor, reticulated python, whip snake, tegu and monitor lizards, and other heavily traded species. It is also essential to track the trade and other potential threats to more

KEEP IN MIND . . .

Products

In comparison to trade in crocodilian leather, the trade in snake and lizard products has fewer problems in terms of illegal trade. But remember: all lizards and some snakes involved in the skin trade are considered threatened. So, if you opt to buy a leather product made of lizard or snake, use the following guidelines:

■ Avoid certain snake skin products, such as those marked "whipsnake," 'boa," or "anaconda." Legal and illegal skins from these snakes are mixed on the international market.

■ Trade in lizard products is largely legal. If you have a choice between lizard and snake, choose the lizard product.

Live

■ Unless you are an experienced collector, or have studied the subject, avoid purchasing live exotic lizards and snakes. They require specialized care, and most die in a novice's hand.

■ Learn as much as you can about reptiles. Join a herpetological society. Two national societies are the American Federation of Herpetoculturists (P.O. Box 1131, Lakeside, CA 92040), which publishes *Vivarium* as its quarterly magazine, and the Society for the Study of Amphibians and Reptiles (Department of Zoology, Miami University, Oxford, OH 45056), which publishes the *Journal of Herpetology* and the *Herpetolocial Review*. Several states, such as Arizona, Ohio, and Virginia, have their own herpetological societies, which you can join. Ask your local zoo for information on these.

■ Some suggested readings:

Halliday, Tim, and Adler, Kraig. *The Encyclopedia of Reptiles and Amphibians*. New York: Facts on File, 1986.
Mehrtens, John J. *Living Snakes of the World in Color*. New York: Sterling, 1987.
Schmidt, Karl P., and Inger, Robert F. *Living Reptiles of the World*. Garden City, N.Y.: Doubleday, 1957.

uncommon or exotic species prized in collecting circles, such as the frilled lizard and certain rattlesnakes.

Armed with better data, governments, the reptile skin industry, and the scientific community could develop conservation programs that better balance fashion demands with concern for lizard and snake species' future in the wild. Better information on the status of "specialty" snakes and lizards also could help wildlife managers develop trade regulations, habitat-protection programs, and captive-breeding operations that conserve truly threatened species and maintain healthy, exploitable populations of species that are more abundant.[82]

In the United States, eastern states with native rare snakes and lizards need to follow the model set by Arizona, California, and Utah in passing strict regulations on commercial collection of wild reptiles. And states such as California and Florida, with rich reptile populations and intensifying development pressures, need to become more knowledgeable about the impact of habitat loss on native reptiles.

It is critically important that worldwide enforcement of existing trade laws be improved, beginning with CITES and national controls imposed by major producer countries, such as Argentina and Paraguay. Since wildlife port authorities are often overworked and in short supply, and are thus able to inspect only a fraction of today's snake and lizard shipments, self-policing within the collecting community and skin-marketing industries is essential. Members of these groups should be well aware of CITES regulations and should make every effort to understand and abide by exporting countries' laws, asking for assistance, if needed from their own federal officials or TRAFFIC network experts.

Consumers, too, can play a vital role in upholding commercial prohibitions on snakes and lizards. When looking for live pets, buyers should deal only with reputable pet shops and should become knowledgeable about the animal they want to buy. They should ask about the source of all animals for sale, refusing to buy any that have illegal or uncertain origins. In addition, reptile collectors should purchase only captive-bred animals or species that are common in the wild. Finally, reptile owners must give their pet snakes and lizards adequate care, including a comfortable living environment and appropriate food. While reptiles make few demands on their owners, they need to be treated well to survive the rigors of captivity.

Since it is nearly impossible for consumers to identify the species or origins of reptiles used to make purses, belts, and other snake and lizard products, the best action citizen conservationists can take to stem the illegal skin trade is to pressure their public officials to improve wildlife trade law enforcement at all levels—from spot inspections of local shops, to increased numbers of federal port inspectors, to broader diplomatic support for a strong CITES treaty.

CHAPTER 22
Turtles

The slow-moving, secretive turtles and tortoises of the world belong to one of the oldest group of living reptiles on earth, the order Testudinata. This order includes sea turtles, land-dwelling tortoises, and freshwater turtles (also called terrapins in some parts of the world). For millions of years, these peaceable creatures have defended themselves against quicker or more aggressive predators by tucking their tails and clawed limbs up into their shells or by swimming quickly away when challenged at sea.

These strategies work well against most furred and fanged pursuers but are virtually useless when trying to escape human beings. Turtles have long been easy targets for two-legged hunters who use their meat, skin, eggs, and shells, as well as for collectors who bring in live specimens for research and the pet trade.

Sea Turtles

The world's sea turtles (families Cheloniidae and Dermochelyidae) have been particularly harmed by exploitation for international trade. Several of these turtles are prized for their mottled amber shells, leathery skin, veal-like meat, and edible cartilage. Their natural habits make them especially vulnerable to hunters. Adult females appear to return to the same natal beaches each year, where they become predictable, defenseless targets. In addition, egg clutches are easy to spot—after laying her eggs, a female sea turtle struggles back to the ocean, leaving an unmistakable trail behind. Because sea turtles probably do not reach sexual maturity for 10 to 30 years in the wild, it may take decades for turtle populations to recover from the effects of heavy hunting and egg collecting.

Green sea turtle (*Chelonia mydas*).
P. Pritchard

Five of the six sea turtle species are now considered endangered. These five include the green (*Chelonia mydas*), hawksbill (*Eretmochelys imbricata*), Kemp's ridley (*Lepidochelys kempii*), olive ridley (*L. olivacea*) and leatherback (*Dermochelys coriacea*) turtles. All these turtles have been heavily hunted, for local meat and egg markets and for international commerce in meat, skin, and shells. A tremendous rise in coastal development along tropical and subtropical nesting beaches has further imperiled them. The sixth species, the loggerhead (*Caretta caretta*), is considered vulnerable throughout its range.[1]

All sea turtle species are listed in Appendix I. Yet large-scale international trade in turtles and turtle products continues at an alarming rate. According to one group of sea turtle conservation experts, "Probably no other group of animals presently protected under Appendix I of CITES is traded more often or in such volume as sea turtles."[2] For instance, over two million hawksbill, green, and olive ridley turtles were imported by Japan, the world's largest consumer of sea turtles, between 1970 and 1986.[3]

MAJOR MARKETS

International trade in sea turtles revolves today around two major markets: "tortoiseshell,"* primarily involving the hawksbill turtle, and

Technically, the term tortoiseshell is a misnomer since tortoises and sea turtles belong to different families in the turtle order.

leather, with the olive ridley turtle being the most popular source of skins. Limited international trade also occurs in sea turtle meat, mostly from the green turtle, and in sea turtle eggs.

Plastic "tortoiseshell" eyeglass frames and hair combs are now widespread in the United States and Europe. Nevertheless, there is still a sizable world market for the real thing, particularly in Far Eastern countries. The thick, richly colored shell of the hawksbill makes it especially prized as tortoiseshell, not just in eyeglass frames and combs but also in hair ornaments, brooches, rings, and other jewelry. An estimated 100,000 hawksbills are killed annually.[4] World exports of raw tortoiseshell run to some 165 tons per year.[5]

Indonesia historically has been the major source for raw tortoiseshell reported in international trade. It exported 40 to 70 percent of the world total between 1979 and 1984, though this pattern appears to have changed in the late 1980s (figure 22.1).[6] Thailand has also been an important source, along with Cuba, Panama, and other Caribbean countries. Indonesia, Thailand, and Panama are all parties to CITES; Cuba is not.

Japan is by far the major tortoiseshell importer, along with Taiwan, China, South Korea, Hong Kong, and Singapore.[7] Between 1970 and 1986, Japan imported about 706 tons of shell, equivalent to more than 600,000 hawksbill turtles.[8] Hawksbill shell, known as "bekko" in Japan,

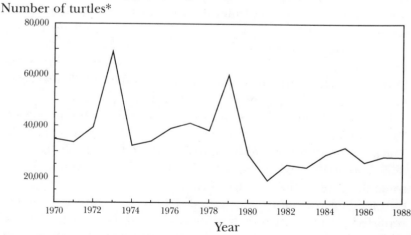

Figure 22.1
Estimated Number of Hawksbill Turtles Involved
in Japanese Imports of Bekko, 1980–1988

*Calculated at 1.06 kilograms of shell per hawksbill turtle.
Source: Japanese Customs statistics.

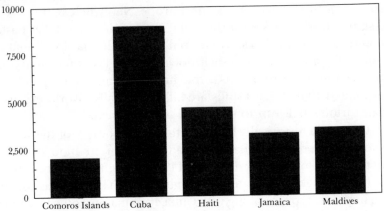

Figure 22.2
Major Exporters of Hawksbill Turtles to Japan, 1988

Number of turtles*

*Calculated at 1.06 kilograms of hawksbill shell per turtle.
Source: Japanese Customs data.

is particularly popular with brides in that country as a traditional decoration for their wedding regalia.

In an average year, Japan's hawksbill shell imports require the slaughter of 28,000 adult turtles (figure 22.2). At least half of the trade is estimated to be illegal, coming from CITES parties that do not have reservations on the species and do not authorize hawksbill exports. Responding to criticism of illegal trade practices, Japanese bekko dealers in 1986 voluntarily agreed not to import bekko from CITES parties. This has curbed the illicit flow somewhat. Evidently, however, Indonesian tortoiseshell was subsequently laundered into Japan via Singapore, at least until it joined CITES in February 1987, and Caribbean tortoiseshell has similarly passed through Jamaica, a nonparty.

Every year, thousands of sea turtles are also killed and processed by artisans or manufacturers in countries where the turtles are native. The turtle products are then exported as worked tortoiseshell, a term that includes not only manufactured tortoiseshell goods but also, in some instances, whole stuffed turtles.

Trade in worked tortoiseshell is difficult to measure. It is usually reported by value, rather than volume, and traders often undervalue shipments to avoid local taxes. Major world exporters of worked tortoiseshell are Indonesia, the Philippines, Taiwan, Fiji, Singapore, and South Korea. Exports from South Korea have jumped particularly dramatically since 1979; by 1983, that country was the world's largest source of worked shell.

Japan, once again, is the largest reported market for worked tortoise-shell, followed by Fiji, which probably sells imported jewelry primarily to tourists.[9] In Japan, the well-established tortoiseshell manufacturing industry produces top-quality, polished combs, eyeglass frames, and other goods from raw tortoiseshell. Most worked tortoiseshell imports are stuffed turtles. The sea turtle symbolizes longevity in Japanese culture, and many Japanese like to adorn the walls of their homes, restaurants, and other establishments with dead sea turtles as a result. This practice apparently began in the 1970s; during the years from 1970 to 1986, Japan imported over 570,000 stuffed hawksbills and another 380,000 to 400,000 stuffed green sea turtles, mostly from Indonesia.[10]

The turtle leather market also threatens sea turtle populations, although the market is declining. In addition to olive ridley turtles, green sea turtles are sometimes killed for their skins. Like other exotic leathers, sea turtle skin began to show up in world markets during the mid-1960s, as alligator and crocodile skins became scarcer.[11] Skin from the turtles' tough, scaly flippers and leathery neck is dried, salted, and processed into boots, shoes, belts, wallets, and handbags.

Mexico is probably the world's major source of processed sea turtle skin, reportedly shipping over 108 tons to Japan, its largest customer, between 1976 and 1986.[12] Most of the estimated 320,000 or more turtles killed to supply this trade were olive ridleys, which nest along Mexico's Pacific coastline.[13] Mexico is not a CITES party and once allowed large-scale harvests of olive ridley sea turtles under a quota system. The olive ridley quotas were greatly reduced in 1986, but earlier harvests apparently took a heavy toll. For instance, the commercial olive ridley catch in the coastal state of Oaxaca dropped from 56,000 in 1982 to 28,000 in 1983, likely a result of a drastic decline in olive ridley populations there.[14]

Two other major sources of sea turtle skins are Indonesia and Ecuador. Indonesia exports bulk shipments of turtle leather, mostly from green sea turtles. Sea turtle flippers are salted and dried for export from Bali and Surabaja.[15] Ecuador officially bans fishing and trade in sea turtles, but its fishery still survives with government sanctions. In 1987, Ecuadorean industry officials allowed two sea turtle processing plants in Manta to reopen and authorized exports of sea turtle products to Mexico.[16]

Japan is the largest turtle skin and leather consumer, fashioning the hides into all kinds of exotic luxury items, including belts, handbags, wallets, and shoes. France, Italy, and West Germany used to be

Butchering a green sea turtle.
Ross

important markets for sea turtle leather, but have reported no imports since 1984, when they outlawed all sea turtle trade in line with newly imposed strict European Economic Community (EEC) rules.[17] Japanese imports of raw and processed skins topped 836 tons between 1970 and 1986, accounting for the lives of at least 490,000 olive ridleys and 38,000 green turtles. Of particular concern to Japanese conservationists is the high volume of illicit olive ridley skins their country imports from Ecuador.[18]

Traditionally, the adult green sea turtle has been esteemed as a flavorful addition to the soup pot. Apparently, however, only limited international trade in green sea turtle meat continues today. Notably, the Cayman Islands still export some meat from green turtles bred in captivity or farmed. In the early 1980s, over 100 tons of meat, flippers, and "calipee" (edible shell cartilage) were exported, mostly to West Germany and the United Kingdom.[19] Because the Cayman Islands are administered by the United Kingdom, Cayman-U.K. trade is considered internal and does not have to be reported directly in CITES trade records.

Domestic consumption of meat from sea turtles remains common in some areas. According to researcher Rodney Salm, "Bali is the single largest trading point for green turtle meat in Indonesia and probably in the world."[20] Indonesian sea turtle meat is often featured in tourist restaurants offering sea turtle steaks.

Finally, a small amount of international trade also is reported in sea turtle eggs. However, most sea turtle eggs, which look much like leathery ping pong balls, are collected specifically for *local* subsistence purposes. In Japan, sea turtle eggs are occasionally sold in urban fish markets, with the eggs believed to come from coastal regions within the country.[21]

CONTINUING TRADE IN APPENDIX I SPECIES

Why are sea turtles still exploited when all species are listed on Appendix I? One reason is that many countries with native sea turtle populations consider turtle fishing an important source of local income and allow some exports, sometimes despite their membership in CITES. Over 80 percent of all raw tortoiseshell exports probably violate CITES. Countries that do not belong to CITES also contribute to turtle exploitation and international trade. For example, Cuba, Haiti, and Vietnam are important tortoiseshell suppliers,[22] and Mexico is a key leather source. Two countries—Jamaica and Singapore—have been singled out in the 1980s as laundering points for illicit sea turtle shipments destined for Japan.[23] Jamaica is not a CITES member; Singapore signed the treaty in 1986.

Even if countries have legal controls on sea turtle exports, they frequently lack the financial means to patrol nesting beaches and foraging areas or to prosecute turtle poachers. Further frustrating these countries' efforts to control all harvests of native sea turtle populations is the fact that the turtles frequently migrate across national boundaries.

Consuming countries are equally responsible for the continuing trade in sea turtle products. As is the case with other species listed in CITES appendices, countries that belong to CITES may trade in sea turtles if the countries have entered reservations on specific species and if all shipments of those species have proper import and export permits. Japan, the largest sea turtle importer in the world, took reservations on green, hawksbill, and olive ridley turtles when it acceded to CITES in 1980, allowing it to import or export these species from other CITES parties holding reservations so long as it obeyed permitting requirements. However, the evidence is clear that Japanese trade officials have failed miserably in abiding by these conditions. TRAFFIC(Japan) has documented persistent, high-volume imports of hawksbill, green, and olive ridley sea turtles arriving without legal CITES export permits from countries that do not hold corresponding reservations, particularly Indonesia, Panama, and Ecuador.[24]

Stopping Japan's illegal trade in sea turtles and sea turtle products

Meat from the green sea turtle is commonly used in sea turtle soup in Japan, while the shell from the hawksbill turtle is used for a variety of bekko products.
TRAFFIC(Japan)

is a top priority for conservationists working to prevent overexploitation of these endangered species. In July 1987, TRAFFIC(Japan) called on the Japanese government to meet CITES requirements for trade in reservation species, to reject sea turtle shipments from Indonesia falsely marked as captive bred, and to drop its reservations on the hawksbill, green, and olive ridley species as soon as possible. TRAFFIC(Japan) recommended strict limits on the trade in the interim.[25] In 1987, Japan dropped its reservation on one species, the green sea turtle.

Only one other CITES party, Suriname, currently is allowed under CITES rules to continue commercial trade. This country has reservations on green and leatherback turtles.

Until 1984, Italy held a reservation to allow trade in green sea turtles, and France had one for both green and hawksbill turtles. As EEC members, however, these countries were obligated to withdraw their reservations by January 1, 1984. Italy still imported over 2,300 pounds of green turtle oil from the Cayman Islands in 1984, but it contended that the oil was from animals raised in captivity and thus exempt from Appendix I prohibitions.[26] France delayed its compliance with the EEC regulation until the end of 1984. CITES records show that France imported roughly 470 pounds of hawksbill turtle shell from Cuba and over 70 pounds from Haiti in 1984.[27]

Overseas colonies and territories of CITES members present another loophole in efforts to control sea turtle trade. Without violating CITES, French citizens may bring home sea turtle souvenirs from Martinique and Guadeloupe, two French territories in the Caribbean.[28] As noted earlier, the United Kingdom imports green turtle products from a farm in the Cayman Islands; in 1984, it reported imports of nearly 13,000 pounds of green turtle meat and more than 1,000 pounds of calipee from that territory.[29]

CITES members often import sea turtles in clear contravention of the treaty, either intentionally or because the shipments are unchecked or unrecognized. As mentioned, Japan regularly accepts shipments with improper documents or with no documents at all.[30] Hong Kong, China, and West Germany have also imported significant quantities of raw tortoiseshell. And Australia, West Germany, and the United States have reportedly imported worked tortoiseshell from the Far East.[31]

Finally, some countries that do not belong to CITES do little to control their sea turtle imports. Notable examples include Taiwan and South Korea.[32]

SEA TURTLE RANCHING AND CAPTIVE BREEDING

Trade control exemptions for sea turtle ranching and captive-breeding operations are among the most widely debated and divisive topics in international wildlife trade. Recently, the subject has come up at every biennial CITES conference, with battle lines quickly drawn. Over the years, CITES treatment of sea turtle ranching and captive-breeding operations has grown increasingly complex.

Turtle-ranching operations collect eggs or hatchlings from the wild and raise them in controlled conditions with the intention of producing sea turtle products for market. CITES parties have agreed to allow commercial trade in ranch-raised animals if the ranching operations meet certain standards and can show that they will actually benefit wild populations. To date, no sea turtle ranches have succeeded in satisfying all of the CITES criteria.

Captive-breeding, or farming, operations must, in principle, go one step further than ranches. They must establish a closed system in which captive-bred animals reliably produce offspring to keep the farm population going without adding breeders from the wild. The farm must produce a generation of turtles from wild breeders *and* a second generation (known in genetics as the F2 generation) that are "grandchildren" of the original breeding group.

Turtle farming and ranching advocates contend that such operations improve the survival rate of eggs and hatchlings in the wild and provide income for local peoples. They also argue that sale of farm- or ranch-raised turtles helps curb demand for wild turtles by supply-

Galápagos tortoise (*Geochelone elephantopus*).
Ginette Hemley

ing substitutes to existing markets.

Opponents argue that existing commercial operations still depend on wild populations and thus do not conserve turtles or meet CITES requirements for opening the trade. Critics also dispute claims that the turtles are sold to benefit local peoples, noting that the animals are costly to raise, so they are not generally farmed by those who need the income most; they are also more expensive than wild-caught specimens, so they are usually sold in foreign industrial countries rather than local food markets.

In practice, no sea turtle farming operation has yet achieved second-generation breeding. The largest turtle farm, Cayman Turtle Farms Ltd. of the Cayman Islands, has hatched and raised hundreds of thousands of green turtle eggs taken from the wild between 1968 and 1978 and has produced thousands of first-generation captive-bred animals. But it has not produced a viable F2 generation from captive-born parents. It has, however, not taken turtles from the wild since 1978, when it last acquired wild eggs or breeding stock.

The United Kingdom has made repeated requests, on behalf of the Cayman Islands, that commercial trade in turtles from this farm be allowed, but participants in the CITES conferences have declined each request. Opponents argue that the United Kingdom's proposals would not take pressure off wild turtle populations but would actually do the reverse—stimulating demand for wild turtles by possibly reopening the U.S. market, which has been closed to green turtle products since 1979.

In 1985, participants at the biennial CITES conference also rejected proposals to approve sea turtle ranching projects in Suriname and Reunion, an island territory of France. The Reunion proposal met similar defeat at the 1987 biennial CITES conference. Ranching and farming proposals are likely to come up again in the future, particularly if turtle-raising techniques prove more successful.

Tortoises

In sharp contrast to the sea turtle trade, most international commerce in tortoises involves live animals destined for pet shops, private collections, or zoos and research facilities. All of the trade is regulated by CITES: the Galápagos tortoise (*Geochelone elephantopus*), the Bolson tortoise (*Gopherus flavomarginatus*), and three other highly endangered species are listed on Appendix I, and all remaining members of the family Testudinidae are on Appendix II.

It may be too late to save some of the rarest tortoises from the combined pressure of habitat loss, hunting, and trade. One such species is the Bolson tortoise, a Mexico native that has almost disappeared. The species is naturally rare, but human predation, illegal trade, and encroaching farms and irrigation projects are pushing it ever closer to extinction. Today, few individuals survive, along a 75-mile strip in north central Mexico. The United States lists the Bolson tortoise as endangered under the Endangered Species Act, in part to help stop trade across the Texas/Mexico border.

Until the EEC banned imports of three tortoise species in 1984, the European pet trade was pressuring wild populations of the spur-thighed tortoise (*Testudo graeca*), found in Morocco, Turkey, and other Mediterranean nations; the Hermann's tortoise (*T. hermanni*), of the northern Mediterranean seaboard; and, to a lesser extent, the marginated tortoise (*T. marginata*), a Greek native not as common in the pet trade. Another species that is still heavily involved in trade is the Afghan or Horsfield's tortoise (*T. horsfieldii*), which comes from Afghan-

---

*Most Horsfield's specimens come from the Soviet Union, where collectors reportedly take in some 150,000 of the slow-breeding animals each year.[34] Many of these are sold in Soviet pet markets, but enormous numbers were exported to Europe in the early 1980s. In 1982, minimum world trade topped 97,000 animals, with the majority going to western Europe. Imports slowed in 1984, the only major trade being 18,000 animals shipped to Italy from Turkey.[35]

istan, Iran, the Soviet Union, and other central and southwest Asian countries.[33]* Collecting of this species as well as the three others is believed to have caused tortoise populations to drop steeply, particularly in Algeria, Bulgaria, France, Morocco, Romania, Spain, and Yugoslavia.[36]

In the 1970s, the Royal Society for the Prevention of Cruelty to Animals and other citizen groups protested against cruel shipping practices used to bring southern tortoises to British markets and the heavy mortality of tortoises in trade. They also voiced concern over the impact of trade on dwindling wild tortoise populations. A study by British herpetologist M. K. Lambert found that over 80 percent of all imported tortoises died within one year of their arrival in northern Europe, victims of the harsh winters, lack of resistance to foreign disease, and their owners' ignorance of their new pets' needs.[37] A later survey of 2,000 tortoises brought into the country in 1982 concluded that 92 percent did not survive beyond three years in captivity.[38]

During the mid- to late 1970s, numerous efforts were made to control the tortoise trade in response to conservation and humanitarian concerns. For instance, all tortoises in the genus *Testudo* were listed on Appendix II in 1975; the United Kingdom's management authority agreed to set overall trade limits on tortoise imports in 1979; and the Convention on the Conservation of European Wildlife and Natural Habitats (popularly known as the Berne Convention), which came into force in 1982, prohibited internal trade and possession of spur-thighed, Hermann's, and marginated tortoises.

Efforts to protect tortoises continued in the 1980s. U.K. authorities issued a directive in 1982 requiring new tortoise owners to sign an agreement when they purchased their pets certifying that they would provide the minimum recommended care. Finally, after EEC member countries outlawed all commercial imports of the three European species in 1984, the tortoise market in Europe began to turn downward. According to CITES records, European imports of spur-thighed tortoises fell from 63,000 or so a year in 1980-83 to approximately 11,000 in 1984. The market for Hermann's tortoise also dropped dramatically, from approximately 17,000 per year before the ban to roughly 7,000 in 1984.[39]

Wildlife trade experts Richard Luxmoore and John Joseph, of the Wildlife Trade Monitoring Unit, are guardedly optimistic about the EEC ban. They report, "It appears that the EEC trade ban has been highly effective in curbing trade in European tortoises."[40] There has been some concern, however, that the market may shift to the United States, although 1984 CITES data show relatively few U.S. imports. In California, Hermann's tortoises imported from Greece reportedly

A single hyacinth macaw
(*Anodorhynchus hyacinthinnus*), the
world's largest parrot, can bring up
to $10,000 in the United States and
elsewhere.
Russell A. Mittermeier / WWF

The endangered St. Lucia parrot
(*Amazona versicolor*) is a victim of
both hunting and habitat loss. On
the small Caribbean island whose
name it bears, it is sought for food
and for capture as a pet.
S. Lousada / VIREO

The scarlet macaw (*Ara macao*) is one of the most popular large parrots in
trade. Efforts to breed this Neotropical species in captivity have increased
since international trade of wild scarlet macaws was banned in 1985.
C. Munn / NYZS / VIREO

The endangered peregrine falcon (*Falco peregrinus*) is one of the most popular species in falconry. It can dive or "stoop" at speeds of 100 or more miles per hour to attack other birds, killing them with sharp claws.
D. & M. Zimmerman / VIREO

Several raptor species are now being bred in captivity. The American kestrel (*Falco sparverius*), for example, is sometimes bred for use in laboratories.
Dave Menke / U.S. Fish and Wildlife Service

Falconers value the northern goshawk (*Accipiter gentilis*) for its audacious hunting behavior. It frequently targets wild rabbits and grouse and occasionally raids hen houses.
D. R. Herr / VIREO

The endangered Orinoco crocodile (*Crocodylus intermedius*), from northern South America, was one of the first crocodilians to be so decimated by hunters that it could not be hunted and traded profitably.
John Thorbjarnarson

Perhaps three-quarters of the 1.5 to 2 million crocodilian skins that reach world markets annually come from the spectacled (or yacare) caiman (*Caiman crocodilus*).
Lawrence E. Naylor

The common (or green) iguana (*Iguana iguana*) has long been one of the most popular lizards in the pet trade.
P. August

The Indian cobra (*Naja naja*) is a popular species in the international pet snake trade. Skins of this species are also used in India for wallets, handbags, and other leather goods for sale to tourists.
WWF-India

For centuries after Europeans first saw the Galápagos Islands in 1535, sailors captured massive numbers of the huge, slow-moving Galápagos tortoise (*Geochelone elephantopus*) as easy sources of meat for the voyages. Today, this tortoise is highly endangered.
Y. J. Rey-Millet

Five of the world's six sea turtle species, including the hawksbill (*Eretmochelys imbricata*), are considered endangered—victims of heavy hunting, both for local meat and egg markets and for international commerce in meat, skin, and shells.
Douglas Faulkner

The European Economic Community, a major market for live butterflies, has banned virtually all trade in the European Apollo butterfly (*Parnassius apollo*) and several other species.
George O. Krizek, M.D.

Flashy morpho butterflies (subfamily Morphinae) are used in their native Latin American countries to make earrings, ornaments, and butterfly-wing "pictures." Taiwan also imports these butterflies for use in bookmarks, coasters, and other works of "art."
J. Smith

Overexploitation of the world's coral resources increasingly concerns conservationists and marine biologists. Excessive removal of corals from the reefs in which several coral species live together can severely affect the fish and other marine animals that depend on the reefs for feeding and spawning grounds.
F. Barnwell

The Great Barrier Reef, off the coast of Australia, is the world's largest coral reef. "Stonies" such as these are harvested in many countries not just for coral collectors but also for use in building materials, road construction, and industry.
S. Earle

The polyps of tube corals, such as these photographed off California's Catalina Island, are extremely sensitive to light. The flash of light from one photograph can cause them to contract entirely.
S. Earle

Trade in living rock cacti (genus *Ariocarpus*) concerns conservationists. This Mexican native grows particularly slowly and has a very restricted natural distribution.
Linda McMahan

The United States is a major exporter, as well as importer, of wild and propagated cacti. The Arizona red claret cactus (*Echinocereus triglochidiatus* var. *arizonicus*) is endemic to the state whose name it bears.
Linda McMahan

South Africa is a major source of wild-collected aloe plants on the world market. Overzealous collectors have snapped up populations of many of the country's rarest species. As a result of trade sanctions imposed against South Africa in 1986, the United States is no longer of significant importer of the country's aloes or other succulents.
WWF-South Africa

Orchid enthusiasts should be careful to purchase only artificially propagated plants. The showy ladyslipper (*Cypripedium reginae*), a North American native, was cultivated in Holland as early as 1737.
William Krebs

High-volume collecting of wild *Cyclamen* in Turkey may threaten the survival of several species of this popular bulb plant.
Megan Epler Wood

Cycads such as the *Cycas circinalis* were in their heyday during the days of the dinosaur. Today, they are considered one of the most threatened plant groups in the world, with at least half the species facing extinction.
J. Lowe

The Venus's flytrap (*Dionaea muscicapula*, above) seems to be holding its own in the wild trade, unlike pitcher plants, the other carnivorous plant popular with collectors.
E. Laverne Smith / OES

have sold for as much as $525 each.[41]

The EEC ban has pushed up prices for pet tortoises in Europe. In the United Kingdom, for instance, spur-thighed and Hermann's tortoises that once sold for $10 to $15 now cost more than $100 each.[42] According to Richard Luxmoore, "These creatures have become true collectors' items." The net result may be beneficial to tortoises, since collectors are more likely to give their animals the care they require.

Tortoise aficionados in Europe are not giving up completely in their search for elegant and exotic pets. Some tortoise species are now being bred in captivity,[43] and some dishonest dealers may still be offering illicit specimens, such as the Ceylon star tortoise (*T. elegans*) of Sri Lanka, which is protected by that country's ban on exports of live wildlife. And, between 1982 and 1985, an Austrian animal dealer illegally imported hundreds of the striking reptiles with forged Filipino permits. Most were eventually reexported to West Germany.[44] A British pet dealer advertised "living gems from Sri Lanka" for £75 each in 1984.[45]

Reptile trade specialists are monitoring world markets to find out whether the European trade ban may cause pet shop owners to turn to Horsfield's tortoise or other less-protected species. So far, CITES records do not show this happening at significant levels,[46] though European traders may be importing the beleaguered Chaco tortoise (*Geochelone chilensis*) of southern South America to help fill the void left by the 1984 ban. Trade pressures are already a serious threat to this hardy yellow-brown native of Argentina, Paraguay, and possibly Bolivia. According to CITES reports, Argentine exports surged from 215 in 1981 to 8,111 in 1984.[47] To combat the threat, Argentina prohibited exports of the Chaco tortoise in 1986 as part of a ban on the export of most live wildlife. Conservationists in Argentina are concerned that illegal exports may now be passing through Chile to the United States.

In addition, one U.S. herpetologist, Kenneth Dodd of the U.S. Fish and Wildlife Service, reports a surge in exports of American box turtles (*Terrapene carolina*) to European markets since the Testudo ban took effect. He claims that some thousands of American box turtles may be shipped to the EEC each year. Florida authorities are considering outlawing all trade in this popular pet from their state.[48]

Freshwater Turtles

TURTLES AS PETS

Most of the world's captive turtles are freshwater species. Although many come from abundant wild or farmed populations, experts warn that U.S., European, and Japanese pet markets may be depleting

KEEP IN MIND . . .

Products

■ Travelers beware! Sea turtle products are available in tourist shops and marketplaces in many tropical countries. It is illegal under the U.S. Endangered Species Act to bring any sea turtle product back into the United States. It will be taken from you without compensation by wildlife officials.

■ Most brands of turtle soup in the United States are OK to eat because they probably contain meat from the freshwater snapping turtle, which is not an endangered species. These turtles are legally harvested in the United States for this purpose. The label should indicate the species name *Chelydra serpentina*.

Live

■ If you want a pet turtle or tortoise, choose it carefully. It is against U.S. health regulations to keep a red-earred slider turtle that is under four inches long since these are known carriers of salmonella.

■ If you decide to keep any species of pet turtle or tortoise, make sure you know how to care for it properly. Most reptiles die quickly after acquisition in inexperienced hands.

■ Learn about turtles and tortoises. Join a herpetological society, such as the American Federation of Herpetoculturists (P.O. Box 1131, Lakeside, CA 92040), which publishes *Vivarium* as its quarterly magazine; the Society for the Study of Amphibian and Reptiles (Department of Zoology, Miami University, Oxford, OH 45056), which publishes the *Journal of Herpetology* and the *Herpetological Review*; and the New York Turtle and Tortoise Society (365 Pacific St., Brooklyn, NY 11217), which publishes the *Plastron Papers*.

■ Some suggested readings:

Ernst, Carl H., and Barbour, Roger W. *Turtles of the United States*. Lexington, Ky.: University Press of Kentucky, 1972.

Halliday, Tim, and Adler, Kraig. *The Encyclopedia of Reptiles and Amphibians*. New York: Facts on File, 1986.

Pritchard, Peter C.H. *Living Turtles of the World*. Neptune City, N.J.: T.F.H., 1979.

Schmidt, Karl P., and Inger, Robert F. *Living Reptiles of the World*. Garden City, N.Y.: Doubleday, 1957.

---

several Latin American species, including the yellow-spotted sideneck (*Podocnemis unifilis*), South American red-lined (*Pseudemys scripta callirostris*), and spiny land (*Heosemys spinosa*) turtles.[49]

In addition to conservation concerns, the pet turtle trade raises health and ethical questions. Pet turtles can carry infectious *Salmonella* bacteria and are often shipped and stored under questionable conditions. Commerce in the red-eared "slider" (*Pseudemys scripta elegans*), a pocket-sized, bright green native of northern South America and the southern United States, illustrates these trade problems.

The red-eared slider, a relatively common and widespread species, is the mainstay of the international pet turtle trade.[50] The United States is the major world supplier of these popular aquarium dwellers, shipping some 5 million hatchlings a year to foreign pet shops.[51] About 55 percent go to Europe, and over 40 percent go to the Far East.[52] Most of these turtles are farmed and raised in humanmade ponds, with the industry annually collecting some 100,000 wild turtles to supplement breeding stocks.[53]

Imports and domestic sales of small sliders (under four inches in shell length) were banned in the United States in 1975, after researchers traced *Salmonella* poisoning in people to infected young pet sliders. Exports are not covered by this policy. Although this is not the only U.S. policy that protects the country's own residents from health hazards without taking similar precautions for overseas consumers, it is a source of controversy in U.S. medical and wildlife trade circles.

The U.S. Food and Drug Administration (FDA) is considering approval of a drug to disinfect red-eared slider eggs, a move that could lead to resumption of domestic sales. Turtle industry spokespersons such as Ralph Boudreaux have expressed hope that the egg treatment, known as the "gentamicin sulfate dip," and a newly created plastic package for storing and shipping young turtles will soon bring an end to the FDA ban. Critics argue that treating eggs does not protect hatchlings from reinfection. Some also consider sterile shipping bubbles to be inhumane "plastic prisons."[54]

TRADE IN FRESHWATER TURTLE MEAT AND SHELLS

Not all of the freshwater turtle trade involves live specimens. Like sea turtles and tortoises, freshwater turtles are sometimes killed for their meat, oil, eggs, and shell, which is used in traditional Oriental medicine. Over 400 years ago, in the days before Europeans reached the Amazon Basin, native people collected freshwater turtles and kept them in ponds as a ready source of meat when fishing was poor.[55] Today, turtles are still eaten in parts of Latin America, causing heavily exploited species such as the South American river turtle (*Podocnemis expansa*) to dwindle despite national protection.

Large-scale trade in freshwater turtles apparently occurs in Southeast Asia, both for local consumption and international shell sales, although this has not been documented.[56] Some concern also exists over U.S. consumption of native species, which are mainly used in Oriental cuisine.[57] In addition, the common snapping turtle (*Chelydra serpentina*), a scrappy, sharp-toothed native of streams and ponds across the eastern United States, is hunted for domestic and European steak and soup sales.

Another U.S. native, the alligator snapping turtle (*Macroclemys teminckii*), is widely hunted in Louisiana and other southeastern states for domestic meat markets, though the extent of any foreign trade is not known. In the late 1960s and early 1970s, the Campbell Soup Company purchased these animals for use in frozen snapper soup.[58] There is also a small domestic market for hatchlings and young snappers as pets, though this is not considered a significant threat to the species. The alligator snapping turtle is probably best known for its powerful jaws, the strongest of all freshwater turtles, and the way it lures prey. Lying still and open-mouthed, the turtle presents a tantalizing worm-like tongue to passing fish, tempting them to venture within snapping range.

Peter Pritchard, one of the world's leading specialists on freshwater turtles, discovered in 1982 that certain populations of the alligator snapping turtle were suffering from trapping and from habitat alteration. He proposed that it be listed as threatened under the U.S. Endangered Species Act, but no federal action has yet been taken.[59] Out of concern for the species' apparent decline, a British group, the People's Trust for Endangered Species, is raising funds for a complete survey of the population throughout its range.[60]

PART VI
Other
Animals

CHAPTER 23
Butterflies

Butterfly collecting, once the sport of wealthy world travelers and long-skirted Victorian ladies, is now estimated to involve perhaps as much as $100 million per year.[1] Many millions of dead butterflies reach world markets annually.[2] Usually, collecting does not endanger butterflies. Most of them, like other insects, reproduce rapidly, showing a remarkable ability to spread themselves about the earth and adapt to varied environments. As a class, insects make up three-quarters of the world's animal species and seem to be holding their own against the human population explosion.

In the past decade, however, entomologists have discovered that some of the world's most elegant and exotic butterfly species are exceptions to this generally healthy picture. For example, some members of the swallowtail butterfly family, Papilionidae, may soon become extinct. According to British scientists Mark Collins and Michael Morris, 78 of the world's 573 swallowtail butterfly species are threatened, largely because human activities are destroying their native habitats.[3]

When a butterfly species not only is losing its habitat but also has a small population and a naturally slow reproductive rate, large-scale collecting can be particularly threatening. Two species in a desperate situation are the beautiful black and lime-green paradise birdwing (*Ornithoptera paradisea*) of Papua New Guinea and the Homerus swallowtail (*Papilio homerus*) of Jamaica.

Trade Controls

The various swallowtail butterflies listed on Appendices I and II are the only insects protected by CITES. Queen Alexandra's birdwing (*Ornithoptera alexandrae*), the Homerus swallowtail, the Corsican

243

swallowtail (*Papilio hospiton*), and the Luzon swallowtail (*P. chikae*) are listed on Appendix I. Appendix II species include all other swallowtails that belong to "birdwing" species (*Ornithoptera, Trogonoptera*, and *Troides spp.*), the Bhutan glories (genera *Bhutanitis*), the Kaiser-I-Hinds (genera *Teinopalpus*), and the European Apollo butterfly (*Parnassius apollo*). Some of the rarest butterflies are also protected in their native countries.

Butterfly trade is difficult to monitor, in part because nearly all trade occurs through the mail. Only in a few cases have trade restrictions been enforced, though experts believe that CITES has cut down on the advertised trade in butterflies listed on the two appendices.[4] In 1985, a butterfly dealer put up a large collection of imported birdwings for auction by Sotheby's, including the Queen Alexandra's birdwing. One of the rarest species in the world, this

---

BUTTERFLY RANCHING IN PAPUA NEW GUINEA

A unique program for breeding and managing various species of birdwing butterflies has earned the island country of Papua New Guinea outspoken praise from conservationists. It has also prompted at least two other countries—Indonesia and the Solomon Islands, where the rest of the world's most prized birdwings are found—to begin plans for their own ranching programs.

Under the program, a government bureau, the Insect Farming and Trading Agency (IFTA), controls Papua New Guinea's birdwing trade and helps local villagers ranch butterflies for healthy profits. Ranchers lure wild butterflies into egg-laying areas by planting garden spots with especially nectarous flora and keeping predators away. After a butterfly lays her eggs in a protected patch, the pupae are collected and raised in cages until they become adult butterflies, when they are sold to IFTA. Ranchers frequently release some of their butterfly "crop" to renew wild populations.

The Papua New Guinea government pays local people for participating in this program, involving the citizenry in conservation efforts and meshing economic development needs with conservation goals. Seventy-five percent of the profits earned by the IFTA on butterfly sales are returned to local villagers. Individuals can earn as much as $1,200 per year, a better than average wage in the region.[1]

Only nonendangered birdwing species can be raised and exported through this program. In 1968, Papua New Guinea outlawed collection of its seven rarest birdwings, including the famous and highly endangered Queen Alexandra's birdwing, which measures 10 inches from wing tip to wing tip and sold for over $2,800 before it was placed on CITES Appendix I, and the stunning paradise birdwing, which was once advertised for as much as $7,000 but now fetches about $200 on the black market.[2]

butterfly is legally protected in the small area of rain forest it occupies in Papua New Guinea. The collection did not have proper CITES import permits (at the time, the Queen Alexandra's birdwing was listed on Appendix II), and the auction house honored official requests to withdraw it.[5]

The European Economic Community (EEC), an important market for butterflies, banned virtually all trade in the three birdwing genera and the European Apollo in 1982. In an unusual twist, after the ban was adopted, some European conservationists argued that it gave birdwings too much protection. They contended that the ban actually hurt conservation efforts by stopping legal imports from Papua New Guinea, the major source of top-quality birdwings. Papua New Guinea has a successful butterfly conservation and management program in which nonendangered butterfly species are captive-raised for export (see box).[6] According to the conservationists, this program effectively protects specific birdwing species while allowing moderate trade. Mark Collins explained, "Preserve enough natural habitat, study and manage the butterflies carefully, and all will be well; even collecting, ranching and trade are perfectly acceptable, so long as they are sustainable and conservation-oriented."[7]

In 1987, EEC leaders responded to the conservationists' argument by loosening restrictions to allow trade in ranched birdwing butterflies. The one exception was the Queen Alexandra's birdwing, trade in which is still banned.

Commercial Trade Routes

Several countries around the world are involved in butterfly exports

Morpho butterly (subfamily Morphinae).
ESA/Ries Memorial Slide Collection

and imports. Taiwan is the world leader in butterfly exports, but Brazil, the Central African Republic, Madagascar, Malaysia, Mexico, Papua New Guinea, the Philippines, and Peru are also major suppliers. The United Kingdom, West Germany, and other European countries are the most significant butterfly importers, but trade is also considerable in the United States and Japan.

Taiwan reportedly ships up to 500 million butterflies each year. It relies not just on 90 of its more than 350 native species but also on thousands of decorative birdwings and iridescent morpho (subfamily Morphinae) butterflies imported from Southeast Asia and South America.[8] In the late 1970s, at the height of Taiwan's butterfly craze, 20,000 people worked in the trade, including some 10,000 collectors. Taiwanese factories processed butterfly wings into colorful bookmarks, coasters, table mats, plastic toilet seats, and even portraits of Mona Lisa and Abraham Lincoln. Millions of leftover butterfly bodies were fed to local pig populations. The Taiwanese trade reportedly is declining, but the island's workers still process large numbers of local and foreign species. One such species is Taiwan's own threatened Maraho swallowtail (*Papilio maraho*), which sells for $150 per female and $75 per male.[9]

Another important player in world butterfly trade, Malaysia, ships over 100 native species. Malaysia is best known for its annual exports of some 125,000 specimens of Rajah Brooke's birdwing (*Trogonoptera brookiana*), an Appendix II species that wholesales for $1 to $3 in Europe and the United States. Recent evidence suggests that most of these shipments leave the country through postal channels without required CITES export permits.[10]

As the world's largest supplier of top-quality birdwing specimens, Papua New Guinea receives more than $60,000 income each year from the butterfly trade. Its birdwing ranching program enables the country to raise and sell the common green birdwing (*Ornithoptera priamus*), a poisonous black and gold birdwing (*Troides oblongomaculatus*), and other native species.

Although Australia has a broad supply of unique native butterflies, some experts believe that it has little commercial trade, largely because Australians are not particularly enthusiastic about butterfly collecting. There is some trade in endemic birdwings and, among others, a swallowtail known as the big greasy butterfly (*Cressida cressida*), named for the way its wing scales rub off on one's fingers.[11] Australia controls the export of all native flora and fauna, including insects, with a few exceptions.[12]

Some of the flashiest butterflies are found in South America. Members of the morpho subfamily, these inhabitants of tropical forests in such countries as Brazil, Colombia, Ecuador, Guyana, Mexico, and Peru come in dazzling shades of metallic blue. Specimens are used to make earrings, ornaments, and even butterfly-wing "pictures." Brazil processed an estimated 50 million per year in the 1970s. Legally, all Brazilian morphos are supposed to be captive-bred, but there is evidence that the market is made up largely of wild butterflies.[13]

Among other Latin American countries, Mexico is very active in butterfly exports, and Peru, a world-renowned center of butterfly species diversity, supplies some 10 million specimens per year to global markets.[14] French Guiana is a minor player in the trade, though some butterflies are collected and exported from St. Laurent, the penal colony made famous for its butterfly-catching convicts chronicled in Henri Charriere's novel *Papillon*.

Parts of Africa also supply growing commercial demand for butterflies. Prized African species include the spectacular African giant swallowtail (*Papilio antimachus*), which sold for $20 per specimen in the United States in 1983, and the rare Kilimanjaro swallowtail (*P. sjoestedti*), advertised for $212. Few African species are protected. Hundreds of thousands of specimens come out of the Central African Republic each year, where collectors can earn about $600 per month, 10 times the average national wage.[15] In Madagascar, some 60 species are collected in large volumes for export. Experts suspect that many butterflies are smuggled off the island to avoid Madagascar's export tax. One severely endangered Malagasy species, the large yellow and black Morondavana swallowtail (*P. morondavana*), sells for up to $150.[16]

Live Butterflies in Commerce

Although most butterflies in trade are "dead-stock" (that is, killed for collections or factory processing), live butterflies are increasingly popular. This is particularly true in the United Kingdom, where "butterfly houses" allow visitors to watch and photograph colorful specimens flying about in lush, tropical greenhouses. Each year, almost 4 million people—or 1 in 15 British residents—flock to that country's butterfly houses. Nearly unheard of until the early 1980s, captive-butterfly watching is now an established industry in the United Kingdom, worth an estimated $9 million per year in ticket sales. Exhibits of live butterflies also are springing up in the United States, the Netherlands, West Germany, Ireland, Sri Lanka, Australia, and elsewhere.[17]

British butterfly houses exhibit one-half million or so live butterflies each year. Approximately two-thirds are purchased from domestic and foreign dealers, while the remainder are bred on the premises.

The Philippines and Malaysia are key overseas suppliers. India, Taiwan, the United States, and, to a lesser extent, Costa Rica, France, Japan, and Sri Lanka also export a significant variety of species to the United Kingdom.[18]

Most live specimens in trade are delivered when they are pupae, rather than adult butterflies. Live butterflies are sometimes shipped in small paper envelopes that restrain their movement, a stressful and possibly cruel procedure that often results in high losses. A 40 percent mortality rate is not unusual. Fortunately, this deplorable practice is becoming less common, although it does still occur.[19]

According to a 1987 study of the United Kingdom's butterfly houses by Mark Collins, none of the species in British establishments is in danger of extinction. Exhibit favorites tend to be large, showy species,

---

KEEP IN MIND . . .

■ Think twice about purchasing curios made of butterflies before you do it. Butterflies are taken in huge numbers in the wild to decorate such tacky items as coasters or toilet seats. Much of this trade is legal, but scientists do not know if this is harming heavily exploited butterfly populations.

■ If you collect dried insects, be warned that many butterfly species offered in mail-order catalogs may have entered the United States illegally. Importers have been known to bypass U.S. wildlife import regulations simply by using the postal system.

■ Visit a butterfly house to learn more about these species. Some butterfly houses in the United States are located at the Cincinnati Zoo, Cincinnati; Marine World Africa USA, Vallejo, California; Callaway Gardens, Pine Mountain, Georgia; and Butterfly World, Fort Lauderdale, Florida.

■ Join a butterfly society and or an invertebrate conservation organizaton to learn more about butterflies. Two of these are the Lepidopterists' Society (257 Common St., Dedham, MA 02026), which publishes *News* and the *Journal*, and the Xerces Society (10 S.W. Ash Street, Portland, OR 97204), which publishes *Wings*. If you are already a member of either society, point out these trade problems to your fellow members.

■ Some suggested readings:

Brewer, Jo, and Winter, Dave. *Butterflies and Moths*. New York: Prentice Hall, 1986.

Preston-Mafham, Rod, and Preston-Mafham, Ken. *Butterflies of the World*. New York: Facts on File, 1988.

Pyle, Robert Michael. *The Audubon Society Handbook for Butterfly Watchers*. New York: Scribner's, 1984.

such as the African monarch butterfly (*Danaus chrysippus*) and the lime/lemon butterfly (*Papilio demoleus*). According to Collins, butterfly houses have the potential to do a great deal for conservation by educating the public about rare butterflies and their habitat needs and by helping to breed rare species for release back into the wild. At present, however, only 1 in 4 British butterfly houses actively promote conservation, and just 1 in 10 are involved in research.[20] Public encouragement could help convince these establishments to make a more concerted contribution to preserving butterflies in the wild.

Live butterfly markets, like the dead-stock trade, also encourage butterfly farms in developing countries, which—if managed wisely—produce income for local people and promote sustainable use of valuable insect populations.

CHAPTER 24
Corals

Ecologists, marine biologists, and conservationists are increasingly concerned about overexploitation of the world's coral resources. Prized for their often colorful, uniquely shaped skeletal secretions, minuscule colonial marine invertebrates known as corals are collected for a variety of uses, ranging from road construction to bangle jewelry to commercial medicinal extracts.[1]

According to marine specialist Sue Wells, who has studied the coral trade and industry extensively, coral beds and reefs that have been overexploited can recover in time, and it is unlikely that any one species of coral could be collected to the point of biological extinction. The degree of damage depends on how rapidly the exploited colonies can recover. Species may become depleted in local areas, however. Black coral stands, for instance, have been picked clean in parts of St. Lucia, Barbados, the Bahamas, and the U.K. Virgin Islands.[2] Precious red coral, once common in the Mediterranean Sea, has been collected heavily, and some of the historical, commercially exploitable beds have been degraded. The Italian coral industry now relies as much on imported coral from Taiwan and Japan as it does on local sources.[3]

Coral reefs provide excellent feeding and spawning grounds for fish and other marine species. Although coral reefs only occur in tropical waters, which are relatively nutrient-poor, coral reef ecosystems are rich in organic matter, such as oxygen-producing algae that live symbiotically with coral as well as sponges, sea urchins, sea anemones, sea squirts, fish, and other organisms. Coral reefs are a favorite habitat for smaller fish because their intricate structure gives protection from deep-ocean predators, such as sharks. Offshore reefs

Coral polyps, Red Sea
S. Earle

create physical barriers that shield beaches and other coastal lands from destructive wave action.

Coral collecting can contribute to reef damage, which also severely affects fish populations that depend on coral reefs and beds and local industries reliant on scuba diving, snorkeling, sightseeing, and other tropical tourist activities. In the Philippines, tourism and the fishing industry have suffered in some areas where reefs have been degraded. An estimated 70 percent of all Philippine reefs have been killed or seriously damaged by a combination of siltation, pollution, fishing with dynamite or cyanide, and, to a lesser extent, overcollection of coral.[4]

There are basically two types of coral: the stony corals, which build hard, calcareous external skeletons, and the soft corals, which have horny internal skeletons that give them a relatively flexible structure. Colonies of individual stony coral animals, known as polyps, form the basis for the world's coral reefs. The reef-building stony corals (order Scleractinia) are collected in many countries in bulk for building materials, road construction, and industrial use. The hard external skeletons of stony coral colonies, which are usually white when dead, are pried or blasted off reefs and crushed to manufacture lime, cement, and other products. Smaller colonies of stony corals are found more and more frequently in trade, particularly those in the genera *Fungia, Acropora, Pocillopora,* and *Porites.*[5]

In addition to stony corals, other hard-coral species in trade include the noncleractinian blue coral (*Heliopora coerulea*), organpipe coral, and the hydrozoan fire corals (*Millepora* spp.)

Soft corals, also called seafans or seawhips, often grow in attractive shades of black, red, blue, yellow, and other colors. Among the soft corals are the precious and semiprecious corals used to make necklaces, cameos, statues, vases, and so forth. Most precious and semiprecious corals are either gorgonian corals (Gorgonacea order) or black corals (Antipathacia order).

Important commercial species include Mediterranean or noble coral (*Corallium rubrum*); in the Far East, oxblood (*C. japonicum*), midway deep sea coral (*C.* sp. nov.), boke or maguy (*C. elatius*), and white (*C. konojoi*) coral; and several Hawaiian species, especially pink or angel skin (*C. secundum*) and gold (*Gerardia* spp.) coral.[6] In the Mediterranean, where red coral has long been hand collected by divers from Spain, France, Italy, and other coastal countries, the introduction of heavy-duty dragging devices in the past two decades and a boom in the coral-diving profession have helped deplete this valuable marine resource in several fishing areas, despite regulatory measures imposed by Spain and France.[7]

The Far East is now the leading center of precious coral processing, supplied in large part by far-ranging Taiwanese and Japanese fishing vessels, as well as by Philippine imports. Taiwan exports some of its "catch" to Japan or Italy but also supports a large domestic coral-carving industry, which makes the island the world's largest black-coral processing center and the leading exporter of both black and pink worked-coral items. Japan, which is involved primarily in the pink coral industry, is also at the hub of the precious coral market. It imports unworked specimens, primarily from Taiwan, for domestic processing and exports worked coral to Italy and other European countries, as well as to Taiwan and India.[8] The Mediterranean, especially Italy, is a third major site for pink-coral processing and trade. Once the world's only supplier, the region is famous for its cameo designs, vases, and other artwork.

In Asia and the Middle East, black corals traditionally have been made into amulets and beads worn to ward off disease or evil spirits.[9] Listed on Appendix II in 1981, the 150 species of black coral now are most often collected and sold in the form of bracelets, earrings, carved figures, and other items to tourists in the Caribbean, Hawaii, and the South Pacific. These semiprecious corals have been particularly hard hit in the Caribbean and are depleted in certain locations.[10] The bulk of raw black coral used in commercial processing comes from the Philippines.[11]

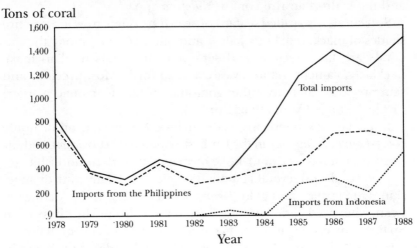

Figure 24.1
U.S. Imports of Crude Corals, 1978–1988

Tons of coral

Total imports

Imports from the Philippines

Imports from Indonesia

Year

Source: U.S. Customs data.

One Indo-Pacific species, a "whip" coral (*Cirrhipathes anguina*), makes up much of the international black-coral trade. Used to make inexpensive bracelets, more than 166,000 items of this species reached the United States in 1985, all but 2,500 from Taiwan. The remainder came from the Philippines. In all, the United States imported over 478,000 black coral items, with a declared value of approximately $365,000, in 1985.[12]

The Philippines supplies the bulk of raw stony corals to the world market, despite a government ban on all coral collection and exports in effect from 1977 to 1986. At the height of the coral trade, in the mid-1970s, the Philippines exported over 1,980 tons in a single year, with three-quarters going to the United States. Trade declined following the 1977 Philippine ban and subsequent efforts to honor it. In 1986, after the ban was lifted, the Philippines exported 689 tons of raw coral to the United States. These imports comprised about half of all U.S. imports that year.[13] Figures for total Philippine exports are not available.

The United States, the largest consumer of raw coral, imported nearly 1,400 tons in 1986.[14] U.S. efforts to enforce the Philippine ban are worth mentioning. In 1981, the United States added corals to the Lacey Act, which meant that it outlawed all coral imports that contravened foreign law. In 1982, the U.S. Fish and Wildlife Service instructed all of its inspectors at designated wildlife entry ports to refuse any shipments of coral from the Philippines. Coral continued

The United States is the world's largest importer of crude corals, many of which are sold in shell shops as tourist trinkets.
David Mack / WWF

to flow in, however, because U.S. authorities were confused about which Philippine agency issued export permits and because traders skirted the designated ports to bring coral in elsewhere. In October 1985, the United States tried to crack down by banning all wildlife imports from the Philippines. The Philippine government was caught off guard by this maneuver and responded quickly with a clear description of its permitting practices and a promise to strengthen enforcement of its wildlife laws. After only one week, the United States rescinded its ban. The next month, the United States imported some 60 tons of Philippine coral, double the average monthly intake, and imports for 1985 topped those of 1984. Although trade data are scarce, statistics show that several European countries, South Africa, Taiwan, and Australia also have active coral markets and imported illegally collected Philippine corals prior to 1986.[15]

Indonesia, Malaysia, Taiwan, Fiji, and India each exported over 50 tons of crude coral to the United States in 1986.[16] Over the past decade, minor suppliers to world markets have included the Dominican Republic, South Africa, Maldives, Tanzania, Kenya, and Kuwait.[17]

Controlling the Trade

Coral exploitation and trade are very hard to control, in part because coral is often collected in offshore areas seldom patrolled by national authorities. When raw coral enters the market, it is difficult—and sometimes impossible—to identify particular species. Coral colonies

Corals

of the same species grow differently, depending on environmental conditions, so even experts sometimes have a tough time recognizing them. And mixed consignments of shell and coral often are labeled as "shell" on trade permits and documents. Once coral is dried and processed, identification becomes even more difficult.

There have been some international efforts to monitor and control trade in certain precious and semiprecious corals. As noted earlier, the black corals were listed in Appendix II in 1981. To protect the most exploited stony corals, CITES parties listed 17 genera on Appendix II in 1985. An export permit is now required for CITES members to trade commercially in bird's nest, cauliflower, mushroom, brain, trumpet, and organpipe (*Tubipora musica*) corals, as well as some two dozen other species commonly found in trade.

To monitor the trade in Mediterranean red coral, Spain proposed listing the species on Appendix II during the CITES meeting in Ottawa in 1987, but this measure was voted down because population and trade data were incomplete. The Philippines, Spain, France, and several other major coral-supplying countries regulate coral exploitation through national export restrictions, collection permit requirements, the establishment of protected areas, and other measures.

Unfortunately, many coral-supplying countries do not control collection or trade at all. National measures, particularly those that allow only sustainable exploitation of corals, are essential to protect this valuable resource. National trade restrictions, and the previously discussed CITES listings, should help monitor and control the trade, but they could be strengthened greatly through improved enforcement on the part of producing and consuming countries. Consumer countries should be careful not to import coral taken,

---

KEEP IN MIND . . .

■ Refrain from buying any corals, including decorative coral and coral jewelry. Unmanaged coral collecting is extremely damaging to marine ecosystems because coral reefs cannot rapidly renew themselves.

■ Some suggested readings:

Faulkner, Douglas, and Chesher, Richard. *Living Corals of the World*. New York: Clarkson N. Potter, 1979.

Goreau, Thomas F.; Goreau, Nora I.; and Goreau, Thomas J. "Corals and Coral Reefs." In *Life in the Sea*. San Francisco: W. H. Freeman, 1982.

transported, or sold in contravention of foreign laws.

Management plans are urgently needed. An example is the plan prepared by the U.S. Western Pacific Regional Fishery Management Council for the Western Pacific Region. This plan will regulate coral diving, dredging, and other collecting operations in a way that ensures the long-term sustainability of the resource.[18]

Until such management plans are in effect, the general public can do a great deal to dampen exploitation pressures by encouraging their governments to support strong coral conservation measures and by refusing to purchase certain corals and coral products. There currently are very few efforts to control international commerce in coral products sold to tourists because processed coral is difficult to recognize and because tourists buy and transport it in small amounts. The informed tourist, however, should ask merchants about the source of their products and should avoid those made from black coral and other often-depleted corals.

CHAPTER 25
Ornamental Fish

Aquarium fish are the most popular—or at least the most numerous—pets in the United States. Americans keep some 340 to 500 million fish, more than three times the number of dogs and cats combined, and tropical fish sales are on the upswing.[1]

Retail sales of live tropical fish are worth at least $215 million a year in the United States alone.[2] Some of the fish come from domestic fish farms, but most are imported—part of the growing international commerce in captive-bred and wild-collected aquarium species. The United States imports some 125 million ornamental fish per year, valued at between $25 and $30 million wholesale.[3]

West Germany, Japan, the Netherlands, and the United Kingdom also import large shares of the estimated 350 million ornamental fish that reach world markets each year.[4] The Japanese trade is probably the most varied of the lot; Japanese importers offer some 2,000 species to satisfy national demand for unusual—rather than simply colorful—specimens.[5] The total annual world market for aquarium fish, estimated at $600 million wholesale, reportedly is growing by 10 to 15 percent per year.[6]

Asian countries supply most of the freshwater aquarium fish on the market today. Singapore, a leading world center for breeding and trade of tropical aquarium fish, annually exports over 150 million guppies (Poeciliidae), mollies (Cyprinodontidae), swordtails (*Xiphophorus helleri*), tetras (*Hyphessobrycon* and other genera), and other popular species worth close to $40 million.[7] Indonesia, the Philippines, Sri Lanka, Taiwan, and Thailand are also important Asian sources. Most of the remaining shipments come from Latin America, particularly Brazil, Colombia, Jamaica, and Peru. A small portion of the world trade are African fish, coming mainly from the rivers and lakes of Burundi, Malawi, Nigeria, and Zaire.

Overall, the aquarium fish trade "is probably one of the most problem-free wildlife markets going," according to Ginette Hemley, director of TRAFFIC(U.S.A.). Hemley explains, "Most pet fish on the world market come from fish farms, so the trade generally poses little threat to wild populations. However, there are some key exceptions."[8] Studies of the fish trade in Japan, the United Kingdom, and the United States all point to the need for improved trade monitoring and CITES protection for certain vulnerable ornamental species still collected from the wild.

Only 17 fish species are listed under CITES. Most are food fish such as sturgeon (Acipenseridae) that are threatened by heavy fishing, habitat loss, and other dangers, but not by commercial trade for the aquarium market.

Trends in the Ornamental Fish Trade

As many as 95 percent of all pet fish come from fresh water rather than the ocean. Most of these freshwater pets—such as guppies, mollies, swordtails, platies (*Xiphophorus maculatus*), catfish (Callichthyidae), algae eaters (*Gyrinocheilus aymonieri*), angelfish (Chaetodontidae), and the ubiquitous goldfish (*Carassius auratus*)— are captive bred in the Far East. Japan, for instance, exports an average of two million captive-bred goldfish and koi carp (*Cyprinus* spp.) to the United States each year.[9]

But trade experts believe that certain wild freshwater fish are being overexploited for the pet-fish market. South American fish are of particular concern. For example, a 1984 study by TRAFFIC(Japan) noted that the wild-caught black arowana (*Osteoglossum ferreirai*) of Brazil, a primitive freshwater species discovered only in 1966, could be depleted by collectors. The Japanese import an estimated 3,000 specimens per year, which might represent a harvest of up to 30,000 fish since as many as 9 out of 10 die in holding tanks before export. The species reportedly is becoming more scarce in the wild, and TRAFFIC(Japan) advocates its listing on Appendix II.[10]

Popular pets such as butterfly fish (Chaetodontidae), angelfish, and damselfish (Pomacentridae) come from the wild, as do some less familiar marine fish in trade, such as the yellow-banded sweetlips (*Plectorhynchus albovittatus*), dash-and-dot goatfish, and striped catfish eel. In general, sea dwellers are very difficult to raise in captivity, although breeders are having increasing success with clown anemonefish (*Amphiprion percula*), neon gobies (*Elacatinus oceanops*), and pygmy sea horses (*Hippocampus zosterae*).

West Germany, Japan, the Netherlands, the United Kingdom, and the United States are major world markets for saltwater species. Popular demand for wild-caught marine fish is growing in many of these countries, principally because hobbyists are developing new ways to care for saltwater species. In the United States in 1986, approximately 10 percent of all retail tropical fish sales involved marine fish.[11]

Indonesia, the Philippines, Singapore, Sri Lanka, and other southeast Asian nations are key exporters of coral-reef fish and other marine ornamentals. Kenya is also an important supplier to fish fanciers in the United Kingdom.[12]

Few controls on the marine-fish trade exist today. Neither CITES nor European Economic Community trade regulations protects marine species, and only a handful of countries restrict their export. Several vulnerable species of butterfly fish, anemonefish (Pomacentridae), and angelfish may merit listing on Appendix II to determine whether they can withstand current market pressures.[13]

Illegal Trade

At least one rare tropical-fish species has produced smuggling problems. The only ornamental fish completely protected under CITES, the Appendix I-listed Asian bonytongue (*Scleropages formosus*), is readily available in Far Eastern black markets. Also called the golden dragon fish, the red arowana, or the emperor fish, this large-scaled, silvery pet is considered a source of good luck in Chinese cultures and a valuable collector's item in Japan, Hong Kong, and Singapore.

Most Asian bonytongues come from still, peat-stained inland waterways of Indonesia, Thailand, and Malaysia. Some also may come

Asian bonytongue (*Scleropages formosus*).
TRAFFIC(Japan)

from Taiwan. They are often shipped to Singapore for sale or reexport. In Singapore, one large specimen prized for its reddish coloring was advertised for over $8,000. Singapore officially banned Asian bony-tongue exports in 1983, but reports indicate that the fish are still smuggled out to markets in Japan, Hong Kong, and the United States.[14] Japan, the major consumer, takes in at least 1,000 Asian bonytongues a year.[15] A single fish in that country could command $3,450 in 1987, up from $700 in the early 1980s.[16] In June 1985, Japanese customs officials in Tokyo uncovered an illicit batch from Singapore tucked inside a shipment of brandy bottles.[17]

Smugglers also pass Asian bonytongues off as other species—such as the arowana (*Osteoglossum bicirrhosum*), an Amazonian native—or mislabel them as captive-bred. Actually, there are no known commercial-breeding operations. One Asian trader claimed, "Put two in the same tank, and they will kill each other."[18] Although some enthusiasts have been more successful in keeping individual fish together in a tank, the species as a whole has proved difficult to breed.

Some ichthyologists question whether the Asian bonytongue actually merits strict legal protection because its population status is little known. Others believe that it is threatened by swamp clearing and dredging in parts of its range, as well as by trade. The species is considered vulnerable by the International Union for Conservation of Nature and Natural Resources.

Other Problems in the Ornamental Fish Trade

According to Elizabeth Wood, a British marine biologist who has stud-ied the coral-reef fish trade in Sri Lanka and the United Kingdom, out of every 1,000 nonfood fish taken from the sea in Sri Lanka, only 850 lived long enough for export, 765 survived shipping, 727 were left to be sold, and then only 363 lived more than six months with their new owners.[19] The death rate for South American freshwater fish collected from the wild is equally perilous. Up to 50 percent may perish between capture and export, and another 10 to 40 percent more may not survive shipping.[20] Marine fish shipments from Hawaii appear to fare better, with one study showing that 42 percent of all fish captured in Hawaiian waters were still alive in their new aquarium homes six months later.[21]

In some areas, unscrupulous coral-reef fish collectors actually poison their catch. In the Philippines and parts of Indonesia and the Caribbean, fishers squirt sodium cyanide, and sometimes other toxic liquids such as chlorine bleach, into coral reef pockets where fish hide.[22] Temporarily narcotized, the fish are captured easily. Most fish later revive, but studies have shown that many sustain permanent

International Wildlife Trade: Whose Business Is It?

physiological damage and do not survive for long. Such toxic fishing practices also damage nontarget fish, invertebrates, and other reef dwellers.[23]

As many as 80 percent of fish once exported by the Philippines were captured using sodium cyanide, despite a longstanding national ban on its use.[24] The government of Philippine President Corazon Aquino has outlawed this practice, however, and launched an educational program and publicity campaign to deter fishermen from using the poison. President Aquino also changed fishing regulations to allow the use of fine-mesh monofilament nets as a substitute.[25] The International Marinelife Alliance, a private conservation organization, has been working with the Philippine government to train fishermen to use nets instead of cyanide.

Poor storing and shipping conditions also kill many marketable tropical fish. After capture, newly-netted fish may catch bacterial and fungal infections during their stay in holding tanks. Or they may die during exportation due to overcrowding, oxygen deprivation, abrupt water temperature changes, or rough handling. Freshwater fish exported from Southeast Asia generally fare better than those from South America and Africa, where shippers are less practiced in dealing with such fragile cargo. The Southeast Asian fish also fare better because they usually come from fish farms located near shipping routes, whereas South American and African ornamentals frequently are taken from rivers and streams in more remote regions and must suffer long and arduous travel before they leave the country.[26]

Butterfly fish (Chaetodontidae).

Ornamental Fish

Aquarium fish can also suffer high death rates because their owners do not take proper care of them. As the *Wall Street Journal* reported, a pet fish is often treated "like a bauble or a plant, and few people appear to care about its health." Unlike dogs, they are easily overfed, starved, suffocated, or otherwise accidentally killed.[27] A 1986 study of the U.S. tropical fish market discovered that one-quarter of all aquarium owners purchase their tanks for "room decoration,"[28] which may not bode well for their fragile pets.

Finally, some fish that have been taken from the wild die even in the care of experienced aquarists simply because they are not suited to captivity. For instance, Dr. Wood found that six Sri Lankan butterfly fish species regularly sold in the United Kingdom are virtually impossible to keep alive because they feed only on coral polyps. She also noted that another short-lived import, the cleaner wrasse, cannot last long once it cleans all parasites from other tank inhabitants.[29]

Thanks to the efforts of Dr. Wood, the International Marinelife Alliance, and the TRAFFIC network, threats to and abuses of wild fish destined for the aquarium trade are now coming to light. Further

---

KEEP IN MIND . . .

- If you are considering setting up your first aquarium, choose freshwater species to fill your tank. These are much easier to keep than marine (i.e., saltwater) species, and most of them are captive bred. Know what you are doing before attempting to keep marine fish.

- Buy responsibly. Ask the aquarium dealer where the fish originated. Be aware that marine fish harvested off the Philippines are often caught with cyanide. This destructive practice ruins the coral reefs and eventually kills the fish.

- Some suggested readings:

  Aquarium Fish magazine. Published bimonthly. Fancy Publications, 3 Burroughs, Irvine, CA 92718.

  Axelrod, Herbert R.; Burgess, Warren E.; and Emmens, Cliff W. *Exotic Marine Fishes.* 5th ed. Neptune City, N.J.: T.F.H., 1979.

  Axelrod, Herbert R., et al. *Exotic Tropical Fishes.* Neptune City, N.J.: T.F.H., n.d.

  Freshwater and Marine Aquarium magazine. Published monthly. R/C Modeler Corp., 144 W. Sierra Madre Blvd., Sierra Madre, CA 91024.

  Tropical Fish Hobbyist magazine. Published monthly. T.F.H. Publications, 1 T.F.H. Plaza, Neptune, NJ 07753.

investigation is needed, but in the meantime exporting countries can act to protect their resources from overexploitation and unnecessary health risks. President Aquino's effort to stop the use of sodium cyanide in the Philippines is an encouraging example of much-needed action. Equally important, the United States, Japan, and other wealthy consumer nations must do their share to curb stress and disease-related mortality and to halt trade in species ill-suited to aquarium life.

Ornamental Fish

CHAPTER 26
Frogs and Other Amphibians

Soaked in brandy, rolled in butter, or deep-fat fried, frog legs are popular in restaurants across Europe and the United States. Tasting much like chicken, the legs usually come from the Indian bullfrog (*Rana tigerina*), captured in the rice paddies and swamps of India, Bangladesh, and Indonesia. Every year, French traders import the legs from at least 100 million Asian frogs, many of which are then repackaged and sold in neighboring West Germany as "French frog legs." The United States imports the legs of some 50 million Asian frogs, the Dutch consume the legs of another 20 million, and the West Germans take in 12 million or so. The Swiss, Belgians, British, and Australians also eat their share, bringing total world imports to upwards of 200 million wild Asian frogs per year.[1]

People have long had a taste for frog legs, but rapid advances in shipping and meat-freezing technologies have contributed to a boom in Asian exports over the past two decades.

Studies of the ecological effects of this trade—which supports an annual Asian harvest of some 250 million wild bullfrogs—document several serious problems. Asian bullfrogs apparently are disappearing at an alarming rate in some collecting regions.[2] The lack of healthy frogs to feed on harmful insects is believed in turn to be causing local population surges among crop-eating pests and malarial mosquitoes.[3] In the early 1980s, mosquito-spread malaria epidemics took the lives of over 3,000 Indians.[4]

According to TRAFFIC(Germany) director Manfred Niekisch, an authority on the international frog legs trade, some of the frog-

Marsh frog (*Rana ridibunda*).
Weber & Hafner / WWF

harvesting countries compound their ecological problems by increasing their use of pesticides, rather than by reducing their harvest of frogs.[5] Bangladesh and India spend more on chemical pest controls than they earn from the frog harvest.[6] This reliance on pesticides can be costly and dangerous to nontarget species, including humans. Moreover, the dependence on DDT or other toxic substances may also drive consumers away from pesticide-ridden frog meat. In 1986, for example, the United States rejected several frog leg shipments from Indonesia out of concern that the meat would be contaminated.[7]

Niekisch indicates that frog leg shipments pose other health concerns as well. Australia has banned frog leg imports from Southeast Asia on several occasions due to the discovery of salmonella bacteria in incoming shipments. In Bangladesh, frog legs are now dipped in a chlorine solution before export, to avoid salmonella problems.[8]

Publicity over the demise of wild Asian frogs apparently has reduced demand for frog legs in some countries. For example, several of the most famous German restaurants have opted to stop serving the delicacy. Overall, the West German market for frog legs has dropped considerably in recent years.[9]

Trade Controls in the Frog Leg Market

In response to reports of diminishing wild frog populations and growing ecological problems, CITES parties listed the Indian bullfrog and another commonly traded Asian species, the six-fingered frog (*R. hexadactyla*), on Appendix II in 1985. These two species account for most of the world's frog leg exports.

Because frog legs can produce valuable returns, some developing countries are not interested in curbing the trade. President Suharto of Indonesia recently urged his country to expand its exports; in 1983, Indonesia's export of the legs of at least 70 million frogs netted over $8.7 million.[10]

Not all developing countries are so reluctant to limit frog exports, however. India, the exporter of legs from some 70 million frogs, and Bangladesh, the source for another 70 million per year in the early 1980s, have each banned frog collecting and export at various times.[11] In 1985, India established an export quota of 2,750 tons per year—equal to approximately 50 million frogs.[12] Following the first World Conference on Trade in Frog Legs in the mid-1980s, and the discovery of conclusive evidence that frogs are important in controlling malaria and agricultural scourges, Indian officials attempted to persuade the European Economic Community to ban imports of the culinary staple.[13] After these efforts failed, India banned the export of frog legs and outlawed commercial frog killing in March 1987.[14] Bangladesh and Indonesia are now the world's major sources of frog legs.

There are no international controls on trade in other frogs valued in the frog legs market, such as the Asian paddy frog (*R. limnocharis*), the American bullfrog (*R. catesbiana*), and the marsh frog (*R. ridibunda*) of central Europe.

Other Amphibian Markets

Most frogs and other amphibians listed on CITES appendices have never been popular in the international frog leg trade. Rather, they are considered threatened because they are naturally rare, because of habitat loss or alteration, because they are popular as food for people native to their habitat, or because of nonfood trade. All together, 14 amphibian species are listed on Appendix I, and 59 are on Appendix II.

Of the Appendix II amphibians, 51 species are the tiny—and toxic—jewels of the live amphibian trade, the Neotropical poison arrow frogs (family Dendrobatidae). So named because native Indians use their skin secretions to make poison arrows, these exotic frogs are increasingly popular with European and American frog keepers. Exports from South and Central America surged in the 1970s, with most going to the Netherlands and West Germany.[15] Little-known but easily recognized by their vibrant colors, which serve to warn potential predators of their unsavory skin, several of these frogs (*Dendrobates* and *Phyllobates spp.*) are legally protected by most Latin American countries.

In some cases, even a small amount of trade can be too much for an amphibious species. For example, the Appendix I giant salamanders (*Andrias spp.*) are naturally rare in their high-altitude habitats in China and Japan. Local food collecting and habitat alteration are major threats to their long-range survival, and the small amount of collecting that is done for export as pets exacerbates an already risky situation.[16]

Captive breeding promises to help save several endangered species of amphibians. For example, the tomato frog (*Dyscophus antongilii*), which occurs only in a few areas of northeastern Madagascar, is listed

---

KEEP IN MIND . . .

Products

■ Think twice before you indulge in that tasty frog leg dinner. Most of the frog legs we consume are imported, and in general the trade is unmanaged. Overharvesting in Bangladesh, for example, has resulted in increases in mosquitos, a frog's natural food, and in higher incidences of malaria and other insect-carried diseases.

Live

■ Don't waste wildlife. Refrain from buying or collecting an amphibian unless you are sure you know how to care for it properly. Gain experience in practical herpetology before buying an exotic pet.

■ Learn all you can about this trade. Join a herpetolgical society and study reptiles and amphibians. Three of these societies are the Society for the Study of Amphibians and Reptiles (Department of Zoology, Miami University, Oxford, OH 45056), which publishes the *Journal of Herpetology* and the *Herpetological Review*; the American Society of Ichthyologists and Herpetologists (Florida State Museum, University of Florida, Gainesville, FL 32611), which publishes *Copeia* as its quarterly journal; and the American Federation of Herpetoculturists (P.O. Box 1131, Lakeside, CA 92040), whose quarterly magazine is *Vivarium*.

■ Some suggested readings:

Cochran, Doris M. *Living Amphibians of the World*. Garden City, N.Y.: Doubleday, 1961.

Halliday, Tim, and Adler, Kraig. *The Encyclopedia of Reptiles and Amphibians*. New York: Facts on File, 1986.

Mattison, Chris. *Frogs and Toads of the World*. New York: Facts on File, 1987.

on Appendix I because of threats it faces from severe habitat alteration and destruction. This bright red, roundish frog has long been popular in international trade as a pet. Until recently, all tomato frogs in trade were caught in the wild, and large numbers were exported to Europe and the United States. Now, however, these frogs are captive bred in sufficient quantities to satisfy commercial demand (and captive bred tomato frogs are less expensive than wild-caught frogs).

As every student who has taken basic biology probably knows, live frogs continue to be in demand for dissection and other scientific uses, though the number of frogs involved is only a fraction of the number of frogs used in the frog leg market. The United States uses an estimated 9 million frogs per year for scientific activities, relying mainly on the leopard frog (*Rana pipiens*) and American bullfrog, neither of which is listed on CITES appendices.[17] Some come from captive-breeding operations or commercially managed ponds in the United States, Brazil, and parts of Asia,[18] but most are taken from the wild.

Amphibians are certain to play an increasing role in scientific research. Of particular importance in the future may be the African clawed toad (*Xenopus laevis*), long used in laboratories for pregnancy tests and dissection. This toad has been found to have a special antibiotic in its system that might assist medical research, especially on AIDS.[19]

Finally, trade experts have uncovered a new market for frogs and toads. Frogskin wallets, toad leather boots, and other exotic amphibian hide products are now showing up in international commerce. In 1985, the United States imported more than 11,000 frog and toad hides and products, worth some $350,000, for the fashion trade.[20] Most imported skins come from the large Malaysian species *R. macrodon*. Also killed for the skin trade are the black-spined toad (*Bufo melanosticus*), the American bullfrog, and the Asiatic painted frog (*Kaloula pulchra*).[21] None of these species is listed on CITES appendices.

CHAPTER 27
Spiders

S piders are regarded as one of the most frightening creatures that walk—or climb—on the earth today. With eight long and often hairy legs, an ability to hide in dark places, and a generally unjustified reputation for nipping human flesh, members of the Arachnid class tend to be very unpopular guests in modern households.

There is one notable exception, however. Members of the poisonous tarantula (Theraphosidae) family are in great demand among

Red-kneed tarantula (*Brachypelma smithi*).
N. Mark Collins

pet lovers in the United States and Europe. Prized for their unmistakable appearance and the surprisingly docile temperament of some species, tarantulas have been collected in the United States for over 50 years. In 1981 and 1982, the United States imported some 30,000 tarantulas from Mexico (*Brachypelma* and *Aphonopelma* spp.) and exported or reexported 31,000 to Japan, Canada, West Germany, and several other nations.[1]

In general, little is known about the total number of tarantulas in international commerce. Experts have determined that the most popular spider pet is probably the red-kneed tarantula (*Brachypelma smithi*). In 1985, CITES parties added this species to Appendix II to aid attempts to monitor trade volumes and help determine whether it could sustain commercial demand. It is the only spider listed under CITES, although several other tarantula species are traded internationally.

A large, bullfrog-sized spider noted for its attractive red-fringed head and legs, the red-kneed tarantula comes from western Mexico. Mexico's 1982 ban on all commercial exports of live wildlife included arachnids, but this ban is not always enforced and the tarantula trade continues. The species ranges in price from $12 per animal in the United States to $30 in the United Kingdom.[2]

Virtually all red-kneed tarantulas in trade come from the wild. Since the species appears to have naturally low reproductive success, losing as much as 98 percent of a typical hatching of 200 to 400 young, conservationists are concerned that uncontrolled collecting could endanger wild populations.[3]

PART VII
Plants

CHAPTER 28
Live Plants

No one knows for certain how many plant species exist on Earth, or how many may be discovered in the coming years. We do know, however, that wild plant species are disappearing at an alarming rate. An estimated 1 in 10 recorded species are now considered either rare or endangered. The most serious pressures come from industrial development, air and water pollution, farming and livestock grazing, and land clearing for timber production and firewood.[1]

The world market for wild plants to decorate gardens and houses, as well as trade among specialty collectors, adds to the peril of species that are both rare and difficult to cultivate. While there are no reliable estimates for global demand, it is safe to say that it is tremendous. The United States alone imported over 250 million garden and house plants in 1984, up from about 180 million plants in 1977 and fewer than 10 million plants in 1970.[2] U.S. imports of foreign bulbs has also shot upward, from 550 million in 1982 to 1 billion in 1987.[3] This enormous rise in plant and bulb imports probably was sparked by an economic boom and the increasing popularity of using diverse, attractive plants in and around the home.[4]

To guard against loss of wild stocks, some of the more popular horticultural plants, including all orchids (*Orchidaceae* spp.) and cacti (*Cactaceae* spp.), several aloes (*Aloe* spp.) and palms (*Palmae* spp.), many cycads (*Cycadaceae* spp.), and a few insectivorous plants (*Sarraceniaceae* and *Nepenthaceae* spp.) were listed under CITES in the 1970s and early 1980s. Many also are now afforded some protection by national or local laws. In the United States, for example, the Endangered Species Act implements CITES, prohibits collecting protected plants on federal lands, and requires a permit for interstate trade in propagated specimens of listed species; the Lacey Act prohibits international or interstate commerce in native wild plants taken in violation of state or federal endangered species law.* There are also numerous state laws protecting native species.

In the past decade, nursery owners, agricultural officials, botanical societies, conservation groups, and other plant enthusiasts have done a great deal to ensure that the majority of plants in commercial trade come from nonthreatened or artificially propagated stock. They have stepped up cultivation efforts, implemented somewhat stronger international and domestic controls on the rare plant market, encouraged self-policing within the trade, and educated consumers about the reasons to avoid purchasing rare species collected in the wild. As a result, less than 1 percent of the world cactus trade, a thriving multimillion-plant business annually, involves specimens taken from the wild.[5] As another example, the majority of U.S. horticultural dealers who sell rare, specialty succulents, such as some *Pachypodium* species of South Africa and Madagascar, reportedly now propagate their wares.[6]

Despite these advances, overcollecting and smuggling still plague the plant trade. Plants other than hallucinogenics often are given scant attention by border officials, and few CITES parties adequately enforce existing controls on plant commerce. Those that make an attempt face an extremely complex task: officials need to be able to identify a vast diversity of species (there are somewhere between 17,000 and 30,000 species in the orchid family alone), as well as plants from different sources that belong to the same species. Commercial trade in artificially propagated specimens of Appendix I species is allowed with proper documents, while trade in wild-collected plants is not. Plants taken from their habitat are sometimes given false propagation papers, and it can be very difficult to notice and verify the fraud. And, at the end of the line, there are still customers who, knowingly or not, purchase protected plants that would be far better off if left to reproduce in the wild.

Cacti and Other Succulents

Without doubt, most horticulturists frown on colleagues who dig cactus plants from the wild.[7] Propagated or nursery-raised cacti are more popular in the mass market, too, because they tend to be healthier—free of bug bites, sunburn, and other imperfections. Of

---

*The Lacey Act prohibits exportation of native wild plants taken in violation of state or federal law. It does not prohibit the import of plants taken contrary to foreign law, as it does with animals.

Field of propagated cacti in Arizona.
Linda McMahan / WWF

the 10 million or so cactus plants in world trade every year, over 99 percent are propagated, often by large-scale nursery operations in the Netherlands, Japan, Brazil, and the western United States. In the United States alone, cactus growers may produce as many as 50 million plants per year for domestic and foreign markets.[8]

That is the good news.

The bad news is that every year an estimated 30,000 cactus plants, including many rare species, are dug from the wild for trade to nurseries and private collections.[9] Many of these plants are protected species that are smuggled or transported blatantly in contravention of state, national, and international regulations. The strangest and least known species are frequent targets because they are often difficult to cultivate.

Cactus and succulent smugglers have been known to mislabel wild plant shipments as propagated specimens, pay off border officials, avoid checkpoints, and launder plants from one country to another with false documents.[10] In Japan, an unscrupulous importer allegedly wrapped a shipment of Appendix I specimens alongside particularly thorny propagated plants, effectively discouraging port authorities from inspecting the shipment by hand.[11] Enforcement agents also have a difficult time catching "cactus rustlers" because species are often hard to identify and agents lack the necessary references to recognize violations, plant laws are sometimes complicated or little known, and the volume of trade greatly outnumbers port inspectors.

Live Plants

CONTROLS ON TRADE

All cactus species are listed on either Appendix I or II of CITES. In addition, some countries to which cacti are native attempt to protect the plants with their own laws. In the United States, some endangered native cacti are protected by the U.S. Endangered Species Act and various state laws. Another major source of cacti, Mexico, while not a CITES party, apparently prohibits plant exportation without a collection and propagation permit, which may be given only to exporters with adequate propagation facilities.[12] However, there is only one major commercial cactus breeding operation in the country— a German-owned facility that specializes in endemic endangered species—and trade controls, which are complicated by confusion over the proper permit-issuing authorities, are often unenforced.[13]

MAJOR CACTUS SUPPLIERS

Nearly all of the world's 2,000 or so cactus species are native to the Western Hemisphere, so it is not surprising that the major world suppliers of wild cacti are all in the Americas.* In addition to the United States, Mexico, and Chile, major cactus exporters include Brazil and Peru. All five countries seem to have some problems with illegal collecting and exporting of the plants.

Brazil reportedly ships mostly propagated plants, though some wild-collected plants do enter trade. In 1985, Dutch officials seized an illegal shipment of Brazilian cacti (*Discocactus* and *Melocactus* spp.) marked as artificially propagated that were actually taken from the wild.

Likewise, Peru, home to "Old Man of the Andes" (*Oreocereus* spp.) and other popular cacti, cultivates much of its cacti in trade. Nonetheless, some specimens taken from the wild have turned up. In one December 1985 incident, CITES authorities in the Netherlands confiscated over 4,000 wild cactus plants exported from Peru with papers for propagated specimens. Over 300 of the plants were actually collected in Chile and laundered via Lima.[15] Chile is well known as a source of illicit cacti; according to a leading Chilean cactus specialist, overcollection has led to the extinction of some of the country's 180 endemic species in recent years.[16]

Mexico has been one of the most troublesome source countries in world cactus trade, although reports suggest that improved enforcement of border controls and the increase in artificial propagation of cacti have cut down on illegal trade between the United States and Mexico.[17] Mexico is home to a substantial portion of the world's most

---

Several species of one cactus genus, Rhipsalis, *are believed to be native to southern Africa, Madagascar, and Sri Lanka.*[14]

unusual cacti. Unfortunately, approximately 200 of Mexico's 600 endemic cactus species are either threatened or their status in the wild is unknown.[18] Mexico supplied at least 800,000 cacti to the United States alone between 1980 and 1984, and virtually all of this trade came from wild rather than propagated stock.[19] Conservationists remain especially concerned about Mexico's heavy trade in vulnerable species of living rock cactus (genus *Ariocarpus*), which resembles surrounding rocks; these cacti grow slowly and don't have the shoots needed for propagation. Another cactus of concern in Mexico is the glory-of-Texas species (*Thelocactus* spp.).[20]

Edward Anderson, a biologist who has been studying Mexican cacti for 30 years, and a team of Mexican botanists in 1986 completed an investigation of some 20 endangered or threatened species in that country. Their conclusion: collecting is a particularly serious threat to the survival of some of the most rare and interesting cacti in Mexico. Anderson and his colleagues visited the only known site of *Neolloydia viereckii*, a spot where Anderson had recorded numerous plants in 1972, and could not find a single specimen. Anderson also reported "one of our most sobering experiences concerned the beautiful pine cone cactus (*Pelecyphora [Encephalocarpus] strobiliformis*). I visited the locality of this species in 1961 and found literally thousands of individuals. . . . On this recent trip we were unable to find a single plant of that species. Local inhabitants said that collectors had removed them." Anderson found that all accessible locations for

These Mexican living rock (*Ariocarpus trigonus*) and Aztec (*Aztekium ritteri*) cacti were among 200 rare cacti seized by U.S. and state agents in coordinated raids in southern California in 1986.
Linda McMahan / WWF

Live Plants

Beds of wild-collected living rock cacti (*Ariocarpus retusus* and *A. fissuratus*) for sale in a south Texas nursery.
Doug Fuller

another rare species, *Thelocactus conothelos* var. *aurantiacus*, had been picked clean, and uprooted plants of the highly threatened hatchet cactus (*Pelecyphora aselliformis*) and *Mammillaria aureilanata* species had been carelessly left lying on the ground.[21] In an innovative effort to combat losses caused by illegal trade, Universidad Autonomo of Tamaulipas, in Ciudad Victoria, Mexico, collects and breeds Sonoran Desert cacti confiscated by border patrols. The university employs local people who once collected rare specimens for sale to collectors.[22]

The United States exports between 150,000 and 200,000 wild and propagated cacti each year. Until recently, this may have included as many as 10,000 plants smuggled into the country from Mexico. According to Faith Campbell, director of the Plant Conservation Program at the Natural Resources Defense Council (NRDC), the United States has made substantial progress in stopping high-volume illegal trade in protected cacti. However, Campbell cautions that a serious problem still exists with continuing instances of commerce in very rare Mexican species that should not be collected commercially at all.[23]

A few countries that are not home to wild cacti have developed positive reputations for their work in propagating and then exporting the plants. An innovator in cactus-grafting and tissue-culture techniques, Japan is an important world supplier of propagated cacti. The Netherlands also exports large volumes of nursery-produced cacti.[24] Other countries that propagate cacti for export include Taiwan and several in Europe.

MAJOR CACTUS IMPORTERS

The United States, Japan, West Germany, the Netherlands, and Belgium are the world's major cacti markets. The United States now imports about 1 to 2 million plants a year, worth at least $1 million.[25] This total represents a steady decline from a peak of 7 million in 1977; rising energy and transportation costs, CITES protection of cacti, and the growth of domestic supplies of propagated plants have all combined to produce this significant reduction.[26]

Japan imported approximately 20,000 cacti in 1984, primarily from the United States, the Netherlands, Taiwan, and Mexico. The trade apparently has declined from over 150,000 plants in 1981, probably in response to U.S. action to curtail laundering of endangered species collected in Mexico, exported to the United States, and then reexported to Japan. While many of Japan's imports from the Netherlands and other European sources are propagated plants, some of the Dutch shipments are known to include Appendix I species taken from the wild in Mexico and South America. Japanese prices for cacti collected from the wild are among the highest in the world, and the Japanese market for such Appendix I and II species reportedly continues to thrive, stimulated by growing demand for the most bizarre and unusually shaped plants.[27] An in-depth study of Japanese cactus imports by TRAFFIC(Japan) discovered a "persistent and substantial trade in violation of CITES." Most alarming was the number of slow-growing, rare Mexican endemic species on sale in

Figure 28.1
U.S. Imports, Exports, and Reexports of
Wild Cacti, 1980–1987

	Imports	Exports	Reexports
1980	588,669	0	33,087
1981	204,730	6	17,531
1982	198,802	16	15,063
1983	839,099	0	18,600
1984	874,780	0	10,643
1985	1,022,545	2,685	2,681
1986	932,214	230	68
1987	1,033,148	318	44

*Includes cacti categorized as wild or as of unreported origin.

Source: U.S. CITES annual reports.

Live Plants

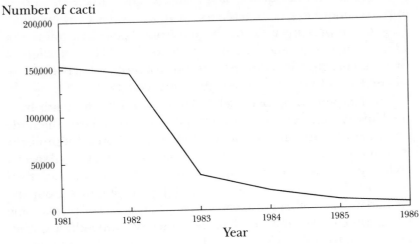

Figure 28.2
Japanese Cactus Imports, 1981–1986

Source: Fuller and Fitzgerald.

Japan, including living rock cactus, hatchet and pine cone cactus, turbinicarpus cactus (genus *Turbinicarpus*), Aztec cactus (*Aztekium ritteri*), and disk cactus (*Strombocactus disciformis*).[28]

In Europe, the cactus trade is fueled in large part by propagated plants from nurseries in Denmark, Spain, and other European countries. According to Steven Brack, a leading U.S. cactus grower, most cactus seed used by nursery owners around the world comes from France and Spain. However, there is still a significant European market for wild-collected plants, including endangered Appendix I species sold by several specialist nurseries in Belgium, the Netherlands, and West Germany. After surveying European nurseries in 1985, Sara Oldfield, a botanical consultant for the Wildlife Trade Monitoring Unit, reported that "there is no doubt that large quantities of Chilean and Brazilian cacti have entered [West] Germany and the Netherlands unrecorded." Oldfield's study also revealed that Appendix I cacti from Mexico often were imported into Europe by way of the United States. She concluded that, while nursery owners were generally interested in promoting effective trade controls to help protect wild cacti, several offenders "appear to operate completely outside conservation controls and cause a disproportionate amount of damage to wild populations."[29]

ENFORCING TRADE CONTROLS

Cactus trade violations are a continuing concern in the United States. In one 1985 incident, 2,500 of the Appendix I teddy bear cactus

(*Backebergia militaris*) entered the United States from Mexico via the Brownsville, Texas, port. Shortly thereafter, two-foot-tall specimens of this cactus, looking suspiciously like Mexican imports, began to appear in American nurseries, priced at $87 each.[30] A 1985 study of the U.S. trade by botanist Douglas Fuller found at least one dozen nursery catalogues advertising Appendix I species such as agave cactus (*Leuchtenbergia principis*), hatchet cactus, and artichoke cactus (*Obregonia denegrii*).[31]

U.S. law enforcement officers are making some progress in stamping out international cactus "rustling." In a landmark plant case, one U.S. nursery owner pleaded guilty and was fined $4,000 for shipping 25 plants of Appendix I- and II-listed cacti to the United Kingdom without the proper permits. In 1986, U.S. Fish and Wildlife Service (FWS) undercover agents in California seized 200 rare cacti and charged nine U.S. collectors and traders with smuggling the plants across the border from Mexico. According to the FWS, the contraband included several highly endangered species, such as Aztec cactus, a species of living rock cactus (*Ariocarpus agavoides*), and artichoke cactus, all on Appendix I.[32] In a plea-bargaining agreement, six of the defendants pleaded guilty to reduced charges; they were fined $1,000 to $3,000 each and placed on probation. Charges against the other three were dismissed.[33]

In Japan, CITES enforcement has been extremely lax, and the market for rare wild cacti is thriving. Appendix I species are advertised frequently by horticulturists, and cactus enthusiasts in the country reportedly pay hefty sums for protected plants—for example, $400 for a large, fasciated artichoke cactus and $650 for a disk cactus, both collected from the wild.[34]

At the urging of TRAFFIC(Japan), Japanese customs authorities stepped up efforts in 1986 to enforce CITES trade controls for cacti. The week after the trade-monitoring group held a press conference highlighting cactus import problems, customs agents stopped two incoming shipments with suspicious origins, one apparently from Mexico that arrived without export permits and another from the United States.[35] The shipments were later released, however.

Some plant conservationists are particularly alarmed about the lack of plant law enforcement in West Germany. The NRDC's Campbell has singled out that country as a major center of the trade in wild-dug cacti. In addition to serving domestic markets, several West German traders are known to ship such cacti and other succulents to the United States using improper propagation certificates.[36]

After compiling evidence from Oldfield and others' investigations of European trade, Campbell determined that there is also cause for concern over the sale of wild-collected cacti in Belgium, Austria, and, at least in the 1980s, the Netherlands.[37] TRAFFIC(Japan) reports that Appendix I and II specimens of wild-collected cacti have been shipped to Japan from the Netherlands, accompanied by certificates saying they were propagated artificially.[38] In 1985, Swiss officials seized a cactus shipment from the Netherlands because nearly half of the 22 plants appeared to be wild-collected, in spite of an accompanying propagation certificate.[39]

OTHER SUCCULENTS IN TRADE

The cacti are the best-known family of succulent plants (that is, plants that store water in their leaves, stems, and roots). However, several other succulents are threatened by international trade and are listed on CITES appendices, including the euphorbias (*Euphorbia spp.*), aloes, several agaves (*Agave* spp.), and ghost men (*Pachypodium* spp.) of southern Africa and Madagascar. Often less well-studied than their cactus relatives, these plant groups are likely to be a major focus of conservation attention in the coming years. Some evidence indicates that several groups featured in the specialty trade, particularly the ghost men and euphorbias, are becoming more popular than cacti.[40]

Although the International Organization for Plant Succulent Study and other floral societies discourage members from buying succulent plants taken from the wild, Appendix I and II succulents reach commercial markets every year. Those found in European nurseries

Wild aloe (*Aloe ukambensis*) in Kenya.
Peter Hill

Right—star cactus (*Astrophytum asterias*).
Linda R. McMahan

often come from Madagascar, home to a rich diversity of rare and unusual succulent species.[41] While these plants are commonly reported as being artificially propagated, there is reason to believe most come from the wild.

According to Oldfield, France is the main entry point for Madagascan succulents destined for European markets. South Africa also has been a major source for wild-collected succulents destined for European, U.S., and Japanese markets. Most of these plants are not listed on CITES appendices, but some are rare and may deserve listing in the future.[42] Today, very few South African and Madagascan succulents are imported into the United States, as U.S. trade sanctions imposed against South Africa in 1986 cut off that supply line and importers have had difficulty finding reputable dealers to ship stock from Madagascar.[43]

Overzealous collectors have snapped up some of the rarest wild succulents. The endangered spiral aloe (*Aloe polyphylla*), popular in some collecting circles, is reportedly down to only 2,500 to 3,500 plants in a few South African sites. Nearly one third of these sites were ravaged recently by collectors. Once believed extinct, over 450 of the newly rediscovered *Euphorbia turbiniformis* of eastern Africa also have been crated off to the United States. Similarly, by 1981, *E. abdelkuri* had declined to only four known wild plants, thanks to commercial "plant-nappers."[44] Fortunately, the species is widely propagated by commercial growers in the United States and other countries.[45]

Orchids

When the wife of Indonesian president Suharto was looking for the perfect gift for her U.S. counterpart, she chose 100 orchid plants named after the former first lady, "Dendrobium Nancy Reagan," worth some $3,500. King Hassan II of Morocco, too, showered Mrs. Reagan with orchids in 1986.[46]

There is a tremendous world market for Orchidaceae, one of the largest families of plants in the world. In 1985, international commerce in wild and artificially propagated members of this diverse and delicate family surpassed 3 million plants. At least one half million of these plants came from the wild, rather than cultivated stock. The United States accounted for some 690,000 orchid imports, roughly half of which were wild plants.[47] The Netherlands supplies nearly one-quarter of the U.S. trade, but Thailand, India, Japan, Brazil, Guatemala, and Honduras are also important sources.[48]*

Recent data show a dramatic increase in imports from several countries, Taiwan in particular. Taiwanese exports to the United States, which totaled only 670 orchids in 1985, exploded to 91,144 in 1986 and 89,024 in 1987.

Virgin orchid (*Diacrium bicornutum*).
Linda R. McMahan

Some orchids are particularly expensive. A single wild *Paphiopedilum rothschildinum* orchid from Borneo can fetch $1,000 in the United States. Perhaps the most expensive wild orchid is *P. sanderinum of Malaysia*, a lady's slipper orchid that sells for $1,500.[49] Top prices and some orchid lovers' thirst for rarer and more exotic plants encourage unscrupulous collectors to uproot endangered species. One rare Chinese orchid, found only on a single knoll in Yunnan Province, *P. armeniacum*, was first discovered in 1982 but could be purchased from nursery owners in California, the United Kingdom, Japan, and Taiwan by 1983. The plant is no longer sold in the United Kingdom but as recently as the mid-1980s was offered for sale in the United States.[50]

This is not a new phenomenon. As Anthony Huxley documented in his book on the world's plant diversity, *Green Inheritance*, a century ago swarms of collectors descended on the Himalayan foothills of India to make off with the lovely blue vanda orchid (*Vanda coerulea*) for shipment home. Sir Joseph Hooker, one of the world's most noted botanists at the time, collected "seven man loads" of what he termed "the rarest and most beautiful of Indian orchids" and sent them to England, recommending that others do the same to clear handsome profits for their efforts. Huxley noted that few of the prized plants remain in the region today.[51]

Trade in specimens of endangered and rare orchid species collected in the wild continues to concern plant conservationists. All orchids are given some protection under CITES, with certain species listed on Appendix I and the remainder on Appendix II. However, as is the case with all plants, these trade controls have proved difficult to enforce and trade officials traditionally have given them little, if any, attention. Enforcement is especially problematic because orchids

Figure 28.3
Recorded International Trade in Orchids,*
1976–1985

	Number in thousands				
Year	World imports (excl. U.S.)	World exports (excl. U.S.)	U.S. imports	U.S. exports	Minimum total trade**
1976	11	1	0	0	11
1977	129	1	n.d. +	2	131
1978	63	4	n.d.	3	66
1979	398	59	71	31	500
1980	3	146	144	36	326
1981	570	332	208	116	894
1982	426	604	257	160	1,021
1983	1,713	821	320	347	2,380
1984	1,125	1,779	395	299	2,473
1985	1,687	1,445	690	968	3,345

*Based in CITES annual reports.
**Estimated by adding the higher of world imports or world exports plus U.S. imports and U.S. exports. Actual total trade is undoubtedly higher.
+ No data available.

Source: McMahan and Walker.

Figure 28.4
Major Exporting and Importing Countries of Orchid Plants,
Listed in Estimated Percentage of Total Trade*

Exporting		Importing	
Country	Estimated percent	Country	Estimated percent
United States	31	Japan	60
Thailand	28	United States	17
Netherlands	21**	Taiwan	5
Taiwan	5	French Polynesia	5
Denmark	4	Korea	5 +
China	3	Netherlands	4
Japan	2	Denmark	4 +

*Estimated based on analysis of shipments of over 1,000 plants. Shipments of this size accounted for 88 percent of world imports (excluding U.S.), 92 percent of world exports (excluding U.S.), 73 percent of U.S. imports, and 80 percent of U.S. exports.
**Although the Netherlands was reported as the exporting country by many importing countries, the Netherlands itself did not record a high number of imports. Based on export figures, the Netherlands is estimated to rank just below the United States and Thailand.
+ Both Denmark and Korea were recorded as the destination by exporting countries to a much higher degree than either recorded receiving orchid plants. Based on export figures, Denmark and Korea's imports are estimated to be roughly 4 and 5 percent of the trade, respectively.

Source: McMahan and Walker.

Live Plants

rarely are traded while in flower, essentially the only time when differing species can be identified.

Further complicating efforts to uphold plant trade laws are the ways that wild-collected specimens of protected species frequently are treated differently from artificially propagated specimens and the difficulty that enforcement officials can have in telling plants from the two sources apart. CITES allows commercial trade in artificially propagated specimens of Appendix I plants but prohibits such trade if the specimens come from the wild. Enforcement becomes complicated when smugglers give falsified propagation papers to plants taken from the wild. TRAFFIC(U.S.A.) estimated that some 10,000 wild orchids were smuggled out of the United States this way in 1981. Wild orchids reportedly are also smuggled out of India and other countries in this manner.[52]

Illicit trade in orchids collected from the wild is also a problem in Japan, where the market for subtropical Chinese endemics belonging to the genus *Paphiopedilum* is particularly strong. Tom Milliken, director of TRAFFIC(Japan), reports that many wild-collected orchids are smuggled into Japan by way of Hong Kong. Japanese orchid merchants have offered specimens from certain *Paphiopedilum* species that are known to occur only at two sites, both within a national park in the Malaysian state of Sabah, on Borneo.[53]

U.S. officials are beginning to crack down on orchid thieves. In 1985, a U.S. federal court convicted a Michigan couple of smuggling over 2,800 protected lady's slipper orchids (genus *Cypripedium*) across state lines, in contravention of the Lacey Act. Over the years, the couple had supplied at least 50,000 wild orchids to nurseries.[54]

Plant conservationists strongly recommend that orchid enthusiasts purchase only propagated specimens. They also advocate self-policing among nursery owners, florists, and others involved in the commercial orchid trade. While these measures cannot be a substitute for government trade controls, they will help limit demand for rare and endangered species.

Bulb Plants

The world bulb trade is the latest commercial plant market area hit by smuggling scandals. In 1986, for instance, U.K. officials fined a plant dealer $2,615 for smuggling over 1,000 cyclamen bulbs and orchid pseudobulbs from Czechoslovakia, Greece, and Japan.[55] This only hints at the extent of the problem. According to one expert, the United States receives many cyclamen bulbs marked as "nursery-grown from the Netherlands" that actually come from wild hillsides in Turkey and Greece but are shipped to the Netherlands for reexport.[56]

A NOTE TO GARDENERS
Many Popular Garden Bulbs May Be
Overcollected from the Wild

American gardeners plant over one *billion* bulbs each year, yet few flower enthusiasts are aware that their gardens may contain wild-collected species that are threatened by trade.

TRAFFIC(U.S.A.), World Wildlife Fund's trade-monitoring arm, together with the Wildlife Trade Monitoring Unit (WTMU), the Natural Resources Defense Council (NRDC), and the Garden Club of America, has launched a study to determine which species are threatened by collection in the wild and the extent to which they are artificially propagated.

Early results show that many popular bulb species may be in trouble because of overcollecting. Gardeners should be aware that bulbs labeled "wild," 'species," or "botanical" and many of the small, early-blooming types *may have been collected* from the wild in Central Asia, South Africa, Portugal, Turkey, or even the United States. While some species are artificially propagated to some extent (particularly in the Netherlands, the world's largest supplier of bulbs), wild-collected bulbs of some species are usually easier and cheaper to obtain.

To avoid buying wild-collected plants, please follow the guidelines below, compiled by Faith Campbell of the NRDC, whose plant trade work is funded by WWF:

Some species are propagated to a limited extent, so it is important to inquire about the origins of the following bulb species. Ask if they were propagated *in the retailer's nursery*, or if the retailer *knows* that the supplier propagated them. Assurances that bulbs were obtained from "commercial sources" or are "nursery-grown" are not adequate: they may still have been collected from the wild.

Try to avoid purchasing the following species:

Amaryllis Family
Galanthus. Avoid *G. elwesii* (always of wild origin).
Leucojum, particularly *L. vernum*. Avoid *L. aestivum*.
Narcissus. Avoid *N. triandrus albus N. bulbocodium conspicuous*. Exercise caution with other small species.
Sternbergia species.

Lily Family
Chionodoxa, especially *C. sardensis*, *C. tmoli*, and *C. lucillae*.
Colchicum species.
Erythronium, except "Pagoda," which is a propagated hybrid.
Fritillaria. Use caution when buying *F. persica* "Adiyamen" and *F. imperialis*. Avoid other species.
Lilium. Many species are propagated, but exercise caution when buying *L. martagon*.

> *Scilla* species. Grows readily in cultivation, but large numbers are still exported from Turkey. Exercise some caution.
> *Trillium*, especially *T. grandiflorum*.
> *Tulipa*. Species that do not offset easily probably come from the wild, particularly *T. hageri, T. praecox*, and *T. pulchella humilis*.
>
> ### Orchid Family
> *Blettia striata*.
> *Pleione* species.
> *Cypripedium*, especially *C. acaule*.
>
> ### Primrose Family
> *Cyclamen*, except from specialized nurseries, which propagate their stock. The rare *C. mirabile* may be exported from Turkey as *C. purpurascens* or *C. europeanum*.
>
> ### Rannunculaceae
> *Anemone*. Blue or mixed stocks of *A. blanda* may be from the wild.
> *Eranthis*, particularly *E. hyemalis* and *E. cilicia*.
>
> *Reprinted from* Focus, *the membership newsletter of World Wildlife Fund, March/April 1989, p. 5. Copyright 1989.*

The bulb-collecting threat is not new. Early in the 20th century, overzealous bulb merchants operating in northern Spain and Portugal purchased large quantities of daffodil bulbs from local collectors, prompting the loss of entire wild populations of *Narcissus moschatus* and other narcissi. Largely as a result, *N. moschatus* may no longer occur in the wild.[57]

Most of the more than 1 billion bulbs imported annually by gardeners in the United States today are tulips, daffodils, hyacinths, and narcissi. Since these bulbs are usually propagated from seed or offsets, often in the Netherlands, they generally do not present problems. The major threats to wild populations arise from world trade in "minor bulbs" favored by collectors, rock gardeners, and others interested in planting unusual wildflowers for dramatic effect. The species of greatest concern in trade include the large-flowered snowdrop (*Galanthus elwesii*) and other snowdrops (*Galanthus* spp.). Also of concern are *Cyclamen mirabile* and other cyclamen, winter aconite (*Eranthis hyemalis*), certain grape hyacinths (*Muscari* spp.), several *Crocus* species, giant summer snowflake (*Leucojum aestivum*), several species of *Sternbergia, Anemone blanda*, and Madonna lily (*Lilium candidum*).[58]

The places where these species are collected from the wild include Italy, Turkey, Spain, South Africa, Central Asia, and even the United

States. The NRDC has alerted U.S. gardeners to the problem of collecting for the bulb trade. "Unless properly regulated, this collecting can force these species to the brink of extinction," the organization warned.[59]

Plant trade experts report that the volume of collecting in Turkey, for example, threatens some of that country's wild flowering cyclamen species, such as the rare, endemic *Cyclamen mirabile*. In 1983, Turkey exported 5 million cyclamen tubers, nearly half of which went to the Netherlands. Other major destinations for Turkish cyclamen exports include Bulgaria, West Germany, and the United Kingdom.[60] The United States is an important market for Turkish cyclamen bulbs reexported from the Netherlands; over 100,000 bulbs were imported through that trade route in 1986.[61]

In 1983, Turkey banned the export of five endemic cyclamen species, including *C. mirabile*, but enforcement of the ban is poor, at best. Botanist Sara Oldfield believes that rare Turkish bulbs often are mistakenly collected and shipped as more common species. In one mix-up, Oldfield says, U.K. customs officials confiscated 50,000 mislabeled Turkish bulbs, all of which turned out to be the rare *C. mirabile*.[62]

Former TRAFFIC(Netherlands) director Minouk van der Plas-Haarsma, who has investigated the Turkish bulb trade, found official reports indicated Turkey exported 600,000 *C. purpurascens* bulbs in 1984. But, because the species does not occur in Turkey, she strongly suspects that many of the exports were actually *C. mirabile*.[63]

All cyclamen species are on Appendix II, which means their trade should be monitored carefully and should comply with CITES permit requirements. Turkey, however, is not a party to the convention, and CITES enforcement for bulbs and tubers in many importing countries is light.[64] To clear up illegal trade problems, the European Economic Community (EEC) halted commercial imports of Turkish cyclamens in late 1985 and then replaced the ban with a combined import quota of 1 million bulbs for all EEC members the following year. The Netherlands exceeded the agreed-upon quota in 1986, importing 1.6 million. In 1989, the EEC quota stands at 1.5 million bulbs. Dr. van der Plas-Haarsma recommends that CITES parties outside the EEC abide by the community's tuber import quota so that the Turkish trade does not simply shift to avoid EEC strictures.[65]

Other Turkish wildflowers also are threatened by the bulb trade. Nonetheless, Turkey continues to export up to 35 million of the plants each year. Trade bans have also been recommended to protect wild populations of other Turkish species, including *Allium roseum*, crown imperial (*Fritillaria imperialis*), *F. persica*, the Madonna lily, certain restricted species of *Muscari*, the sea daffodil (*Pancratium maritimum*), all six native species of *Sternbergia*, and *Tulipa humilis*.[66]

Aside from the Turkish problem, experts are concerned about the large number of *Narcissus* and other wild-collected bulbs exported from Spain and Portugal. There is little hard information available about this high-volume trade, however.

In some instances, illegal trade occurs because the parties involved are unaware of legal protections or the rarity of what they are deal-ing with. In 1984 a group of Italian monks sold some 75,000 bulbs of *Cyclamen neapolitanum*, an Appendix II species, taken from their woodlands for export to the Netherlands. Not knowing CITES require-ments, the monks sold the bulbs to a Dutch importer for less than half a cent apiece. The Italian Scientific Authority was informed of the transaction and stopped further exports, and the Italian minis-ter of agriculture requested limits on bulb collection in the area. Unfortunately, the plants' habitat had already been ruined.[67] Italy banned all cyclamen exports in 1985.

Cycads

Cycads—hardy, palmlike plants belonging to the Cycadeles order—were in their heyday some 150 to 200 million years ago, dominating the plant kingdom in the days of the brontosaurus and tyrannosaurus rex. Unlike the dinosaurs, a few cycads managed to survive the ensuing climatic turbulence. They persevered in mild, tropical regions at the same time as flowering plants began to take over much of the earth.[68]

Wild cycad (*Encephalartos barteri* spp. *allochrous*) in Nigeria.
Coll. L. E. Newtonizoa

In the past century, humans have eradicated many wild cycads. Florida resort builders, Mexican ranchers, Australian farmers, and other landowners have dug up or plowed over them. Cycad leaves are poisonous to livestock, so ranchers have gone after them with a particular vengeance. As cycads have become popular "status plants," collectors, too, have decimated whole populations in Africa, Asia, and Central America. In 1983, plant traders snapped up one of only two known populations of *Ceratozamia norstogii* from Chiapas in Mexico.[69]

Today, cycads are considered one of the most threatened plant groups in the world. At least half of the members of the order are facing extinction.[70] The genera *Ceratozamia* and *Encephalartos* are on Appendix I, along with the species *Microcycas calocoma*, fern-leaved cycad (*Stangeria eriopus*), and beddome cycad (*Cycas beddonci*). All other cycads are on Appendix II. South Africa, Zimbabwe, and Australia have tough laws to protect their native populations, but Mexico, the Dominican Republic, Thailand, Malaysia, and other countries with native cycad populations either lack such laws or fail to enforce them. In Mexico, particularly, experts believe that trade pressures tip the balance toward extinction for wild cycads.

The United States, Europe, Japan, and South Africa are major cycad importers. Some of the cycad supply comes from nursery or botanical garden stock, not from the wild. South Africa and Japan export most of the world's artificially propagated or seed-grown cycads. Mexico, the Dominican Republic, Australia, Thailand, and Malaysia are major exporters of wild cycads.[71]

Cycads grow only an inch or so a year, and mature plants can sell for $475 per yard. As a result, opportunistic commercial traders find it much cheaper to take plants from the wild rather than grow their own.[72] In addition, many of the rarest and most sought-after species are found only in the wild—where they may be stolen by cycad aficionados who are unwilling to wait for propagated specimens to become available.

Cycad thieves often go to great lengths for their prey. One wily collector, masquerading as a "Dr. Jacobs," toured South Africa picking up plants from local people who believed he would use the specimens to make an anticancer drug. Plant robbers sneaked into the Durban Botanical Garden in Durban, South Africa, and made off with one of the last surviving bread palm cycads (*Encephalartos woodii*), even though the base of the plant had been embedded in concrete. On a single Latin American escapade, one American collector singlehandedly eliminated nearly an entire wild population of *Zamiav pseudoparasitica*.[73]

Cycad theft and illicit trade are persistent problems in South Africa.

According to *Encephalartos*, the journal of the Cycad Society of South Africa, private gardens and botanical collections, including the internationally recognized Durban Botanical Gardens, suffered frequent losses to cycad robbers in 1986. The journal also reported that cycad smuggling could decimate the Natal province cycad population in the next few years. South Africa outlaws possession of cycads without permits, and illegal possession can bring fines of up to $858 or 2,000 days in jail. Black marketeers face additional penalties of $1,286 or 12 months in prison for trade offenses. Strengthened by new cycad legislation, South African authorities reportedly are cracking down on known illegal trade routes for the highly endangered plants.[74]

One country whose trade in wild cycads especially concerns conservationists is Mexico, where demand for the plants has been fueled by high prices for rare species in U.S. markets. The *Ceratozamia* genus, notably bamboo cycad (*C. hildae*) and *C. norstogii*, are especially at risk.[75] Mexico reportedly prohibits commercial plant collection, but the law is seldom enforced. To help protect *Ceratozamia*, CITES parties listed the entire genus on Appendix I in 1985. Nevertheless, the United States imported a large number of *Ceratozamia* that year, with the majority arriving *after* the genus was placed on Appendix I.[76]

Carnivorous Plants

With spiked "jaws" or deep, nectarous, and inviting leaf pools, carnivorous plants lure and capture all manner of live insects and aquatic invertebrates. They are also known to digest small amphibians and even birds. This unusual fare allows them to survive in mineral-poor habitats, such as bogs and swamps.[77]

Two carnivorous plants are particularly popular in the plant trade: the brightly colored pitcher plants (*Sarracenia* spp. and *Nepenthes* spp.), which ensnare prey in their long sticky spouts, and the Venus's flytrap (*Dionaea muscicapula*), which clamps shut its spiny leaves on passing insects. Several of the pitcher plants are depleted by trade, particularly the green pitcher plant (*Sarracenia oreophila*), the mountain sweet pitcher plant (*S. jonesii*), and the giant pitcher plant (*Nepenthes rajah*).[78] The Venus's flytrap, on the other hand, seems to be holding its own despite sales of 1 to 4 million plants a year, a large percentage of which are taken from the wild.[79]

The green pitcher plant, found only in Alabama and Georgia, is on Appendix I and is listed as endangered under the U.S. Endangered Species Act. (This law prohibits the import, export, interstate sale, or taking of listed plants on federal land but does not protect those growing on private land.) FWS and state officials may be able to

Green pitcher plant (*Sarracenia oreophilia*).
Don Schnell / OES

identify propagated sources for people wanting their own green pitcher plants.[80] Another U.S. species listed on Appendix I, the mountain sweet pitcher plant, also is dwindling due to private and commercial collection. All other North American pitcher plants were listed on Appendix II in 1987.

Smugglers in Borneo reportedly are stripping the island of its giant pitcher plant, one of the largest of all carnivorous plants. This spectacular Appendix I species, whose pitcher is large enough to hold a football, is found only on one mountain in Borneo.[81] Plant trade experts are also concerned about the remaining 70 or so wild *Nepenthes* species that were not protected under CITES until very recently— particularly *N. villosa*, another Borneo endemic, and *N. khasiana* of India.[82] In 1987, *N. khasiana* was listed on Appendix I, while *N. villosa* and all other *Nepenthes* species were listed on Appendix II.

American Ginseng

The United States exports some 50 tons of wild ginseng root (*Panax quinquefolius*) every year, largely to supply medicinal markets in Hong Kong, Singapore, Taiwan, and other Far Eastern countries. The root of the ginseng plant, found throughout the eastern half of the United States, purportedly cures indigestion, rheumatism, tuberculosis, and other maladies. Some ginseng root in trade comes from cultivated stock, but wild roots fetch the highest prices because they are con-

KEEP IN MIND . . .

- Buy propagated plants for your garden, and buy only from dealers who sell such plants. Remember: "nursery-raised" does not mean that it is an artificially propagated plant. If in doubt, don't buy!

- Refrain from collecting plants from the wild.

- Join a plant society. There are specialist groups concerned with bulbs, orchids, cacti and succulents, and cycads. Many of these societies work seriously to conserve plants. Several of these are the American Daffodil Society (2302 Rt. 3, Byhalia Road, Hernando, MS 38632), the American Orchid Society (6000 S. Olive Ave., West Palm Beach, FL 33405), the American Rock Garden Society (15 Fairmead Rd., Darien, CT 06820), the Cactus and Succulent Society of America (2631 Fairgreen Ave., Arcadia, CA 91006), and the Cycad Society (1161 Phyllis Ct., Mountain View, CA 94040).

- If you are already a member of a plant society, encourage it to pursue conservation and propagation efforts and discourage collection from the wild.

- Learn all you can about the plant trade. Contact World Wildlife Fund's Plant Conservation Program (1250 Twenty-Fourth Street, N.W., Washington, DC 20037) for more information. The international and domestic trade in wild plants flourishes because of the large market for wild plants and the public's lack of knowledge about the effects of trade.

- Some suggested readings:

   Center for Plant Conservation. *Plant Conservation Resource Book*. Available from the Center for Plant Conservation, 125 Arborway, Jamaica Plain, MA 02130

   Fuller, Douglas, and Fitzgerald, Sarah, eds. *Conservation and Commerce of Cacti and Other Succulents*. Washington, D.C.: World Wildlife Fund, 1987.

   Garden magazine. Published bimonthly. Garden Society, New York Botanical Garden, Bronx, NY 10458.

   Gibson, Thomas, et al. *International Trade in Plants: Focus on U.S. Exports and Imports*. Washington, D.C.: World Wildlife Fund, 1981.

   Huxley, Anthony. *Green Inheritance: The World Wildlife Fund Book of Plants*. Garden City, N.Y.: Doubleday, 1985.

   Kramer, Jack. *The World Wildlife Fund Book of Orchids*. New York: Abbeville, 1989.

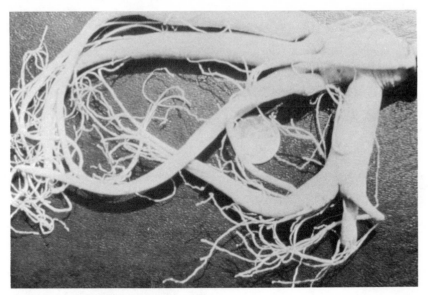

American ginseng (*Panax quinquefolius*) root.
Ron Singer / U.S. Fish and Wildlife Service

sidered more potent. A single human-shaped ginseng root—which connotes special powers—reportedly sells for as much as $50,000 in Hong Kong, if it is in especially good condition.[83]

American ginseng is listed on Appendix II, which allows authorities to keep track of the effects of such heavy trade on wild ginseng populations. FWS monitors ginseng harvests throughout the country and authorizes exports on a state-by-state basis using data from state surveys. According to a 1986 TRAFFIC(U.S.A.) survey by staff botanist Douglas Fuller, states do not always provide the FWS with complete trade and harvest information. Fuller called for more data on harvested-root weights, ages, and sizes to get a true reading of the health of American ginseng populations.[84]

Illegal trade in ginseng is a significant problem in several states, although the FWS has had some success in enforcing ginseng trade controls. In 1986, for instance, an Illinois man was placed on probation and fined $5,000 after he admitted to the illicit sale of approximately 270 pounds of ginseng, worth $47,000, and the purchase of 150 pounds at $25,000.[85] In 1987, a Pennsylvania wildlife trading company was found guilty of illegally exporting ginseng using falsified state harvest certificates. The company, which netted some $900,000 on the illicit ginseng, also was convicted of illegal trade in animal pelts for profits exceeding $1.3 million, and received a $10,000 fine for its infractions.[86]

Live Plants

CHAPTER 29
Tropical Timber

The world loses 27 to 37 million acres of tropical forest, an area roughly the size of Pennsylvania, every year. This translates into more than 76,000 acres a day, or 54 acres (more than 20 football fields) per minute. At this rate, all remaining tropical forests, save those in legally protected areas, may be lost over the next 30 to 80 years. The forces behind this destruction are complex and many, but experts generally agree that the major activity causing tropical deforestation is "slash-and-burn" subsistence agriculture. Other significant contributing factors include cattle ranching, local fuelwood consumption, and timber extraction for foreign and domestic markets. All these factors are often interdependent. For instance, the logging roads built by commercial timber operations often facilitate more land clearing by opening forested areas to settlement and agriculture.[1]

International timber trade plays an important role in tropical deforestation. Commercial logging operations reportedly clear 12 million acres of closed tropical forest each year, and one-quarter of the resulting wood resources are exported.[2] International trade in tropical timber is valued at roughly $7 to $8 billion yearly.[3]

Although there are ways to extract timber without causing massive deforestation, these are seldom employed by tropical logging operations. Modern loggers often use ecologically destructive techniques to extract target tree species and fail to manage the lands they have perturbed for future logging or conservation. The result is soil erosion, wildlife habitat loss, and deforestation.

Selective logging—the extraction of one or a few commercially valuable tree species—is the most common method used to exploit

Slash-and-burn clearing for pasture in Brazil.
R. Bierregard / WWF

tropical timber. According to Robert Buschbacher, tropical forest program officer for World Wildlife Fund (WWF), "Selective logging is inherently one of the least environmentally damaging forms of disturbance to which tropical forests are subjected." In a typical operation, only the prime individual tree specimens are harvested. Selective harvesting depletes commercially valuable species but tends to leave the overall ecosystem reasonably intact. However, Buschbacher cautions, greater damage often still occurs because the selective logging is carried out carelessly and inefficiently. Logging companies frequently have little financial incentive to care for an area because they seldom take a second crop from the same spot. In Sabah, Malaysia, selective harvesting damages or destroys as many as three-quarters of the trees left behind. Selectively logged forests are also more susceptible to fire, invasion by squatters, expansion of cattle-grazing lands, and illegal harvesting of remaining trees for construction poles, railroad ties, and other uses.[4]

The timber trade involves a relatively small number of economically valuable species. In southeast Asia, commercial operations use fewer than 100 species, and the export trade involves mainly a dozen or so. In Amazonia, loggers target only 50 of the region's many thousand species. In Africa, the export trade involves just 35 species, 10 of which comprise nearly three-quarters of total trade.[5]

Little tree planting is going on to replenish or take pressure off natural forests, even when required by law. In the developing countries, only 2.7 million acres are planted for commercial tropical timber each year.[6] The plantations that have been established have little genetic variation, weakening their innate ability to withstand threats from pests, disease, and other natural disasters. The notorious failure of the Henry Ford rubber plantations in Brazil during the 1930s is a classic example of the problems with pestilence: a tropical fungus (*Dothidella ulei*) attacked the American automobile mogul's newly planted stands, prompting Ford to abandon his hopes of producing low-cost, high-yield commercial rubber.[7] Despite advances in forest management since Ford's day, problems in planting monocultures of fast-growing, even-aged tree species continue. For instance, the massive Jari Plantation in Brazil, which required the clearing of hundreds of thousands of acres of native tropical forest, has been ravaged by another fungus (*Ceratocystis fimbriata*).[8]

According to Sara Oldfield, a botanical consultant who has completed an analysis of the tropical timber trade, "There is no doubt that industrial forest resources have not been well managed in the tropics. . . . A recent review of tropical rain forest management systems has shown that, although 'sustainable integrated management of the tropical mixed forest is technically feasible,' it has scarcely been achieved anywhere in the world because of problems concerning land-use policy, socioeconomic conditions, and political realities. . . . As a result of the lack of forest management, the virtual disappearance of commercially productive natural tropical rain forests is imminent in some countries, such as Ivory Coast, Ghana, Nigeria, and Thailand."[9] Once a major wood exporter, Nigeria has already become a net importer, as has Thailand.[10]

Trade Routes and Patterns

Southeast Asia supplies more tropical logs, sawed wood, and plywood to foreign markets than does any other region in the world.[11] Over the past 20 years, Southeast Asian tropical timber exports have increased substantially, as have those of Latin America, while the African trade has remained constant. According to WWF sources, "Africa's forests are the most depleted and Asia's forests are currently being depleted very rapidly. Some countries such as Thailand have exhausted their ability to export timber and are now importers."[12]

The major world exporters of tropical hardwood logs—which comprise the bulk of the trade—are Malaysia (63 percent of total exports), Indonesia (10 percent), the Ivory Coast (7 percent), the Philippines (5 percent), Papua New Guinea (3 percent), and Gabon (3 percent) (figure 29.1). In total, over 90 percent of the world's trade in tropical hardwood logs comes from these six developing countries.[13]

Japan, the European Economic Community (EEC), and the United States are the largest consumers of tropical timber. Measured by value,

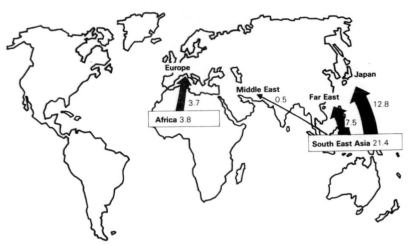

Figure 29.1
Tropical Hardwood Log Trade Flows, 1986
(in million cubic meters)

World tropical hardwood log exports = 25.2 milllion cubic meters.
Source: Nectoux and Dudley.

their share of trade is nearly equal: Japan imported $2.4 billion worth of timber and timber products in 1984, and the United States and EEC each imported $2.2 billion. However, Japan imports a higher percentage of timber as logs (68 percent in 1987), rather than processed wood, and thus accounts for nearly 50 percent of all timber imports by volume. The bulk of Japan's imports are turned into plywood and used in construction. Japan enforces an import tariff on sawed and processed wood, and this helps protect its domestic processing industry. Japan's most important suppliers of tropical timber are Malaysia, Indonesia, the Philippines, and Papua New Guinea. U.S. imports are primarily processed wood and finished goods from Hong Kong, Singapore, and other manufacturing centers (which, for the most part, have imported raw logs from Malaysia and other producer countries). The European trade falls somewhere in between; France, for instance, imports a large percentage of tropical logs, while the United Kingdom imports mainly processed wood.[14]

The form in which tropical hardwoods are exported is an important issue for trading powers as well as conservationists. Producing countries generally bring in less foreign currency from a given stand of forest if they export logs than if they export processed wood, which has a higher value per cubic foot and generates income and employment for local processors as well as domestic loggers (figures 29.2 and 29.3). According to the international WWF network, export-

International Wildlife Trade: Whose Business Is It?

Figure 29.2
Tropical Sawed Hardwood Trade Flows, 1986
(in million cubic meters)

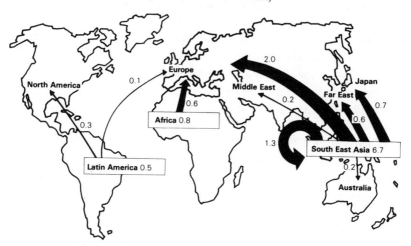

World tropical sawed hardwood log exports = 8.0 milllion cubic meters.
Source: Nectoux and Dudley.

Figure 29.3
Tropical Plywood and Veneers Trade Flows, 1986
(in million cubic meters)

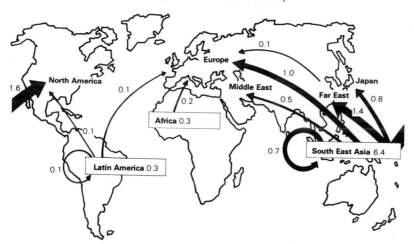

World tropical plywood and veneers exports = 7.0 milllion cubic meters.
Source: Nectoux and Dudley.

Notes: These maps present a simplified view of tropical timber trade flows; some flows are not shown, especially intra-regional ones.
Far East Region includes South Korea, China, Hong Kong, Taiwan, Macau. Singapore is included into South East Asia (which includes Pacific islands such as Png and Solomon Islands).
Central America is included in Latin America (for which Paraguay, Chile, and Argentina are excluded).

Tropical Timber   307

ing processed wood "increases the value of the tropical forest resource and may encourage producer countries to manage it on a longer-term basis. It is important, however, to bear in mind that there is as yet no evidence that enough value can actually be added to timber exports to slow and even stop deforestation."[15] In addition, government subsidies for local processing are expensive. Indonesia is still losing money on its government-subsidized plywood industry.

Producer countries have little control over world timber prices, which have fluctuated dramatically over the past 20 years. In an effort to increase their market power and income, and to protect depleted timber resources, several producer countries have banned or reduced log exports and are developing local processing industries. In 1981, for instance, Indonesia banned log exports by all foreign companies except those that would invest in domestic plywood-production operations. As a result, Indonesian log exports fell from 21 million cubic yards in 1978 to 3.5 million cubic yards in 1982, and the number of local plywood mills has since increased substantially.[16] In 1985, the country banned the export of logs except in conjunction with manufactured products, and Indonesia now has declared that it will stop all log exports by 1989. The Philippines and Thailand have also banned log exports, and Malaysia has restricted export of logs from 16 species.[17]* Honduras and Brazil also prohibit the export of raw logs, although these measures sometimes are circumvented by squaring off logs, cutting them on one side, or applying other minimal "processing" procedures.[19]

*The situation regarding Malaysia is somewhat complicated. In peninsular Malaysia, log exports are virtually banned, while authorities in the states of Sabah and Sarawak "have repeatedly pledged that they will continue to supply Japan with a steady flow of logs."[18] These two states together supply 89 percent of Japan's tropical log requirement.

Factory making plywood from mahogany in Quintana Roo, Mexico.
R. Buschbacher / WWF

International Wildlife Trade: Whose Business Is It?

Species in Trade

Conservation concern over the tropical timber trade focuses primarily on the harmful ecological effects of deforestation and the fact that logging often opens previously forested areas to settlers rather than on the threat that tree species in trade may become extinct. This is in part because the impact on biologically rich tropical ecosystems can be so severe and in part because commercial forces rarely push tree species to the point of actual extinction. Once a species becomes particularly rare, it is usually no longer economically feasible for the industry to harvest and process that species. The species becomes "commercially extinct," and the market moves on to other species. Nevertheless, a few valuable species with particularly limited ranges may disappear altogether, such as *Diospyros hemiteles*, an ebony wood that grows only on the island of Mauritius.[20]

Although extinction is unlikely for most trees, overexploitation remains a serious problem for some of the most valuable and desirable tropical hardwoods. Among these trees are species of popular luxury woods known in the trade as ebony, mahogany, rosewood, and teak. According to the United Nations Food and Agriculture Organization (FAO), at least 41 tropical timber species in commercial trade are being so overexploited that they are now endangered. These trees include afrormosia (*Pericopsis elata*) of West Africa, one of the world's most valuable tropical hardwoods; klinki pine (*Araucaria hunsteinii*) of Papua New Guinea; and Brazilian rosewood (*Dalbergia nigra*), a favorite wood of European cabinetmakers since the mid-1600s.[21]

Mahogany is a general term applied to several unrelated dark red tropical hardwoods long prized for their beauty and resistance to

Mahogany tree in Mexico.
R. Buschbacher / WWF

water and pests. The fate of all these trees is now of serious conservation concern. International trade in mahogany was first recorded in the late 16th century, when Spanish explorers brought Spanish mahogany (*Swietenia mahogani*) back from the West Indies. The trade continued to grow in the 17th century, as British settlers began to exploit rich stands in West African rain forests (*Khaya* spp.). The world mahogany market continued to expand until the last half of the 20th century, when dwindling supplies caused rapid price increases and forced importers to exploit other sources, particularly Philippine mahogany (family Dipterocarpaceae). In 1983, Fauna and Flora Preservation Society researchers Sabrina Knees and Martin Gardner recommended listing all "true" mahoganies—the Neotropical American mahoganies (*Swietenia* species) and the African mahoganies (*Khaya* species)—on Appendix II of CITES to monitor the trade.[22] As of 1988, only one species was listed—Pacific Coast mahogany (*Swietenia humilis*), on Appendix II. That species, however, is not considered important in international trade.[23]

International Trade Controls

Two international trade agreements provide the legal framework to help conserve tropical timbers, CITES and the International Tropical Timber Agreement (ITTA).

CITES currently is used to monitor trade volumes and control exploitation of a few depleted species. Most of the 12 timber species listed on Appendix I and the 4 species on Appendix II are not important in international trade, with the exception of two South American species—Chilean false larch (*Fitzroya cupressoides*), listed on Appendix I in 1973 and then downlisted to Appendix II in 1983, and hoop pine or monkey puzzle tree (*Araucaria araucana*), listed on Appendix II except for the Chilean population, which is on Appendix I.[24]

Forty-one countries, which are responsible for over 95 percent of the world timber market, are parties to the ITTA, which entered into force April 1, 1985. A commodity agreement established under the United Nations Convention on Trade and Development (UNCTAD) to coordinate tropical timber trade policy, the ITTA has great potential for conservation of commercial forest resources. The agreement has strong environmental provisions, reinforced in the work program for the agreement's coordinating body, the International Tropical Timber Organization (ITTO). The ITTO work program includes several important conservation projects, particularly the creation of a data base on scarce and potentially endangered tropical hardwood species in international trade by the World Conservation Monitoring

Center. Other projects with potential conservation benefits include a study of the development of primary-forest logging techniques to minimize damage to remaining trees, a study of the conservation impact of increased commercialization of "lesser known species," and model projects in Brazil and Bolivia to promote commercial forest development on a sustained-yield basis.

Housed in Yokohama, Japan, the ITTO is a relatively new institution, so it is too soon to evaluate its practical value to tropical forest conservation. Financial constraints may hamper initial ITTO efforts. According to WWF, the ITTO needs $20 million to finance critically important conservation, reforestation, and sustainable management efforts.[25] As of 1988, the organization had less than $4 million in pledges, including $2 million from Japan, $1 million from Switzerland, $600,000 from the Netherlands, and $12,000 from WWF and other conservation organizations. In addition, the United States had yet to pay its $50,000 in dues, and other countries owed the ITTO more than $550,000.

Additional Conservation Measures

It is critically important to phase out conventional, ecologically destructive logging in primary forests and to promote sustainable management of forest resources. Because the ITTO presents a useful mechanism for achieving these objectives, its role should be expanded dramatically in the next decade.*

From a trade standpoint, perhaps the most immediate need is to increase the number of tree species that are commercially valuable, thus diversifying the tropical timber market. WWF's Buschbacher considers this one of the most critical conditions for improving tropical forest management. It would give forest managers greater flexibility over the cutting that takes place and the nature of stands left behind, and thus would improve their ability to help a given area regenerate. It also would mean that a greater number of valuable trees could be harvested in a concentrated area, curbing the need to deforest new territory. Exporting countries could require more diverse

---

*In a position paper prepared for the 1987 ITTO meeting, WWF called for ITTA parties to do the following: create a fund specifically to protect forest areas; adopt codes of conduct for producers and consumers that would phase out current, unsustainable logging systems; establish a pricing system for timber that would increase logging efficiency and provide exporting countries with funds for conservation and reforestation; establish a tariff and quota system on imports of tropical timber that promote imports of processed wood, rather than logs; approve a product-marking system that would allow consumers to identify timber from sustainably managed sources; and outlaw trade in tree species that would be further endangered by international trade, such as some mahoganies.[26]

Tropical rain forest in Costa Rica.
R. Buschbacher / WWF

timber extraction and promote the use of "secondary" species. The timber industry and consumer countries, too, could help by supporting research on secondary species and aggressively encouraging markets for such products. Development of local, small-scale processing industries is an additional, critically important measure. Such operations would benefit rural economies and help build local support for conservation and sound management of tropical forests.[27] Taken together, these and other policy reforms must increase the economic benefits of forest harvesting and ensure that those benefits are distributed to local populations. Economic decision making must be based on long-term productivity rather than short-term windfalls and must recognize the value of a wide range of goods and services that forests provide, including but not limited to timber.

CONCLUSION

Wildlife trade is clearly a business with severe problems. Despite nearly 15 years under CITES, smuggling of wildlife and wildlife products is rampant. Violators continue to find and exploit the weakest links among trading nations. Sophisticated black marketeers steal permits, blatantly falsify information on trade documents, pay off border guards, and abuse free-port privileges. In almost every country, customs officers are overworked and undereducated when it comes to checking wildlife shipments; they can hardly be expected to keep up with changing national laws or to know the difference between "farmed" and wild animals that few biologists can tell apart. And tourists continue to purchase—simply through ignorance or lack of concern—jewelry, artifacts, and curios made from endangered or protected species.

But there is cause for optimism as well. With 99 members, CITES is more widely accepted than any other conservation treaty. All major wildlife-consuming countries and most key producers are now parties. According to Michael Bean, head of the Environmental Defense Fund's wildlife program, "CITES clearly reflects an unprecedented consensus among the nations of the world."[1]

Leading "black holes" for wildlife smuggling are being cleaned up. For instance, in October 1986, Singapore, considered the linchpin in illicit Asian traffic at the time, banned all rhino horn trade. The next month, Singapore acceded to the convention. Both moves came in response to international conservation pressure.

Wildlife trade monitoring is also improving. More countries now submit annual trade reports to the Secretariat, and these reports are more complete. The TRAFFIC network of experts tracking wildlife commerce is larger and more comprehensive. Authorities are gaining a better idea of how the market affects rare wildlife, though population information for many species is still scarce. The Wildlife Trade Monitoring Unit (WTMU), in conjunction with the Secretariat, now produces estimates of Appendix II species' endangerment by trade, based on world import and export data and best available population figures. A preventive measure, WTMU's reports are designed to identify trouble spots before these species are on their last legs and before they merit listing on Appendix I. Overall, as World Wildlife Fund's (WWF) David Mack points out, "Wildlife trade monitoring has become a science over the past 10 years."[2]

Individual countries are making headway against big-time smugglers. For example, customs officials in Rio de Janeiro seized the largest illegal shipment of caiman skins ever recorded—nine tons worth over $4.5 million—in 1985; the following year, Belgian port authorities uncovered nearly 2,000 illicit elephant tusks, worth nearly $1.5 million, in boxes marked "beeswax" and headed for Dubai.[3] Since 1980, U.S. undercover investigations have broken open nationwide smuggling rings for parrots, birds of prey, big game animals, rare snakes, black bear parts, and endangered plants. In 1986, state and federal wildlife agents in California capped a year-long probe into illegal cactus traffic along the Mexican border with a series of arrests and seizure of over 200 prized specimens.[4]

Countries also are strengthening their trade laws and imposing stiffer penalties. In 1985, for instance, Australia outlawed all commercial exports of wildlife, except those for which there are management programs, to stop further loss of rare parrots, marsupials, and valuable reptiles.

One of the most significant developments in cleaning up the illegal wildlife trade is the increasing involvement of the industry with supporting conservation projects for commercially valuable species. Responsible industry representatives are beginning to see that well-controlled trade and sustainable harvest programs make not only conservation sense. They also make business sense, ensuring long-term returns for both the species and the legal businesses involved. Wildlife traders have been especially involved in funding WWF and CITES studies of Latin American caiman and tegu lizard populations to determine their status and conservation needs. in the face of woefully inadequate government trade controls, support for such projects and self-policing by the industry itself will be increasingly critical to the long-term success of CITES.

The next 10 years will be crucial to many of the world's exotic plants and animals. Rhinos, black caimans, golden lion tamarins, hyacinth macaws, and other trade-pressured species may disappear forever. On the other hand, saltwater crocodiles, sea otters, vicuñas, and other carefully managed species may continue to recover. The new leopard quota system will be tested severely, as will African elephant tusk trade controls and last-ditch efforts to protect dwindling rhino populations.

Much will depend on consumer countries' ability to curb their appetite for precious specimens. Will the Japanese shut down traditional markets for sea-turtle shell? Can U.S. cactus lovers help stop the flow of rare and protected cacti from Mexico? Will West German fashion mavens stop buying fur coats made from rare cat pelts? The deterioration of the sealskin industry in the early 1980s due to U.S. and European protests against the killing of baby seals is not necessarily a conservation model, but it does indicate the power of consumer demand in driving the wildlife trade.

In the developing world, wildlife trade controls and conservation measures, for the most part, will have to include economic incentives to succeed in the face of intense pressure to exploit wildlife resources. Ranching operations that help local people, such as Papua New Guinea's crocodile-raising scheme, and national parks with strong tourist appeal, such as Rwanda's mountain gorilla reserve, will be increasingly necessary to justify species protection in the face of growing human needs.

APPENDICES

APPENDIX A
How CITES Works

With its 99 member countries, the Convention on International Trade in Endangered Species of Wild Fauna and Flora (CITES) is the most widely accepted wildlife conservation agreement in the world. Most major wildlife-consuming nations belong. Most large-scale wildlife-exporting countries are also members, with a few noteworthy exceptions.

CITES Appendices

CITES lists species of plants and animals in three "appendices." Inclusion in these appendices obligates parties to institute specific controls on listed species.*

Appendix I contains species that are threatened with extinction and are or may be affected by trade. Included are all rhinos, sea turtles, great apes, great whales, most large cats, and over 600 other endangered species. CITES bans all commercial trade in Appendix I species and allows noncommercial trade in them only in exceptional circumstances if it will not damage their chances for survival. All transactions in Appendix I species require an export permit from the country where the wildlife originates or a reexport certificate from the reexporting country, and an import permit from the recipient country. The import permit must be issued *before* any transaction involving an Appendix I species can occur. This permit can be granted only if (*a*) the importation will not be for purposes detrimental to the species' survival, (*b*) it will not be primarily commercial, and (*c*) if live wildlife is involved, the specimen is assured of a suitable home. An export permit can be issued only if (*a*) the wildlife was obtained legally, (*b*) the wildlife will not be harmed during shipping, and (*c*) an import permit has already been granted.

See appendix C for a complete listing of species covered by Appendices I, II, and III.

Through its Appendix II listings, CITES regulates commerce in wildlife that is not already threatened with extinction but may become so if trade is not controlled. The convention permits commercial trade in species listed on Appendix II, provided that the country of origin or country of reexport has issued an export permit or reexport certificate. The exporting country may not issue an export permit unless the proper government agency has certified that the export will not be detrimental to the species' survival. Import permits are not required. More than 2,300 animal species and over 24,000 plants are now listed on Appendix II.

Both Appendices I and II include "look-alike" species that are not threatened themselves but closely resemble other Appendix I or II species. An entire genus, family, or order might also be listed if most species in the group are threatened and if it is difficult to identify them individually. Listing these species helps ease the burden on enforcement officers who are responsible for singling out CITES-listed wildlife and wildlife products from those that may not be covered by the convention. For example, Appendix II covers all parrots, cats, crocodilians, boas, orchids, and cacti not already listed on Appendix I; this helps customs officers know that any shipments containing these species should be checked. Of the 24,000-plus plants on Appendix II, over 20,000 are orchid species, and 1,500 are cacti. Most of these are listed for look-alike reasons.[1]

Finally, CITES gives parties the option of listing on a third appendix native species that are already protected within their own borders. This is intended to help CITES members to gain other nations' cooperation in enforcing their own wildlife trade regulations. Canada, for example, lists the walrus in Appendix III because the government regulates trade in the species and wants other countries to refuse imports of walrus from Canada unless they have proper export permits. Trade in Appendix III species requires an export permit from the listing country or a certificate of origin when the specimen is exported from other countries.[2]

Obligations of CITES Parties

When nations become parties to CITES, they agree to fulfill certain obligations. They must set up management and scientific authorities to regulate trade and submit annual reports on trade, and are requested to attend biennial conferences to review implementation of the convention as well as amend its appendices as necessary. Parties are also obligated to confiscate smuggled goods or send them back to their country of origin and to penalize violators. As is the case with most other international agreements, CITES leaves it up to individual countries to decide the specifics of how they meet these obligations. CITES can only be enforced by its individual members, and national efforts to do so are vital to its success.

NATIONAL LEGISLATION TO IMPLEMENT CITES

After a country accedes to CITES, it must take appropriate measures, usually by passing legislation, to implement the convention. The legislation must, at a minimum, commit the country to abide by all CITES mandates, but it may also incorporate measures stricter than the convention itself. Venezuela and Brazil, for example, have CITES-implementing laws that prohibit the export of virtually all wildlife, even though many of their native species are given only Appendix II protection by CITES.

The United States implements CITES via the Endangered Species Act of 1973 (ESA). Regulations prescribed by the act prohibit import, export, or reexport of Appendix I, II, or III species without the required CITES permits and also forbid the possession of any species imported, exported, or reexported into or from the United States in contravention of the convention. Those who knowingly violate CITES, whether for personal or commercial reasons, may have their goods confiscated and receive penalties of up to one year in jail and as much as $50,000 in fines per violation.*

MANAGEMENT AND SCIENTIFIC AUTHORITIES

CITES parties are required to set up one or more "management authorities" to regulate trade and "scientific authorities" to deliberate on scientific issues related to wildlife trade. The management authority issues import and export permits and compiles information on annual trade. The scientific authority advises whether particular imports and exports will be detrimental to the survival of the species involved, determines whether captive conditions are suitable for live animals in trade, monitors export volumes and their impact

---

*For a civil violation, the fine may be up to $25,000 per violation. A criminal violation carries a maximum $50,000 fine. U.S. wildlife trade cases are also subject to national sentencing guidelines that establish relatively uniform sentencing practices throughout the country. The guidelines require the courts to give certain points (based on the value of wildlife involved, whether quarantine requirements were evaded, whether the species was endangered or threatened, and other case characteristics) to establish an overall "offense level." Each offense level has a specific range of fines and terms of imprisonment. The actual penalty can also be adjusted based on the violator's criminal record, whether the violator acted alone or as the ringleader of a larger smuggling operation, his or her plea, and other individual considerations. A typical first-time offender who is a commercial wildlife dealer involved in illegal imports is likely to have an offense level of 10 to 12. At level 10, he or she could receive probation or 6 to 12 months in jail and a $2,000 to $20,000 fine. At level 12, jail terms are 10 to 16 months and fines range from $3,000 to $30,000.³

on protected native species, and oversees other scientific matters. In addition, the scientific authority often reviews permit applications and proposed changes to the CITES appendices.

Management authority responsibilities are usually undertaken by a single government office. In the United States, the appropriate office is the Office of Management Authority of the Fish and Wildlife Service, in the Department of the Interior. In the United Kingdom, it is the Department of the Environment. In Nepal, the management authority is the Chief National Park and Wildlife Conservation Office for trade in animals, and the director general of the Department of Medicinal Plants for plants, while in Japan, it is the Ministry of International Trade and Industry.

The scientific authority is often a mixture of experts from the government, academia, zoos, and other institutions. The United Kingdom, for example, relies on the Nature Conservancy Council for animals and the Royal Botanic Gardens at Kew for plants. The United States uses the Office of the Scientific Authority of the Fish and Wildlife Service.

NATIONAL REPORTS

To help enforce the convention and identify trouble spots, CITES parties are obliged to submit yearly reports on all trade in CITES-listed wildlife that crosses their borders. These reports are expected to cover all incoming and outgoing trade and to detail where shipments come from or go to, how many items they contain, and why the goods are in trade (for example, for personal use, scientific research, commercial sale, zoos, or other exhibits).

In reality, only about half of all parties typically report on trade, and their efforts are often incomplete. According to a review by the Wildlife Trade Monitoring Unit, 52 percent of all CITES parties reported on trade in 1985.[4] To illustrate the problem of omissions, TRAFFIC(Germany) director Manfred Niekisch reports that West Germany failed to report on plants from 1981 through 1983; this reporting gap occurred because the country was not monitoring plant imports and exports at the time.[5]

In addition, shipments reported by importing countries seldom correlate with those reported by exporting countries. In 1985, importing and exporting country records of individual shipments of CITES-listed animals agreed for only about 25 percent of all shipments reported by CITES member nations.[6] Such discrepancies often are due to reporting errors, omissions, differences in methods for measuring shipments, or illegal trade. Another major factor, however, is the tremendous worldwide shortage of port inspectors and data collectors needed to track the thousands of legal wildlife shipments that cross national borders every day.

In general, experts believe that CITES annual reports are best used to gauge the *minimum*, rather than actual, number of specimens in trade.[7] The data are also helpful in showing general routes and patterns that wildlife and wildlife products follow in international trade.

DESIGNATED PORTS

CITES recommends that parties specify particular international ports through which all shipments containing CITES species entering or leaving the country must flow. This allows a party to concentrate its wildlife inspectors and record-keepers at those ports dealing with the majority of the nation's wildlife trade.

The United States restricts ports of entry for all commercial shipments of wildlife. These "designated ports" are Chicago, Dallas-Ft. Worth, Honolulu, Los Angeles, Miami, New Orleans, New York, San Francisco, and Seattle, as well as additional "border ports" through which shipments to and from Mexico and Canada may flow. The United Kingdom, Japan, and many other countries also limit ports of entry for wildlife.

FINANCES

CITES is financed primarily by contributions from member countries. Each party's requested annual payment is based on the United Nations contributions scale. Requested payments range from $150 or so for the smaller, poorer members to nearly $400,000 for the wealthiest.[8]* The moneys support the CITES Secretariat—the convention's coordinating body—and activities that help countries regulate their wildlife resources. In recent years, CITES funds have partially financed training seminars for officials from Latin America, Africa, and Asia, at which technical "nuts and bolts" advice on implementing CITES trade controls was offered and ways for countries to work on cooperative measures to stop smugglers were suggested.

As with other international programs financed by voluntary contributions, CITES is continually short on funds. In recent years, as many as one-third of the parties have not paid their annual share.[9] Some parties are suffering such severe economic woes and domestic political problems that their neglect is perhaps understandable, but some of the biggest backsliders (for example, the Soviet Union) are neither poor nor unstable.

---

*The United States has the highest payment on the scale. The next are $160,000 for the Soviet Union and $130,000 for West Germany.

ENFORCEMENT

Parties are obliged to confiscate wildlife contraband and set whatever fines or other penalties they choose. Confiscation can be a very real punishment when it involves valuable species. For example, the U.S. seizure of an illicit shipment of 98 palm cockatoos cost smugglers a potential $1 million since the birds could fetch $10,000 to $15,000 each on the black market at that time. Once goods are confiscated, however, it can sometimes be difficult to dispose of them, particularly when they are live birds or other fragile live wildlife. Conservationists have had only limited success in returning tropical birds and endangered monkeys to their native lands. Some zoos, herbaria, aquaria, and other scientific institutions have been extremely helpful in caring for confiscated live wildlife, often with little or no financial assistance from government wildlife agencies. In some countries, traders are legally obliged to pay the expense of caring for confiscated wildlife.

Fines and jail sentences are sometimes ridiculously low in comparison with the value and status of the species involved. But Australia, the United Kingdom, the United States, and others are beginning to impose stiffer penalties. For example, the United States in 1988 raised fines for CITES violations under the Endangered Species Act.

In some parts of the country, such as Miami and San Diego, the courts and federal prosecutors have taken an aggressive position on Lacey Act and ESA violations. For example, in November 1988, four Miami residents were convicted of attempting to smuggle 243 threatened or endangered birds into the United States from Cuba. One received a two-year jail sentence, and another was sentenced to 18 months in prison. The U.S. attorney's office in San Diego has brought several major parrot smugglers to trial in the late 1980s. One smuggling kingpin, long considered a primary source of illegal Central American parrots, was sentenced in June 1988 to four years in prison for smuggling and conspiracy. His operation brought yellow-naped parrots across the Mexican border to a safe house in southern California.

Customs officials or wildlife inspectors are usually in charge of inspecting shipments and seizing contraband. Wildlife agents also investigate illegal trade schemes in many countries. In the United States, the Fish and Wildlife Service's Division of Law Enforcement takes the lead in investigations; the Customs Service, Department of Justice, Department of State, and other agencies also participate.

Any shipment containing CITES-listed wildlife or wildlife products must have a separate permit. The convention recommends specific formats for these trade documents, but countries usually produce their own. It is sometimes difficult to recognize authentic papers, particularly because dishonest traders occasionally falsify the necessary documents. Permit theft also complicates efforts to control the trade.

This difficulty in identifying falsified or stolen permits helps make laundering a serious problem in wildlife trade. Frequently, smugglers take a species from one country where it is protected and ship it to another country where it is not or where trade controls are lax. They then obtain fraudulent export documents indicating that the shipment originated in the intermediary country. Or the smugglers export protected wildlife from its country of origin using false trade papers. Wildlife laundering, much like illegal currency transactions or gunrunning, conceals the goods' true identity or origin. Laundering is very hard to stop, in part because it is frequently difficult to pinpoint exactly where a species' came, or could have come, from. In addition, the commerce commonly involves complex routes with multiple points of entry and exit, and wildlife goods are altered en route through tanning, manufacturing, and other processes. As a result, authorities often find it extremely complicated and burdensome to verify trade documents or to prove with certainty that suspect shipments are illegal. According to Ginette Hemley, director of TRAFFIC(U.S.A.), "the ivory, live bird, and reptile skin trades have been especially prone to laundering practices."[10]

Another troublesome smuggling ploy involves mislabeling shipments of protected species as a nonprotected relative or even as another kind of item altogether. In addition, zones such as free ports through which shipments may pass legally with little or no customs control can make it difficult to enforce CITES and national wildlife trade regulations.

Exceptions to CITES Rules

CITES has several exemptions to allow trade in listed species without the usual permits. Some exemptions depend on what the traders intend to do with their goods, some depend on how the wildlife is grown or raised, and others are based on which countries are involved. Although these exceptions were designed to help make CITES more effective in the long run, some of them also expose weaknesses in the convention.

1) *Traveling exhibits.* Traveling circuses and other mobile wildlife exhibits may move their stock without regular CITES permits, at the discretion of management authorities.[11]

2) *Noncommercial trade.* Scientists and museums, research centers, zoos, and other scientific institutions are allowed to ship or exchange

wildlife for "noncommercial" purposes, provided that the scientists or institutions involved are registered for such activities with management authorities in their countries. This exemption is helpful in allowing zoos to share their breeding stock of gorillas, tigers, or other endangered species. It is open to abuse, however. As Jonathan Barzdo, head of the Wildlife Trade Monitoring Unit and a former zookeeper himself, points out, "Unscrupulous wildlife dealers call themselves zoos to avoid CITES controls, and private profit-making zoos are known to import animals for purely monetary reasons. Since zoos tend to trade in some of the more endangered wildlife, this exception has serious implications and may need to be refined."[12]

3) *Personal items.* People traveling with personal items or household effects from Appendix II species—such as a pet yellow-naped amazon, a favorite stuffed tortoise, or a pair of iguana-skin basketball shoes—generally do not need CITES permits to transport such items. However, this is not a blanket rule, and there are instances where permits are required. For example, individuals need a CITES export permit to bring home any Appendix II wildlife acquired in its country of origin when that country requires export permits for such transactions. Travelers should be aware that interpretation of the exception for personal goods varies from one country to another, so they should check with authorities before attempting to purchase or bring home any exotic wildlife items from abroad. In addition, Appendix I plants and animals acquired in a foreign country cannot be brought home by individuals without CITES export and import permits, even if the specimens can be considered "personal effects."[13]

In practice, the personal effects exemption is complex and difficult to enforce. Abuses undoubtedly occur, but there has been little information collected on this type of trade.[14]

4) *Goods in transit.* Wildlife shipments going from one country to another do not need CITES permits for countries they pass through along the way, if those goods remain "in customs control" and are on their way to specific importers. For instance, a crate of American ginseng root going from Seattle via the Tokyo airport to Hong Kong needs an Appendix II export permit from the United States but not from Japan.

5) *Preconvention specimens.* Any animal or plant acquired before CITES took effect in 1975 or before the species was listed in its appendices is generally exempt from CITES controls. A CITES party may also apply this preconvention exemption to wildlife items that were obtained before the country became a party to CITES. This exemption can be difficult to enforce. In practice, it is a well-known avenue for laundering newly collected skins, ivory, sea turtle shell, and other

products into commerce.

Enforcement is particularly troublesome when importers stockpile protected species just before their country accedes to CITES. In the United Kingdom, for example, traders more than doubled their intake of ocelot skins in the few months before CITES took effect in 1976.[15]

6) *Captive breeding.* Captive-bred animals and artificially propagated plants are exempt from prohibitions on commercial trade in Appendix I species. They are treated as Appendix II specimens and thus need only an export permit or reexport certificate for trade. Strict criteria for determining which specimens come under this exemption, however, were established during the Second Conference of the Parties in San Jose in 1979. A captive animal population maintained for commercial export, referred to as a "farm" under CITES, must be managed so that it is capable of reliably producing second-generation offspring, known as the "F2 generation," and the breeding program must not rely on specimens from wild populations. Similarly, artificially propagated plants, such as certain cacti and orchids, must come from an operation designed to maintain the stock indefinitely, through growth from cuttings or seeds. The CITES Secretariat maintains a registry of institutions that have met the criteria for captive-breeding or artificial propagation of Appendix I species.

Attempts by sea turtle farming operations to qualify for the captive-breeding exemption have been the subject of heated debate among CITES parties since the late 1970s. Sea turtles mature very slowly, and no commercial operation has yet reliably produced F2 offspring in captivity. (Chapter 22 includes a discussion of sea turtle farming and ranching issues.)

7) *Ranched wildlife.* A "ranched" population of an Appendix I species may be transferred to Appendix II to allow commercial trade, provided certain conditions are met. These criteria, established during the Third Conference of the Parties in New Delhi in 1981, generally require that the population no longer be endangered and that the ranching operation contribute to conservation of the wild population involved.[16] Wildlife ranching differs from farming in that it is not a "closed system" but depends on regular supplies from wild populations. Eggs or young are collected from the wild and then raised in a controlled environment. Successful ranching operations can benefit threatened species by improving the yield for each batch of eggs or young, returning some stock to the wild, and creating economic incentives to protect wild populations and their habitats. Two species populations that CITES Parties have downlisted from Appendix I to Appendix II in recognition of successful ranching operations are

the Nile crocodile population in Zimbabwe and the saltwater crocodile population in Australia.

8) *Reservations.* Parties may grant themselves exceptions to CITES
controls by taking "reservations" on individual species listed in Appendices I and II. Once a reservation is taken, a party may act as though
it does not belong to CITES when dealing with imports or exports
of that species. Any country may lodge a reservation when it accedes
to CITES or within 90 days of the time that the "objectionable" species
is listed on or transferred to a particular appendix. (A complete list
of reservations is shown in appendix D.)

The reservation exemption was a debated compromise to encourage support for CITES. The rationale for the provision is that
it gives each country a chance to protect its own trading interests
while continuing to technically uphold the convention. However,
reservations—especially on Appendix I species—weaken CITES' ability to protect endangered wildlife. Simon Lyster, an authority on international wildlife law, states that reservations can be damaging because
"not only can reserving Parties trade freely with non-Parties, but reservations sometimes encourage trade to continue, albeit illegally, with
other Parties."[17]

Administration of the Convention

Not surprisingly, an international agreement as large and complicated as CITES requires careful, detailed administration and the full
involvement of its parties in decision making. The two main elements
in CITES' ongoing execution are its biennial Conferences of the Parties and its Secretariat.

CONFERENCE OF THE PARTIES

CITES parties meet every two years to review how well the convention is working, amend its appendices, and resolve policy issues. These
sessions help the parties to keep up with changes in species' biological status and alert each other to new wildlife-smuggling ploys. Convening parties also review captive- breeding successes and other scientific advances that may affect wildlife trade.

Meeting results are often referred to by location rather than date.
For instance, the standards for listing and delisting species are referred
to as the "Berne Criteria" because they were adopted at the first CITES
meeting in Berne, Switzerland, in 1976. When trade officials men-
tion a ruling "from Buenos Aires," they are talking about an action
taken during the fifth biennial meeting, held in Argentina in 1985.

Nations that have not joined CITES may participate as observers
in the biennial meetings, but they may not vote. In addition, nongovernmental organizations and special interest groups may par-

ticipate as observers if they obtain permission from their national authorities.

THE SECRETARIAT

CITES is one of the few conservation treaties that provides for a permanent secretariat.[18] The CITES Secretariat coordinates international efforts to carry out or implement the convention. The Secretariat provides parties with trade information and scientific and technical support, organizes meetings of the Conference of the Parties, and informs governments and the public about wildlife trade developments. Housed in Lausanne, Switzerland, and administered through the United Nations Environment Programme, the Secretariat is a trade and conservation sentinel, detecting and publicizing possible CITES violations and trade threats to wildlife. In addition, it frequently takes on special projects, such as monitoring the African elephant ivory trade and the number of wild elephants killed each year (see chapter 6).

A relatively small operation, the Secretariat is comprised of a secretary general, several professional officers, and support staff. In 1988, the Secretariat's approved budget was approximately $1.4 million.[19] The Secretariat's mailing address is:

CITES Secretariat
6, rue du Maupas
Case Postale 78
1000 Lausanne 9
Switzerland

The Role of Nongovernmental Organizations

Nongovernmental organizations (NGOs) are a crucial force in promoting strong implementation of CITES. Traditionally, NGOs representing conservationists, various wildlife and industry interests, and the scientific community, have been active participants in the biennial Conferences of the Parties, although they are not allowed to vote.

NGOs make important financial contributions to CITES activities. They occasionally pay travel expenses for conference delegates from developing countries; contribute to the Secretariat's work, such as financing the printing of export permits on special security paper; and help finance and organize training seminars for wildlife trade enforcement officers from developing countries.[20] They also provide technical support to trade officials and carry out public awareness campaigns to end illegal wildlife trade. Their most important contributions, however, may be as watchdogs: conservation NGOs alert government officials to potential infractions, investigate illicit trade routes and operations, and pressure authorities in importing and exporting countries alike to improve their laws and enforcement efforts. As Laura Kosloff and Mark Trexler, two U.S. wildlife trade law experts, concluded in a 1987 evaluation of the convention, "NGO oversight of Parties' implementing actions under CITES has been a key variable in achieving whatever success CITES has achieved. In the absence of NGO participation, CITES would very likely have followed the route of many other international wildlife measures into obscurity."[21]

THE TRAFFIC NETWORK

Only one NGO focuses solely on international wildlife trade. That organization, TRAFFIC, is an international network of wildlife professionals and trade experts that tracks wildlife imports and exports around the world. (TRAFFIC stands for Trade Record Analysis of Flora and Fauna in Commerce.) TRAFFIC staff collect and analyze data on the volume and types of wildlife in trade and promote public awareness of commercial threats to plant and animal species. They regularly provide advice on these topics to governments, international agencies, conservation groups, wildlife traders, and others.

World Wildlife Fund (WWF) finances the network, which is jointly overseen by the International Union for Conservation of Nature and Natural Resources (IUCN). TRAFFIC's work is coordinated by TRAFFIC(International), based at the World Conservation Monitoring Centre (WCMC) in Cambridge, United Kingdom. Another branch of the WCMC, the Wildlife Trade Monitoring Unit (WTMU), processes trade statistics and undertakes research projects in collaboration with the TRAFFIC network. The expanding network has offices in Australia, Austria, Belgium, France, West Germany, Italy, Japan, Netherlands, the United States, and Uruguay. The Australian office covers trade issues throughout Oceania, and the office in Uruguay covers the entire South American continent. Several of these offices, including the U.S. office, are integral programs of WWF national organizations. This supportive relationship gives TRAFFIC access to scientists, government officials, and key trade experts around the world. (For a complete list of addresses of TRAFFIC offices, see appendix E.)

The *Traffic Bulletin*, published by TRAFFIC(International), reports on international trade issues, providing news and in-depth studies of commerce in plants and animals. *TRAFFIC(U.S.A.)*, a newsletter put out by the U.S. office of WWF, focuses on the United States' wildlife trade.

WTMU's mother organization, the World Conservation Monitoring Centre (CMC), collects and analyzes global data on a broad range of conservation topics and is a valuable source for information on threatened wildlife and threatened habitats. Staff scientists regularly report on species they consider endangered or rare, describing how these species are affected by international trade, habitat loss, hunting, and other threats.

WILDLIFE TRADE INDUSTRY GROUPS

Many organizations representing segments of the wildlife trade industry work hard to comply with CITES and domestic regulations. Some industry groups even contribute directly to projects that strengthen trade controls. For instance, the Japanese ivory traders organization has contributed generously to establish and maintain the CITES Ivory Unit, a technical arm of the CITES Secretariat that tracks African elephant ivory trade and helps implement tusk-marking and export quota procedures. (See chapter 6.) Similarly, representatives of the reptile skin trade recently provided funds for a study of caiman crocodile populations in Brazil, Bolivia, and Paraguay and of tegu lizards in Argentina.

Wildlife Trade Control Agreements and Laws Other Than CITES

Although CITES is the sole international convention specifically covering trade in endangered species, it is not the only agreement or law that in some way affects commerce in endangered species. Other treaties protect specific groups of animals, and numerous national laws other than CITES-implementing legislation protect wildlife and regulate the use of their products.

OTHER INTERNATIONAL TREATIES

CITES does not generally affect provisions of other treaties that affect endangered species, such as the International Convention for the Regulation of Whaling and the International Agreement for the Conservation of Polar Bears. Rather, for example, in cases involving Appendix II marine mammals covered by other international treaties, such as the beluga whale or polar bear, CITES expressly exempts parties from convention provisions with respect to trade in such animals.

There are also national, regional, and international health and customs regulations that control plant and animal transactions. For example, U.S. Department of Agriculture regulations require that all live birds entering the United States undergo a 30-day quarantine period to inspect for bird-borne diseases (see chapter 16).

NATIONAL WILDLIFE TRADE CONTROLS

Many nations have laws, in addition to CITES-implementing legislation, that control wildlife imports and exports. A growing number of African, Asian, and Latin American countries have trade controls to stem the drain on their wildlife resources. Some—among them, Australia, Brazil, Ecuador, and Paraguay—ban the export of most native species. Others, such as South Africa and Costa Rica, have detailed restrictions on trade in native species.

In the past, national wildlife trade laws were seldom well known to officials in other countries. Now, however, summaries of all Latin American wildlife trade laws are available through WWF, in Washington, D.C., while similar summaries of African laws have been prepared by IUCN's Environmental Law Centre in Bonn, West Germany. A summary of Asian wildlife trade laws is expected to be available from WWF in 1990.

Like CITES, the success of national trade laws depends largely on enforcement. Without active border guards, alert and well-informed customs agents, trustworthy permit officers, and courts that punish violators, wildlife laws do little more than gather library dust.

U.S. WILDLIFE TRADE LAWS

The United States has four key laws that regulate trade in endangered plants and animals. The previously described Endangered Species Act of 1973, the nation's CITES-implementing legislation, regulates trade in species listed on the convention's three appendices. It also covers some species not listed by CITES, such as certain kangaroos. The Marine Mammal Protection Act (MMPA) bans commercial imports of all marine mammals and products, including those from polar bears, whales, and sea otters.* And the Migratory Bird Treaty Act restricts trade in wild native birds.

Another U.S. law, the Lacey Act, is one of the most important trade laws ever passed by a major wildlife-consuming country. This act supports other countries' efforts to protect their native wildlife, making it a federal crime to import animals or animal products taken or exported in violation of foreign law. (The act does not apply to foreign plants.) Designed to reduce the black market for protected—but frequently smuggled—animals such as Indonesian palm cockatoos and Brazilian anacondas, the Lacey Act commits U.S. financial and human resources to stopping such trade.

THE EUROPEAN ECONOMIC COMMUNITY

The 12 member nations of the European Economic Community

---

*The MMPA provides several exceptions to the ban, primarily for imports intended for scientific research or public display. The act also treats imports of northern fur seals differently by giving precedence over trade controls to the Interim Convention on Conservation of North Pacific Fur Seals, an international agreement which, until recently, governed the animals' harvest and trade. Finally, the act allows native peoples in the northernmost regions of the country to hunt marine mammals to create and sell native handicrafts and clothing; in combination with CITES, which gives precedence to the MMPA, this exception effectively allows export of marine mammal products crafted into authentic native articles, such as scrimshaw from walrus ivory.

(EEC)* include some of the top wildlife consumers in the world. West Germany, France, Italy, and Spain, for instance, are key markets for imported reptile skins, spotted cat skins, wild birds, and frog legs.

Using regional—rather than national or international—regulations, the EEC plays a unique role in influencing wildlife trade. For instance, when the community banned all imports of whale products in 1982, it effectively closed down one of the world's biggest markets for sperm whale oil. Similarly, the EEC's 1987 ban on imports of four small spotted cat species from Latin America should help countries in that region enforce national export restrictions, especially as the EEC has been the key market for those species in recent years.

The EEC is now working to mesh its approach with CITES, which was designed for national, not regional, use. The community intends to become a CITES party in its own right if and when the convention is amended to allow this. Such an amendment was approved at the 1983 Conference of the Parties, but it cannot enter into force until two-thirds of the parties at the time formally accept it. To date, only a small share of the necessary 54 parties have ratified the amendment. In the meantime, since January 1984 the EEC has required member nations to implement CITES whether or not they are parties to the convention.

According to Simon Lyster, the EEC approach has some advantages. The regulations force EEC-member countries that have not joined CITES—Greece and Ireland—to comply with the convention's controls and may also encourage these countries to join CITES on their own. Moreover, the EEC regulations give greater protection to some plants and animals than they receive under CITES. First, under the regulations, some Appendix II species (termed "C1" species), such as the spur-thighed tortoise and the Caribbean flamingo, are treated as if they were in Appendix I. Second, the EEC regulations set special standards for allowable imports of certain other Appendix II species (known as "C2" species), such as the African elephant, margay, and parrots.† Third, the import into an EEC country of any species covered by the regulations requires an import permit. Finally, the regulations prohibit selling within the EEC, offering for sale, publicly displaying for commercial purposes, or otherwise commercially using

---

Members are Belgium, Denmark, France, West Germany, Greece, Ireland, Italy, Luxembourg, Netherlands, Portugal, Spain, and the United Kingdom.

†Importers must show that "C2"-listed animals or plants were collected legally and that their capture does not have a harmful effect on conservation of the species. EEC traders also must obtain import permits from the intended country of import for C2-listed species and prove that incoming live animals on the "C2 list" will receive adequate care.[22]

Appendix I and C1 species, subject to certain exemptions which member states may grant.

Appendix I and C1 species, subject to certain exemptions which member states may grant.

But Lyster and several other conservationists also point out two critical weaknesses in the EEC regulations: they do not restrict internal EEC trade in C2 species, and, more important, they do not require that member states report intracommunity trade in their annual CITES reports. In line with EEC policy on other nonwildlife commodities, the community allows these two weaknesses to promote the free flow of goods between member nations. This policy makes it difficult to track wildlife shipments and may encourage traders to funnel illegal shipments through the weakest links in the system.

APPENDIX B
Parties to CITES

As of May 1989, the following 99 countries are parties to the Convention on International Trade in Endangered Species of Wild Fauna and Flora (CITES).

Country	Effective Date
Afghanistan	January 28, 1986
Algeria	February 21, 1984
Argentina	April 8, 1981
Australia	October 27, 1976
Austria	April 27, 1982
Bahamas	September 18, 1979
Bangladesh	February 18, 1982
Belize	September 21, 1981
Belgium	January 1, 1984
Benin	May 28, 1984
Bolivia	October 4, 1979
Botswana	February 12, 1978
Brazil	November 4, 1975
Burundi	November 6, 1988
Cameroon	September 3, 1981
Canada	July 9, 1975
Central African Republic	November 25, 1980
Chad	May 3, 1989
Chile	July 1, 1975
China, People's Republic of	April 8, 1981
Colombia	November 29, 1981
Congo	May 1, 1983
Costa Rica	September 28, 1975
Cyprus	July 1, 1975
Denmark	October 24, 1977
Dominican Republic	March 17, 1987
Ecuador	July 1, 1975
Egypt	April 4, 1978
El Salvador	July 29, 1987

Country	Effective Date
Finland	August 8, 1976
France	August 9, 1978
Gabon	May 15, 1989
Gambia	November 24, 1977
German Democratic Republic	January 7, 1976
Germany, Federal Republic of	June 20, 1976
Ghana	February 12, 1976
Guatemala	February 5, 1980
Guinea	December 20, 1981
Guyana	August 25, 1977
Honduras	June 13, 1985
Hungary	August 27, 1985
India	October 18, 1976
Indonesia	March 28, 1979
Iran	November 1, 1976
Israel	March 17, 1980
Italy	December 31, 1979
Japan	November 4, 1980
Jordan	March 14, 1979
Kenya	March 13, 1979
Liberia	June 9, 1981
Liechtenstein	February 28, 1980
Luxembourg	March 12, 1984
Madagascar	November 18, 1975
Malawi	May 6, 1982
Malaysia	January 18, 1978
Mauritius	July 27, 1975
Monaco	July 18, 1978
Morocco	January 14, 1976
Mozambique	June 23, 1981
Nepal	September 16, 1975
Netherlands	July 18, 1984
Nicaragua	November 4, 1977
Niger	December 7, 1975
Nigeria	July 1, 1975
Norway	October 25, 1976
Pakistan	July 19, 1976
Panama	November 15, 1978
Papua New Guinea	March 11, 1976
Paraguay	February 13, 1977
Peru	September 25, 1975
Philippines	November 16, 1981
Portugal	March 11, 1981
Rwanda	January 18, 1981
St. Lucia	March 15, 1983
St. Vincent and Grenadines	February 28, 1989
Senegal	November 3, 1977
Seychelles	May 9, 1977
Singapore	February 28, 1987
Somalia	March 2, 1986

Country	Effective Date
South Africa	October 13, 1975
Spain	August 28, 1986
Sri Lanka	August 2, 1979
Sudan	January 24, 1983
Suriname	February 15, 1981
Sweden	July 1, 1975
Switzerland	July 1, 1975
Tanzania	February 27, 1980
Thailand	April 21, 1983
Togo	January 21, 1979
Trinidad & Tobago	April 18, 1984
Tunisia	July 1, 1975
Union of Soviet Socialist Republics	December 8, 1976
United Kingdom	October 31, 1976
United States of America	July 1, 1975
Uruguay	July 1, 1975
Venezuela	January 22, 1978
Zaire	October 18, 1976
Zambia	February 22, 1981
Zimbabwe	August 17, 1981

APPENDIX C

Species Listed on CITES Appendices

Appendix I *(as of October 22, 1987)*

Scientific name	English common name
FAUNA	**ANIMALS**
Mammalia	*Mammals*
MARSUPIALIA	
Dasyuridae	
Sminthopsis longicaudata	Long-tailed dunnart
S. psammophila	Sandhill dunnart
Thylacinidae	
* Thylacinus cynocephalus	Thylacine
Peramelidae	
* Chaeropus ecaudatus	Pig-footed bandicoot
Perameles bougainville	Western barred bandicoot
Thylacomyidae	
Macrotis lagotis	Greater bilby
M. leucura	Lesser bilby
Vombatidae	
Lasiorhinus krefftii	Northern hairy-nosed wombat
Macropodidae	
Bettongia spp.	Bettongs
* Caloprymnus campestris	Desert rat-kangaroo
Lagorchestes hirsutus	Rufous hare-wallaby
Lagostrophus fasciatus	Banded hare-wallaby
Onychogalea fraenata	Bridled nailtail wallaby
O. lunata	Crescent nailtail wallaby

Scientific name	English common name
PRIMATES	
Lemuridae spp.	Lemurs, gentle lemurs, sportive lemurs
Cheirogaleidae spp.	Dwarf lemurs, mouse lemurs, fork-marked lemurs
Indriidae spp.	Indris, sifakas, woolly lemurs
Daubentoniidae	
Daubentonia madagascariensis	Aye-aye
Callithricidae	
Callithrix jacchus aurita	White-eared marmoset
C. j. flaviceps	Buff-headed marmoset
Leontopithecus spp.	Golden tamarins
Saguinus bicolor	Bare-faced tamarin
S. leucopus	White-footed tamarin
S. oedipus	Cotton-headed tamarin
Callimiconidae	
Callimico goeldii	Goeldi's marmoset
Cebidae	
Alouatta palliata	Mantled howler
Ateles geoffroyi frontatus	Black-browed spider monkey
A. g. panamensis	Red spider monkey
Brachyteles arachnoides	Woolly spider monkey
Cacajao spp.	Uakaris
Chiropotes albinasus	White-nosed saki
† *Lagothrix flavicauda*	Yellow-tailed woolly monkey
Saimiri oerstedii	Central American squirrel monkey
Cercopithecidae	
Cercocebus galeritus galeritus	Tana River mangabey
† *Cercopithecus diana*	Diana guenon
Colobus pennantii kirki	Zanzibar red colobus
C. rufomitratus	Tana River colobus
Macaca silenus	Lion-tailed macaque
Nasalis spp.	Pig-tailed langur, proboscis monkey
† *Papio leucophaeus*	Drill
† *P. sphinx*	Mandrill
Presbytis entellus	Hanuman langur
P. geei	Golden langur
P. pileata	Capped langur
P. potenziani	Mentawai langur
† *Pygathrix* spp.	Douc/snub-nosed monkeys
Hylobatidae spp.	Gibbons, siamang
Pongidae spp.	Chimpanzees, gorilla, orangutan
EDENTATA	
Dasypodidae	
Priodontes maximus	Giant armadillo

Scientific name	English common name
PHOLIDOTA	
Manidae	
Manis temminckii	Temminck's ground pangolin
LAGOMORPHA	
Leporidae	
Caprolagus hispidus	Hispid hare
Romerolagus diazi	Volcano rabbit
RODENTIA	
Sciuridae	
Cynomys mexicanus	Mexican prairie dog
Muridae	
Leporillus conditor	Greater stick-nest rat
Pseudomys praeconis	Shark bay mouse
Xeromys myoides	False water-rat
Zyzomys pedunculatus	Central rock-rat
Chinchillidae	
† *Chinchilla* spp. (South American populations)	Chinchillas
CETACEA	
Platanistidae	
Lipotes vexillifer	White flag dolphin
Platanista spp.	Susus
Ziphiidae	
† *Berardius* spp.	Fourtooth whales
† *Hyperoodon* spp.	Bottlenose whales
Physeteridae	
† *Physeter macrocephalus*	Sperm whale
Delphinidae	
Sotalia spp.	Tucuxis
Sousa spp.	Hump-backed dolphins
Phocoenidae	
Neophocaena phocaenoides	Finless porpoise
Phocoena sinus	Cochito
Eschrichtidae	
Eschrichtius robustus	Gray whale
Balaenopteridae	
† *Balaenoptera acutorostrata* (all populations except Greenland)	Minke whale
† *B. borealis*	Sei whale
† *B. edeni*	Bryde's whale
B. musculus	Blue whale
† *B. physalus*	Fin whale
Megaptera novaeangliae	Humpback whale

Appendix C

Scientific name	English common name
Balaenidae	
Balaena spp.	Right whales, bowhead whale
† *Caperea marginata*	Pygmy right whale
CARNIVORA	
Canidae	
† *Canis lupus* (populations of Bhutan, India, Nepal, and Pakistan	Grey wolf
Speothos venaticus	Bush dog
Ursidae	
Ailuropoda melanoleuca	Giant panda
Helarctos malayanus	Sun bear
Selenarctos thibetanus	Asiatic black bear
Tremarctos ornatus	Spectacled bear
Ursus arctos isabellinus	Himalayan brown bear
U. a. nelsoni	Mexican grizzly bear
U. a. pruinosus	Tibetan brown bear
Mustelidae	
† *Aonyx congica* (populations of Cameroon and Nigeria)	Cameroon clawless otter
Enhydra lutris nereis	Southern sea otter
Lutra felina	Marine otter
L. longicaudis	South American river otter
L. lutra	Eurasian otter
L. provocax	Southern river otter
Mustela nigripes	Black-footed ferret
Pteronura brasiliensis	Giant otter
Viverridae	
Prionodon pardicolor	Spotted linsang
Hyaenidae	
Hyaena brunnea	Brown hyaena
Felidae	
Acinonyx jubatus	Cheetah
† *Felis bengalensis bengalensis* (all except Chinese population)	Bengal leopard cat
† *F. caracal* (Asian population)	Caracal
F. concolor coryi	Florida puma
F. c. costaricensis	Costa Rican puma
F. c. cougar	Eastern puma
F. jacobita	Andean cat
F. marmorata	Marbled cat
F. nigripes	Black-footed cat
F. pardalis mearnsi	Costa Rican ocelot
F. p. mitis	South Brazilian ocelot
F. planiceps	Flat-headed cat
† *F. rubiginosa* (Indian population)	Rusty-spotted cat
F. rufa escuinapae	Central Mexican bobcat

Scientific name	English common name
F. temmincki	Asiatic golden cat
F. tigrina oncilla	Costa Rican little spotted cat
F. wiedii nicaraguae	Central American margay
F. w. salvinia	Guatemalan margay
† *F. yagouaroundi* (populations of North and Central America)	Jaguarundi
Neofelis nebulosa	Clouded leopard
Panthera leo persica	Asiatic lion
P. onca	Jaguar
P. pardus	Leopard
P. tigris	Tiger
P. uncia	Snow leopard

PINNIPEDIA

Otariidae
  Arctocephalus townsendi — Guadalupe fur seal

Phocidae
  Monachus spp. — Monk seals

PROBOSCIDEA

Elephantidae
  Elephas maximus — Asian elephant

SIRENIA

Dugongidae
  † *Dugong dugon* (except Australian population) — Dugong

Trichechidae
  Trichechus inunguis — Amazonian manatee
  T. manatus — Caribbean manatee

PERISSODACTYLA

Equidae
  Equus africanus — African wild ass
  E. grevyi — Grevy's zebra
  E. hemionus hemionus — Mongolian wild ass
  E. h. khur — Indian wild ass
  E. przewalskii — Przewalski's horse
  E. zebra zebra — Cape Mountain zebra

Tapiridae spp. (all species not listed on Appendix II) — Tapirs

Rhinocerotidae spp. — Rhinoceroses

ARTIODACTYLA

Suidae
  Babyrousa babyrussa — Babirusa
  Sus salvanius — Pygmy hog

Tayassuidae
  Catagonus wagneri — Chacoan peccary

Scientific name	English common name
Camelidae	
† *Vicugna vicugna* (except for parts of populations of Chile and Peru)	Vicuña
Cervidae	
Blastocerus dichotomus	Marsh deer
Cervus dama mesopotamicus	Persian fallow deer
C. duvauceli	Swamp deer
C. elaphus hanglu	Kashmir red deer
C. eldi	Thamin
C. porcinus annamiticus	Indochinese hog deer
C. p. calamianensis	Calamian hog deer
C. p. kuhli	Kuhl's hog deer
Hippocamelus spp.	Huemuls
Moschus spp. (populations of Afghanistan, Bhutan, Burma, India, Nepal, and Pakistan)	Musk deer
Muntiacus crinifrons	Black muntjac
Ozotoceros bezoarticus	Pampas deer
Pudu pudu	Southern pudu
Bovidae	
Addax nasomaculatus	Addax
Antilocapra americana peninsularis	Baja pronghorn
A. a. sonoriensis	Sonoran pronghorn
Bison bison athabascae	Wood bison
Bos gaurus	Gaur
B. mutus	Yak
B. sauveli	Kouprey
Bubalus depressicornis	Lowland anoa
B. mindorensis	Tamarau
B. quarlesi	Mountain anoa
Capra falconeri chialtanensis	Chiltan markhor
C. f. jerdoni	Suleman markhor
C. f. megaceros	Kabul markhor
Capricornis sumatraensis	Mainland serow
Gazella dama	Dama gazelle
Hippotragus niger variani	Giant sable antelope
Nemorhaedus goral	Common goral
Oryx dammah	Scimitar-horned oryx
O. leucoryx	Arabian oryx
Ovis ammon hodgsoni	Tibetan argali
O. orientalis ophion	Cyprus mouflon
O. vignei	Urial
Pantholops hodgsoni	Chiru
Rupicapra rupicapra ornata	Abruzzi chamois

Scientific name	English common name
Aves	*Birds*

STRUTHIONIFORMES

Struthionidae

† *Struthio camelus* (populations of   Ostrich
Algeria, Burkina Faso, Cameroon,
Central African Republic,
Chad, Mali, Mauritania,
Morocco, Niger, Nigeria,
Senegal, and Sudan)

RHEIFORMES

Rheidae

| *Pterocnemia pennata* | Lesser rhea |

TINAMIFORMES

Tinamidae

| *Tinamus solitarius* | Solitary tinamou |

SPHENISCIFORMES

Spheniscidae

| *Spheniscus humboldti* | Humboldt penguin |

PODICIPEDIFORMES

Podicipedidae

| *Podilymbus gigas* | Atitlan grebe |

PROCELLARIIFORMES

Diomedeidae

| *Diomedea albatrus* | Short-tailed albatross |

PELECANIFORMES

Pelecanidae

| *Pelecanus crispus* | Dalmatian pelican |

Sulidae

| *Sula abbotti* | Abbott's booby |

Fregatidae

| *Fregata andrewsi* | Christmas Island frigatebird |

CICONIIFORMES

Ciconiidae

Ciconia ciconia boyciana	Oriental white stork
Jabiru mycteria	Jabiru
Mycteria cinerea	Milky stork

Threskiornithidae

| *Geronticus eremita* | Northern bald ibis |
| *Nipponia nippon* | Japanese crested ibis |

ANSERIFORMES

Anatidae

| *Anas aucklandica nesiotis* | Campbell Island brown teal |
| *A. laysanensis* | Laysan duck |

Scientific name	English common name
A. oustaleti	Marianas duck
Branta canadensis leucopareia	Aleutian goose
B. sandvicensis	Hawaiian goose
Cairina scutulata	White-winged wood duck
* Rhodonessa caryophyllacea	Pink-headed duck

FALCONIFORMES

Cathartidae
Gymnogyps californianus	California condor
Vultur gryphus	Andean condor

Accipitridae
Aquila heliaca	Imperial eagle
Chondorhierax uncinatus wilsonii	Cuban hook-billed kite
Haliaeetus albicilla	White-tailed eagle
H. leucocephalus	Bald eagle
Harpia harpyja	South American harpy eagle
Pithecophaga jefferyi	Philippine eagle

Falconidae
Falco araea	Seychelles kestrel
F. jugger	Laggar falcon
F. newtoni aldabranus	Aldabra kestrel
F. peregrinus	Peregrine falcon
F. punctatus	Mauritius kestrel
F. rusticolus	Gyr falcon

GALLIFORMES

Megapodiidae
Macrocephalon maleo	Maleo

Cracidae
Aburria jacutinga	Black-fronted piping guan
A. pipile pipile	Trinidad piping guan
Crax blumenbachii	Red-billed curassow
C. mitu mitu	Greater razor-billed curassow
Oreophasis derbianus	Horned guan
Penelope albipennis	White-winged guan

Phasianidae
Catreus wallichii	Cheer pheasant
Colinus virginianus ridgwayi	Masked bobwhite
Crossoptilon crossoptilon	White-eared pheasant
C. mantchuricum	Brown-eared pheasant
Lophophorus spp.	Monals
Lophura edwardsi	Edwards' pheasant
L. imperialis	Imperial pheasant
L. swinhoii	Swinhoe's pheasant
Polyplectron emphanum	Palawan peacock-pheasant
Rheinartia ocellata	Crested argus pheasant
Syrmaticus ellioti	Elliot's pheasant
S. humiae	Hume's pheasant
S. mikado	Mikado pheasant

Scientific name	English common name
Tetraogallus caspius	Caspian snowcock
T. tibetanus	Tibetan snowcock
Tragopan blythii	Blyth's tragopan
T. caboti	Cabot's tragopan
T. melanocephalus	Western tragopan
Tympanuchus cupido attwateri	Attwater's prairie chicken

GRUIFORMES

Gruidae
Grus americana	Whooping crane
G. canadensis nesiotes	Cuban sandhill crane
G. c. pulla	Mississippi sandhill crane
G. japonensis	Red-crowned crane
G. leucogeranus	Siberian crane
G. monacha	Hooded crane
G. nigricollis	Black-necked crane
G. vipio	White-naped crane

Rallidae
Tricholimnas sylvestris	Lord Howe wood rail

Rhynochetidae
Rhynochetos jubatus	Kagu

Otididae
Chlamydotis undulata	Houbara bustard
Choriotis nigriceps	Great Indian bustard
Houbaropsis bengalensis	Bengal florican

CHARADRIIFORMES

Scolopacidae
Numenius borealis	Eskimo curlew
N. tenuirostris	Slender-billed curlew
Tringa guttifer	Nordmann's greenshank

Laridae
Larus relictus	Relict gull

COLUMBIFORMES

Columbidae
Caloenas nicobarica	Nicobar pigeon
Ducula mindorensis	Mindoro imperial pigeon

PSITTACIFORMES

Psittacidae
Amazona arausiaca	Red-necked amazon
A. barbadensis	Yellow-shouldered amazon
A. brasiliensis	Red-tailed amazon
A. dufresniana rhodocorytha	Red-crowned amazon
A. guildingii	St. Vincent amazon
A. imperialis	Imperial amazon
A. leucocephala	Cuban amazon
A. pretrei	Red-spectacled amazon
A. versicolor	St. Lucia amazon

Scientific name	English common name
A. vinacea	Vinaceous amazon
A. vittata	Puerto Rican amazon
Anodorhynchus spp.	Blue macaws
Ara ambigua	Buffon's macaw
A. glaucogularis	Blue-throated macaw
A. macao	Scarlet macaw
A. militaris	Military macaw
A. rubrogenys	Red-fronted macaw
Aratinga guarouba	Golden conure
Cyanopsitta spixii	Spix's macaw
Cyanoramphus auriceps forbesi	Forbes' yellow-fronted parakeet
C. novaezelandiae	Red-fronted parakeet
* *Geopsittacus occidentalis*	Night parrot
Neophema chrysogaster	Orange-bellied parrot
Ognorhynchus icterotis	Yellow-eared conure
Opopsitta diophthalma coxeni	Coxen's double-eyed fig parrot
Pezoporus wallicus	Ground parrot
Pionopsitta pileata	Brazilian pileated parrot
Probosciger aterrimus	Palm cockatoo
Psephotus chrysopterygius	Golden-shouldered parrot
* *P. pulcherrimus*	Paradise parrot
Psittacula echo	Mauritius parakeet
Psittacus erithacus princeps	Principe grey parrot
Pyrrhura cruentata	Blue-throated conure
Rhynchopsitta spp.	Thick-billed parrots
Strigops habroptilus	Kakapo

STRIGIFORMES

Tytonidae
    Tyto soumagnei — Madagascar owl

Strigidae
    Athene blewitti — Forest owlet
    Ninox novaeseelandiae royana — Norfolk Island boobook owl
    N. squampila natalis — Christmas Island boobook owl
    Otus gurneyi — Mindanao owl

APODIFORMES

Trochilidae
    Glaucis dohrnii — Hook-billed hermit

TROGONIFORMES

Trogonidae
    Pharomachrus mocinno — Resplendent quetzal

CORACIIFORMES

Bucerotidae
    Buceros bicornis homrai — Northern great hornbill
    Rhinoplax vigil — Helmeted hornbill

Scientific name	English common name
PICIFORMES	
Picidae	
Campephilus imperialis	Imperial woodpecker
Dryocopus javensis richardsi	Tristram's white-bellied woodpecker
PASSERIFORMES	
Cotingidae	
Cotinga maculata	Banded cotinga
Xipholena atropurpurea	White-winged cotinga
Pittidae	
Pitta kochi	Whiskered pitta
Atrichornithidae	
Atrichornis clamosus	Noisy scrub-bird
Muscicapidae	
* *Dasyornis broadbenti litoralis*	Western rufous bristlebird
* *D. longirostris*	Western bristlebird
Picathartes spp.	Picathartes
Zosteropidae	
Zosterops albogularis	White-chested white-eye
Meliphagidae	
Meliphaga cassidix	Helmeted honeyeater
Fringillidae	
Carduelis cucullata	Red siskin
Sturnidae	
Leucopsar rothschildi	Rothschild's myna

Reptilia — *Reptiles*

TESTUDINATA	
Emydidae	
Batagur baska	Common batagur
Geoclemys hamiltonii	Black pond turtle
Kachuga tecta tecta	Indian tent turtle
Melanochelys tricarinata	Three-keeled land turtle
Morenia ocellata	Burmese swamp turtle
Terrapene coahuila	Aquatic box turtle
Testudinidae	
Geochelone elephantopus	Galapagos giant tortoise
G. radiata	Radiated tortoise
G. yniphora	Madagascar tortoise
Gopherus flavomarginatus	Bolson tortoise
Psammobates geometricus	Geometric tortoise
Cheloniidae spp.	Marine turtles
Dermochelyidae	
Dermochelys coriacea	Leatherback turtle

Scientific name	English common name
Trionychidae	
Lissemys punctata punctata	Indian flap-shell turtle
Trionyx ater	Black soft-shell turtle
T. gangeticus	Ganges soft-shell turtle
T. hurum	Peacock-marked soft-shell turtle
T. nigricans	Dark soft-shell turtle
Chelidae	
Pseudemydura umbrina	Short-necked turtle

CROCODYLIA

Alligatoridae	
Alligator sinensis	Chinese alligator
Caiman crocodilus apaporiensis	Rio Apaporis spectacled caiman
C. latirostris	Broad-nosed caiman
Melanosuchus niger	Black caiman
Crocodylidae	
Crocodylus acutus	American crocodile
† *C. cataphractus*	Sharp-nosed crocodile
C. intermedius	Orinoco crocodile
C. morelitii	Morelet's crocodile
† *C. niloticus*	Nile crocodile
C. novaeguineae mindorensis	Mindoro crocodile
C. palustris	Mugger crocodile
† *C. porosus*	Estuarine crocodile
C. rhombifer	Cuban crocodile
C. siamensis	Siamese crocodile
† *Osteolaemus tetraspis*	West African dwarf crocodile
Tomistoma schlegelii	False gharial
Gavialidae	
Gavialis gangeticus	Gharial

RHYNCHOCEPHALIA

Sphenodontidae	
Sphenodon punctatus	Tuatara

SAURIA

Iguanidae	
Brachylophus spp.	Fiji iguanas
Cyclura spp.	West Indian rock iguanas
Sauromalus varius	San Esteban Island chuckwalla
Lacertidae	
Gallotia simonyi	Hierro giant lizard
Varanidae	
Varanus bengalensis	Bengal monitor
V. flavescens	Yellow monitor
V. griseus	Desert monitor
V. komodoensis	Komodo dragon

Scientific name	English common name
SERPENTES	
Boidae	
Acrantophis spp.	Madagascar boas
Boa constrictor occidentalis	Argentine boa constrictor
Bolyeria multocarinata	Round Island boa
Casarea dussumieri	Keel-scaled boa
Epicrates inornatus	Puerto Rican boa
† *E. monensis*	Mona Island boa
E. subflavus	Jamaican boa
Python molurus molurus	Indian rock python
Sanzinia madagascariensis	Madagascar tree boa
Viperidae	
† *Vipera ursinii* (population of Europe, excluding the USSR)	Ursini's viper

Amphibia — *Amphibians*

Scientific name	English common name
CAUDATA	
Cryptobranchidae	
Andrias spp.	Giant salamanders
ANURA	
Bufonidae	
Atelopus varius zeteki	Golden frog
Bufo superciliaris	Cameroon toad
Nectophrynoides spp.	Viviparous African toads
Microhylidae	
Dyscophus antongilii	Tomato frog

Pisces — *Fish*

Scientific name	English common name
ACIPENSERIFORMES	
Acipenseridae	
Acipenser brevirostrum	Shortnose sturgeon
A. sturio	Common sturgeon
OSTEOGLOSSIFORMES	
Osteoglossidae	
Scleropages formosus	Asian bony-tongue
CYPRINIFORMES	
Cyprinidae	
Probarbus jullieni	Ikan temoleh
Catostomidae	
Chasmistes cujus	Cui ui
SILURIFORMES	
Schilbeidae	
Pangasianodon gigas	Giant catfish

Appendix C

Scientific name	English common name
PERCIFORMES	
Sciaenidae	
Cynoscion macdonaldi	Totoaba
Insecta	*Insects*
LEPIDOPTERA	
Papilionidae	
Ornithoptera alexandrae	Queen Alexandra's birdwing
Papilio chikae	Luzon swallowtail
P. homerus	Homerus swallowtail
P. hospiton	Corsican swallowtail
Mollusca	*Mollusks*
UNIONOIDA	
Unionidae	
Conradilla caelata	Birdwing pearly mussel
Dromus dromas	Dromedary pearly mussel
Epioblasma curtisi	Curtis' pearly mussel
E. florentina	Yellow-blossom pearly mussel
E. sampsoni	Sampson's pearly mussel
E. sulcata perobliqua	White catspaw mussel
E. torulosa gubernaculum	Green-blossom pearly mussel
E. t. torulosa	Tubercled-blossom pearly mussel
E. turgidula	Turgid-blossom pearly mussel
E. walkeri	Brown-blossom pearly mussel
Fusconaia cuneolus	Fine-rayed pigtoe pearly mussel
F. edgariana	Shiny pigtoe pearly mussel
Lampsilis higginsi	Higgins' eye pearly mussel
L. orbiculata orbiculata	Pinck mucket pearly mussel
L. satura	Plain pocketbook pearly mussel
L. virescens	Alabama lamp pearly mussel
Plethobasus cicatricosus	White warty-back pearly mussel
P. cooperianus	Orange-footed pimpleback mussel
Pleurobema plenum	Rough pigtoe pearly mussel
Potamilus capax	Fat pocketbook pearly mussel
Quadrula intermedia	Cumberland monkey-face pearly mussel
Q. sparsa	Appalachian monkey-face pearly mussel
Toxolasma cylindrella	Pale lilliput pearly mussel
Unio nickliniana	Nicklin's pearly mussel
U. tampicoensis tecomatensis	Tampico pearly mussel
Villosa trabalis	Cumberland bean pearly mussel
STYLOMMATOPHORA	
Achatinellidae	
Achatinella spp.	Oahu tree snails

International Wildlife Trade: Whose Business Is It?

Scientific name	English common name
FLORA	**PLANTS**

AGAVACEAE
Agave arizonica	New River agave
A. parviflora	Little princess agave
Nolina interrata	Dehesa beargrass

APOCYNACEAE
Pachypodium namaquanum

ARACEAE
Alocasia sanderiana
A. zebrina

ARAUCARIACEAE
| *Araucaria araucana* | Monkey-puzzle tree |
| (Chinese population) | |

CACTACEAE
Ancistrocactus tobuschii	Tobusch's fishhook cactus
Ariocarpus agavoides	Tamaulipas living-rock cactus
A. scapharostrus	Nuevo Leon living-rock cactus
A. trigonus	
Astrophytum asterias	Star cactus
Aztekium ritteri	Aztec cactus
Backebergia militaris	Teddy-bear cactus
Coryphantha minima	Nellie's cory cactus
C. sneedii	Sneed's pincushion cactus
C. werdermanii	Jabali pincushion cactus
Echinocereus lindsayi	Lindsay's cactus
E. erectocentrus	Needle-spined pineapple cactus
E. mariposensis	Mariposa cactus
Leuchtenbergia principis	Agave cactus
Mammillaria pectinifera	
M. plumosa	Feather cactus
M. solisioides	
Nopalxochia macdougallii	MacDougal's cactus
Obregonia denegrii	Artichoke cactus
Pediocactus bradyi	Brady's pincushion cactus
P. despainii	Despain's cactus
P. knowltonii	Knowlton's cactus
P. papyracanthus	Grama-grass cactus
P. paradinei	Paradine's cactus
P. peeblesianus	Peebles' Navajo cactus
P. sileri	Siler's pincushion cactus
P. winkleri	Winklers cactus
Pelecyphora spp.	Hatchet cactus, pine-cone cactus
Sclerocactus glaucus	Uinta Basin hookless cactus
S. mesae-verdae	Mesa Verde cactus
S. pubispinus	Great Basin fishhook cactus
S. wrightiae	Wright's fishhook cactus
Strombocactus disciformis	Disk cactus

Scientific name	English common name
Turbinicarpus laui	
T. lophophoroides	
T. pseudomacrochele	
T. pseudopectinatus	
T. schmiedickeanus	
T. valdezianus	
Wilcoxia schmollii	Lamb's-tail cactus

CARYOCARACEAE
Caryocar costaricense

COMPOSITAE
Saussurea lappa   Kuth

CRASSULACEAE
Dudleya stolonifera   Laguna Beach dudleya
D. traskiae   Santa Barbara Island dudleya

CUPRESSACEAE
Fitz-Roya cupressoides   Alerce
Pilgerodendron uviferum

CYCADACEAE
Cycas beddomei   Beddomes's cycad

FOUQUIERIACEAE
Fouquieria fasciculata
F. purpusii

GENTIANACEAE
Prepusa hookeriana   Scarlet-flowered prepusa

HUMIRIACEAE
Vantanea barbourii

JUGLANDACEAE
Engelhardtia pterocarpa

LEGUMINOSAE
Cynometra hemitomophylla
Platymiscium pleiostachyum
Tachigalia versicolor

LILIACEAE
Aloe albida
A. pillansii
A. polyphylla   Spiral aloe
A. thorncroftii
A. vossii

MELASTOMATACEAE
Lavoisiera itambana

MELIACEAE
Guarea longipetiola

MORACEAE
Batocarpus costaricensis

Scientific name	English common name
NEPENTHACEAE	
Nepenthes khasiana	Indian pitcher-plant
N. rajah	Kanabalu pitcher-plant
ORCHIDACEAE	
Cattleya skinneri	White nun orchid
C. trianae	Christmas orchid
Didiciea cunninghamii	
Laelia jongheana	
L. lobata	
Lycaste skinneri var. *alba*	
Paphiopedilum druryi	Drury's slipper orchid
Peristeria elata	Holy ghost orchid
Renanthera imschootiana	Red vanda orchid
Vanda coerulea	Blue vanda orchid
PINACEAE	
Abies guatemalensis	Guatemalan fir
PODOCARPACEAE	
Podocarpus costalis	
P. parlatorei	Parlatore's podocarp
PROTEACEAE	
Orothamnus zeyheri	Marsh rose protea
Protea odorata	
RUBIACEAE	
Balmea stormiae	Ayuque
SARRACENIACEAE	
Sarracenia alabamensis ssp. *alabamensis*	Alabama canebrake pitcher-plant
S. jonesii	Mountain sweet pitcher-plant
S. oreophila	Green pitcher-plant
STANGERIACEAE	
Stangeria eriopus	Hottentot's head
WELWITSCHIACEAE	
Welwitschia bainesii	Welwitschia
ZAMIACEAE	
Ceratozamia spp.	
Encephalartos spp.	Bread-palms
Microcycas calocoma	Palma corcho
ZINGIBERACEAE	
Hedychium philippinense	Ginger lily

---

* Possibly extinct.

† Specific populations, subspecies, or species.

Scientific name	English common name

FAUNA

ANIMALS

Mammalia

Mammals

MONOTREMATA

Tachyglossidae
   Zaglossus spp. — Long-beaked echidnas

MARSUPIALIA

Phalangeridae
   Phalanger maculatus — Common spotted cuscus
   P. orientalis — Grey cuscus

Burramyidae
   Burramys parvus — Mountain pygmy-possum

Macropodidae
   Dendrolagus bennettianus — Bennett's tree-kangaroo
   D. inustus — Grizzled tree-kangaroo
   D. lumholtzi — Lumholtz' tree-kangaroo
   D. ursinus — Vogelkop tree-kangaroo

CHIROPTERA

Pteropodidae
+ *Pteropus insularis* — Truk flying-fox
+ *P. macrotis* — Big-eared flying-fox
+ *P. mariannus* — Marianas flying-fox
+ *P. molossinus* — Ponape flying-fox
+ *P. phaeocophalus* — Mortlock flying-fox
+ *P. pilosus* — Large Palau flying-fox
+ *P. samoensis* — Samoan flying-fox
+ *P. tokudae* — Guam flying-fox
+ *P. tonganus* — Insular flying-fox

PRIMATES

All nonhuman primates not listed on Appendix I

EDENTATA

Myrmecophagidae
   Myrmecophaga tridactyla — Giant anteater
   Tamandua tetradactyla chapadensis — Mato Grosso collared anteater

Bradypodidae
   Bradypus variegatus — Brown-throated sloth

PHOLIDOTA

Manidae
   Manis crassicaudata — Indian pangolin
   M. javanica — Malayan pangolin
   M. pentadactyla — Chinese pangolin

Scientific name	English common name

RODENTIA

Sciuridae
  Ratufa spp.   Oriental giant squirrels

CETACEA

All cetacean species and populations not listed on Appendix I

CARNIVORA

Canidae
† *Canis lupus* (populations not   Grey wolf
   listed on Appendix I)
  Chrysocyon brachyurus   Maned wolf
  Cuon alpinus   Dhole
  Dusicyon culpaeus   Colpeo fox
  D. griseus   Argentine grey fox
  D. gymnocercus   Pampas fox
  Vulpes cana   Blanford's fox
  V. zerda   Fennec fox

Ursidae
† *Ursus arctos* (subspecies not   Brown bear
   listed on Appendix I)
  U. maritimus   Polar bear

Procyonidae
  Ailurus fulgena   Lesser panda

Mustelidae
  Conepatus humboldtii   Patagonian hog-nosed skunk
  Lutrinae spp. (species not   Otters
   listed on Appendix I)

Viverridae
  Cryptoprocta ferox   Fossa
  Cynogale bennettii   Otter-civet
  Eupleres goudotii   Falanouc
  Fossa fossa   Malagasy civet
  Hemigalus derbyanus   Banded palm civet
  Prionodon linsang   Banded linsang

Felidae spp. (all species and   Cats
   populations not listed on
   Appendix I)

PINNIPEDIA

Otariidae
  Arctocephalus spp. (all species   Fur seals
   not listed on Appendix I)

Phocidae
  Mirounga angustirostris   Northern elephant-seal
  M. leonina   Southern elephant-seal

Appendix C   359

Scientific name	English common name
TUBULIDENTATA	
Orycteropodidae	
Orycteropus afer	Aardvark
PROBOSCIDEA	
Elephantidae	
Loxodonta africana	African elephant
SIRENIA	
Dugongidae	
† *Dugong dugon* (Australian population)	Dugong
Trichechidae	
Trichechus senegalensis	African manatee
PERISSODOCTYLA	
Equidae	
Equus hemionus (subspecies not listed on Appendix I)	Asiatic wild ass
E. zebra hartmannae	Hartmann's mountain zebra
Tapiridae	
Tapirus terrestris	Brazilian tapir
ARTIODACTYLA	
Tayassuidae spp. (all species not listed on Appendix I, except U.S. populations)	Peccaries
Hippopotamidae	
Choeropsis liberiensis	Pygmy hippopotamus
Camelidae	
Lama guanicoe	Guanaco
† *Vicugna vicugna* (parts of populations of Chile and Peru)	Vicuña
Cervidae	
Cervus elaphus bactrianus	Bactrian red deer
Moschus spp. (populations not listed on Appendix I)	Musk deer
Pudu mephistophiles	Northern pudu
Bovidae	
Ammotragus lervia	Barbary sheep
Antilocapra americana mexicana	Mexican pronghorn
Budorcas taxicolor	Takin
Capra falconeri	Markhor
Cephalophus dorsalis	Bay duiker
C. jentinki	Jentink's duiker
C. monticola	Blue duiker
C. ogilbyi	Ogilby's duiker
C. sylvicultor	Yellow-backed duiker

Scientific name	English common name
C. zebra	Banded duiker
Damaliscus dorcas dorcas	Bontebok
Hippotragus equinus	Roan antelope
Kobus leche	Lechwe
† *Ovis ammon* (except for subspecies listed on Appendix I)	Argali
† *O. canadensis* (populations of Mexico, Canada, and the U.S.)	Bighorn

Aves — *Birds*

RHEIFORMES

Rheidae

Rhea americana albescens	Argentine greater rhea

TINAMIFORMES

Tinamidae

Rhynchotus rufescens maculicollis	Bolivian rufous tinamou
R. r. pallescens	Argentine rufous tinamou
R. r. rufescens	Brazilian rufous tinamou

SPHENISCIFORMES

Spheniscidae

Spheniscus demersus	Jackass penguin

CICONIIFORMES

Balaenicipitidae

Balaeniceps rex	Shoebill

Ciconiidae

Ciconia nigra	Black stork

Threskiornithidae

Eudocimus ruber	Scarlet ibis
Geronticus calvus	Southern bald ibis
Platalea leucorodia	White spoonbill

Phoenicopteridae spp.	Flamingos

ANSERIFORMES

Anatidae

Anas aucklandica aucklandica	Auckland Island brown teal
A. a. chlorotis	New Zealand brown teal
A. bernieri	Madagascar teal
Branta ruficollis	Red-breasted goose
Coscoroba coscoroba	Coscoroba swan
Cygnus columbianus jankowskii	Jankowski's swan
C. melanocoryphus	Black-necked swan
Dendrocygna arborea	West Indian whistling duck
Oxyura leucocephala	White-headed duck
Sarkidiornis melanotos	Comb duck

Scientific name	English common name

FALCONIFORMES — Birds of prey

All Falconiformes species not listed on Appendix I, except Cathartidae spp. (New World vultures)

GALLIFORMES

Phasianidae

Argusianus argus	Great argus pheasant
Cyrtonyx montezumae mearnsi (except U.S. population)	Mexican Mearns' Montezuma quail
C. m. montezumae	Southern Montezuma quail
Francolinus ochropectus	Djibouti francolin
F. swierstrai	Swierstra's francolin
Gallus sonneratii	Grey junglefowl
Ithaginis cruentus	Blood pheasant
Pavo muticus	Green peafowl
Polyplectron bicalcaratum	Grey peacock-pheasant
P. germaini	Germain's peacock-pheasant
P. malacense	Malaysian peacock-pheasant

GRUIFORMES

Turnicidae

Turnix melanogaster	Black-breasted buttonquail

Pedionomidae

Pedionomus torquatus	Plains-wanderer

Gruidae spp. (all species not listed on Appendix I) — Cranes

Rallidae

Gallirallus australis hectori	Buff weka

Otididae spp. (all species not listed on Appendix I) — Bustards

COLUMBIFORMES

Columbidae

Gallicolumba luzonica	Luzon bleeding-heart dove
Goura spp.	Crowned pigeons

PSITTACIFORMES

All parrot species not listed on Appendix I, except *Melopsittacus undulatus* (Budgerigar), *Nymphicus hollandicus* (Cockatiel), and *Psittacula krameri* (Rose-ringed parakeet)

CUCULIFORMES

Musophagidae

Tauraco corythaix	Knysna turaco
T. porphyreolophus	Purple-crested turaco

STRIGIFORMES

All owl species not listed on Appendix I

APODIFORMES

Trochilidae spp. (all species not listed on Appendix I) — Hummingbirds

Scientific name	English common name
CORACIIFORMES	
Bucerotidae	
Aceros narcondami	Narcondam hornbill
Buceros bicornis (all subspecies not listed on Appendix I)	Southern great hornbill
B. hydrocorax hydrocorax	Luzon rufous hornbill
B. rhinoceros rhinoceros	Malayan rhinoceros hornbill
PASSERIFORMES	
Cotingidae	
Rupicola spp.	Cocks-of-the-rock
Pittidae	
Pitta brachyura nympha	Fairy pitta
Hirundinidae	
Pseudochelidon sirintarae	White-eyed river martin
Muscicapidae	
Niltava ruecki	Rueck's blue flycatcher
Emberizidae	
Gubernatrix cristata	Yellow cardinal
Paroaria capitata	Yellow-billed cardinal
P. coronata	Red-crested cardinal
Fringillidae	
Carduelis yarrellii	Yellow-faced siskin
Estrildidae	
Poephila cincta cincta	Southern black-throated finch
Paradisaeidae spp.	Birds of paradise

Reptilia — *Reptiles*

TESTUDINATA	
Dermatemydidae	
Dermatemys mawii	Central American river turtle
Emydidae	
Clemmys muhlenbergi	Bog turtle
Testudinidae spp. (all species and subspecies not listed on Appendix I)	Tortoises
Pelomedusidae	
Erymnochelys madagascariensis	Madagascar sideneck turtle
Peltocephalus dumeriliana	Parrot-beaked turtle
Podocnemis spp.	South American river turtles
CROCODYLIA	

All crocodilian species not listed on Appendix I (subject to specific annual export quotas for some species and countries)

Scientific name	English common name

SAURIA

Gekkonidae
    Cyrtodactylus serpensinsula   Serpent Island gecko
    Phelsuma spp.   Day geckos

Agamidae
    Uromastyx spp.   Spiny-tailed lizards

Chamaeleonidae
    Bradypodion spp.   Dwarf chameleons
    Chamaeleo spp.   Chameleons

Iguanidae
    Amblyrhynchus cristatus   Galapagos marine iguana
    Conolophus spp.   Galapagos land iguanas
    Iguana spp.   Green iguanas
    Phrynosoma coronatum blainvillei   San Diego horned lizard

Lacertidae
    Podarcis lilfordi   Lilford's wall lizard
    P. pityusensis   Ibiza wall lizard

Cordylidae
    Cordylus spp.   Girdled lizards
    Pseudocordylus spp.   Crag lizards

Teiidae
    Cnemidophorus hyperythrus   Orange-throated whiptail
    Crocodilurus lacertinus   Dragon lizardet
    Dracaena guianensis   Caiman lizard
    Tupinambis spp.   Tegus

Helodermatidae
    Heloderma spp.   Gila monster, beaded lizard

Varanidae
† *Varanus* spp. (all species not   Monitors
    listed on Appendix I)

SERPENTES

Boidae spp. (all species not listed   Boas and pythons
on Appendix I)

Colubridae
    Clelia clelia   Mussurana
    Cyclagras gigas   False cobra
    Elachistodon westermanni   Indian egg-eating snake

Elapidae
    Hoplocephalus bungaroides   Broad-headed snake

Amphibia   *Amphibians*

CAUDATA

Ambystomidae
    Ambystoma dumerilii   Achoque
    A. mexicanum   Axolotl

Scientific name	English common name

ANURA

Bufonidae
  Bufo retiformis Sonoran green toad

Dendrobatidae
  Dendrobates spp. Poison-arrow frogs
  Phyllobates spp. Poison-arrow frogs

Myobatrachidae
  Rheobatrachus spp. Platypus frog/gastric-brooding frog

Ranidae
  Rana hexadactyla Six-fingered frog
  R. tigerina Indian bullfrog

Pisces *Fish*

CERATODIFORMES

Ceratodidae
  Neoceratodus forsteri Australian lungfish

COELACANTHIFORMES

Coelacanthidae
  Latimeria chalumnae Coelacanth

ACIPENSERIFORMES

Acipenseridae
  Acipenser oxyrhynchus Atlantic sturgeon

OSTEOGLOSSIFORMES

Osteoglossidae
  Arapaima gigas Pirarucu

CYPRINIFORMES

Cyprinidae
  Caecobarbus geertsi African blind barb fish

ATHERINIFORMES

Cyprinodontidae
  Cynolebias constanciae Pearlfish
  C. marmoratus Ginger pearlfish
  C. minimus Minute pearlfish
  C. opalescens Opalescent pearlfish
  C. splendens Splendid pearlfish

Insecta *Insects*

LEPIDOPTERA

Papilionidae
  Bhutanitis spp. Bhutanitis swallowtails
  Ornithoptera spp. (all species Birdwing butterflies
    not listed on Appendix I)
  Parnassius apollo Mountain apollo

Scientific name	English common name
Teinopalpus spp.	Kaiser-I-Hinds
Trogonoptera spp.	Birdwing butterflies
Troides spp.	Birdwing butterflies

Arachnida — Arachnids

ARANEAE

Theraphosidae
   Brachypelma smithi — Mexican red-kneed tarantula

Annelida — Annelids

ARHYNCHOBDELLAE

Hirudinidae
   Hirudo medicinalis — Medicinal leech

Mollusca — Mollusks

VENEROIDA

Tridacnidae spp. — Giant clams

UNIONOIDA

Unionidae
   Cyprogenia aberti — Edible pearly mussel
   Epioblasma torulosa rangiana — Tan-blossom pearly mussel
   Fusconaia subrotunda — Long solid mussel
   Lampsilis brevicula — Ozark lamp pearly mussel
   Lexingtonia dolabelloides — Slab-sided pearly mussel
   Pleurobema clava — Club pearly mussel

STYLOMMATOPHORA

Camaenidae
   Papustyla pulcherrima — Manus green tree snail

Paryphantidae
   Paryphanta spp. — Amber snails
   (all New Zealand species)

Anthozoa — Anthozoans

ANTIPATHARIA spp. — Black corals

SCLERACTINIA

Pocilloporidae
   Pocillopora spp. — Brown stem cluster corals
   Seriatopora spp. — Birds nest corals
   Stylophora spp. — Cauliflower corals

Acroporidae
   Acropora spp. — Branch corals

Agariciidae
   Pavona spp. — Cactus corals

Scientific name	English common name
Fungiidae	
Fungia spp.	Mushroom corals
Halomitra spp.	
Polyphyllia spp.	Feather corals
Faviidae	
Favia spp.	Brain corals
Platygyra spp.	Brain corals
Merulinidae	
Merulina spp.	Merulina corals
Mussidae	
Lobophyllia spp.	Brain root corals
Pectiniidae	
Pectinia spp.	Lettuce corals
Caryophylliidae	
Euphyllia spp.	Brain trumpet corals

Hydrozoa · *Hydrozoans*

ATHECATA

Milleporidae
   Millepora spp. · Wello fire corals

Alcyonaria · *Alcyonarians*

COENOTHECALIA

Helioporidae
   Heliopora spp. · Blue corals

STOLONIFERA

Tubiporidae
   Tubipora spp. · Organpipe corals

FLORA · PLANTS

AGAVACEAE
   Agave victoriae-reginae · Queen agave

APOCYNACEAE
   Pachypodium spp. (all species not listed on Appendix I) · Elephant's trunks

ARALIACEAE
   Panax quinquefolius · American ginseng

ARAUCARIACEAE
   Araucaria araucana (except Chinese population) · Monkey-puzzle tree

ASCLEPIADACEAE
   Ceropegia spp. · Rosary vines
   Frerea indica

Scientific name	English common name
BYBLIDACEAE	
Byblis spp.	Byblises
CACTACEAE spp. (all species not listed on Appendix I)	Cacti
CEPHALOTACEAE	
Cephalotus follicularis	Albany pitcherplant
CYATHEACEAE spp.	Tree ferns
CYCADACEAE spp. (all species not listed on Appendix I)	Cycads
DIAPENSIACEAE	
Shortia galacifolia	Oconee-bells
DICKSONIACEAE spp.	
DIDIEREACEAE spp.	
DIOSCOREACEAE	
Dioscorea deltoidea	
ERICACEAE	
Kalmia cuneata	White wicky
EUPHORBIACEAE	
Euphorbia spp. (excluding species that are not succulents)	Euphorbias
FAGACEAE	
Quercus copeyensis	Copey oak
FOUQUIERIACEAE	
Fouquieria columnaris	Boojum tree
LILIACEAE	
Aloe spp. (all species not listed on Appendix I)	Aloes
MELIACEAE	
Swietenia humilis	Mexican mahogany
NEPENTHACEAE	
Nepenthes spp. (all species not listed on Appendix I)	Pitcher-plants
ORCHIDACEAE spp. (all species not listed on Appendix I)	Orchids
PALMAE	
Areca ipot	
Chrysalidocarpus decipiens	
Neodypsis decaryi	
Phoenix hanceana var. *philippinensis*	
Salacca clemensiana	
PORTULACACEAE	
Anacampseros spp.	
Lewisia cotyledon	Siskiyou lewisia
L. maguirei	Maguire's lewisia

Scientific name	English common name
L. serrata	Saw-toothed lewisia
L. tweedyi	Tweedy's lewisia
PRIMULACEAE	
Cyclamen spp.	Cyclamens
SARRACENIACEAE	
Darlingtonia californica	California pitcher-plant
Sarracenia spp. (all species not listed on Appendix I	North American pitcher-plants
STERCULIACEAE	
Pterygota excelsa	
THEACEAE	
Camellia chrysantha	Jinhuacha
ZAMIACEAE spp. (all species not listed on Appendix I)	Zamias
ZYGOPHYLLACEAE	
Guaiacum sanctum	Tree of life

+ Dead specimens only.

† Specific populations, subspecies, or species.

Scientific name	English common name	Party listing species
FAUNA	**ANIMALS**	
Mammalia	*Mammals*	
CHIROPTERA		
Phyllostomidae		
Vampyrops lineatus	White-lined bat	UY
EDENTATA		
Myrmecophagidae		
Tamandua tetradactyla	Collared anteater	GT
Choloepidae		
Choloepus hoffmanni	Hoffman's two-toed sloth	CR
Dasypodidae		
Cabassous centralis	Northern naked-tailed armadillo	CR
C. tatouay	Greater naked-tailed armadillo	UY
PHOLIDOTA		
Manidae		
Manis gigantea	Giant pangolin	GH
M. tetradactyla	Long-tailed pangolin	GH
M. tricuspis	Tree pangolin	GH
RODENTIA		
Sciuridae		
Epixerus ebii	Temminck's giant squirrel	GH
Sciurus deppei	Deppe's squirrel	CR
Anomaluridae		
Anomalurus beecrofti	Beecroft's flying squirrel	GH
A. derbianus	Lord Derby's flying squirrel	GH
A. peli	Pel's flying squirrel	GH
Idiurus macrotis	Long-eared flying squirrel	GH
Hystricidae		
Hystrix cristata	North African crested porcupine	GH
Erethizontidae		
Sphiggurus mexicanus	Mexican tree porcupine	HN
S. spinosus	Spiny tree porcupine	UY
Agoutidae		
Agouti paca	Spotted paca	HN
Dasyproctidae		
Dasyprocta punctata	Central American agouti	HN
CARNIVORA		
Ursidae		
Melursus ursinus	Sloth bear	IN[s]

Scientific name	English common name	Party listing species
Procyonidae		
Bassaricyon gabbii	Bushy-tailed olingo	CR
Bassariscus sumichrasti	Central American cacomistle	CR
Nasua nasua	Coati	HN
N. n. solitaria	South Brazilian coati	UY
Potos flavus	Kinkajou	HN
Mustelidae		
Eira barbara	Tayra	HN
Galictis vittata	Greater grison	CR
Mellivora capensis	Ratel	GH, BW
Viverridae		
Civettictis civetta	African civit	BW
Protelidae		
Proteles cristatus	Aardwolf	BW
PINNIPEDIA		
Odobenidae		
Odobenus rosmarus	Walrus	CA
ARTIODACTYLA		
Hyppopotamidae		
Hippopotamus amphibius	Hippopotamus	GH
Tragulidae		
Hyemoschus aquaticus	Water chevrotain	GH
Cervidae		
Cervus elaphus barbarus	Barbary red deer	TN
Mazama americana cerasina	Guatemalan red brocket	GT
Odocoileus virginianus mayensis	Guatemalan white-tailed deer	GT
Bovidae		
Antilope cervicapra	Blackbuck	NP
Boocercus eurycerus	Bongo	GH
Bubalus bubalis	Water buffalo	NP, TN
Damaliscus lunatus	Tsessebi	GH
Gazella cuvieri	Edmi gazelle	TN
G. dorcas	Dorcas gazelle	TN
G. leptoceros	Sand gazelle	TN
Tetracerus quadricornis	Four-horned antelope	NP
Tragelaphus spekei	Sitatunga	GH

Aves — *Birds*

RHEIFORMES		
Rheidae		
Rhea americana	Greater rhea	UY
CICONIIFORMES		
Ardeidae		
Ardea goliath	Goliath heron	GH
Bubulcus ibis	Cattle egret	GH

Scientific name	English common name	Party listing species
Casmerodius albus	Great egret	GH
Egretta garzetta	Little egret	GH
Ciconiidae		
Ephippiorhynchus senegalensis	Saddlebill stork	GH
Leptoptilos crumeniferus	Marabou stork	GH
Threskiornithidae		
Hagedashia hagedash	Hadada ibis	GH
Lampribis rara	Spot-breasted ibis	GH
Threskiornis aethiopicus	Sacred ibis	GH
ANSERIFORMES		
Anatidae		
Alopochen aegyptiacus	Egyptian goose	GH
Anas acuta	Northern pintail	GH
A. capensis	Cape teal	GH
A. clypeata	Northern shoveler	GH
A. crecca	Common teal	GH
A. penelope	Eurasion wigeon	GH
A. querquedula	Garganey	GH
Aythya nuroca	Ferruginous duck	GH
Cairina moschata	Muscovy duck	HN
Dendrocygna autumnalis	Black-bellied whistling duck	HN
D. bicolor	Fulvous whistling duck	GH, HN
D. viduata	White-faced whistling duck	GH
Nettapus auritus	African pygmy goose	GH
Plectropterus gambensis	Spur-winged goose	GH
Pteronetta hartlaubii	Hartlaub's duck	GH
FALCONIFORMES		
Cathartidae		
Sarcoramphus papa	King vulture	HN
GALLIFORMES		
Cracidae		
Crax alberti	Blue-billed curassow	CO
C. daubentoni	Yellow-knobbed curassow	CO
C. globulosa	Wattled curassow	CO
C. pauxi	Helmeted curassow	CO
C. rubra	Great curassow	CO, CR, GT, HN
Ortalis vetula	Plain chachalaca	GT, HN
Penelope purpurascens	Crested guan	HN
Penelopina nigra	Highland guan	GT
Phasianidae		
Agelastes meleagrides	White-breasted guineafowl	GH
Agriocharis ocellata	Ocellated turkey	GT
Arborophila brunneopectus	Bar-backed partridge	MY
A. charltonii	Chestnut-necklaced partridge	MY
Caloperdix oculea	Ferruginous wood-partridge	MY
Lophura erythrophthalma	Crestless fireback pheasant	MY

Scientific name	English common name	Party listing species
L. ignita	Crested fireback pheasant	MY
Melanoperdix nigra	Black wood-partridge	MY
Polyplectron inopinatum	Mountain peacock-pheasant	MY
Rhizothera longirostris	Long-billed partridge	MY
Rollulus rouloul	Crested wood partridge	MY
Tragopan satyra	Satyr tragopan	NP

CHARADRIIFORMES

Burhinidae
Burhinus bistriatus	Double-striped thick-knee	GT

COLUMBIFORMES

Columbidae
Columba guinea	Speckled pigeon	GH
C. iriditorques	Western bronze-naped pigeon	GH
C. livida	Rock pigeon	GH
C. unicincta	Afep pigeon	GH
Nesoenas mayeri	Pink pigeon	MU
Oena capensis	Namaqua dove	GH
Streptopelia decipiens	Mourning collared dove	GH
S. roseogrisea	African collared dove	GH
S. semitorquata	Red-eyed dove	GH
S. senegalensis	Laughing dove	GH
S. turtur	Western turtle dove	GH
S. vinacea	Vinaceous dove	GH
Treron calva	African green pigeon	GH
T. waalia	Bruce's green pigeon	GH
Turtur abyssinicus	Black-billed wood dove	GH
T. afer	Blue-spotted wood dove	GH
T. brehmeri	Blue-headed wood dove	GH
T. tympanistria	Tambourine dove	GH

PSITTACIFORMES

Psittacidae
Psittacula krameri	Rose-ringed parakeet	GH

CUCULIFORMES

Musophagidae
Corythaeola cristata	Great blue turaco	GH
Crinifer piscator	Western grey plantain-eater	GH
Musophaga violacea	Violet turaco	GH
Tauraco macrorhynchus	Crested turaco	

PICIFORMES

Ramphastidae
Ramphastos sulfuratus	Keel-billed toucan	GT

PASSERIFORMES

Cotingidae
Cephalopterus ornatus	Amazonian umbrellabird	CO
C. penduliger	Long-wattled umbrellabird	CO

Scientific name	English common name	Party listing species
Pittidae		
Pitta guajana	Banded pitta	TH
P. gurneyi	Gurney's pitta	TH
Muscicapidae		
Bebrornis rodericanus	Rodrigues warbler	MU
Tchitrea bourbonnensis	Mascarene paradise flycatcher	MU
Icteridae		
Xanthopsar flavus	Saffron-cowled blackbird	UY
Fringillidae		
Serinus gularis	Streaky-headed canary	GH
S. leucopygius	White-rumped canary	GH
S. mozambicus	Yellow-fronted canary	GH
Estrildidae		
Amadina fasciata	Cut-throat	GH
Amandava subflava	Orange-breasted waxbill	GH
Estrilda astrild	Common waxbill	GH
E. caerulescens	Lavender waxbill	GH
E. melpoda	Orange-cheeked waxbill	GH
E. troglodytes	Black-rumped waxbill	GH
Lagonosticta larvata	Black-faced firefinch	GH
L. rara	Black-bellied firefinch	GH
L. rubricata	Brown-backed firefinch	GH
L. rufopicta	Bar-breasted firefinch	GH
L. senegala	Red-billed firefinch	GH
Lonchura bicolor	Black-breasted mannikin	GH
L. cucullata	Bronze mannikin	GH
L. fringilloides	Magpie mannikin	GH
L. malabarica	Silverbill	GH
Mandingoa nitidula	Green-backed twinspot	GH
Nesocharis capistrata	White-cheeked oliveback	GH
Nigrita bicolor	Chestnut-breasted negro-finch	GH
N. canicapilla	Grey-crowned negro-finch	GH
N. fusconota	White-breasted negro-finch	GH
N. luteifrons	Pale-fronted negro-finch	GH
Ortygospiza atricollis	Common quail-finch	GH
Parmoptila woodhousei	Antpecker	GH
Pholidornis rushiae	Tiny tit	GH
Pyrenestes ostrinus	Black-bellied seedcracker	GH
Pytilia hypogrammica	Red-faced pytilia	GH
P. phoenicoptera	Red-winged pytilia	GH
Spermophaga haematina	Western bluebill	GH
Uraeginthus bengalus	Red-cheeked cordon-bleu	GH
Ploceidae		
Amblyospiza albifrons	Thick-billed weaver	GH
Anomalospiza imberbis	Cuckoo weaver	GH
Bubalornis albirostris	Black buffalo-weaver	GH
Euplectes afer	Yellow-crowned bishop	GH
E. ardens	Red-collared widowbird	GH

Scientific name	English common name	Party listing species
E. hordeaceus	Red-crowned bishop	GH
E. macrourus	Yellow-shouldered widowbird	GH
E. orix	Red bishop	GH
Malimbus cassini	Black-throated malimbe	GH
M. malimbicus	Crested malimbe	GH
M. nitens	Blue-billed malimbe	GH
M. rubriceps	Red-headed malimbe	GH
M. rubricollis	Red-necked malimbe	GH
M. scutatus	Red-vented malimbe	GH
Passer griseus	Grey-headed sparrow	GH
Petronia dentata	Bush sparrow	GH
Plocepasser superciliosus	Chestnut-crowned sparrow-weaver	GH
Ploceus albinucha	White-naped weaver	GH
P. aurantius	Orange weaver	GH
P. cucullatus	Village weaver	GH
P. heuglini	Heuglin's weaver	GH
P. luteolus	Little weaver	GH
P. melanocephalus	Black-headed weaver	GH
P. nigerrimus	Black weaver	GH
P. nigricollis	Black-necked weaver	GH
P. pelzelni	Slender-billed weaver	GH
P. preussi	Golden-backed weaver	GH
P. superciliosus	Compact weaver	GH
P. tricolor	Yellow-mantled weaver	GH
P. velatus	Common masked weaver	GH
Quelea erythrops	Red-headed quelea	GH
Sporopipes frontalis	Speckle-fronted weaver	GH
Vidua chalybeata	Village indigobird	GH
V. interjecta	Uelle paradise whydah	GH
V. larvaticola	Bako indigobird	GH
V. macroura	Pin-tailed whydah	GH
V. paradisaea	Common paradise whydah	GH
V. raricola	Jambandu indigobird	GH
V. togoensis	Togo paradise whydah	GH
V. wilsoni	Wilson's lovebird	GH

Reptilia — Reptiles

TESTUDINATA

Trionychidae

Trionyx triunguis	Nile soft-shell turtle	GH

Pelomedusidae

Pelomedusa subrufa	Helmeted turtle	GH
Pelusios adansonii	Adanson's mud turtle	GH
P. castaneus	West African mud turtle	GH
P. gabonensis	African forest turtle	GH
P. niger	West African black forest turtle	GH

SERPENTES
Colubridae
Atretium schistosum	Olive keelback watersnake	IN
Cerberus rhynchops	Dog-faced watersnake	IN
Ptyas mucosus	Asiatic rat snake	IN
Xenochrophis piscator	Chequered keelback watersnake	IN

Elapidae
Micrurus diastema	Atlantic coral snake	HN
M. nigrocinctus	Black-banded coral snake	HN
Naja naja	Asiatic Cobra	IN
Ophiophagus hannah	King cobra	IN

Viperidae
Agkistrodon bilineatus	Cantil	HN
Bothrops asper	Barba amarilla	HN
B. nasutus	Horned hog-nosed pit viper	HN
B. nummifer	Jumping viper	HN
B. ophryomegas		HN
B. schlegelii	Horned palm viper	HN
Crotalus durissus	Tropical rattlesnake	HN
Vipera russellii	Russell's viper	IN

FLORA   PLANTS

GNETACEAE
Gnetum montanum	NP

MAGNOLIACEAE
Talauma hodgsonii	NP

PAPAVERACEAE
Meconopsis regia	NP

PODOCARPACEAE
Podocarpus neriifolius	NP

TETRACENTRACEAE
Tetracentron sinense	GH

---

*Coding guide for parties listing species:
BW—Botswana	IN—India
CA—Canada	MU—Mauritius
CO—Colombia	MY—Malaysia
CN—China	NP—Nepal
CR—Costa Rica	TH—Thailand
GH—Ghana	TN—Tunisia
GT—Guatemala	UY—Uruguay
HN—Honduras	

APPENDIX D
Reservations Listed by CITES Parties

Specific Reservations Entered by CITES Parties for Appendix I Species
(as of April 26, 1989)

Species	Party with Reservations
MAMMALS	
Physeter macrocephalus sperm whale	Japan, Norway
Berardius spp. fourtooth whales	USSR
B. bairdii Northern fourtooth whale	Japan
Hyperoodon spp. bottlenose whales	USSR
Balaenoptera acutorostrata minke whale	Brazil,* Japan,* Norway,* Peru,* USSR*
B. borealis sei whale	Japan,* Norway,* USSR*
B. edeni Bryde's whale	Brazil, Japan, Peru, USSR
B. physalus fin whale	Japan, Norway,* USSR*
Magaptera novaengliae humpback whale	St. Vincent and the Grenadines
Caperea marginata pygmy right whale	Brazil, Peru
Canis lupus† grey wolf	Switzerland*
Ursus arctos isabellinus Himalayan brown bear	Switzerland

Species	Party with Reservations
Lutra lutra Eurasian otter	USSR
Felis caracal† caracal	Switzerland*
F. rubiginosa rusty-spotted cat	Switzerland*
Catagonus wagneri chacoan peccary	Liechtenstein, Switzerland
Pantholops hodgsoni chiru	Switzerland

BIRDS

Chlamydotis undulata houbara bustard	Switzerland
Caloenas nicobarica Nicobar pigeon	Switzerland
Ara macao scarlet macaw	Liechtenstein, Suriname, Switzerland

REPTILES

Chelonia mydas green turtle	Suriname*
Eretmochelys imbricata hawksbill turtle	Japan, St. Vincent and the Grenadines
Lepidochelys olivacea olive ridley turtle	Japan
Dermochelys coriacea leatherback turtle	Suriname
Crocodylus niloticus† Nile crocodile	Botswana,* Sudan*
C. porosus† estuarine or saltwater crocodile	Japan,* Singapore*
Varanus bengalensis Bengal monitor	Japan
V. flavescens yellow monitor	Japan
Vipera ursinii Ursini's viper	Liechtenstein,* Switzerland*

AMPHIBIANS

Dyscophus antongilii tomato frog	Liechtenstein, Switzerland

PLANTS

Fitz-Roya cupressoides alerce	Chile*

Species	Party with Reservations
Renanthera imschootiana red vanda orchid	Switzerland
Vanda coerulea blue vanda orchid	Switzerland

MAMMALS

Species	Party with Reservations
Canis lupus† grey wolf	USSR*
Felis lynx lynx	USSR

BIRDS

Species	Party with Reservations
Pedionomus torquatus plains-wanderer	Switzerland
Agapornis spp. lovebirds	Liechtenstein, Switzerland
Amazonia aestiva blue-fronted amazon	Liechtenstein, Switzerland
Amazona ochrocephala yellow-crowned amazon	Liechtenstein, Switzerland
Aratinga spp. conures	Liechtenstein, Switzerland
Cacatua galerita sulphur-crested cockatoo	Liechtenstein, Switzerland
Cyanoliseus patagonus Patagonian conure	Liechtenstein,* Switzerland (except for *C. p. byroni*)
Eolophus roseicapillus galah	Liechtenstein, Switzerland
Myiopsitta monachus monk parakeet	Liechtenstein, Switzerland
Nandayus nenday nanday conure	Liechtenstein, Switzerland
Platycercus eximius eastern rosella	Liechtenstein, Switzerland
Poicephalus senegalus Senegal parrot	Liechtenstein, Switzerland
Psittacula cyaocephala plum-headed parakeet	Liechtenstein, Switzerland
Psittacus erithacus African grey parrot	Liechtenstein, Switzerland
Pyrrhua spp. conures	Liechtenstein, Switzerland
Trochilidae spp. hummingbirds	Liechtenstein, Switzerland

Species	Party with Reservations
REPTILES	
Caiman crocodilus crocodilus spectacled caiman	Singapore
Crocodylus novaeguineae novaeguineae New Guinea crocodile	Singapore
Crocodylus porosus† estuarine or saltwater crocodile	Singapore*
Podarcis lilfordi Lilford's wall lizard	Liechtenstein, Switzerland
Podarcis pityusensis Ibiza wall lizard	Liechtenstein, Switzerland
Varanus salator Malayan water monitor	Thailand
AMPHIBIANS	
Dendrobates spp. poison-arrow frogs	Liechtenstein, Switzerland
Phyllobates spp. poison-arrow frogs	Liechtenstein, Switzerland
FISH	
Caecobarbus geertsi African blind barb fish	Liechtenstein, Switzerland
PLANTS	
Cactaceae spp. cacti	Austria*
MAMMALS	
Marmota caudata long-tailed marmot	Denmark, West Germany, Italy, Luxembourg
M. himalana Himalayan marmot	Denmark, West Germany, Italy, Luxembourg
Sphiggurus mexicanus Mexican porcupine	Austria
Agouti paca spotted paca	Austria
Dasyprocta punctata Central American gouti	Austria
Canis aureus golden jackal	Denmark, West Germany, Italy, Liechtenstein, Luxembourg, Switzerland
Vulpes bengalensis Bengal fox	Denmark, West Germany, Italy, Luxembourg
V. vulpes griffithi *V. v. montana* *V. v. pusilla* red fox subspecies	Denmark, West Germany, Italy, Liechtenstein, Luxembourg, Switzerland

Species	Party with Reservations
Nasua nasua coati	Austria
Potos flavus kinkajou	Austria
Eira barbara tayra	Austria
Martes flavigula yellow-throated marten	Denmark, West Germany, Italy, Luxembourg
Martes foina intermedia beech marten	Denmark, West Germany, Italy, Liechtenstein, Luxembourg, Switzerland
Mustela altaica mountain weasel	Denmark, West Germany, Italy, Liechtenstein, Luxembourg, Switzerland
Mustela erminea stoat or ermine	Denmark, West Germany, Italy, Liechtenstein, Luxembourg, Switzerland
Mustela kathiah yellow-bellied weasel	Denmark, West Germany, Italy, Liechtenstein, Luxembourg, Switzerland
Mustela sibirica Siberian weasel	Denmark, West Germany, Italy, Liechtenstein, Luxembourg, Switzerland
Arctictis binturong binturong	Denmark, West Germany, Italy, Luxembourg
Paguma larvata masked palm civet	Denmark, West Germany, Italy, Luxembourg
Paradoxurus hermaphroditus common palm civet	Denmark, West Germany, Italy, Luxembourg
Pardoxurus jerdoni Jerdon's palm civet	Denmark, West Germany, Italy, Luxembourg
Viverra megaspila large spotted civet	Denmark, West Germany, Italy, Luxembourg
Viverra zibetha large Indian civet	Denmark, West Germany, Italy, Luxembourg
Viverricula indica small Indian civet	Denmark, West Germany, Italy, Luxembourg
Herpestes auropunctatus Small Indian mongoose	Denmark, West Germany, Italy, Luxembourg
Herpestes edwardsi Indian grey mongoose	Denmark, West Germany, Italy, Luxembourg
Herpestes fuscus Indian brown mongoose	Denmark, West Germany, Italy, Luxembourg
Herpestes smithii ruddy mongoose	Denmark, West Germany, Italy, Luxembourg
Herpestes urva crab-eating mongoose	Denmark, West Germany, Italy, Luxembourg

Species	Party with Reservations
Herpestes vitticollis stripe-necked mongoose	Denmark, West Germany, Italy, Luxembourg

BIRDS

Species	Party with Reservations
Cairina moschata Muscovy duck	Austria
Dendrocygna autumnalis red-billed or black-bellied whistling duck	Austria
D. bicolor fulvous whistling duck	Austria*
Sarcoramphus papa king vulture	Austria
Crax rubra great curassow	Austria*
Ortalis vetula plain chachalaca	Austria
Penelope purpurascens crested guan	Austria
Psittacula krameri rose-ringed parakeet	Liechtenstein, Switzerland

REPTILES

Species	Party with Reservations
Micrurus diastema Atlantic coral snake	Austria
M. nigrocinctus black-banded coral snake	Austria
Agkistrodon bilineatus tropical moccasin, cantil	Austria
Bothrops asper lance-headed viper, barba amarilla	Austria
B. nasutus horned hog-nosed pit viper	Austria
B. nummifer jumping viper	Austria
B. ophryomegas western hog-nosed viper	Austria
B. schlegelii Schlegel's pit, horned palm, or eyelash viper	Austria
Crotalus durissus South American rattlesnake	Austria

* Only certain populations of the species are covered by the reservation.
† Species has populations listed on both Appendices I and II.

APPENDIX E
TRAFFIC Offices

TRAFFIC(International)

World Conservation Monitoring Centre, 219c Huntingdon Road, Cambridge CB3 ODL, United Kingdom. Tel: (223) 277427. Fax: (223) 277136. Tlx: 817036 SCMU G.

TRAFFIC(Austria)

WWF-Austria, Ottakringerstr. 114-116/9, Postfach 1, 1162 Wien, Austria. Tel: (222) 461463. Fax: (222) 453648. Tlx: 114900 OBRAU A.

TRAFFIC(Belgium)

Chaussee de Waterloo 608, B-1060 Brussels, Belgium. Tel: (2) 347 01 11. Fax: (2) 344 05 11. Tlx: 23986 WWFBEL B.

TRAFFIC(France)

WWF-France, 151 Boulevard de la Reine, 78000, Versailles, France. Tel: (1) 3950 75 14. Fax: (1) 39 53 04 46. Tlx: 699153 soria.

TRAFFIC(Germany)

WWF-Germany, Hedderichstrasse 110, 6000 Frankfurt 70, F.R. Germany. Tel: (69) 60 50 030. Fax: (69) 60 50 03 26. Tlx: 0 505 990 217 WWF.

TRAFFIC(Italy)

WWF-Italy, Via Salaria 290, 00199 Rome, Italy. Tel: (6) 85 24 92. Fax: (6) 86 83 34 (manually operated).

TRAFFIC(Japan)

7th Fl., Nihonseimei Akabanebashi Bldg., 3-1-4 Shiba Minato-Ku, Tokyo 105, Japan. Tel: (3) 769 1716. Fax: (3) 769 1717. Tlx: 242 8231 WWFJPN J.

TRAFFIC(Netherlands)

Postbus 7, 3700 AA Zeist, The Netherlands. Tel: (3404) 19 438. Fax: (3404) 12064. Tlx: 76122 W N F NL.

TRAFFIC(Oceania)

P.O. Box 799, Manly 2095 NSW, Australia. Tel: (2) 977 4786. Fax: (2) 977 3437. Tlx: 176177 BTATS AA.

TRAFFIC(South America)

Carlos Roxlo 1496/301, Montevideo, Uruguay. Tel: (2) 49 33 84. Fax: (2) 60 0351 ["Attn: Juan S. Villalba, Tel. 493384"]. Tlx: 398901 P. BOOTH UY ["Attn: Juan S. Villalba, Tel. 493384"].

TRAFFIC(U.S.A.)

1250 24th St. N.W., Washington, DC 20037, USA. Tel: (202) 293 4800. Fax: (202) 293 9211. Tlx: 64505 PANDA.

APPENDIX F
Glossary of Wildlife Trade

accession—The step by which countries become members to the Convention on International Trade in Endangered Species of Wild Fauna and Flora (CITES) and other treaties. To join CITES, a country deposits an "instrument of accession" with the convention's depositary government, Switzerland, whereupon it becomes a party to the treaty.

antique wildlife products—Antiques made from or containing parts of wildlife protected under the Endangered Species Act (ESA) can be imported into the United States if they meet certain criteria. They must be at least 100 years old and should not have been modified after December 28, 1973 (the date the ESA came into effect). Wildlife antiques must enter through a port designated by the U.S. Fish and Wildlife Service and be accompanied by documents authenticating their age.

APHIS—The Animal and Plant Health Inspection Service of the U.S. Department of Agriculture is charged with inspecting live animals, birds, and plants that enter the United States. APHIS controls the USDA quarantine stations where certain imported wild and domestic animals must undergo quarantine because of the possibility of disease introduction. APHIS personnel inspect all imported plant material and issue permits for certain plant material brought into the United States, including fruits, vegetables, and plants intended for growing.

Appendix I (CITES)—A list of endangered animal and plant species that the parties to the Convention on International Trade in Endangered Species (CITES) have agreed may become extinct if commercial trade in those species is not controlled. In general, trade in wild specimens of Appendix I species is prohibited except under exceptional circumstances, and all transactions must be accompanied by permits from both the importing and exporting countries. Examples of Appendix I species are: all great apes, all sea turtles, all great whales, the giant panda, the Asian elephant, the cheetah, the tiger, all rhinos, and several species of crocodile, birds of prey, orchids, and parrots.

Appendix II (CITES)—A list of threatened animal and plant species that the parties to the Convention on International Trade in Endangered Species (CITES) have agreed may become endangered if commercial trade in those species is not controlled. CITES parties generally allow commercial transactions in wild specimens of Appendix II species only after issuing special permits acknowledging that the trade will not harm wild populations. Examples of Appendix II species are: the African elephant, birds of paradise, black corals, birdwing butterflies, and all taxa of primates, cats, otters, whales, tortoises, crocodiles, birds of prey, parrots, and orchids not already on Appendix I.

Appendix III (CITES)—A list of animal and plant species formally identified by any party to the Convention on International Trade in Endangered Species (CITES) as endangered or threatened in that country. Trade in these species requires special permits, similar to those necessary for trade in Appendix II species. Appendix III species must have an export permit, if exported from the listing country, or a certificate of origin, if exported from another country. Countries that have listed species on Appendix III include: Botswana, Canada, Costa Rica, Ghana, Guatemala, India, Malaysia, Mauritius, Nepal, Tunisia, and Uruguay.

artificial propagation—Artificially contained or induced breeding or reproduction of either plants or animals (the term is more commonly used with plants). Under the Convention on International Trade in Endangered Species, artificial propagation refers to plants grown from seeds, cuttings, callus tissue, spores, or other propagules, under controlled conditions.

ban (wildlife trade)—The action taken to temporarily or indefinitely stop the import or export of any or all wildlife either to or from a particular country or countries, or of a particular species or group of species.

bekko—The Japanese term for the shell of the hawksbill sea turtle (*Eretmochelys imbricata*).

captive-bred wildlife—Animals born from either wild or captive-bred parents in controlled conditions, such as in zoos or on breeding farms.

captive-raised wildlife—Animals taken as young or eggs from the wild and raised in controlled conditions.

certificate of origin (CITES)—An official document verifying the country of origin of wildlife or wildlife product being traded. Required for trade in species listed on Appendix III of the Convention on International Trade in Endangered Species that do not come from the country that lists it on Appendix III.

certificate, reexport (CITES)—An official document that is required for the reexport of wildlife listed on Appendix II of the Convention on International Trade in Endangered Species.

CITES—The Convention on International Trade in Endangered Species of Wild Fauna and Flora, which was signed in 1973 and came into force in 1975. The treaty regulates international trade in endangered and threatened species primarily through a system of permits. Today nearly 100 countries are members of CITES.

CITES Secretariat—The coordinating office of the Convention on International Trade in Endangered Species (CITES). The Secretariat coordinates communication among all parties, organizes the biennial Conference of the Parties, acts as the central unit of distribution and compilation of all CITES documentation in English, Spanish, and French, and oversees other CITES activities. The Secretariat is based in Lausanne, Switzerland, and operates under the auspices of the United Nations Environment Program.

Conference of the Parties—Biennial meeting of the parties to the Convention on International Trade in Endangered Species (CITES) held to review implementation of CITES and to add, transfer, or delete species from the CITES appendices.

country of export—The country that exports a wildlife specimen.

country of import—The country that imports a wildlife specimen.

country of origin—The country from which a wildlife specimen was taken from its natural habitat, propagated, or bred in captivity.

country of reexport—The country that imports a wildlife specimen from one country and then reexports it to another.

Customs Service, U.S.—Bureau of the U.S. Department of the Treasury that is responsible for assessing and collecting revenue (fees, penalties, and taxes) for imported goods. The service also enforces customs laws, seizes contraband, processes carriers and cargo into and out of the United States, and administers certain navigation laws, among other duties. The service cooperates with and assists numerous government agencies, including the U.S. Fish and Wildlife Service and the Animal and Plant Health Inspection Service in enforcing requirements relating to international wildlife trade.

declared value (wildlife)—The monetary value of the wildlife or wildlife product as reported by the importer or exporter on trade documents.

depopulate—A term used by the U.S. Department of Agriculture's Animal and Plant Health Inspection Service to describe a group of birds in a quarantine station that is destroyed due to disease or infection.

Eagle Protection Act, U.S.—The U.S. law enacted in 1940 that fully protects the two species of eagle that occur in the United States, the bald eagle (*Haliaeetus leucocephalus*) and the golden eagle (*Aquila chrysaetos*). This law makes it illegal to import, export, buy, or sell any live bald or golden eagles, their parts, products, nests, or eggs. Penalties for violation are up to $20,000 and 2 years imprisonment. The U.S. Fish and Wildlife Service has primary responsibility for enforcement of the Eagle Protection Act.

ecosystem—A natural area of any size that is made up of living and nonliving entities that interact and exchange materials with each other to produce a stable system.

endangered (ESA)—A classification under the Endangered Species Act that means a species is in danger of extinction. A species can be designated as endangered if the survival of its population is detrimentally affected by: habitat or range destruction that can result from agricultural or industrial development; over-hunting or over-exploitation; disease; or natural predation. Generally, no endangered species may be imported or exported except under strict conditions and with special permits.

endangered, due to similarity of appearance (ESA)—A classification under the Endangered Species Act for a species that so closely resembles a species or population listed as "endangered" that it is difficult for enforcement personnel to distinguish one from the other. Species listed under this classification are subject to ESA rules to ensure that the endangered species is fully protected.

Endangered Species Act of 1973, U.S. (ESA)—The U.S. law that places restrictions on a wide range of activities involving endangered and threatened species to help ensure their continued survival.

Among other restrictions, the ESA regulates U.S. import, export, and protection of animals and plants classified as "endangered" or "threatened." In addition, the ESA requires that *all* wildlife imported into the United States for commercial purposes be declared upon entry on special forms, be made available for government inspection and clearance, and be brought through specially designated wildlife ports. The ESA requires wildlife traders to obtain special licenses from the U.S. Fish and Wildlife Service if the value of their imports or exports exceeds $25,000 annually.

Appendix F   387

The ESA also serves as legislation for the implementation of the Convention on International Trade in Endangered Species in the United States. Penalties for violation of the ESA are up to $20,000 and one year imprisonment. The U.S. Fish and Wildlife Service is primarily responsible for enforcement of the ESA.

Endangered Species List—An alphabetical list of U.S. and foreign animals and plants grouped by taxonomic order and classified as either "endangered" or "threatened" under the Endangered Species Act (ESA). The list is updated and published regularly by the U.S. Fish and Wildlife Service.

farming (CITES)—Under the Convention on International Trade in Endangered Species, the practice whereby animal species are bred in captivity primarily for commercial export. For Appendix I species, special exemptions may be granted for trade in "farmed" specimens if certain requirements are met. The parental breeding stock may be initially removed from the wild if such removal is not harmful to the wild populations and the government of the country where these wild populations occur approves the removal. No further augmentation from the wild is allowed except for occasional additions to protect the captive population from inbreeding. The operation must be designed to keep the breeding stock indefinitely.

Fish and Wildlife Service, U.S.—Agency of the U.S. Department of the Interior that is primarily responsible for implementation and enforcement of the Endangered Species Act and other wildlife laws, and of the Convention on International Trade in Endangered Species. The FWS oversees protection of migratory birds, endangered species, and certain marine mammals. Its program includes the preparation and update of endangered species lists; development of endangered species recovery plans; consultation with foreign governments on endangered species programs; and law enforcement.

harvest(-ing, wildlife)—A term frequently used to describe the killing or collection of wildlife from wild populations for domestic or commercial use. The term is based on the principle that wildlife is a renewable resource.

hunting trophies—Wildlife taken primarily by hunters that is intended for personal use or display. Depending on the species and country involved, special permits are often required to hunt and trade wildlife as trophies.

import (ESA)—According to the Endangered Species Act (ESA), the term meaning "to bring wildlife or wildlife products into any place under the jurisdiction of the United States."

injurious species—Species, often nonnative, determined to be potential disease carriers or to have other potentially harmful effects on a native wild species' population, habitat, or food source. Species such as the fruit bat, mongoose, walking catfish, and the java sparrow are considered injurious species in the United States. Their import is strictly regulated.

introduction from the sea (CITES)—According to the Convention on International Trade in Endangered Species (CITES), the transportation of a species from a marine environment that is not under the jurisdiction of any country into another country.

IUCN—The International Union for Conservation of Nature and Natural Resources, based in Gland, Switzerland, was established in 1948 to promote scientifically based conservation of wild living resources. It has voting members in 114 countries and maintains a global network of more than 2,000 scientists and professionals organized into 6 commissions. The IUCN publishes the *Red Data Book* series.

ivory—The modified teeth or tusks taken from the Asian or African elephant, walrus, narwal, or sperm whale or the products made from them.

The Asian elephant is an endangered species according to the Endangered Species Act (ESA) and the Convention on International Trade in Endangered Species (CITES), and its ivory cannot be traded. The African elephant is a threatened species according to the ESA and CITES, and its ivory can be legally traded from certain countries and with CITES permits. U.S. import and export of sperm whale, walrus, and narwhal ivory are prohibited under the Marine Mammal Protection Act. Antique ivory can generally be traded with special permits, and mammoth ivory is not covered under any wildlife protection laws.

CITES generally recognizes two types of ivory: raw ivory, which includes whole, uncarved tusks or parts of tusk; and worked ivory, which includes tusks with carved surfaces or smaller carved items, such as jewelry.

Lacey Act, U.S.—The U.S. wildlife law originally passed in 1900 and amended in 1981 to become one of the strongest laws in the world designed to curb illegal wildlife trade. It was originally intended to prohibit interstate commerce of illegally killed animals and prevent importation of injurious wildlife. One important amendment to the Lacey Act prohibits the import of animals or products that were illegally killed, collected, or exported from another country. Another amendment allows the government to seize wildlife and wildlife products that enter the United States illegally, whether or not the importer had prior knowledge of the laws of another country. Under the Lacey Act, an importer may be required to produce documents and permits required by the laws of the country where the wildlife originated. Violation of the act can bring penalties of up to $20,000 or five years imprisonment. The U.S. Fish and Wildlife Service is responsible for enforcement of the Lacey Act.

launder(-ing, wildlife)—Method used by traders to illegally transport wildlife either by smuggling wildlife from a country that prohibits export to another country where fraudulent export documents may be obtained; inaccurately declaring a species name, country of origin, or purpose of trade on documents or permits; or obtaining falsified or forged trade documents from exporting or reexporting countries.

Management Authority—A government office or agency designated by a country that is a member of the Convention on International Trade in Endangered Species that oversees implementation of CITES and issues CITES permits for that country. All new parties, at the time of joining CITES, must designate the name and address of their national management authority. The management authority of the United States is the Secretary of the Interior. Two principal agencies in the U.S. Department of the Interior's Fish and Wildlife Service administer CITES: the Office of Management Authority issues CITES permits and regulations; and the Division of Law Enforcement enforces wildlife import and export laws.

Marine Mammal Protection Act of 1972, U.S.—The U.S. law establishing a moratorium on the taking and importation of marine mammals, including parts and products, in all waters and lands under the jurisdiction of the United States. This includes the transport, purchase, or sale of any marine mammal, including dolphin, dugong, manatee, polar bear, porpoise, seal, sea lion, sea otter, walrus, and whale. The act provides limited exceptions, such as taking for scientific study or educational display. Violations of the act can bring penalties of up to $20,000 and one year imprisonment. The National Marine Fisheries Service has primary responsibility for enforcement of the Marine Mammal Protection Act.

Migratory Bird Treaty Act—This U.S. law, passed in 1918 and amended several times since, makes it unlawful to harm, kill, buy, sell, or own any migratory bird, including feathers or other parts, nests, eggs, or products made from such birds. Exceptions are granted for special scientific purposes and for quail, ducks, geese, etc., which can be taken in season under other regulations. Violations of the act can bring penalties of up to $2,000 and two years imprisonment. The U.S. Fish and Wildlife Service is responsible for enforcement of the Migratory Bird Treaty Act.

National Marine Fisheries Service, U.S. Department of Commerce—This agency has broad responsibilities for controlling and regulating marine fish within the U.S. 200-mile fishing zone. It also governs importation and interstate commerce of marine mammals. Under the Marine Mammal Protection Act, the service regulates protection of all marine mammals that are found in U.S. waters. The service is also responsible for protecting endangered and threatened sea turtles when they are in coastal waters, while the U.S. Fish and Wildlife Service is responsible for protection of the turtles when they are on land.

Newcastle disease—(see "VVND.")

NGO—Refers to any nongovernmental organization such as environmental, wildlife conservation, or trade associations. NGOs may participate as observers in most meetings of the Convention on International Trade in Endangered Species after gaining accreditation or approval from their national governments.

notification (CITES)—An official, written advisement from the Secretariat of the Convention on International Trade in Endangered Species (CITES) to all treaty members on changes and additions to the CITES appendices, quotas, and administrative policy and on law enforcement problems or items of special interest relating to CITES activities worldwide.

party(-ies, CITES)—A country that is a member of the Convention on International Trade in Endangered Species (CITES) and has agreed, by accession to the treaty, to abide by its terms. Nearly 100 countries are party to CITES.

permit (CITES)—An official national document required for trade (import or export) in species listed on the appendices of the Convention on International Trade in Endangered Species (CITES). Information printed on such permits must include: the CITES name; the name and any identifying stamp of the national management authority granting it; and a control number assigned by the same national management authority. Permits should list the purpose of the transaction, country of origin, scientific name, quantity, and source of specimens—i.e., captive bred or wild.

pest species—Species that potentially threaten the survival of native species, their habitat, or food source; or species that pose a threat to humans or to horticultural and agricultural practices.

poach(-ing)—The capture, removal, or killing of wildlife in a forbidden area or by illicit methods, or the capture, removal, or killing of protected wildlife.

population—Individuals of a species that occupy the same area, utilize the same food and space resources, and are geographically isolated from other groups of that same species by physical barriers such as mountain ranges or rivers. Sometimes these segregated populations are designated by scientists as subspecies of a particular species.

ports (CITES)—Ports designated by a party upon accession to the Convention on International Trade in Endangered Species (CITES) as those ports where CITES-listed species may enter or leave its borders. Designation of ports is required when a country joins CITES.

Appendix F

ports, FWS designated—Ports designated by the U.S. Fish and Wildlife Service through which commercial shipments of wildlife and wildlife products must be imported or exported except under special circumstances. The U.S. ports designated by the FWS are Chicago, Dallas/Fort Worth, Honolulu, Los Angeles, Miami, New Orleans, New York, San Francisco, and Seattle. The FWS also designates special border ports for wildlife or wildlife products imported from or exported to Canada and Mexico.

purpose of transaction—A term commonly used in wildlife trade to clarify the intent of the transaction, such as for commercial purposes, scientific or education purposes, or personal use. Required on many trade documents, including CITES permits.

quarantine (wildlife)—Term describing the period during which some live animals—domestic and exotic—entering the United States must be held in facilities approved by the U.S. Department of Agriculture (USDA). Animals are held for 30 days to be screened for infectious diseases. USDA quarantine facilities are located in the following cities: Brownsville, Texas; El Paso, Texas; Honolulu; Laredo, Texas; Los Angeles; New York; Nogales, Arizona; Miami; and San Ysidro, California.

ranching (CITES)—According to the Convention on International Trade in Endangered Species, a practice whereby animal species are raised in captivity, often for commercial export, from eggs or young taken from wild populations. Special exemptions for trade in specimens from "ranched" populations may be granted when it is determined that such removal of eggs or young from the wild is not harmful to the wild populations, and the country in which these wild populations occur allows their removal.

Red Data Book, IUCN—Publications published by the International Union for Conservation of Nature and Natural Resources on mammals, amphibians, reptiles, plants, invertebrates, swallowtail butterflies, birds, fish, and certain ecosystems. These publications summarize information on threatened species and habitats and categorize them as "commercially threatened," "extinct," "indeterminate," "insufficiently known," "out of danger," "rare," "threatened community," "threatened phenomenon," or "vulnerable."

reservation (CITES)—Under the Convention on International Trade in Endangered Species, a party may enter a reservation on a CITES-listed species when it first joins CITES or when a species is first listed on an Appendix. By this action, a party does not have to abide by regular CITES requirements for that species. This clause allows a country to continue commercial trade in Appendix I species and technically still comply with the treaty.

resolution (CITES)—A change in or addition to the implementation requirements of the Convention on International Trade in Endangered Species as formally approved and agreed upon by the majority of CITES parties at the biennial Conference of the Parties.

scientific authority—An office or agency designated by a party to the Convention on International Trade in Endangered Species to oversee the scientific aspects of CITES implementation and trade in that country. All new parties, at the time of their accession, must designate a scientific authority. The scientific authority of the United States is the Office of Scientific Authority, Fish and Wildlife Service, U.S. Department of the Interior.

scrimshaw—A carved or engraved article, or the art of carving or engraving an article, usually made from ivory. Historically, scrimshaw involved whale ivory, whale bone, and walrus tusks that were crafted by whalemen while on long voyages. Today, scrimshaw involves a variety of materials including African elephant ivory, hippopotamus teeth, wild cat teeth, fossil mastodon ivory, staghorn, legal antique ivory of endangered animals, and artifical ivory made of plastic and natural composites.

smuggle (-ing, wildlife)—The illegal movement of wildlife or wildlife products from or into a country either by passing the wildlife through unguarded borders; deliberately misidentifying the species, subspecies, or country of origin on trade documents; or concealing illicit wildlife or wildlife products from government authorities, such as by disguising shipping containers.

species—The unit of taxonomic classification defining a group of animals or plants that interbreed and share common attributes. Strictly defined, members of one species are isolated from those of another by their ability to produce viable offspring with each other. As defined by the Convention on International Trade in Endangered Species, the term *species* includes all species, subspecies, or geographically separate populations of a species or a subspecies.

specimen—Generally refers to an animal or plant individual or part that is typical of that animal or plant species. As defined by the Convention on International Trade in Endangered Species, a specimen is any live or dead animal or plant, or part thereof. The term also refers to individual products, raw or manufactured, derived from a particular species.

SSC—The Species Survival Commission of the International Union for Conservation of Nature and Natural Resources (IUCN). The SSC was formed in 1949 to identify endangered or vulnerable wildlife and to determine the threats or potential threats to such wildlife populations. It now consists of 65 specialist groups that address the conservation needs of wildlife.

stockpile (wildlife)—Wildlife or wildlife products held by governments or private traders, sometimes claimed to have been obtained before a country's accession to the Convention on International Trade in Endangered Species, or before a species became protected. If held by a government, stockpiles are often composed of confiscated shipments.

subspecies—A population of one species that is geographically separate from other members of its species and, over a period of time, develops unique physical or behavioral differences not typical in the species. It is not considered a separate species because it can naturally produce viable offspring with other individuals of the species.

sustainable use—The principle whereby the earth's resources— land, forests, water, wildlife, etc.—are used in such a manner and maintained at such levels that they are not depleted but rather can renew themselves. The *World Conservation Strategy* urges all nations to utilize their natural resources in this fashion.

threatened (ESA)—A formal classification under the Endangered Species Act that includes any species that is likely to become an endangered species within the forseeable future. In general, threatened species cannot be traded except for educational or scientific purposes or for zoological exhibition.

threatened, due to similarity of appearance (ESA)—A classification under the Endangered Species Act for a species that so closely resembles a species or population listed as "threatened" that it is difficult for enforcement personnel to distinguish one from the other. Species listed under this classification are subject to rules of the ESA to ensure that the threatened species is fully protected.

tortoiseshell—Generally, products made from the scales or scutes of the carapace (shell top) or plastron (shell bottom) of sea turtles, principally the hawksbill sea turtle (*Eretmochelys imbricata*).

trade (excessive, wildlife)—Generally refers to the lawful, but potentially detrimental, volume of trade in wildlife that may threaten the long-term survival of a species.

trade (illegal, wildlife)—The trade of wildlife or wildlife products in violation of national or international laws or agreements.

trade (wildlife)—The transfer of wildlife or wildlife products from one point to another, generally through export, reexport, import, or introduction from the sea. Wildlife trade can occur for a variety of purposes.

TRAFFIC—Trade Records Analysis of Flora and Fauna in Commerce. An organization established in 1976 to monitor international trade in wild animals and plants, especially those protected under the Convention on International Trade in Endangered Species. A program of World Wildlife Fund and cooperating with the International Union for Conservation of Nature and Natural Resources, the TRAFFIC network now includes offices in Australia, Austria, Belgium, France, West Germany, Italy, Japan, Netherlands, Uruguay, the United Kingdom, and the United States.

TRAFFIC(U.S.A.)—The U.S. office of the international TRAFFIC network. It is a program of World Wildlife Fund and the principal source of objective information on international wildlife trade for the U.S. government, Congress, private nongovernmental organizations, and traders. TRAFFIC(U.S.A.) produces a quarterly newsletter of the same name.

TRAFFIC Bulletin—The quarterly newsletter of the TRAFFIC network, published by the IUCN Wildlife Trade Monitoring Unit, located in Cambridge, United Kingdom.

transship(-ment, wildlife)—The process of transporting wildlife or wildlife products through a country that has no intention of importing that wildlife. Such a shipment may also be referred to as "in-transit."

U.S. Department of Agriculture (USDA)—For wildlife trade purposes, the U.S. agency responsible for safeguarding the environment through inspection programs for imported wildlife. Such programs protect domestic and wild native plant and animal species from the introduction into the United States of potentially harmful diseases or nonnative species. The USDA agency in charge of these programs is the Animal and Plant Health Inspection Service.

U.S. Department of the Interior (DOI)—The principal U.S. authority responsible for implementation of the Convention on International Trade in Endangered Species and for programs associated with the development, conservation, and utilization of fish and wildlife resources. The DOI agency with principal responsibility for the protection of endangered and threatened species is the U.S. Fish and Wildlife Service.

VVND—Viscerotropic velogenic Newcastle disease. A highly contagious viral disease of poultry and other birds, causing high mortality. Symptoms in birds are not immediately recognizable and infected birds can remain carriers for months. The U.S. government requires that imported birds be held in quarantine for 30 days to be screened for VVND and other diseases. Birds testing positive for VVND are immediately "depopulated" (killed).

WCMC—The World Conservation Monitoring Centre, established by the International Union for Conservation of Nature and Natural Resources and based in Cambridge, United Kingdom, collects, analyzes, interprets, and disseminates data on species, wildlife trade, and habitats. These data are used by the IUCN and World Wildlife Fund to determine conservation priorities. Among WCMC's functions are the compilation of the *Red Data Book* series.

WTMU—Wildlife Trade Monitoring Unit of the International Union for Conservation of Nature and Natural Resources' World Conservation Monitoring Centre. WTMU is a principal data source for the TRAFFIC network and is based in Cambridge, United Kingdom.

Washington Convention—Another name for the Convention on International Trade in Endangered Species of Wild Fauna and Flora (CITES), so called because the CITES signatory meeting was held in Washington, D.C., in March 1973.

wildlife—As used in wildlife trade, a term that describes nondomesticated animals and plants, whether they are wild, captive-bred, or captive-raised.

Wildlife Trade Campaign—A joint effort between World Wildlife Fund, the U.S. government, and wildlife-user industries to curb the flourishing illegal trade in wildlife and wildlife products.

World Conservation Strategy (WCS)—Published by the International Union for Conservation of Nature and Natural Resources in 1980, this document is a long-range plan for preserving the earth's living resources by ensuring that development is carried out on a sustained basis. The WCS integrates conservation and development and calls on all nations to adopt conservation policies at home and abroad that make wise use of natural resources.

APPENDIX G
Suggested Readings

BOOKS AND BOOKLETS

Abbott, R. Tucker. *Shell Trade in Florida*. Washington, D.C.: World Wildlife Fund, 1980.

Bean, Michael J. *The Evolution of National Wildlife Law*. Rev. ed. New York: Praeger, 1983.

Boardman, Robert. *International Organization and the Conservation of Nature*. Bloomington, Ind.: Indiana University Press, 1981.

Collar, N. J., and Stuart, S. N. *Threatened Birds of Africa and Related Islands: The ICBP/IUCN Red Data Book*. Part 1. 3rd ed. Gland, Switzerland: International Union for Conservation of Nature and Natural Resources, and Cambridge: International Council for Bird Preservation, 1984.

Collins, N. Mark, and Morris, Michael G. *Threatened Swallowtail Butterflies of the World: The IUCN Red Data Book*. Gland, Switzerland: International Union for Conservation of Nature and Natural Resources, 1985.

Dixon, Alexandra. *Evaluation of the Psittacine Importation Process in the United States*. Washington, D.C.: World Wildlife Fund, 1986.

Durrell, Lee. *State of the Ark: An Atlas of Conservation in Action*. New York: Doubleday, 1986.

Ehrlich, Paul, and Ehrlich, Anne. *Extinction: The Causes and Consequences of the Disappearance of Species*. New York: Random House, 1981.

Farrand, John, Jr., ed. *The Audubon Society Encyclopedia of Animal Life*. New York: Alfred A. Knopf, 1982.

Freiberg, M., and Walls, J. G. *The World of Venomous Snakes*. Neptune, N.J.: T.F.H. Publications, 1984.

Fuller, Douglas, and Fitzgerald, Sarah, eds. *Conservation and Commerce of Cacti and Other Succulents*. Washington, D.C.: World Wildlife Fund, 1987.

Fuller, Kathryn S., and Swift, Byron. *Latin American Wildlife Trade Laws*. Rev. ed. Washington, D.C.: World Wildlife Fund, 1985.

Gibson, Thomas, et al. *International Trade in Plants: Focus on U.S. Exports and Imports*. Washington, D.C.: World Wildlife Fund, 1981.

The Golden Guide series. New York: Houghton-Mifflin.

Groombridge, Brian. *The IUCN Amphibia-Reptilia Red Data Book.* Part 1. *Testudines-Crocodylia-Rhynocephalia.* Gland, Switzerland: International Union for Conservation of Nature and Natural Resources, 1982.

Grzimek's Animal Life Encyclopedia. 13 vols. New York: Van Nostrand Reinhold, 1974.

Hemley, Ginette, and Gaski, Andrea. *Travelling Tropicals: A Study of the U.S.-International Ornamental Fish Trade.* Washington, D.C.: World Wildlife Fund, 1988.

―――――――――――――, and Thomsen, Jorgen. *The World Trade in Birds of Prey.* Washington, D.C.: World Wildlife Fund, forthcoming.

Huxley, Anthony. *Green Inheritance: The World Wildlife Fund Book of Plants.* Garden City, N.Y.: Doubleday, 1985.

Inskipp, Tim, and Wells, Sue. *International Trade in Wildlife.* London: International Institute for Environment and Development, 1979.

International Union for Conservation of Nature and Natural Resources. *African Wildlife Laws.* Bonn: Environmental Law Centre, 1986.

―――――――――――――, Conservation Monitoring Centre. *1986 IUCN Red List of Threatened Animals.* Gland, Switzerland: International Union for Conservation of Nature and Natural Resources, 1986.

King, Stephen T., and Schrock, John R. *Controlled Wildlife: A Three-Volume Guide to U.S. Wildlife Laws and Permit Procedures.* Lawrence, Kans.: Association of Systematics Collections, 1985.

King, Warren B. *Endangered Birds of the World: The ICBP Bird Red Data Book.* Cambridge: International Council for Bird Preservation, 1981.

Kosloff, Laura H., and Trexler, Mark C. *The Wildlife Trade and CITES: An Annotated Bibliography for the Convention on International Trade in Endangered Species of Wild Fauna and Flora.* Washington, D.C.: World Wildlife Fund, 1987.

Lucas, G., and Synge, H. *The IUCN Plant Red Data Book.* Gland, Switzerland: International Union for Conservation of Nature and Natural Resources, 1978.

Lyster, Simon. *International Wildlife Law.* Cambridge: Grotius Publications, 1985.

Mack, David, and Mittermeier, Russell A., eds. *The International Primate Trade.* Vol. 1. Washington, D.C.: World Wildlife Fund, 1984.

Martin, Esmond Bradley. *The Japanese Ivory Industry.* Tokyo: World Wildlife Fund-Japan, 1985.

―――――――――――――, and Martin, Chrysee Bradley. *Run Rhino Run.* London Chatto and Windus, 1982.

Medem, Federico. *Crocodile Skin Trade in South America.* Washington, D.C.: World Wildlife Fund, 1985.

National Audubon Society. *Audubon Wildlife Report.* Published annually.

National Wildlife Federation. *Conservation Directory.* Washington, D.C.: National Wildlife Federation. Published annually.

Nichols, John. *The Animal Smugglers.* New York: Facts on File, 1987.

Nilsson, Greta. *The Bird Business: A Study of the Commercial Cage Bird Trade.* 2d ed. Washington, D.C.: Animal Welfare Institute, 1981.

―――――――――――――. *Facts about Furs.* 3rd ed. Washington, D.C.: Animal Welfare Institute, 1981.

Parker, I., and Amin, M. *Ivory Crisis.* London: Chatto and Windus, 1983.

The Peterson Field Guide series. New York: Houghton Mifflin.

Prescott-Allen, Robert, and Prescott-Allen, Christine. *What's Wildlife Worth?* London: International Institute for Environment and Development, 1982.

The Simon and Schuster Field Guide series. New York: Simon and Schuster.

Thornback, Jane, and Jenkins, Martin. *The IUCN Mammal Red Data Book.* Gland, Switzerland: International Union for Conservation of Nature and Natural Resources, 1981.

Tropical Agricultural Training Center (CATIE). *Status and Trends in International Trade and Local Utilization of Wildlife in Central America.* 1984.

U.S. Central Intelligence Agency. *The World Factbook.* Washington, D.C.: U.S. Government Printing Office. Published annually.

Wells, Susan M.; Pyle, Robert M.; and Collins, N. Mark. *The IUCN Invertebrate Red Data Book.* Gland, Switzerland: International Union for Conservation of Nature and Natural Resources, 1983.

Wood, Elizabeth. *Exploitation of Coral Reef Fishes for the Aquarium Trade.* Ross-on-Wye, Great Britain: Marine Conservation Society, 1985.

CHAPTERS AND ARTICLES

Hemley, Ginette. "International Wildlife Trade." In Chandler, William J., ed.. *Audubon Wildlife Report 1988/1989.* San Diego: Academic Press, 1988. Pp. 337-74.

Jackson, D. D. "Pursued in the Wild for the Pet Trade, Parrots Are Perches on a Risky Limb." *Smithsonian* 16, no. 1 (1985):59-67.

King, F. Wayne. "The Wildlife Trade." In H. P. Brokaw, ed. *Wildlife and America: Contributions to an Understanding of American Wildlife and Its Conservation.* Washington, D.C.: U.S. Government Printing Office, 1978. Pp. 253-77.

Kosloff, Laura H. "For Sale: Parrots, Leopard Skin Coats, and Crocodile Shoes." *Environs* 9, no. 1 (1985):7-10.

——————————, and Trexler, Mark C. "The Convention on International Trade in Endangered Species: No Carrot, but Where's the Stick?" *Environmental Law Reporter* 17 (1987):10222-36.

Muller, Peter. "Preposterous Pets Have Always Been Our Status Symbols." *Smithsonian.* 11, no. 6 (1980):82-90.

Schonfield, A. "International Trade in Wildlife: How Effective Is the Endangered Species Treaty?" *California Western International Law Journal* 15 (1985):110-160.

Turner, John L. "The Deadly Wild Bird Trade." *Defenders* 60, no. 6 (1985):20-29.

Weichart, H. J. "Impressions of a Journey to Southeast Asia." *Animals International* 3, no. 10 (1983):7-11.

Williams, Ted. "Small Cats: Forgotten, Exploited." *Audubon* 87, no. 6 (1985):34-40.

PERIODICALS

Endangered Species Technical Bulletin. Published monthly by the U.S. Department of the Interior, Washington, D.C.

IUCN Bulletin. Published quarterly by the International Union for Conservation of Nature and Natural Resources, Gland, Switzerland.

Oryx. Published quarterly by Flora and Fauna Preservation Society of London, United Kingdom.

Appendix G

Species: Newsletter of the SSC. Published by the Species Survival Commission of the International Union for Conservation of Nature and Natural Resources, Gland, Switzerland.

Threatened Plants Newsletter. Published by the Conservation Monitoring Centre of the International Union for Conservation of Nature and Natural Resources, Surrey, United Kingdom.

TRAFFIC Bulletin. Published quarterly by the Wildlife Trade Monitoring Unit of the International Union for Conservation of Nature and Natural Resources, Cambridge, United Kingdom.

TRAFFIC(U.S.A.). Quarterly newsletter published by World Wildlife Fund, Washington, D.C.

MISCELLANEOUS

TRAFFIC(U.S.A.). "Factsheets." Washington, D.C.: World Wildlife Fund. Subjects available include "CITES," "CITES Parties," "Elephant Ivory Trade," "Flower Bulb Trade," "Fur Trade," "Monitoring Wildlife Trade—The TRAFFIC Network," "Primate Trade," "Psittacine Trade," "Rhinoceros Trade," "U.S. Imports of Wildlife," "Watch Out for Wildlife Products—Mexico," "Watch Out for Wildlife Products—The Caribbean," "World Trade in Wildlife," and "World Wildlife Fund's Campaign to Stop Illegal Wildlife Trade."

REFERENCES

1. International Trade in Wildlife—What It Is, What It Means

1. TRAFFIC(U.S.A.), "Elephant Ivory Trade Factsheet" and "World Trade in Wildlife Factsheet," World Wildlife Fund, Washington, D.C., 1986.
2. Michael Green, personal communication.
3. "Rare Plants Smuggled," *Traffic Bulletin* 6, no. 5 (1985):83.
4. "Who Says Invertebrates Are Worthless?" *TRAFFIC(U.S.A.)* 7, nos. 2&3 (1987):35.
5. Esmond Bradley Martin, "Investigating and Combating the Rhino Horn Trade, 1985-1986," unpublished manuscript, 1986.
6. Robert Singer, personal communication.
7. Tom Milliken, "Japan's Trade in Cat Skins," report to International Union for Conservation of Nature and Natural Resources (IUCN) Species Survival Commission Cat Specialist Group, Kanha, India, April 1984.
8. International Union for Conservation of Nature and Natural Resources, *World Conservation Strategy* (Gland, Switzerland: IUCN, 1980).
9. Committee for the Conservation and Care of Chimpanzees, *Current Threats to the Survival of Chimpanzees in Equatorial Africa* (Washington, D.C.: CCCC, 1987).
10. Tim Inskipp and Sue Wells, *International Trade in Wildlife* (London: International Institute for Environment and Development, 1979).
11. "Of Butterfly Ranchers and Crocodile Catchers," *The Economist*, March 1, 1986, pp. 73-74.
12. "Pesticides Contaminating Frogs," *Oryx* 20, no. 2 (1986):118.
13. "Of Butterfly Ranchers and Crocodile Catchers."
14. TRAFFIC(U.S.A.), "World Trade in Wildlife Factsheet."
15. Paul Ehrlich and Anne Ehrlich, *Extinction: The Causes and Consequences of the Disappearance of Species* (New York: Random House, 1981).
16. Ibid.
17. Mark J. Plotkin, "No Further than Your Breakfast Table," *Focus* 10, no. 1 (1988):8.
18. Robert Prescott-Allen and Christine Prescott-Allen, *What's Wildlife Worth?* (London: International Institute for Environment and Development, 1982).
19. Ehrlich and Ehrlich, *Extinction*.
20. Ginette Hemley, "Alligator Exports Boom in '86," *TRAFFIC(U.S.A.)* 8, no. 1 (1988):3.

21. Jorgen B. Thomsen, "Recent U.S. Imports of Certain Products from the African Elephant," TRAFFIC(U.S.A.), World Wildlife Fund, Washington, D.C., August 31, 1987.

22. John A. Burton, review of *International Wildlife Law* by Simon Lyster, *Oryx* 20, no. 1 (1986):57.

23. Simon Lyster, *International Wildlife Law* (Cambridge: Grotius Publications, 1985).

24. Ibid.

25. Michael J. Bean, *The Evolution of National Wildlife Law*, rev. ed. (New York: Praeger, 1983).

26. Lyster, *International Wildlife Law*.

27. Ibid.

28. Ibid.

29. Laura H. Kosloff and Mark C. Trexler, "The Convention on International Trade in Endangered Species: No Carrot, But Where's the Stick?" *Environmental Law Reporter* 17 (1987):10222-36.

Figures

1.1. TRAFFIC(U.S.A.), "World Trade in Wildlife Factsheet," World Wildlife Fund, Washington, D.C., 1986; U.S. Department of the Interior, unpublished data.

1.2. TRAFFIC(U.S.A.), "World Trade in Wildlife Factsheet"; U.S. Department of the Interior, unpublished data.

2. CITES in Action

1. CITES Secretariat, "Interpretation and Implementation of the Convention: Implementation of the Convention in Certain Countries," *Proceedings of the Sixth Meeting of the Conference of the Parties*, Ottawa, Canada, July 12-24, 1987 (Lausanne, Switzerland: CITES Secretariat, 1989), Doc. 6.20.

2. Ginette Hemley, "Curbing Illegal Wildlife Trade: A Turning Point in Ottawa?" press release, World Wildlife Fund, Washington, D.C., 1987.

3. Erik Eckholm, "Despite Setbacks, World Control of Trade in Wildlife Expands Influence," *New York Times*, July 28, 1987, p. C1.

4. African Elephant and Rhino Specialist Group, "Elephant Population Estimates, Trends, Ivory Quotas and Harvests," report to the CITES Secretariat, *Proceedings of the Sixth Meeting of the Conference of the Parties*, Doc. 6.21, Annex 2.

5. CITES Secretariat, "Interpretation and Implementation of the Convention: Implementation of the Convention in Certain Countries."

6. CITES Secretariat, "Interpretation and Implementation of the Convention: Review of Alleged Infractions," *Proceedings of the Sixth Meeting of the Conference of the Parties*, Doc. 6.19.

7. Tom Milliken, press conference, July 6, 1987.

8. William K. Reilly, interview with Japanese Ministry of International Trade and Industry official, June 1987.

9. CITES Secretariat, "Interpretation and Implementation of the Convention: Implementation of the Convention in Certain Countries."

10. Ibid.

11. Juan S. Villalba-Macias, press conference, July 6, 1987.

12. CITES Secretariat, "Interpretation and Implementation of the

Convention: Implementation of the Convention in Certain Countries."

13. Juan S. Villalba-Macias, personal communication.
14. CITES Secretariat, "Interpretation and Implementation of the Convention: Implementation of the Convention in Certain Countries."
15. Ibid.
16. Juan S. Villalba-Macias, "South American Exports of Crocodile Skins," paper presented to the International Union for Conservation of Nature and Natural Resources Crocodile Specialist Group meeting in Quito, Ecuador, October 1986.
17. CITES Secretariat, "Interpretation and Implementation of the Convention: Review of Alleged Infractions"; "Hyacinth Macaw Decline Documented," *TRAFFIC(U.S.A.)* 8, no. 1 (1988):18.
18. CITES Secretariat, "Interpretation and Implementation of the Convention: Review of Alleged Infractions."
19. TRAFFIC(U.S.A.), "U.S. Imports of Wildlife Factsheet," World Wildlife Fund, Washington, D.C., 1987.
20. Ginette Hemley, press conference, July 6, 1987.
21. Larry Rohter, "Mexico Is Serving as Hub for Wildlife Smugglers," *New York Times*, July 26, 1987.
22. World Wildlife Fund, "WWF Position Statement, Sixth Meeting of the Conference of the Parties to CITES, 12-24 July 1987."
23. African Elephant and Rhino Specialist Group, "Elephant Population Estimates, Trends, Ivory Quotas and Harvests."
24. "A Program to Save the African Elephant," *World Wildlife Fund Letter*, no. 2, 1989, p. 12.
25. Eckholm, "Despite Setbacks, World Control of Trade in Wildlife Expands Influence."
26. Manfred Niekisch, press conference, July 6, 1987.

Box: "Links to the Drug Trade"
1. John Nichols, *The Animal Smugglers* (New York: Facts on File, 1987).
2. John L. Turner, "The Deadly Wild Bird Trade," *Defenders* 60, no. 6 (1985):20-29.
3. Nichols, *The Animal Smugglers*.

Figures
2.1. TRAFFIC(U.S.A.), World Wildlife Fund.
2.2. U.S. Department of the Interior, Fish and Wildlife Service, unpublished data.

3. Bears

1. Steven C. Amstrup, "Polar Bear," in National Audubon Society, *Audubon Wildlife Report 1986* (New York: National Audubon Society, 1986), pp. 791-804.
2. Jane Thornback and Martin Jenkins, *The IUCN Mammal Red Data Book*, part 1 (Gland, Switzerland: International Union for Conservation of Nature and Natural Resources, 1982).
3. Amstrup, "Polar Bear."
4. Ibid.
5. Ibid.; Thornback and Jenkins, *The IUCN Mammal Red Data Book*.
6. Amstrup, "Polar Bear."
7. Ibid.; Thornback and Jenkins, *The IUCN Mammal Red Data Book*.

8. Amstrup, "Polar Bear."
9. Steve Amstrup, personal communication with Joel Rhymer, March 1988.
10. TRAFFIC(Japan).
11. "Polar Bears to be Ranched?" *Oryx* 20, no. 4 (1986):252.
12. "Two Arrested in Inquiry into Sales of Wildlife," *New York Times*, January 31, 1987.
13. TRAFFIC(Japan).
14. U.S. Fish and Wildlife Service, "Wildlife Law Enforcement Agents Serve Warrants in Alaska and Other States," press release, January 29, 1987.
15. "Gall Bladder Capers," *TRAFFIC(U.S.A.)* 6, no. 4 (1988):18; Marc Reisner, "Bad News, Bears," *California Magazine* 12, no. 3 (1987):71.
16. Tom Milliken, "Concern over Japanese Bear Trade," *Traffic Bulletin* 7, no. 1 (1985):5-8.
17. Ibid.
18. Ibid.
19. Ibid.
20. "Gall Bladder Capers."
21. Reisner, "Bad News, Bears"; Michael Pelton, "The Black Bear," in Roger L. DiSilvestro, ed., *Audubon Wildlife Report 1987* (Orlando, Fla.: Academic Press, 1987), pp. 520-29.
22. Confidential source, Alaska Department of Fish and Game, personal communication.
23. I. McT. Cowan, "The Status and Conservation of Bears (Ursidae) of the World," in *International Conference on Bear Research and Management* 2 (1972):342-67; cited in Pelton, "The Black Bear."
24. Pelton, "The Black Bear."
25. "Gall Bladder Capers."
26. Reisner, "Bad News, Bears."
27. "Gall Bladder Capers."
28. Reisner, "Bad News, Bears."
29. Gary Griggs, personal communication, May 31, 1988.
30. Art Paul, personal communication, May 31, 1988.
31. U.S. Department of the Treasury, Customs Service, 1985.
32. Ronald M. Nowak and John L. Paradiso, *Walker's Mammals of the World*, 4th ed., vol. 2 (Baltimore: Johns Hopkins University Press, 1983).

4. Big Cats

1. Simon Lyster, *International Wildlife Law* (Cambridge: Grotius Publications, 1985).
2. Tim Inskipp and Sue Wells, *International Trade in Wildlife* (London: International Institute for Environment and Development, 1979).
3. Tom Milliken, "Japan's Trade in Cat Skins," report to International Union for Conservation of Nature and Natural Resources (IUCN) Species Survival Commission Cat Specialist Group, Kanha, India, April 1984.
4. Peter Jackson, "World Tiger Populations," *BBC Wildlife*, September 1986, p. 417.
5. Peter Jackson, in Ronald Tilson and Ulysses S. Seal, eds., *Tigers of the World: The Biology, Biopolitics, Management, and Conservation of an Endangered Species* (Park Ridge, N.J.: Noyes, 1988).

6. Jackson, "World Tiger Populations" and personal communication; Ronald L. Tilson and Ulysses S. Seal, "Dilemma in Tigerland: A Problem of Small Population Numbers," in American Association of Zoological Parks and Aquariums, *AAZPA 1986 Annual Conference Proceedings*, Minneapolis, Minnesota, September 14-18, 1986, pp. 13-19.

7. Jackson, personal communication; Inskipp and Wells, *International Trade in Wildlife*.

8. Jackson, "World Tiger Populations."

9. Raleigh Blouch, in Peter Jackson, *Cat News* 1 (July 1984).

10. Denis D. Gray, "Hunters Threaten Southeast Asian Big Cats," *Los Angeles Times*, December 20, 1984.

11. *Straits Times*, December 19, 1985.

12. Unpublished correspondence to CITES Secretariat, 1985.

13. Jasper Becker, "China Fights the Animal Smugglers," *New Scientist*, February 13, 1986, p. 19.

14. Jeffrey A. McNeely and Paul Spencer Wachtel, "They Use Everything but the Cat's Meow," *International Wildlife* 11, no. 3 (1981):14-19.

15. CITES annual reports.

16. International Species Information System (ISIS), *Species Distribution Report Abstract*, December 31, 1987.

17. International Union for Conservation of Nature and Natural Resources (IUCN), *The 1988 IUCN Red List of Threatened Animals* (Cambridge: IUCN Conservation Monitoring Centre, 1988); Jackson, personal communication.

18. Pier-Lorenzo Florio, personal communication.

19. Jackson, *Cat News*.

20. Gillian Kerby, "The Cheetah," in *Our Precious Planet*, Department of Zoology, University of Oxford, Oxford, United Kingdom.

21. Tom Milliken, personal communication.

22. CITES annual reports; Kerby, "The Cheetah."

23. IUCN, *1988 Red List*; Charles Santiapillai and Kenneth R. Ashby, "The Clouded Leopard in Sumatra," *Oryx* 22, no. 1 (1988):44-45.

24. Milliken, "Japan's Trade in Cat Skins."

25. Jackson, *Cat News*.

26. Rodney Jackson, "A Report on the Wildlife and Hunting in the Namlang (Langu) Valley of West Nepal," submitted to Government National Parks and Wildlife Conservation Office, Katmandu, Nepal, 1978.

27. Jackson, *Cat News*.

28. Jackson, "A Report on the Wildlife and Hunting in the Namlang (Langu) Valley of West Nepal."

29. Jackson, *Cat News*.

30. Peter Jackson, "Summary of Conservation Status of the Jaguar: Wildlife Management in Neotropical Moist Forest," Manaus, Brazil, April 4-5, 1986; Rafael Hoogesteign, 1986, quoted by Jackson, personal communication.

31. J. Lobao Tello, "The Situation of the Wild Cats (Felidae) in Bolivia," report prepared for CITES, 1986.

32. Jane Thornback and Martin Jenkins, *The IUCN Mammal Red Data Book*, part 1 (Gland, Switzerland: International Union for Conservation of Nature and Natural Resources, 1982).

References   403

33. Florio, personal communication.
34. R. B. Martin and T. De Meulenaer, "Survey of the Status of the Leopard (*Panthera pardus*) in Sub-Saharan Africa," abbreviated version, in CITES Secretariat, "Interpretation and Implementation of the Convention: Trade in Leopard Skins," *Proceedings of the Sixth Meeting of the Conference of the Parties*, Ottawa, Canada, July 12-24, 1987 (Lausanne, Switzerland: CITES Secretariat, 1989), Doc. 6.26, annex.
35. Ibid.
36. Ibid.
37. Ronald M. Nowak and John L. Paradiso, *Walker's Mammals of the World*, 4th ed., vol. 2 (Baltimore: Johns Hopkins University Press, 1983).
38. Ibid.
39. ISIS, *Species Distribution Report Abstract*.

5. Small Cats

1. CITES annual reports, 1984.
2. J. Lobao Tello, "The Situation of the Wild Cats *(Felidae)* in Bolivia," report prepared for CITES, 1986.
3. Kathryn S. Fuller and Byron Swift, *Latin American Wildlife Trade Laws*, rev. ed. (Washington, D.C.: World Wildlife Fund, 1985).
4. Steven Broad, *The Harvest of and Trade in Latin American Spotted Cats* (Felidae) *and Otters* (Lutrinae) (Cambridge: Wildlife Trade Monitoring Unit/International Union for the Conservation of Nature and Natural Resources, 1987).
5. Ted Williams, "Small Cats: Forgotten, Exploited," *Audubon* 87, no. 6 (1985):34-40.
6. CITES annual reports, 1984.
7. Ginette Hemley, personal communication.
8. CITES annual reports, 1984.
9. Jorgen Thomsen, personal communication.
10. Pier-Lorenzo Florio, personal communication.
11. Jane Thornback and Martin Jenkins, *The IUCN Mammal Red Data Book*, part 1 (Gland, Switzerland: International Union for Conservation of Nature and Natural Resources, 1982).
12. Patricia Daniels, "Prowlers on the Mexican Border," *National Wildlife* 21, no. 6 (1983):15-16.
13. Broad, *The Harvest of and Trade in Latin American Spotted Cats* (Felidae) *and Otters* (Lutrinae).
14. Linda McMahan, "The International Cat Trade," in S. Douglas Miller and Daniel D. Everett, eds., *Cats of the World: Biology, Conservation and Management*, proceedings of the 2d International Cat Symposium, October 4-6, 1982 (Washington, D.C.: National Wildlife Federation, 1986).
15. Williams, "Small Cats."
16. John A. Burton, "Wildlife Imports in Britain 1975," *Oryx* 13, no. 4 (1976):330-31.
17. Broad, *The Harvest of and Trade in Latin American Spotted Cats* (Felidae) *and Otters* (Lutrinae).
18. Manfred Niekisch, personal communication.
19. Broad, *The Harvest of and Trade in Latin American Spotted Cats* (Felidae) *and Otters* (Lutrinae).

20. Hilario Moreno, personal communication.
21. Broad, *The Harvest of and Trade in Latin American Spotted Cats* (Felidae) *and Otters* (Lutrinae).
22. Ute Grimm, personal communication.
23. Broad, *The Harvest of and Trade in Latin American Spotted Cats* (Felidae) *and Otters* (Lutrinae).
24. Grimm, personal communication.
25. Broad, *The Harvest of and Trade in Latin American Spotted Cats* (Felidae) *and Otters* (Lutrinae).
26. S. D. Miller, E. P. Hill, and M. S. O'Brien, "Bobcat (*Lynx rufus*)," in Eugene F. Deems, Jr., and Duane Pursley, eds., *North American Furbearers: A Contemporary Reference* (Washington, D.C.: International Association of Fish and Wildlife Agencies, in cooperation with the Maryland Department of Natural Resources-Wildlife Administration, 1983).
27. Gary Koehler, "The Bobcat," in Roger L. DiSilvestro, ed., *Audubon Wildlife Report 1987* (Orlando, Fla.: Academic Press, 1987), pp. 399-409.
28. CITES annual reports, 1984.
29. Richard Mitchell, personal communication.
30. Koehler, "The Bobcat."
31. Ibid.
32. T. N. Bailey, untitled, in David W. Macdonald, ed., *The Encyclopedia of Mammals* (New York: Facts on File, 1984).
33. Stephen DeStefano, "The Lynx," in DiSilvestro, *Audubon Wildlife Report 1987*, pp. 411-22.
34. L. Boddicker and B. P. Saunders, "Lynx (*Felis canadensis*)," in Deems and Pursley, *North American Furbearers*, pp. 189-93.
35. DeStefano, "The Lynx."
36. Ibid.
37. C. J. Brand and L. B. Keith, "Lynx Demography during a Snowshoe Hare Decline in Alberta," *Journal of Wildlife Management* 48 (1979):827-49.
38. DeStefano, "The Lynx."
39. Boddicker and Saunders, "Lynx (*Felis canadensis*)."
40. CITES annual reports, 1984.
41. Boddicker and Saunders, "Lynx (*Felis canadensis*)."
42. DeStefano, "The Lynx."
43. Niekisch, personal communication.
44. Ronald M. Nowak and John L. Paradiso, *Walker's Mammals of the World*, 4th ed., vol. 2 (Baltimore: Johns Hopkins University Press, 1983).
45. CITES annual reports, 1984.
46. Tom Milliken, "Japan's Trade in Cat Skins," report to International Union for Conservation of Nature and Natural Resources (IUCN) Species Survival Commission Cat Specialist Group, Kanha, India, April 1984; Grimm, personal communication.
47. DeStefano, "The Lynx."
48. M. Delibes, "The Lynx in the Iberian Peninsula," Bulletin Mens. OH. Nation. Chase No. Sp. Scien. Tech. le Lynx., pp. 41-46. (In French, Eng. summary), cited in DeStefano, "The Lynx."
49. CITES annual reports, 1984.
50. Ibid.
51. Nowak and Paradiso, *Walker's Mammals of the World*.
52. CITES annual reports, 1984.

References 405

Figures

5.1. West German CITES annual reports.

5.2. CITES annual reports.

5.3. U.S. CITES annual reports.

6. Elephants

1. Tim Inskipp and Sue Wells, *International Trade in Wildlife* (London: International Institute for Environment and Development, 1979).

2. Jane Thornback and Martin Jenkins, *The IUCN Mammal Red Data Book*, part 1 (Gland, Switzerland: International Union for Conservation of Nature and Natural Resources, 1982).

3. Ivory Trade Review Group, "The Ivory Trade and the Future of the African Elephant," unpublished report prepared for the 2nd meeting of the CITES African Elephant Working Group, Gaborne, Botswana, July 4-8, 1989.

4. I. Douglas-Hamilton, "African Elephants: Population Trends and Their Causes," *Oryx* 21, no. 1 (1987):11-24.

5. J. R. Caldwell, "The Effect of Recent Legislative Changes on the Pattern of the World's Trade in Raw Ivory," *Traffic Bulletin* 9, no. 1 (1987):6-10.

6. John Caldwell, personal communication; Jorgen Thomsen, personal communication.

7. Douglas-Hamilton, "African Elephants."

8. Inskipp and Wells, *International Trade in Wildlife*.

9. Paul Spencer Wachtel, "Crackdown on Poachers," *WWF News*, no. 38 (1985):3.

10. Marilyn Achiron, "Africa: The Last Safari?" *Newsweek*, August 18, 1986, pp. 40-42.

11. John Caldwell and Jonathan Barzdo, "The World Trade in Raw Ivory, 1983 and 1984," report of the Wildlife Trade Monitoring Unit to the CITES Secretariat, 1985.

12. Tom Milliken, "Japan's Ivory Trade," *Traffic Bulletin* 7, nos. 3/4 (1985):43.

13. Ibid.; Caldwell, "The Effect of Recent Legislative Changes on the Pattern of the World's Trade in Raw Ivory."

14. Caldwell, "The Effect of Recent Legislative Changes on the Pattern of the World's Trade in Raw Ivory."

15. Japanese Customs data.

16. R. Shimpo, *Los Angeles Times*, December 12, 1986.

17. "Biggest Ivory Seizures . . . outside Africa," *Traffic Bulletin* 8, no. 2 (1986):23.

18. Caldwell, "The Effect of Recent Legislative Changes on the Pattern of the World's Trade in Raw Ivory."

19. African Elephant and Rhino Specialist Group (AERSG), "Elephant Population Estimates, Trends, Ivory Quotas and Harvests," report to the CITES Secretariat, *Proceedings of the Sixth Meeting of the Conference of the Parties*, Ottawa, Canada, July 12-24, 1987 (Lausanne, Switzerland: CITES Secretariat, 1989), Doc. 6.21, annex 2.

20. Jorgen B. Thomsen, "Recent U.S. Imports of Certain Products from the African Elephant," a report to the Subcommittee on Fisheries and Wildlife Conservation and the Environment, Merchant Marine and Fisheries Committee, U.S. House of Representatives, from TRAFFIC(U.S.A.), Washington, D.C., 1987.

21. "Endangered Species Convention: Prohibition on Importation of Burundi Ivory," *Federal Register* 53, no. 83 (1988):15468.
22. Ibid.
23. AERSG, "Elephant Population Estimates, Trends, Ivory Quotas and Harvests"; John Caldwell, personal communication.
24. Caldwell, "The Effect of Recent Legislative Changes on the Pattern of the World's Trade in Raw Ivory."
25. Douglas-Hamilton, "African Elephants."
26. Caldwell, "The Effect of Recent Legislative Changes on the Pattern of the World's Trade in Raw Ivory"; Paul Evan Ress, "Saving Elephants: A Mammoth Task," CITES Secretariat, August 1986.
27. Caldwell, personal communication.
28. WWF Hong Kong, "WWF Hong Kong Welcomes Ivory Control Moves," press release, July 26, 1988.
29. Ibid.; unclassified telegram, from U.S. consulate, Hong Kong, to U.S. secretary of state, no. 00932, May 6, 1988.
30. "Hong Kong's Ivory Carvers Seem an Endangered Species," *Asian Business*, February 1986; Caldwell, personal communication.
31. R. B. Martin, J. R. Caldwell, and J. G. Barzdo, *African Elephants, CITES, and the Ivory Trade* (Lausanne, Switzerland: CITES Secretariat, 1986).
32. Ibid.
33. Thomsen, "Recent U.S. Imports of Certain Products from the African Elephant."
34. Jonathan Barzdo, "The Worked Ivory Trade," *Traffic Bulletin* 6, no. 2 (1984):21-26.
35. Thomsen, "Recent U.S. Imports of Certain Products from the African Elephant"; TRAFFIC(U.S.A.), "Elephant Ivory Trade Factsheet," World Wildlife Fund, Washington, D.C., 1987.
36. Thomsen, "Recent U.S. Imports of Certain Products from the African Elephant."
37. Jorgen B. Thomsen, "Conserving the African Elephant: CITES Fails— U.S. Acts," *TRAFFIC(U.S.A.)* 9, no. 1 (1989):1.
38. Thomsen, "Recent U.S. Imports of Certain Products from the African Elephant."
39. Ginette Hemley, personal communication.
40. Thomsen, "Recent U.S. Imports of Certain Products from the African Elephant."
41. Ibid.; Hemley, personal communication.
42. Thomsen, "Recent U.S. Imports of Certain Products from the African Elephant."
43. Douglas-Hamilton, "African Elephants," and personal communication.
44. AERSG, "Elephant Population Estimates, Trends, Ivory Quotas and Harvests."

Figures

6.1. Charles Santiapillai, "Action Plan for Asian Elephant Conservation: A Country by Country Analysis," draft (Bogor, Indonesia: World Wildlife Fund, 1987).
6.2. "A Program to Save the African Elephant," *World Wildlife Fund Letter*, 1989, no. 2.
6.3. CITES Secretariat.

6.4. Japanese Customs data; J. R. Caldwell, "The Effect of Recent Legislative Changes on the Pattern of the World Trade in Raw Ivory," *Traffic Bulletin* 9, no. 1 (1987):6.

6.5. U.S. CITES annual reports.

7. Kangaroos and Other Macropods

1. *Kangaroo Management Programs of the Australian States* (Canberra, Australia: Commonwealth of Australia, 1984).
2. "Kangaroo Management in New South Wales," in ibid.
3. Frank Antram, personal communication.
4. Lee Durrell, *State of the Ark: An Atlas of Conservation in Action* (New York: Doubleday, 1986).
5. "Kangaroo Bar," *New Scientist,* June 26, 1986, p. 26.
6. Ibid.; "Australia Suspends Wildlife Exports," *Traffic Bulletin* 8, no. 2 (1986):24.
7. Antram, personal communication.
8. Alexandra M. Dixon, "The European Trade in Kangaroo Products," *Traffic Bulletin* 6, no. 5 (1985):73-82.
9. Ibid.
10. International Wildlife Coalition, "Coalition Hails Passage of Kangaroo and Wallaby Resolution by the European Parliament," press release, 1987.
11. Antram, personal communication; Dixon, "The European Trade in Kangaroo Products."
12. Andrea L. Gaski, "'Roo Update: A Short History of U.S. Kangaroo Skin and Product Imports, 1984-1987," *TRAFFIC(U.S.A.)* 8, no. 2 (1988):1-5.
13. Dixon, "The European Trade in Kangaroo Products."
14. Ibid.

Figure

7.1. A. M. Dixon, "The European Trade in Kangaroo Products," *Traffic Bulletin* 6, no. 5 (1985):73-82; Australian Bureau of Statistics.

8. Musk Deer

1. "Japan Stockpiles Musk," *TRAFFIC(U.S.A.)* 8, no. 1 (1988):17.
2. Michael Green and Richard Taylor, "The Musk Connection," *New Scientist,* June 20, 1986.
3. Michael J. B. Green, "The Distribution, Status and Conservation of the Himalayan Musk Deer (*Moschus chrysogaster*)," *Biological Conservation* 35 (1986):347-75.
4. Ibid.; Green and Taylor, "The Musk Connection."
5. Green and Taylor, "The Musk Connection"; Tom Milliken, personal communication.
6. Green and Taylor, "The Musk Connection."
7. Milliken, personal communication.
8. "Japan Stockpiles Musk."
9. Milliken, personal communication.
10. Green and Taylor, "The Musk Connection."
11. Ibid.; Green, "The Distribution, Status and Conservation of the Himalayan Musk Deer (*Moschus chrysogaster*)."

Figure

8.1.   TRAFFIC(Japan).

9. Primates

1.   David Mack and Russell A. Mittermeier, "Introduction," in David Mack and Russell A. Mittermeier, eds., *The International Primate Trade*, vol. 1 (Washington, D.C.: World Wildlife Fund, 1984), pp. 15-17.
2.   Russell A. Mittermeier, "Effects of Hunting on Rain Forest Primates," in Clive W. Marsh and Russell A. Mittermeier, eds., *Primate Conservation in the Tropical Rain Forest* (New York: Alan R. Liss, 1987), pp. 147-77.
3.   Russell A. Mittermeier and Dorothy L. Cheney, "Conservation of Primates and Their Habitats," in Barbara B. Smuts et al., eds., *Primate Societies* (Chicago: University of Chicago Press, 1987), pp. 477-90.
4.   Mittermeier, "Effects of Hunting on Rain Forest Primates."
5.   Tim Inskipp and Sue Wells, *International Trade in Wildlife* (London: International Institute for Environment and Development, 1979); Michael Kavanagh, Ardith A. Eudey, and David Mack, "The Effects of Live Trapping and Trade on Primate Populations," in Marsh and Mittermeier, *Primate Conservation in the Tropical Rain Forest*; Jeremy Cherfas, "Chimps in the Laboratory: An Endangered Species," *New Scientist*, March 27, 1986.
6.   N. Wade, "New Vaccine May Bring Man and Chimpanzees into Tragic Conflict," *Science* 200 (1978):1027-30; cited in Committee for the Conservation and Care of Chimpanzees (CCCC), "Current Threats to the Survival of Chimpanzees in Equatorial Africa," Washington, D.C., 1987.
7.   Mack and Mittermeier, "Introduction."
8.   Michael Kavanagh, "A Review of the International Primate Trade," in Mack and Mittermeier, *The International Primate Trade*, vol. 1, pp. 49-89.
9.   Mack and Mittermeier, "Introduction."
10.   Julian Oliver Caldecott and Michael Kavanagh, "Use of Primates and Captive Breeding Programs Outside the United States," in Mack and Mittermeier, *The International Primate Trade*, vol. 1, pp. 137-52.
11.   Inskipp and Wells, *International Trade in Wildlife*; Kavanagh, Eudey, and Mack, "The Effects of Live Trapping and Trade on Primate Populations."
12.   Kavanagh, Eudey, and Mack, "The Effects of Live Trapping and Trade on Primate Populations."
13.   Inskipp and Wells, *International Trade in Wildlife*.
14.   Jorgen Thomsen, personal communication.
15.   Kavanagh, Eudey, and Mack, "The Effects of Live Trapping and Trade on Primate Populations."
16.   Tom Milliken, personal communication.
17.   Geza Teleki, personal communication, June 1989.
18.   Kavanagh, Eudey, and Mack, "The Effects of Live Trapping and Trade on Primate Populations."
19.   Shirley McGreal, personal communication, June 2, 1988.
20.   Russell A. Mittermeier et al., "Primate Conservation," in G. Mitchell and Joe Erwin, eds., *Comparative Primate Biology*, vol. 2A, *Behavior, Conservation, and Ecology* (New York: Alan R. Liss, 1986), pp. 3-72.

21. David Mack, "Trends in Primate Imports into the United States, 1981," *ILAR News* 25, no. 4 (1982):10-13.

22. Kavanagh, Eudey, and Mack, "The Effects of Live Trapping and Trade on Primate Populations."

23. Humane Society of the United States (HSUS), "To Upgrade the Chimpanzee (*Pan troglodytes*) from Threatened to Endangered Status pursuant to the Endangered Species Act of 1973, as Amended," petition before the U.S. Department of the Interior, Fish and Wildlife Service, November 4, 1987.

24. Mittermeier and Cheney, "Conservation of Primates and Their Habitats."

25. Cherfas, "Chimps in the Laboratory."

26. TRAFFIC(Austria), personal communication.

27. HSUS, "To Upgrade the Chimpanzee (*Pan troglodytes*) from Threatened to Endangered Status."

28. David Mack and Ardith Eudey, "A Review of the U.S. Primate Trade," in Mack and Mittermeier, *The International Primate Trade*, vol. 1, pp. 91-136; Douglas Fuller, "Trends in Primate Imports into the United States, 1984," *ILAR News* 28, no. 4 (1985):4-7.

29. Michael Kavanagh, "Simians for Science: The United Kingdom and the Worldwide Trade in Primates," in D. Harper, ed., *Proceedings of the Symposium on the Conservation of Primates and Their Habitats* (Leicester: University of Leicester, 1983), pp. 149-81; John A. Burton, "Primate Imports into the United Kingdom 1965-1975," in D. J. Chivers and W. Lane-Petter, eds., *Recent Advances in Primatology*, vol. 2 (London: Academic Press, 1978), pp. 137-45.

30. "Japanese Imports of Primates," *Traffic Bulletin* 1, nos. 8&9 (1979):5-7; Kavanagh, "A Review of the International Primate Trade"; Japanese Customs data.

31. Kavanagh, "A Review of the International Primate Trade."

32. Kavanagh, Eudey, and Mack, "The Effects of Live Trapping and Trade on Primate Populations"; "New Kenyan Legislation," *Traffic Bulletin* 3, no. 6 (1982):69.

33. Russell A. Mittermeier, personal communication.

34. Kavanagh, "A Review of the International Primate Trade."

35. Ibid.

36. Ardith Eudey and David Mack, "Use of Primates and Captive Breeding Programs in the United States," in Mack and Mittermeier, *The International Primate Trade*, vol. 1, pp. 153-80; Cherfas, "Chimps in the Laboratory"; Kavanagh, "A Review of the International Primate Trade."

37. Mack and Mittermeier, "Summary, Update, and Conclusions," in Mack and Mittermeier, *The International Primate Trade*, vol. 1, pp. 181-85; Mack and Eudey, "A Review of the U.S. Primate Trade."

38. Mack and Mittermeier, "Summary, Update, and Conclusions."

39. Kavanagh, "A Review of the International Primate Trade."

40. Cherfas, "Chimps in the Laboratory."

41. Mack and Mittermeier, "Summary, Update, and Conclusions."

42. Kavanagh, "A Review of the International Primate Trade."

43. Kavanagh, Eudey, and Mack, "The Effects of Live Trapping and Trade on Primate Populations."

44. CCCC, "Current Threats to the Survival of Chimpanzees in Equatorial Africa."
45. Teleki, personal communication, June 1989.
46. CCCC, "Current Threats to the Survival of Chimpanzees in Equatorial Africa."
47. Cherfas, "Chimps in the Laboratory."
48. Jane Goodall, "A Plea for the Chimps," *New York Times Magazine*, May 17, 1987, pp. 108ff.
49. Ibid.
50. Teleki, personal communication, June 2, 1988.
51. International Species Inventory System (ISIS), "Species Distribution Report Abstract," Apple Valley, Minnesota, December 31, 1987.
52. CCCC, "Current Threats to the Survival of Chimpanzees in Equatorial Africa."
53. Ian Redmond, "Law of the Jungle," *BBC Wildlife*, June 1986.
54. Cherfas, "Chimps in the Laboratory."
55. "Chimpanzees Cause Controversy," *TRAFFIC(U.S.A.)* 7, nos. 2&3 (1987):25.
56. Kavanagh, Eudey, and Mack, "The Effects of Live Trapping and Trade on Primate Populations."
57. Kavanagh, "A Review of the International Primate Trade."
58. Mittermeier and Cheney, "Conservation of Primates and Their Habitats."
59. Alexandra Dixon, "Congo Gorillas to U.K.," *Traffic Bulletin* 8, no. 4 (1987):56; Thomas O. McShane, personal communication.
60. Dixon, "Congo Gorillas to U.K."
61. McGreal, personal communication.
62. ISIS, "Species Distribution Report Abstract."
63. Fuller, "Trends in Primate Imports into the United States, 1984."
64. Caldecott and Kavanagh, "Use of Primates and Captive Breeding Programs Outside the United States."
65. Eudey and Mack, "Use of Primates and Captive Breeding Programs in the United States."
66. Milliken, personal communication.
67. Cherfas, "Chimps in the Laboratory."
68. Russell A. Mittermeier, "Colobus Monkeys and the Tourist Trade," *Oryx* 12, no. 1 (1973):113-17; R. Dunbar and E. Dunbar, "Guereza Monkeys: Will They Become Extinct in Ethiopia?" *Walia* 6 (1975):14-15.
69. Mittermeier, "Effects of Hunting on Rain Forest Primates."
70. Wildlife Trade Monitoring Unit, Appendix II study of *Colobus queraza*, 1986.
71. Kavanagh, "A Review of the International Primate Trade."
72. Milliken, personal communication.
73. James J. Moore, "Chimpanzees in Mali," *WWF Monthly Report*, July 1985, p. 156.

Figures

9.1. U.S. Customs data.
9.2. Japanese Customs data.

10. Rhinoceroses

1. Esmond Bradley Martin, "Status of Rhino Populations and Associated Trade in Rhino Products," report prepared on behalf of the African Elephant and Rhino Specialist Group of the International Union for Conservation of Nature and Natural Resources Species Survival Commission, *Proceedings of the Sixth Meeting of the Conference of the Parties*, Ottawa, Canada, July 12-24, 1987 (Lausanne, Switzerland: CITES Secretariat, 1989), Doc. 6.25, annex 1.
2. Esmond Bradley Martin and Chrysee Bradley Martin, "Horns of a Dilemma," *BBC Wildlife* 3, no. 3 (1985):127-31.
3. Esmond Bradley Martin, *Rhino Exploitation: The Trade in Rhino Products in India, Indonesia, Malaysia, Burma, Japan, and South Korea* (Hong Kong: World Wildlife Fund-Hong Kong), 1983; Esmond Bradley Martin, "Religion, Royalty, and Rhino Conservation in Nepal," *Oryx* 19, no. 1 (1985):11-16.
4. Martin, "Status of Rhino Populations and Associated Trade in Rhino Products."
5. "IUCN Update: Scientific Tests Fail to Show Rhino Horn Effective as Medicine," *IUCN Bulletin* 14, nos. 1-3 (1983):2.
6. Esmond Bradley Martin, testimony before the Subcommittee on Natural Resources, Agriculture, and Environment, Committee on Science and Technology, U.S. House of Representatives, September 25, 1986; Martin, "Status of Rhino Populations and Associated Trade in Rhino Products."
7. John Hanks, untitled discussion paper on the need for a continental strategy for the conservation of the rhinoceros in Africa, WWF International, Gland, Switzerland, 1987.
8. Martin, "Status of Rhino Populations and Associated Trade in Rhino Products."
9. Martin, testimony before the Subcommittee on Natural Resources, Agriculture, and Environment; Esmond Bradley Martin, personal communication.
10. Martin, testimony before the Subcommittee on Natural Resources, Agriculture, and Environment; Martin, "Status of Rhino Populations and Associated Trade in Rhino Products."
11. TRAFFIC(U.S.A.), "Rhino Factsheet," World Wildlife Fund, Washington, D.C., 1986.
12. Martin, "Status of Rhino Populations and Associated Trade in Rhino Products."
13. Ibid.; "Rhino Poaching in Zimbabwe," *Pachyderm*, no. 6 (1986):18.
14. Willie Nduku, "The Rhino Conservation Strategy in Zimbabwe: Code Name 'Operation Stronghold,' " statement for the Subcommittee on Natural Resources, Agriculture, and Environment, Committee on Science, Space, and Technology, U.S. House of Representatives, June 22, 1988.
15. "Run Poacher Run," *TRAFFIC(U.S.A.)* 8, no. 1 (1988):19.
16. Esmond Bradley Martin, "Rhinos and Daggers: A Major Conservation Problem," *Oryx* 19, no. 4 (1985):198-201.
17. "North Yemen Bans Importation of Rhino Horn," *Traffic Bulletin* 4, nos. 4&5 (1982):39.
18. Martin, "Rhinos and Daggers."
19. Martin, "Status of Rhino Populations and Associated Trade in Rhino Products."

20. Martin, personal communication.
21. Martin, "Status of Rhino Populations and Associated Trade in Rhino Products."
22. Ibid.
23. Tom Milliken, personal communication.
24. CITES Secretariat, "Interpretation and Implementation of the Convention: Review of Alleged Infractions," *Proceedings of the Sixth Meeting of the Conference of the Parties*, Doc. 6.19.
25. Martin, "Status of Rhino Populations and Associated Trade in Rhino Products."
26. Martin, personal communication, total based on his estimate that the average horn weighs 3.5 pounds.
27. Esmond Bradley Martin, "Investigating and Combating the Rhino Horn Trade, 1985-1986," unpublished manuscript, 1986.
28. "Run Poacher Run."
29. Martin, "Status of Rhino Populations and Associated Trade in Rhino Products."
30. Esmond Bradley Martin, "South Korea Stops Rhino Horn Imports," *Traffic Bulletin* 8, no. 2 (1986):28.
31. "Asian Rhino Horn Imports," *Traffic Bulletin* 8, no. 1 (1986):12.
32. Ibid.; Martin, "Status of Rhino Populations and Associated Trade in Rhino Products."
33. Martin, "Status of Rhino Populations and Associated Trade in Rhino Products."
34. World Wildlife Fund, "Wildlife Trade Violations Stir International Debate," press release, Washington, D.C., July 1987.
35. Martin, "Status of Rhino Populations and Associated Trade in Rhino Products."

Figures

10.1. Lili Sheeline, "Is There a Future in the Wild for Rhinos?" *TRAFFIC(U.S.A.)* 7, no. 4 (1987):1-6, 24.
10.2. Ibid.; John Hanks, unpublished data, 1987; Lucy Vigue and Esmond Bradley Martin, "Kenya Tries to Save Its Rhinos," *Quagga*, no. 15 (Spring 1986):11-12; David Western and Lucy Vigne, "The Deteriorating Status of African Rhinos," *Oryx* 19, no. 4 (1985)215-20.
10.3. D. Cumming, "Zimbabwe and the Conservation of Black Rhino," *The Zimbabwe Science News* 21, nos. 5/6 (1987):59-62.
10.4. Malcolm Penny, *Rhinos: Endangered Species* (New York: Facts on File, 1988), p. 37.
10.5. Ibid., pp. 49, 59.
10.6. Ibid., p. 65.

11. Vicuñas

1. Jane Thornback and Martin Jenkins, *The IUCN Mammal Red Data Book*, part 1 (Gland, Switzerland: International Union for Conservation of Nature and Natural Resources, 1982).
2. Ibid.
3. Margot Hornblower, "Noble Sentiments, Sharp Disagreements," *Audubon* 81, no. 4 (1979):108-15.
4. Thornback and Jenkins, *The IUCN Mammal Red Data Book*, part 1.

5. Ibid.
6. Ibid.
7. Carlos Saavedra, personal communication.
8. Barbara d'Achille, "Salvar la Vicuña: Una Vieja Preocupacion," *El Comercio*, Lima, Peru, July 17, 1986; William L. Franklin, "The Biology, Ecology and Relationship to Man of the South American Camelid," in Michael A. Mares and Hugh Genoways, eds., *Mammalian Biology in South America*, Pymatuning Laboratory of Ecology, Special Publication Series, vol. 6 (Pittsburgh: University of Pittsburgh, 1981), pp. 457-89.

12. Otters

1. C. F. Mason and S. M. MacDonald, *Otters: Ecology and Conservation* (Cambridge: Cambridge University Press, 1986); Paul Chanin, *The Natural History of Otters* (New York: Facts on File, 1985).
2. Chanin, *The Natural History of Otters*.
3. Karl W. Kenyon, *The Sea Otter in the Eastern Pacific Ocean* (New York: Dover, 1975).
4. Ibid.
5. Ronald M. Nowak and John L. Paradiso, *Walker's Mammals of the World*, 4th ed., vol. 2 (Baltimore: Johns Hopkins University Press, 1983).
6. CITES annual reports.
7. Ibid.
8. J. Thornback and M. Jenkins, *The IUCN Mammal Red Data Book*, part 1 (Gland, Switzerland: International Union for Conservation of Nature and Natural Resources, 1982).
9. Juan S. Villalba-Macias, personal communication.
10. Steven Broad, *The Harvest of and Trade in Latin American Spotted Cats (Felidae) and Otters (Lutrinae)* (Cambridge: Wildlife Trade Monitoring Unit/International Union for the Conservation of Nature and Natural Resources, 1987).
11. Villalba-Macias, personal communication.
12. N.J.H. Smith, "Caimans, Capybaras, Otters, Manatees, and Man in Amazonia," *Biological Conservation* 19 (1980-81):177-87.
13. J. Lobao Tello, "The Situation of the Wild Cats *(Felidae)* in Bolivia," report prepared for CITES, 1986.
14. Juan S. Villalba-Macias, unpublished report on French Guiana, 1986.
15. Villalba-Macias, personal communication.
16. Broad, *The Harvest of and Trade in Latin American Spotted Cats* (Felidae) *and Otters* (Lutrinae)
17. Thornback and Jenkins, *The IUCN Mammal Red Data Book*, part 1.
18. Mason and MacDonald, *Otters*.
19. T. Pacheco, "Effectos Positivos y Negativos de la Veda de Caza de 1973 en la Amazonia Peruana," report for the Universidad Nacional Agraria la Molina, Lima, Peru, 1983.
20. Broad, *The Harvest of and Trade in Latin American Spotted Cats* (Felidae) *and Otters* (Lutrinae).
21. Chanin, *The Natural History of Otters*.
22. CITES annual reports, 1984.
23. Nowak and Paradiso, *Walker's Mammals of the World*.
24. Peter Dollinger, ed., *CITES Identification Manual*, vol. 1, *Mammalia* (Lausanne, Switzerland: CITES Secretariat, 1983).

25. E. P. Hill and R.R.P. Stardom, "River Otter (*Lutra canadensis*)," in Eugene F. Deems, Jr., and Duane Pursley, eds., *North American Furbearers: A Contemporary Reference* (Washington, D.C.: International Association of Fish and Wildlife Agencies, in cooperation with the Maryland Department of Natural Resources-Wildlife Administration, 1983), pp. 177-81.
26. Ibid.
27. Jorgen Thomsen, personal communication.
28. Mason and MacDonald, *Otters.*
29. Wildlife Trade Monitoring Unit, significant trade studies.

13. Seals

1. Simon Lyster, *International Wildlife Law* (Cambridge: Grotius Publications, 1985).
2. Judith E. King, *Seals of the World* (Ithaca, N.Y.: Cornell University Press, 1983).
3. Ibid.
4. Ibid.
5. Georgia Cranmore, personal communication.
6. King, *Seals of the World.*
7. Ibid.
8. Michael Weisskopf, "Plastic Reaps a Grim Harvest in the Oceans of the World," *Smithsonian* 18, no. 12 (1988):58-66.
9. Charles Fowler, personal communication.
10. Lyster, *International Wildlife Law.*
11. Ibid.
12. Ibid.; Michael J. Bean, *The Evolution of National Wildlife Law* (New York: Praeger Publishers, 1983).
13. King, *Seals of the World.*
14. Lyster, *International Wildlife Law.*
15. CITES annual reports, 1985.
16. Alexandra M. Dixon, "The European Trade in Sealskins," *Traffic Bulletin* 6, nos. 3&4 (1984):54-65.
17. Bean, *The Evolution of National Wildlife Law.*
18. Dixon, "The European Trade in Sealskins."
19. Ibid.
20. Ibid.
21. "Seal Fur Dressing Plant to Close," *Traffic Bulletin* 5, nos. 5&6 (1984):64.
22. Dixon, "The European Trade in Sealskins."
23. Jonathan Barzdo, *International Trade in Harp and Hooded Seals* (London: Fauna and Flora Preservation Society and the International Fund for Animal Welfare, 1980).
24. Dixon, "The European Trade in Sealskins."
25. Ibid.; Jonathan Barzdo and John Caldwell, "A Review of the International Trade in Marine Mammals," *Traffic Bulletin* 4, nos. 4&5 (1982):40-60.
26. Dixon, "The European Trade in Sealskins."
27. Ibid.
28. Ibid.
29. Barzdo and Caldwell, "A Review of the International Trade in Marine Mammals."

References   415

30. Dixon, "The European Trade in Sealskins."
31. Jorgen Thomsen, personal communication.
32. Steve Koplin, "U.S. Exports of Sealskins (Dressed)," Fisheries Statistics, National Marine Fisheries Service, Washington, D.C., 1987.
33. Dixon, "The European Trade in Sealskins."
34. Cranmore, personal communication.
35. Ibid.
36. Dixon, "The European Trade in Sealskins."
37. "Industria Lobera y Pesquera del Estado Gevencia de Loberia y Curtiembre," Departmento Cientifico y Tecnologico, Montevideo, Uruguay, 1986; King, *Seals of the World*.
38. "Industria Lobera y Pesquera del Estado"; Dixon, "The European Trade in Sealskins"; CITES annual report for the European Economic Commission, 1985.
39. "Industria Lobera y Pesquera del Estado."
40. "Block on Soviet Seal Hunt," *New Scientist*, August 6, 1987.
41. King, *Seals of the World*.

Figure

13.1. Steve Koplin, "U.S. Exports of Sealskins (Dressed)," Fisheries Statistics, National Marine Fisheries Service, Washington, D.C., 1987.

14. Walruses

1. Francis H. Fay, "Walrus," in David W. Macdonald, ed., *The Encyclopedia of Mammals* (New York: Facts on File, 1984); E. H. Miller, "Walrus Ethology. I. The Social Role of Tusks and Applications of Multidimensional Scaling," *Canadian Journal of Zoology* 53 (1975):590-613.
2. Francis H. Fay, B. P. Kelly, and John L. Sease, "Managing the Exploitation of Pacific Walruses: A Tragedy of Delayed Response and Poor Communication," 1987.
3. Fay, "Walrus."
4. Francis H. Fay et al., *Modern Populations, Migrations, Demography, Trophics, and Historical Status of the Pacific Walrus*, final report, R.U. #611 (Anchorage, Alaska: National Oceanic and Atmospheric Administration Outer Continental Shelf Environmental Assessment Program, 1984).
5. John L. Sease and Francis H. Fay, "The Walrus," in Roger L. DiSilvestro, ed., *Audubon Wildlife Report 1987* (Orlando, Fla.: Academic Press, 1987), pp. 357-68.
6. J. R. Gilbert, report to U.S. Fish and Wildlife Service, in R. Hinman, Alaska Department of Fish and Game, letter to Amie L. Brautigam.
7. R. R. Reeves, *Atlantic Walrus (Odobenus rosmarus rosmarus): A Literature Survey and Status Report*, U.S. Fish and Wildlife Service Research Report no. 10 (Washington, D.C.: U.S. Fish and Wildlife Service, 1987.)
8. Sease and Fay, "The Walrus."
9. TRAFFIC Network, "Positions on Proposals to Amend the Appendices of CITES at the 6th Meeting of the Conference of the Parties," Ottawa, Canada, July 12-24, 1987.

15. Whales and Small Cetacea

1. International Whaling Commission (IWC), *Thirty-Seventh Report of the International Whaling Commission* (Cambridge: IWC, 1987); quoted in "Jap-

anese Quits Whale Group," *New York Times,* June 27, 1987.

2. Rebecca Roots, letter to Sarah Fitzgerald, June 23, 1988.

3. Ibid.

4. Dean Swanson, personal communication, April 24, 1989.

5. Clyde Haberman, "Japan, Defying Protests, Pushes Whaling Plan, *New York Times,* August 1, 1987.

6. U.S. Department of Commerce, "Statement: United States and Iceland Negotiations," *U.S. Department of Commerce News,* September 16, 1987.

7. Swanson, personal communication, May 22, 1988.

8. Swanson, personal communication, April 24, 1989.

9. World Wildlife Fund, "World Wildlife Fund Seeks to End Japan's Whaling," press release, Washington, D.C., September 1, 1987.

10. Swanson, personal communication, May 22, 1988.

11. Ralph Osterwoldt, "International Law and Politics of Conservation: Two Conventions and the Whales," submitted in fulfillment of the requirements for the Masters of Lit. (Politics), University of Oxford, St. Anne's College, 1984.

12. Japanese customs data.

13. Ibid.

14. "Not Quite a Moratorium," *Oryx* 20, no. 1 (1986):2-3.

15. Swanson, personal communication, May 22, 1988.

16. "Philippine Pirate Whaling Exposed," *Monitor Meeting Agenda,* Washington, D.C., June 15, 1987, p. 1.

17. Roots, letter.

18. Asahi News Service, "Two Arrested for Allegedly Smuggling Whale Meat into Japan," June 30, 1987.

19. Ibid.

20. Philip Shabecoff, "U.S. Declares Japan in Violation on Whaling and May Curb Trade," *New York Times,* February 11, 1988.

21. Japanese customs data.

22. Osterwoldt, "International Law and Politics of Conservation."

23. Tom Milliken, personal communication.

24. Tom Ashbrook, "Japan Gets Set for Last Whale Hunt," *Boston Globe,* October 28, 1986, p. 2.

25. Roots letter.

26. IWC, *Thirty-Seventh Report.*

27. *Japanese Whaling in the Philippines* (London: Greenpeace UK, 1987).

28. Roots, letter.

29. Swanson, personal communication, April 24, 1989.

30. Lee Durrell, *State of the Ark: An Atlas of Conservation in Action* (Garden City, N.Y.: Doubleday, 1986).

31. Rebecca Roots, personal communication.

32. Roots, letter.

33. Ibid.

34. International Wildlife Coalition.

35. Nathalie F. R. Ward, "The Whales of Bequia," *Oceanus* 30, no. 4 (1987/1988):89-83.

36. Robert Campbell, personal communication, June 22, 1988.

37. Wildlife Trade Monitoring Unit, Appendix II study on narwhal (*Monodon monoceros*), 1986.

References   417

38. Steven Broad, Richard Luxmoore, and Martin Jenkins, eds., *Significant Trade in Wildlife: A Review of Selected Species in CITES Appendix II*, vol. 2, *Mammals* (Gland, Switzerland: International Union for Conservation of Nature and Natural Resources, 1988).

39. Campbell, personal communication.

40. Broad, Luxmoore, and Jenkins, *Significant Trade in Wildlife*, vol. 2, *Mammals*.

41. Paul Brodie, "White Whales," in David W. Macdonald, ed., *The Encyclopedia of Mammals* (New York: Facts on File, 1984).

42. Jonathan Barzdo and John Caldwell, "A Review of the International Trade in Marine Mammals," *Traffic Bulletin* 4, nos. 4&5 (1982):40-60.

43. Miguel Stutzin, personal communication to Nancy Hammond, March 11 and 16, 1987.

44. "UK Bans Dolphin Imports," *Traffic Bulletin* 8, no. 2 (1986):23.

Figures

15.1. Japanese Customs data.

15.2. Heathcote Williams, *Whale Nation* (London: Jonathan Cape, 1988).

16. Parrots

1. J. Serpell, "Parrots, Lories and Cockatoos," in Christopher Perrins and Alex L. Middleton, eds., *The Encyclopedia of Birds* (New York: Facts on File, 1985), pp. 220-27.

2. Ibid.

3. TRAFFIC(U.S.A.), "Parrot Trade Factsheet" and "World Trade in Wildlife Factsheet," World Wildlife Fund, Washington, D.C., 1986.

4. Charles A. Munn, Jorgen B. Thomsen, and Carlos Yamashita, "Survey and Status of the Hyacinth Macaw (*Anodorhynchus hyacinthinus*: Psittacidae) in Brazil, Bolivia, and Paraguay," report prepared for the CITES Secretariat, Lausanne, Switzerland, 1987.

5. Jorgen B. Thomsen and Charles A. Munn, "*Cyanopsitta spixii:* A Non-Recovery Report," *Parrotletter* 1, no. 1 (1988):6-7.

6. World Wildlife Fund, "WWF Position Statement, Sixth Meeting of the Conference of the Parties to CITES, 12-24 July 1987.

7. G. Randy Milton, "Investigation of Parrots on Bacan (North Molucca) and Waxmar (Southeast Molucca) Islands, Indonesia," *Parrotletter* 1, no. 1 (1988):6-7.

8. Wildlife Trade Monitoring Unit (WTMU), unpublished Appendix II studies for the hyacinth macaw, African grey parrot, chattering lory, blue-streaked lory, and salmon-crested cockatoo, 1986; Milton, "Investigation of Parrots on Bacan (North Molucca) and Waxmar (Southeast Molucca) Islands, Indonesia."

9. WTMU, unpublished Appendix II study for the chattering lory.

10. Milton, "Investigation of Parrots on Bacan (North Molucca) and Waxmar (Southeast Molucca) Islands, Indonesia."

11. Paolo Bertagnolio, cited in Pier-Lorenzo Florio, personal communication.

12. Amanda Jorgenson and Jorgen B. Thomsen, "Neotropical Parrots Imported by the United States, 1981 to 1985," *TRAFFIC(U.S.A.)* 7, nos. 2&3 (1987):3-4.

13. Greta Nilsson, *Importation of Birds into the United States, 1980-1984*, vols. 1

& 2 (Washington, D.C.: Animal Welfare Institute, 1985).

14. U.S. Department of Agriculture, Animal and Plant Health Inspection Service, "Exotic Newcastle Disease: A Deadly Form of a Familiar Poultry Disease," PA 1414, 1988.

15. "VVND Kills Birds," *TRAFFIC(U.S.A.)* 8, no. 1 (1988):20-21.

16. TRAFFIC(U.S.A.), "Parrot Trade Factsheet."

17. Tim Inskipp, personal communication.

18. CITES annual reports; Jorgen B. Thomsen and Ginette Hemley, "Bird Trade . . . Bird Bans," *TRAFFIC(U.S.A.)* 7, nos. 2&3 (February 1987); D. D. Jackson, "Pursued in the Wild for the Pet Trade, Parrots Are Perched on a Risky Limb," *Smithsonian* 16, no. 1 (1985):59-67.

19. Inskipp, personal communication.

20. Jorgenson and Thomsen, "Neotropical Parrots Imported by the United States, 1981 to 1985."

21. Amanda Jorgenson and Jorgen B. Thomsen, "The World Trade in African Parrots, 1984," *TRAFFIC(U.S.A.)* 7, nos. 2&3 (1987):9-14.

22. Steven Broad, "Imports of Psittacines into the UK (1981-1984)," *Traffic Bulletin* 8, no. 3 (1986):36-44.

23. Emily Roet and Tom Milliken, *The Japanese Psittacine Trade, 1981-1982* (Washington, D.C.: World Wildlife Fund, 1985).

24. Jorgenson and Thomsen, "The World Trade in African Parrots, 1984."

25. TRAFFIC(U.S.A.) estimate.

26. Jorgenson and Thomsen, "The World Trade in African Parrots, 1984."

27. Thomsen and Hemley, "Bird Trade . . . Bird Bans."

28. Donald Carr, personal communication.

29. Jackson, "Pursued in the Wild for the Pet Trade, Parrots Are Perched on a Risky Limb"; TRAFFIC(U.S.A.), "Parrot Trade Factsheet."

30. Douglas Fuller, "Central American Wildlife Trade Update," *TRAFFIC(U.S.A.)* 6, no. 3 (1985):4-6.

31. Jorgenson and Thomsen, "The World Trade in African Parrots, 1984."

32. Ngiam Tong Hai, "124 Rare Birds Seized," *The Straits Times*, September 6, 1983, p. 48.

33. U.S. Department of the Interior, "Valuable Bird Shipment Forfeited to the U.S. Fish and Wildlife Service," news release, February 29, 1984.

34. Bob Bottom, "Rustling Feathers," Australian *Penthouse*, February 1984.

35. Frank Antram, personal communication.

36. Judith Judd, "Rare Birds in Danger," *The Observer*, February 3, 1980.

37. Thomsen and Munn, "*Cyanopsitta spixii:* A Non-Recovery Report"; World Wildlife Fund, "Raid Nets Parrot Smugglers in Paraguay," press release, Washington, D.C., March 26, 1987.

38. Jorgen Thomsen, personal communication.

39. Munn, Thomsen, and Yamashita, "Survey and Status of the Hyacinth Macaw in Brazil, Bolivia, and Paraguay."

40. Ibid.

41. TRAFFIC(U.S.A.), "Parrot Trade Factsheet"; Nilsson, *Importation of Birds into the United States, 1980-1984*, vols. 1 & 2.

42. Munn, Thomsen, and Yamashita, "Survey and Status of the Hyacinth Macaw in Brazil, Bolivia, and Paraguay."

43. CITES Secretariat, "Interpretation and Implementation of the Convention: Review of Alleged Infractions," *Proceedings of the Sixth Meeting of the Conference of the Parties*, Ottawa, Canada, July 12-24, 1987

References   419

(Lausanne, Switzerland: CITES Secretariat, 1989), Doc. 6.19.

44. Juan S. Villalba-Macias, personal communication.
45. TRAFFIC Network, "Positions on Proposals to Amend the Appendices of CITES at the Sixth Meeting of the Conference of the Parties," Ottawa, Canada, July 12-24, 1987.
46. Thomsen, personal communication.
47. Ginette Hemley, "One View of Buenos Aires: Handling of Elephants, Macaws, and Crocodiles Reflects Varied Responses to Trade Problems," *TRAFFIC(U.S.A.)* 6, no. 3 (1985).
48. Robert S. Ridgely, "The Current Distribution and Status of Mainland Neotropical Parrots," in Roger F. Pasquier, *Conservation of New World Parrots*, Proceedings of the ICBP Parrot Working Group Meeting, St. Lucia, 1980 (Washington, D.C.: Smithsonian Institution Press, 1981), pp. 223-384.
49. Jorgenson and Thomsen, "The World Trade in African Parrots, 1984"; WTMU, unpublished Appendix II studies for the African grey parrot.
50. Alexandra Dixon, *Evaluation of the Psittacine Importation Process in the United States* (Washington, D.C.: World Wildlife Fund, 1986).

Figure
16.1. CITES annual reports.

17. Raptors

1. Deborah Barnes and Ginette Hemley, "The International Trade in Raptors," *Traffic Bulletin* 7, no. 5 (1986):64-71.
2. Ian Newton, "Shell Shock: Pesticides and Birds of Prey," in Christopher Perrins and Alex L. Middleton, eds., *The Encyclopedia of Birds* (New York: Facts on File, 1985), pp. 122-27.
3. Barnes and Hemley, "The International Trade in Raptors."
4. Warren B. King, *The IUCN Aves Red Data Book*, vol. 2 (Morges, Switzerland: International Union for Conservation of Nature and Natural Resources, 1979).
5. TRAFFIC(Austria), personal communication.
6. Robert B. Berry, testimony to the Subcommittee on Environmental Pollution, Committee on Environment and Public Works, U.S. Senate, 1985.
7. Barnes and Hemley, "The International Trade in Raptors"; Paul D. Goriup, letter to Jonathan Barzdo, January 9, 1985.
8. Paul D. Goriup, personal communication; Goriup, letter to Barzdo.
9. Barnes and Hemley, "The International Trade in Raptors."
10. Manfred Niekisch, personal communication.
11. Barnes and Hemley, "The International Trade in Raptors."
12. Ibid.
13. Ibid.
14. Robert B. Berry, *Commercialism of Domestically Produced Raptors* (North American Raptor Breeders' Association, 1986).
15. Barnes and Hemley, "The International Trade in Raptors."
16. John Gavitt, personal communication.
17. Robert E. Taylor, "When These Falcons Flew to Saudi Arabia, They Traveled by Jet," *Wall Street Journal*, August 8, 1986.
18. Ibid.

19. Barnes and Hemley, "The International Trade in Raptors."
20. "Falconer Convicted in U.K.," *Traffic Bulletin* 7, nos. 3&4 (1985):58.
21. Barnes and Hemley, "The International Trade in Raptors."
22. "Goshawks Returned to Europe," *Traffic Bulletin* 7, nos. 3&4 (1985):58.
23. "Egg Smugglers Arrested," *Traffic Bulletin* 8, no. 1 (1986):6.
24. Jan Raath, "Eagle Scandal Exposed," *The Observer*, October 21, 1984.

18. Songbirds

1. Jorgen B. Thomsen and Ginette Hemley, "Bird Trade . . . Bird Bans," *TRAFFIC(U.S.A.)* 7, nos. 2&3 (February 1987).
2. Stewart M. Evans, "The Mouse of the Avian World," in Christopher Perrins and Alex L. Middleton, eds., *The Encyclopedia of Birds* (New York: Facts on File, 1985), p. 422.
3. Paolo Bertagnolio, cited in Pier-Lorenzo Florio, personal communication.
4. Sadie Coats and William H. Phelps, Jr., "The Venezuelan Red Siskin: Case History of an Endangered Species," in P. A. Buckley et al, eds., *Neotropical Ornithology* (Washington, D.C.: American Ornithologists Union, 1985), pp. 977-85.
5. R. L. Bruggers, "The Exportation of Cage Birds from Senegal," *Traffic Bulletin* 4, no. 2 (1982):12-23.
6. Ibid.
7. Greta Nilsson, *Importation of Birds into the United States, 1980-1984*, vols. 1 & 2 (Washington, D.C.: Animal Welfare Institute, 1985).
8. Phillippe Ruelle and Richard L. Bruggers, "Senegal's Trade in Cage Birds, 1979-81," U.S. Fish and Wildlife Service Leaflet 515, 1983.
9. Tim Inskipp, "The Indian Bird Trade," *Traffic Bulletin* 5, nos. 3&4 (1983):26-46.
10. Ibid.

19. Other Birds in Trade

1. Jorgen B. Thomsen and Ginette Hemley, "Bird Trade . . . Bird Bans," *TRAFFIC(U.S.A.)* 7, nos. 2&3 (February 1987).
2. R. L. Bruggers, "The Exportation of Cage Birds from Senegal," *Traffic Bulletin* 4, no. 2 (1982):12-23.
3. Thomsen and Hemley, "Bird Trade . . . Bird Bans."
4. N. M. Meyers, "National Cage and Aviary Bird Improvement Plan Status Report," in *Proceedings of the 87th Annual Meeting of the U.S. Animal Health Association* (Richmond, Va.: U.S. Animal Health Association, 1983), pp. 425-30.
5. Tim Inskipp, "Hummingbird Trade and Protection," *Traffic Bulletin* 9, no. 1 (1987):12-28.
6. Ecuadorean proposal to list hummingbirds in Appendix II, presented to 6th meeting of the Conference of the Parties, Ottawa, Canada, July 12-24, 1987.
7. Inskipp, "Hummingbird Trade and Protection."
8. Ibid.
9. Jorgen Thomsen, personal communication.
10. U.S. Fish and Wildlife Service, declarations data.
11. "Recent Trends in U.S. Skin Imports," *TRAFFIC(U.S.A.)* 5, no. 2 (1983):6.

12. Ibid.
13. Juan S. Villalba-Macias, personal communication.
14. Andrea Gaski, personal communication.
15. Villalba-Macias, personal communication.
16. Tim Inskipp and Sue Wells, *International Trade in Wildlife* (London: International Institute for Environment and Development, 1979).
17. Ibid.
18. Villalba-Macias, personal communication.
19. TRAFFIC Network, "Positions on Proposals to Amend the Appendices of CITES at the Sixth Meeting of the Conference of the Parties," Ottawa, Canada, July 12-24, 1987.
20. French proposal to list *Eudocimus ruber* in Appendix I, amendments to Appendices I and II of the Convention, presented to 6th meeting of the Conference of the Parties, Ottawa, Canada, July 12-24, 1987.

Figure
19.1. Jorgen B. Thomsen and Ginette Hemley, "Bird Trade . . . Bird Bans," *TRAFFIC(U.S.A.* 7, nos. 2&3 (February 1987):21.

20. Crocodiles, Alligators, and Caimans

1. Tim Inskipp and Sue Wells, *International Trade in Wildlife* (London: International Institute for Environment and Development, 1979).
2. F. Wayne King, "The Wildlife Trade," in H. P. Brokaw, ed., *Wildlife and America: Contributions to an Understanding of American Wildlife and Its Conservation* (Washington, D.C.: U.S. Government Printing Office, 1978), pp. 253-77.
3. Ibid.
4. Peter Brazaitis, "The Caiman of the Pantanal: Past, Present, and Future," paper presented to the International Union for Conservation of Nature and Natural Resources Crocodile Specialist Group meeting in Quito, Ecuador, October 1986.
5. Andrea L. Gaski and Ginette Hemley, "The Ups and Downs of the Crocodilian Skin Trade," *TRAFFIC(U.S.A.)* 8, no. 1 (February 1988).
6. Randall Hyman, "Brazil Wages War on Poachers," *International Wildlife* 15, no. 1 (1985):5-11.
7. R. A. Luxmoore et al., *A Directory of Crocodilian Farming Operations* (Cambridge: International Union for Conservation of Nature and Natural Resources, 1985).
8. Romulus Whitaker, P. Sukran, and C. Hartono, "The Crocodile Resource in Irian Jaya," 1985; cited in R. A. Luxmoore, "Exploitation of the Saltwater Crocodile in Indonesia," *Traffic Bulletin* 7, no. 5 (1986):78-80.
9. Gaski and Hemley, "The Ups and Downs of the Crocodilian Skin Trade."
10. Ibid.
11. Ginette Hemley, "Alligator Exports Boom in '86," *TRAFFIC(U.S.A.)* 8, no. 1 (February 1988).
12. Ibid.
13. Federico Medem, *Crocodile Skin Trade in South America* (Washington, D.C.: World Wildlife Fund, 1985).
14. J. L. Tello, "The Situation of the Wild Cats in Bolivia," report prepared for the CITES Secretariat, 1986.

15. Medem, *Crocodile Skin Trade in South America.*
16. Ginette Hemley and John Caldwell, *Crocodile Skin Trade since 1979* (Washington, D.C.: World Wildlife Fund, 1984); Hyman, "Brazil Wages War on Poachers."
17. Gaski and Hemley, "The Ups and Downs of the Crocodilian Skin Trade."
18. Peter Brazaitis, personal communication.
19. Ginette Hemley, personal communication.
20. Brazaitis, personal communication.
21. Venezuela, Notification to the Parties no. 457, CITES Secretariat, Lausanne, Switzerland, May 7, 1986.
22. Tom Milliken, personal communication.
23. Gaski and Hemley, "The Ups and Downs of the Crocodilian Skin Trade."
24. Hyman, "Brazil Wages War on Poachers."
25. Ibid.
26. Brazaitis, "The Caiman of the Pantanal."
27. Guatemala, Notification to the Parties no. 386, CITES Secretariat, Lausanne, Switzerland, May 7, 1986.
28. Gaski and Hemley, "The Ups and Downs of the Crocodilian Skin Trade."
29. Ibid.
30. Brazaitis, "The Caiman of the Pantanal."

Figures

20.1. U.S. Department of the Interior, Fish and Wildlife Service, "Declaration for Importation or Exportation of Fish or Wildlife," Forms 3-177, obtained from unedited computerized data.
20.2. CITES annual reports.

21. Lizards and Snakes

1. International Union for Conservation of Nature and Natural Resources (IUCN) Conservation Monitoring Centre (CMC), Appendix II studies for water monitor, savannah lizard, tupinambis, Nile monitor, blood python, reticulated python, anaconda, yellow anaconda, boa constrictor, and Indian python.
2. Ginette Hemley, "Tracking Argentina's Wildlife Trade," *TRAFFIC(U.S.A.)* 7, no. 1 (1986):1.
3. IUCN CMC Appendix II studies.
4. Ginette Hemley, "Reptiles as Popular as Ever," *TRAFFIC(U.S.A.)* 5, no. 2 (1984):4; Brian Groombridge, *World Checklist of Threatened Amphibians and Reptiles* (Peterborough, U.K.: Nature Conservancy Council, 1988).
5. Ginette Hemley, personal communication.
6. Hemley, "Reptiles as Popular as Ever."
7. IUCN CMC Appendix II studies.
8. Hemley, "Tracking Argentina's Wildlife Trade."
9. Ibid.
10. Hemley, personal communication.
11. "International Trade in Skins of Monitor and Tegu Lizards, 1975-80," *Traffic Bulletin* 4, no. 6 (1983):71-73.
12. Walter Auffenberg, "Interim Report, 1987 Pakistan Project."

13. Xotic Pets Ltd., "Stock List no. 5," Alfreton, United Kingdom, November 1984.

14. U.S. Department of the Interior, Fish and Wildlife Service, unpublished data, 1985.

15. Tim Inskipp, "World Trade in Monitor Lizard Skins, 1977-1982," *Traffic Bulletin* 6, nos. 3&4 (1984):51-53.

16. IUCN CMC Appendix II studies.

17. U.S. Fish and Wildlife Service, unpublished data, 1985.

18. IUCN CMC Appendix II studies.

19. Walter Auffenberg, "Catch a Lizard, Use a Lizard," *International Wildlife* 12, no. 6 (1982):16-19.

20. IUCN CMC Appendix II studies.

21. U.S. Fish and Wildlife Service, unpublished data, 1985.

22. Auffenberg, "Catch a Lizard, Use a Lizard."

23. Hemley, personal communication.

24. IUCN CMC Appendix II studies.

25. Ibid.; Manfred Niekisch, personal communication.

26. Hemley, personal communication.

27. Henry S. Fitch, Robert W. Henderson, and David M. Hillis, "Exploitation of Iguanas in Central America," in Gordon M. Burghardt and A. Stanley Rand, eds., *Iguanas of the World: Their Behavior, Ecology and Conservation* (Park Ridge, N.J.: Noyes, 1982), pp. 397-417.

28. Andrea Gaski, personal communication.

29. Ginette Hemley, "International Reptile Skin Trade Dependent on Few Species," *TRAFFIC(U.S.A.)* 5, no. 2 (1983); C. Kenneth Dodd, Jr., "Importation of Live Snakes and Snake Products into the United States, 1977-1983," *Herpetological Review* 17, no. 4 (1986):76-79.

30. C. Kenneth Dodd, Jr., "Status, Conservation and Management," in Richard A. Seigel, Joseph T. Collins, and Susan S. Novak, eds., *Snakes: Ecology and Evolutionary Biology* (New York: Macmillan, 1987), pp. 488.

31. Ibid., pp. 498, 505.

32. CITES, "Proposal to List *Vipera ursinii* in Appendix I. The French Republic and the Italian Republic. Amendments to Appendices I and II of the Convention," presented to 6th meeting of the Conference of the Parties, July 12-24, 1987, Ottawa, Canada.

33. U.S. Fish and Wildlife Service, unpublished data, 1985.

34. Andrea Gaski, personal communication.

35. U.S. Fish and Wildlife Service, unpublished data, 1985.

36. Dodd, "Status, Conservation and Management," p. 502.

37. Ibid.

38. IUCN CMC Appendix II studies.

39. Pier-Lorenzo Florio, personal communication.

40. "Seizures," *Traffic Bulletin* 9, nos. 2&3 (1987):33.

41. IUCN CMC Appendix II studies; Gaski, personal communication.

42. U.S. Fish and Wildlife Service, unpublished data, 1985.

43. IUCN CMC Appendix II studies.

44. Ibid.

45. Ibid.; U.S. Fish and Wildlife Service, unpublished data, 1985.

46. Dodd, "Importation of Live Snakes and Snake Products into the United States, 1977-1983."

47. IUCN CMC Appendix II studies.

48. Gaski, personal communication.
49. "Python Skin Shoes Draw $15,000 Fine," *Geosphere,* June 1981.
50. IUCN CMC Appendix II studies.
51. U.S. Fish and Wildlife Service, unpublished data, 1985.
52. Ibid.
53. Ibid.
54. Howard Hall, "A Deadly Business," *International Wildlife,* July/August 1987.
55. Keith Scholey, "Sea Snakes," *BBC Wildlife,* October 1985.
56. Hall, "A Deadly Business."
57. Frank Antram, "The Australian Sea Snake Industry," *Traffic Bulletin* 8, no. 3 (1986):51.
58. Hall, "A Deadly Business."
59. Antram, "The Australian Sea Snake Industry."
60. Dodd, "Importation of Live Snakes and Snake Products into the United States, 1977-1983."
61. Dodd, "Status, Conservation and Management."
62. IUCN CMC Appendix II studies.
63. Ibid.
64. IUCN CMC Appendix II studies; Hemley, personal communication.
65. Gaski, personal communication.
66. John H. Trestrail III, " 'The Underground Zoo'—The Problem of Exotic Venomous Snakes in Private Possession in the United States," *Veterinary and Human Toxicology* 24 (1982):144-49.
67. Dodd, "Status, Conservation and Management."
68. Ibid.
69. S. Bruno, "Anfibi d'Italia (Studi sullar Fauna erpetologica italiana XVII)," *Natura Soc. It. sc. Nat. Museo Civ. St. Nat. et. Acquario Civ. Milano* 64 (1973):209-450; cited in Dodd, "Importation of Live Snakes and Snake Products into the United States, 1977-1983."
70. H. A. Reid, "Bites by Foreign Venomous Snakes in Britain," *British Medical Journal* 1 (1978):1598-1600.
71. "International Snake Trade," *Hamadryad* 12, no. 1 (1987):6.
72. C. Kenneth Dodd, Jr., personal communication.
73. Jeff Greenwald, "Large Scale Obsession," *Image,* August 30, 1987.
74. "Dragons Fly First Class," *TRAFFIC(U.S.A.)* 8, no. 1 (1988):19.
75. Frank Antram, "Australian Prosecutions," *Traffic Bulletin* 9, nos. 2&3 (1987):54.
76. Michael Bender, "Sting Operation Reveals Massive Illegal Trade," *Endangered Species Technical Bulletin* 6, no. 8 (1981):1,4.
77. "Seizures."
78. Sharon Begley, "The Snakescam Sting," *Newsweek,* July 27, 1981.
79. "Two, Four, Six Reptiles, a Dollar?" *TRAFFIC(U.S.A.)* 7, no. 4 (1987):13.
80. "Tuataras Traded for Drugs," *Oryx* 21, no. 2 (1987):125.
81. "Papua New Guinea Suspends Exports," *Traffic Bulletin* 9, nos. 2&3 (1987):31.
82. Dodd, "Status, Conservation and Management."

Box: "Problems in the Indian Snake Trade"
1. Romulus Whitaker, "Introduction, Aims and Objectives of the Snake Specialist Group," in *Proceedings of the IUCN/SSC Snake Group Meeting,* Madras, India, November 8-12, 1982.

2. Anne Joseph, "Indian Snake Skin Trade," in *Proceedings of the IUCN/SSC Snake Group Meeting.*
3. Josephine Andrews and Chris Birkinshaw, "India's Snakeskin Trade," *Traffic Bulletin* 9, no. 4 (1988):66-77.
4. Tim Inskipp, "Indian Trade in Reptile Skins," report for the Wildlife Trade Monitoring Unit/International Union for Conservation of Nature and Natural Resources, 1981.
5. Jonathan Barzdo, personal communication.
6. "International Snake Trade," *Hamadryad* 12, no. 1 (1987):6.
7. Andrews and Birkinshaw, "India's Snakeskin Trade."
8. Tim Inskipp, "Indian Trade in Reptile Skins," report for the Wildlife Trade Monitoring Unit/International Union for Conservation of Nature and Natural Resources, 1981; Andrews and Birkinshaw, "India's Snakeskin Trade."
9. Inskipp, "Indian Trade in Reptile Skins."
10. Andrews and Birkinshaw, "India's Snakeskin Trade."
11. "Bid to Smuggle Snakeskins to S'pore," *Straits Times*, September 11, 1985.
12. Andrews and Birkinshaw, "India's Snakeskin Trade."
13. Ibid.

Figures
21.1. Richard Luxmoore, Brian Groombridge, and Steven Broad, eds., *Significant Trade in Wildlife: A Review of Selected Species in CITES Appendix II*, vol. 2, *Reptiles and Invertebrates* (Cambridge: International Union for Conservation of Nature and Natural Resources, 1988), p. 175.
21.2. Ibid., pp. 187, 202, 212.
21.3. CITES annual reports.

22. Turtles

1. Brian Groombridge, *The IUCN Amphibia-Reptilia Red Data Book*, Part I (Gland, Switzerland: International Union for Conservation of Nature and Natural Resources, 1982).
2. M. Weber et al., *Sea Turtles in Trade: An Evaluation* (Washington, D.C.: Center for Environmental Education, 1983).
3. Tom Milliken and Hideomi Tokunaga, *The Japanese Sea Turtle Trade, 1976-1986* (Tokyo: TRAFFIC(Japan)/Center for Environmental Education, 1987).
4. Richard Luxmoore, personal communication.
5. J. Canin and R. Luxmoore, *International Trade in Sea Turtle Shell, 1979-1984* (Cambridge: Wildlife Trade Monitoring Unit, 1985).
6. Ibid.
7. Ibid.
8. Milliken and Tokunaga, *The Japanese Sea Turtle Trade, 1976-1986.*
9. Canin and Luxmoore, *International Trade in Sea Turtle Shell, 1979-1984.*
10. Milliken and Tokunaga, *The Japanese Sea Turtle Trade, 1976-1986.*
11. Tim Inskipp and Sue Wells, *International Trade in Wildlife* (London: International Institute for Environment and Development, 1979).
12. Milliken and Tokunaga, *The Japanese Sea Turtle Trade, 1976-1986*; Roderic Mast and Amie Brautigam, "Mexico's Sea Turtles: Trade the Major Threat to Their Survival," *TRAFFIC(U.S.A.)* 6, no. 4 (1986):14-15.
13. Milliken and Tokunaga, *The Japanese Sea Turtle Trade, 1976-1986.*

14. Kim Cliffton, unpublished report submitted to World Wildlife Fund, 1984.
15. Rodney Salm, "IUCN/WWF Conservation Project, Sea Turtle Trade in Indonesia," IUCN/WWF Report no. 5, Bogor, Indonesia.
16. "Ecuador's Backward Step for Turtles," *Oryx* 21, no. 4 (1987):255.
17. "The EEC Annual CITES Report for 1984: A Preliminary Assessment of the Implementation of CITES in the European Economic Community" (Washington, D.C.: World Wildlife Fund, 1986).
18. Milliken and Tokunaga, *The Japanese Sea Turtle Trade, 1976-1986*.
19. "Exports for Cayman Turtle Farm (1980-1983), Ltd.," unpublished document, 1984.
20. Salm, "IUCN/WWF Conservation Project, Sea Turtle Trade in Indonesia."
21. Luxmoore, personal communication.
22. Canin and Luxmoore, *International Trade in Sea Turtle Shell, 1979-1984*.
23. Milliken and Tokunaga, *The Japanese Sea Turtle Trade, 1976-1986*.
24. Ibid.
25. Ibid.
26. "EEC Annual CITES Report for 1984"; Italian Management Authority, via Pier-Lorenzo Florio, personal communication.
27. "EEC Annual CITES Report for 1984."
28. A. Meylan, "The Ecology and Conservation of the Caribbean Hawksbill (*Eretmochelys imbricata*)," final report, World Wildlife Fund project no. 1499.
29. "EEC Annual CITES Report for 1984."
30. Milliken and Tokunaga, *The Japanese Sea Turtle Trade, 1976-1986*.
31. Canin and Luxmoore, *International Trade in Sea Turtle Shell, 1979-1984*.
32. Ibid.
33. Richard Luxmoore and John Joseph, "UK Trade in Tortoises," *Traffic Bulletin* 8, no. 3 (1986):46-48.
34. Wildlife Trade Monitoring Unit, unpublished data.
35. Luxmoore and Joseph, "UK Trade in Tortoises"; Florio, personal communication.
36. Luxmoore and Joseph, "UK Trade in Tortoises."
37. M.R.K. Lambert, "The Mediterranean Spur-Thighed Tortoise, *Testudo graeca*, in the Wild and in Trade," in J. Coburn, ed., *Proceedings of the European Herpetology Symposium* (Oxford: 1980), pp. 17-23.
38. K. Lawrence, "Arguments for the Tortoise Ban," 1986; cited in Luxmoore and Joseph, "UK Trade in Tortoises."
39. Luxmoore and Joseph, "UK Trade in Tortoises."
40. Ibid.
41. J. Joseph, "An Investigation into the United Kingdom Trade in Tortoise and Terrapins," submitted as part of the requirement for the degree of B.Sc., Environmental Studies, the Hatfield Polytechnic.
42. Luxmoore, personal communication.
43. Luxmoore and Joseph, "UK Trade in Tortoises."
44. TRAFFIC(Austria), personal communication.
45. Xotic Pets Ltd., "Stock List no. 5," Alfreton, United Kingdom, November 1984.
46. Luxmoore and Joseph, "UK Trade in Tortoises."
47. Wildlife Trade Monitoring Unit, significant trade study, 1986.

References   427

48. Kenneth Dodd, personal communication.
49. Freshwater Chelonian Specialist Group, "Progress Report," International Union for Conservation of Nature and Natural Resources, Gland, Switzerland, 1981.
50. Peter C.H. Pritchard, *Encyclopedia of Turtles* (Neptune City, N.J.: T.F.H., 1979.
51. Townsend Feehan, "Turtle Trade Controversy Reignited," *TRAFFIC(U.S.A.)* 7, no. 1 (1986):4-5.
52. Clifford Warwick, "Red-eared Terrapin Farms and Conservation," *Oryx* 20 (October 1986):237-40.
53. C. Warwick, "Wildtrack: The Truth about the Terrapin Trade," *BBC Wildlife*, September 1984.
54. Feehan, "Trutle Trade Controversy Reignited."
55. Russell Kyle, *A Feast in the Wild* (Kidlington, U.K.: KUDU Publishing, 1987), p. 153.
56. Luxmoore, personal communication.
57. Ginette Hemley, personal communication.
58. Peter C.H. Pritchard, "The Biology and Status of the Alligator Snapping Turtle (*Macroclemys temmincki*) with Research and Management Recommendations," Florida Audubon Society, 1982.
59. Ibid.
60. Tim Kirby, "Too Much Thunder for the Alligator Snapper," *BBC Wildlife* 4, no. 2 (1986)80.

Figures

22.1. Japanese Customs data.
22.2. Ibid.

23. Butterflies

1. N. Mark Collins and Michael G. Morris, *Threatened Swallowtail Butterflies of the World* (Gland, Switzerland: International Union for Conservation of Nature and Natural Resources, 1985).
2. N. M. Collins, *Butterfly Houses in Britain: The Conservation Implications* (Gland, Switzerland: International Union for Conservation of Nature and Natural Resources, 1987).
3. Collins and Morris, *Threatened Swallowtail Butterflies of the World*.
4. Ibid.
5. "The FFPS Steps in to Stop Illegal Butterfly Sale," *Oryx* 20, no. 1 (1986):65.
6. N. Mark Collins, "Catching No Harm," *The Guardian*, February 14, 1986.
7. Quoted in Paul Ress, "Swallowtails Emerge from Their Cocoons," press release, United Nations Environment Programme, 1986.
8. Collins and Morris, *Threatened Swallowtail Butterflies of the World*.
9. Andrea Gaski, personal communication.
10. N. Mark Collins, personal communication; Collins and Morris, *Threatened Swallowtail Butterflies of the World*.
11. Collins and Morris, *Threatened Swallowtail Butterflies of the World*.
12. Frank Antram, personal communication.
13. Collins and Morris, *Threatened Swallowtail Butterflies of the World*.
14. Collins, personal communication.

15. F. Quilici and M. P. Quaglia, "The World of Butterflies," *Tax*, November 1986.
16. Collins and Morris, *Threatened Swallowtail Butterflies of the World*.
17. Collins, *Butterfly Houses in Britain*.
18. Ibid.
19. Ibid.
20. Ibid.

Box: "Butterfly Ranching in Papua New Guinea"
1. N. Mark Collins, "Catching No Harm," *The Guardian*, February 14, 1986; N. Mark Collins and Michael G. Morris, *Threatened Swallowtail Butterflies of the World* (Gland, Switzerland: International Union for Conservation of Nature and Natural Resources, 1985).
2. "Quick, the Butterfly Net," *Audubon* 89, no. 4 (1987):22.

24. Corals

1. Susan M. Wells, *International Trade in Corals* (London: International Union for Conservation of Nature and Natural Resources Conservation Monitoring Centre, 1981.)
2. Ibid.
3. C. C. Carleton and P. W. Philipson, "Report on a Study of the Marketing and Processing of Precious Coral Products in Taiwan, Japan, and Hawaii," unpublished report by South Pacific Forum Fisheries Agency, Honiara, Solomon Islands, 1987.
4. Edgardo D. Gomez, A. C. Alcala, and A. C. San Diego, *Status of Philippine Coral Reefs—1981*, vol. 1, Proceedings of the 4th International Coral Reef Symposium, Manila, the Philippines, 1981, pp. 275-82.
5. Wells, *International Trade in Corals.*
6. Ibid.
7. CITES Secretariat, "Proposed Amendments to Appendices I and II of the Convention," presented to 6th Meeting of the Conference of the Parties, Ottawa, Canada, July 12-24, 1987.
8. Carleton and Philipson, "Marketing and Processing of Precious Coral Products."
9. T. S. Douglas, *The Wealth of the Sea* (London: John Gifford, 1947); cited in in Wells, *International Trade in Corals.*
10. Susan M. Wells, Robert M. Pyle, and N. Mark Collins, *The IUCN Invertebrate Red Data Book* (Gland, Switzerland: International Union for Conservation of Nature and Natural Resources, 1983).
11. Carleton and Philipson, "Marketing and Processing of Precious Coral Products."
12. U.S. Fish and Wildlife Service, "U.S. Imports of Black Coral and Products, Law Enforcement Declarations Data, 1985.
13. U.S. trade data, 1987.
14. Ibid.
15. Susan M. Wells, "Stony Corals: A Case for CITES," *Traffic Bulletin* 7, no. 1 (1985):9-11.
16. U.S. trade data, 1987.
17. Wells, "Stony Corals."
18. Wells, *International Trade in Corals.*

Figure

24.1. U.S. Customs data.

25. Ornamental Fish

1. Michael J. McCarthy, "Pity the Pet Fish: It May be Desired, But It Isn't Loved," *The Wall Street Journal*, October 23, 1986.
2. David Kowalski, "The 1986 Pet Retail Sales/Profit Picture," *Pet/Supplies/Marketing* 41, no. 6 (1987):40-53.
3. Ginette Hemley and Andrea Gaski, *Travelling Tropicals: A Study of the U.S.-International Ornamental Fish Trade* (Washington, D.C.: World Wildlife Fund, 1988).
4. Ibid.
5. Shinobu Matsumura and Tom Milliken, "The Japanese Trade in Bonytongue and CITES-listed Asian Fish," *Traffic Bulletin* 6, nos. 3&4 (1984):42-50.
6. Richard Seah, "Farms to Put Singapore in the Swim," *Business Times*, October 15, 1986.
7. Ibid.
8. Ginette Hemley, personal communication.
9. Hemley and Gaski, *Travelling Tropicals*.
10. Matsumura and Milliken, "The Japanese Trade in Bonytongue and CITES-listed Asian Fish."
11. Kowalski, "The 1986 Pet Retail Sales/Profit Picture."
12. Elizabeth Wood, *Exploitation of Coral Reef Fishes for the Aquarium Trade* (Ross-on-Wye, U.K.: Marine Conservation Society, 1985).
13. Ibid.
14. John Joseph, Diana Evans, and Steven Broad, "International Trade in Asian Bonytongues," *Traffic Bulletin* 7, no. 5 (1986):73-76.
15. Matsumura and Milliken, "The Japanese Trade in Bonytongue and CITES-listed Asian Fish."
16. TRAFFIC Network, "Positions on Proposals to Amend the Appendices of CITES at the Sixth Meeting of the Conference of the Parties," Ottawa, Canada, July 12-24, 1987.
17. Joseph, Evans, and Broad, "International Trade in Asian Bonytongues."
18. *Asian Business*, August 1984.
19. Wood, *Exploitation of Coral Reef Fishes for the Aquarium Trade*.
20. D. A. Conroy, *An Evaluation of the Present Status of World Trade in Ornamental Fish*, FAO Fisheries Technical Paper no. 146 (Rome: Food and Agriculture Organization, 1975).
21. H. Walter Van Poollen and Alfonso M. Obara, *Hawaii's Marine Aquarium Fish Industry Profile*, Ocean Resources Office Contribution No. 14, (Honolulu: State of Hawaii, Department of Planning and Economic Development, 1984).
22. Steve Robinson, "Fishing with Poison," *TRAFFIC(U.S.A.)* 6, no. 3 (1985):10; Pratt, personal communication.
23. Robinson, "Fishing with Poison."
24. Ibid.
25. "Philippines Approves New Fish Collecting Program," *TRAFFIC(U.S.A.)* 7, nos. 2&3 (1987):26.
26. Hemley and Gaski, *Travelling Tropicals*.
27. McCarthy, "Pity the Pet Fish."

28. "1986 Market Study—Industry Is Growing," *Tetra Topics*, May/June 1986.

29. Wood, *Exploitation of Coral Reef Fishes for the Aquarium Trade.*

26. Frogs and Other Amphibians

1. Manfred Niekisch, "Verhangnisvolle Gaumenfreuden—Ausverkauf der Frosche in Asien," *WWF-Journal*, April 1984; Manfred Niekisch, personal communication.

2. Manfred Niekisch, "The International Trade in Frogs' Legs," *Traffic Bulletin* 8, no. 1 (1986):7-10.

3. "Frogs to Keep Legs, Eat Mosquitoes," *BBC Wildlife* 5, no. 5 (1987):250.

4. Ibid.; "Mosquitos Save Frogs," *TRAFFIC(U.S.A.)* 8, no. 1 (1988):21.

5. Niekisch, "The International Trade in Frogs' Legs."

6. Paul Spencer Wachtel, "In a Stew over Frog Legs," *International Wildlife* 15, no. 3 (1985):24.

7. "Pesticides Contaminating Frogs," *Oryx* 20, no. 2 (1986):118.

8. Niekisch, personal communication.

9. Ibid.

10. "Pesticides Contaminating Frogs"; TRAFFIC(U.S.A.) estimate based on Amanda Jorgenson, "Biologists Express Concern for Huge Trade in Bullfrogs," *TRAFFIC(U.S.A.)* 6, no. 2 (1985):25-26.

11. Niekisch, "Verhangnisvolle Gaumenfreuden—Ausverkauf der Frosche in Asien"; Niekisch, "The International Trade in Frogs' Legs."

12. Niekisch, "Verhangnisvolle Gaumenfreuden—Ausverkauf der Frosche in Asien"; Niekisch, "The International Trade in Frogs' Legs."

13. "Frogs' Legs Export Ban," *Oryx* 21, no. 4 (1987):251.

14. "India Bans Export of Frogs' Legs," *Traffic Bulletin* 9, no. 1 (1987):1.

15. Republic of Suriname, "Inclusion of All Members of the Genus *Dendrobates* in Appendix II," presented to the 6th Meeting of Conference of the Parties, Ottawa, Canada, July 12-24, 1987, Doc. 6.46, no. 47.

16. Gaski, personal communication.

17. Tim Inskipp and Sue Wells, *International Trade in Wildlife* (London: International Institute for Environment and Development, 1979).

18. Jorgenson, "Biologists Express Concern for Huge Trade in Bullfrogs."

19. David Helton, "Aids Sets Off Biological Treasure Hunt," *BBC Wildlife* 5, no. 11 (1987):612-13.

20. TRAFFIC(U.S.A.), "1985 Amphibian Imports to U.S.," unpublished.

21. "Recent Trends in U.S. Skin Imports," *TRAFFIC(U.S.A.)* 5, no. 2 (1983):6.

27. Spiders

1. Ginette Hemley, "Spotlight on the Red-Kneed Tarantula Trade," *TRAFFIC(U.S.A.)* 6, no. 4 (1986):16-17.

2. Ibid.; Susan M. Wells, Robert M. Pyle, and N. Mark Collins, *The IUCN Invertebrate Red Data Book* (Gland, Switzerland: International Union for Conservation of Nature and Natural Resources, 1983).

3. Wells, Pyle, and Collins, *The IUCN Invertebrate Red Data Book*; Hemley, "Spotlight on the Red-Kneed Tarantula Trade."

28. Live Plants

1. Tim Inskipp and Sue Wells, *International Trade in Wildlife* (London: International Institute for Environment and Development, 1979).

2. "U.S. Customs Data on Orchids," *TRAFFIC(U.S.A.)* 6, no. 4 (1986):3.
3. World Wildlife Fund, "As Trade Blooms, Wild Species Are at Risk," press release, Washington, D.C., March 3, 1988.
4. "U.S. Customs Data on Orchids."
5. Faith Campbell, personal communication with author, June 8, 1988.
6. B. Ballard, personal communication with author, June 8, 1988.
7. Mariella Pizzetti, *The Macdonald Encyclopedia of Cacti* (London: Macdonald & Co., Ltd., 1985).
8. Douglas Fuller, "U.S. Cactus and Succulent Business Moves toward Propogation," *TRAFFIC(U.S.A.)* 6, no. 2 (1985):1.
9. Campbell, personal communication.
10. Tom Milliken, Kazuko Yokoi, and Shinobu Matsumura, "The Japanese Trade in Cacti," in Douglas Fuller and Sarah Fitzgerald, eds., *Conservation and Commerce of Cacti and Other Succulents* (Washington, D.C.: World Wildlife Fund, 1987), pp. 66-125; Douglas Fuller, "The U.S. Cactus Business, 1987," in Fuller and Fitzgerald, eds., *Conservation and Commerce of Cacti and Other Succulents*, pp. 185-225; B. Monroe, "Oregonian Rewarded for Help in Stopped Trade in Rare Cacti," *The Oregonian*, February 8, 1987.
11. Milliken, Yokoi, and Matsumara, "The Japanese Trade in Cacti."
12. Kathryn Fuller and Byron Swift, *Latin American Wildlife Trade Laws*, rev. ed. (Washington, D.C.: World Wildlife Fund, 1985).
13. Alfonso Delgado, personal communication with Mario Ramos, World Wildlife Fund, July 1, 1988.
14. Katharine McCarthy, "International Trade in Succulent Plants: An Analysis of U.S. Fish and Wildlife Service Data," in Fuller and Fitzgerald, *Conservation and Commerce of Cacti and Other Succulents*, pp. 126-84.
15. "Netherlands Seizes Cacti," *Traffic Bulletin* 8, no. 1 (1986):6.
16. TRAFFIC(Japan), "TRAFFIC(Japan) Uncovers Vast Illegal Trade in CITES-Protected Cactus Species," press release, April 19, 1986.
17. R. Reinhold, "For Rustlers, Cactus is the Big Cash Crop," *New York Times*, August 30, 1987, p. 4.
18. International Union for Conservation of Nature and Natural Resources, Threatened Plant Unit.
19. McCarthy, "International Trade in Succulent Plants."
20. Faith Campbell, "Mexican Cacti Exports Decline," *TRAFFIC(U.S.A.)* 6, no. 4 (1986):12-13.
21. Edward F. Anderson, letter to Philip Espinosa, assistant United States attorney, U.S. Department of Justice, July 22, 1986.
22. Reinhold, "For Rustlers, Cactus is the Big Cash Crop."
23. Campbell, personal communication.
24. TRAFFIC(U.S.A.), "World Trade in Wildlife Factsheet," World Wildlife Fund, Washington, D.C., 1986.
25. TRAFFIC(U.S.A.), "U.S. Imports of Wildlife Factsheet," World Wildlife Fund, Washington, D.C., 1986.
26. Fuller, "U.S. Cactus and Succulent Business Moves toward Propogation"; Niall McCarten, "Commercial Trade in Plants since 1980," *TRAFFIC(U.S.A.)* 6, no. 2 (1985):12; TRAFFIC(U.S.A.), "U.S. Imports of Wildlife Factsheet."
27. Milliken, Yokoi, and Matsumara, "The Japanese Trade in Cacti."
28. TRAFFIC(Japan), press release.

29. Sara Oldfield, "The Western Trade in Cacti and Other Succulents," in Fuller and Fitzgerald, *Conservation and Commerce of Cacti and Other Succulents,* pp. 32-65.
30. Douglas Fuller, personal communication.
31. Fuller, "U.S. Cactus and Succulent Business Moves toward Propogation."
32. "USA Seizes Rare Cacti," *Traffic Bulletin* 8, no. 2 (1986):32.
33. Faith T. Campbell, memo to Endangered Species Act contacts, November 13, 1986.
34. Shinobu Matsumara, "Endangered Cacti Popular in Japan," *Traffic Bulletin* 6, no. 5 (1985):83.
35. Milliken, Yokoi, and Matsumara, "The Japanese Trade in Cacti."
36. Faith T. Campbell, memo to International Union for Conservation of Nature and Natural Resources Plant Working Group, June 12, 1986.
37. Ibid.
38. Milliken, Yokoi, and Matsumara, "The Japanese Trade in Cacti."
39. Campbell, memo of IUCN Plant Working Group.
40. Ballard, personal communication.
41. Oldfield, "The Western Trade in Cacti and Other Succulents."
42. Ibid.
43. Ballard, personal communication.
44. Thomas Gibson et al., *International Trade in Plants: Focus on U.S. Exports and Imports* (Washington, D.C.: World Wildlife Fund, 1981).
45. Ballard, personal communication.
46. Sarah Booth Conroy, "Gifts to the White House: From Daggers to Jellybeans," *Washington Post,* March 5, 1987, p. B3.
47. TRAFFIC(U.S.A.) estimate, based on U.S. customs data, 1986.
48. "U.S. Customs Data on Orchids," *TRAFFIC(U.S.A.)* 6, no. 2 (1986):15.
49. A. Atkinson, personal communication, June 7, 1988.
50. Marcus Chown, "Rare Plants Piled High and Sold Cheap," *New Scientist,* March 7, 1985, p. 10.
51. Anthony Huxley, *Green Inheritance: The World Wildlife Fund Book of Plants* (Garden City, N.Y.: Doubleday, 1985).
52. TRAFFIC(U.S.A.), "Flower Bulb Trade Factsheet," World Wildlife Fund, Washington, D.C., 1986.
53. Tom Milliken, personal communication.
54. "Michigan Orchid Case: First Plant Conviction under Lacey Act," *TRAFFIC(U.S.A.)* 6, no. 4 (1986):17.
55. "UK and USA Fine Plant Smugglers," *Traffic Bulletin* 8, no. 1 (1986).
56. "WWF-U.S. Funds *Cyclamen* Bulb Study," *TRAFFIC(U.S.A.)* 6, no. 2 (1985):27.
57. Huxley, *Green Inheritance.*
58. Joan Lee Faust, "An Insecure Future for Some Bulbs," *New York Times,* July 19, 1987, p. 45.
59. Ibid.
60. Minouk van der Plas-Haarsma, *Cyclamen in Trade* (Zeist, The Netherlands: TRAFFIC[Netherlands], 1987).
61. Thompson, *in litt.*
62. Chown, "Rare Plants Piled High and Sold Cheap."
63. Van der Plas-Haarsma, *Cyclamen in Trade.*
64. "WWF-U.S. Funds *Cyclamen* Bulb Study."
65. Van der Plas-Haarsma, *Cyclamen in Trade.*

References   433

66. Ibid.
67. Pier-Lorenzo Florio, personal communication.
68. Sheryl Gilbert, *Cycads: Status, Trade, Exploitation, and Protection, 1977-1982* (Washington, D.C.: World Wildlife Fund, 1984).
69. "U.S. Proposal to List *Ceratozamia* spp. on Appendix I," 5th meeting of the Conference of the Parties, Buenos Aires, Argentina, April 22-May 3, 1985.
70. Sara Oldfield, "More Protection for Cycads?" *Oryx* 19, no. 3 (1985):132.
71. Gilbert, *Cycads*.
72. "Cycad Crimes Climb," *TRAFFIC(U.S.A.)*, 7, nos. 2-3 (1987):32.
73. Gilbert, *Cycads*.
74. *Encephalartos*, March 1986, cited in "Cycad Crimes Climb."
75. Oldfield, "More Protection for Cycads?"
76. Campbell, personal communication.
77. E. LaVerne Smith, "The Green Pitcher Plant," in Roger L. DiSilvestro, ed., National Audubon Society, *Audubon Wildlife Report 1985* (New York: National Audubon Society, 1985), pp. 533-39.
78. Gibson et al., *International Trade in Plants*; Sara Oldfield, "Disappearing Pitcher Plants," *Oryx* 19, no. 2 (1985):71-72.
79. Robert Sutter, "Venus Flytrap Threatened Primarily by Habitat Loss," *TRAFFIC(U.S.A.)* 6, no. 2 (1985):13.
80. Ibid.
81. Adrian Slack, *Carnivorous Plants* (Cambridge, Mass.: MIT Press, 1980); Oldfield, "Disappearing Pitcher Plants."
82. Oldfield, "Disappearing Pitcher Plants"; Gibson et al., *International Trade in Plants*.
83. Robert Singer, personal communication.
84. Douglas Fuller, "American Ginseng: Harvest and Export, 1982-1984," *TRAFFIC(U.S.A.)* 7, no. 1 (1986):3.
85. *Endangered Species Technical Bulletin Reprint* 4, nos. 2&3 (December 1986/January 1987).
86. *USA* v. *Hershey's Hides & Furs, Inc.*, sentence and sentencing memorandum, U.S. District Court, Middle District of Pennsylvania, May 4, 1987.

Figures

28.1. Douglas Fuller and Sarah Fitzgerald, eds., *Conservation and Commerce of Cacti and Other Succulents* (Washington, D.C.: World Wildlife Fund, 1987), pp. 167-70; U.S. CITES annual reports.
28.2. Japanese CITES annual reports, cited in Fuller and Fitzgerald, *Conservation and Commerce of Cacti and Other Succulents*, p. 98.
28.3. Linda R. McMahan and Kerry S. Walker, "The International Orchid Trade," in William J. Chandler, ed., *Audubon Wildlife Report 1988/1989* (San Diego: Academic Press, 1988), pp. 376-92.
28.4. Ibid.

29. Tropical Timber

1. WWF International, *WWF Position Paper on Forest Conservation and the International Tropical Timber Agreement* (Gland, Switzerland: WWF International, 1987).
2. Sara Oldfield, *Report of a Feasibility Study for a Conservation Database on the Tropical Timber Trade*, (Cambridge: International Union for Conservation

of Nature and Natural Resources Conservation Monitoring Centre, 1987).

3. Robert Buschbacher, personal communication.

4. Robert Buschbacher, "Ecological Analysis of Natural Forest Management in the Humid Tropics," paper presented at The Application of Ecology to Enhancing Economic Development in the Humid Tropics symposium, sponsored by the Ecological Society of America, August 12, 1987.

5. Oldfield, *Report of a Feasibility Study for a Conservation Database on the Tropical Timber Trade.*

6. J. P. Lanly, *Tropical Forest Resources,* Food and Agriculture Organization Forestry Paper no. 30 (Rome: U.N. Food and Agriculture Organization, 1982).

7. Harold Sioli, "Recent Human Activities in the Brazilian Amazon Region and Their Ecological Effects," in Betty J. Meggers, E. S. Ayensu, and W. D. Duckworth, eds., *Tropical Forest Ecosystems in Africa and South America: A Comparative Review* (Washington, D.C.: Smithsonian Institution Press, 1973), pp. 321-34.

8. P. M. Fearnside and J. M. Rankin, "Jari Revisited: Changes and the Outlook for Sustainability in Amazonia's Largest Silviculture Estate," *Intercienia* 10, no. 3 (1985):121-29.

9. Oldfield, *Report of a Feasibility Study for a Conservation Database on the Tropical Timber Trade;* including citation from R. C. Schmidt, "Current Programmes of Tropical Rain Forest Management," paper for International Workshop on Rain Forest Regeneration and Management, Guri, Venezuela, November 24-28, 1986.

10. François Nectoux and Nigel Dudley, *A Hard Wood Story: An Investigation into the European Influence on Tropical Forest Loss* (London: Friends of the Earth, 1987).

11. François Nectoux, *Timber! An Investigation of the UK Tropical Timber Industry* (London: Friends of the Earth, 1985).

12. WWF International, *WWF Position Paper on Forest Conservation and the International Tropical Timber Agreement.*

13. Ibid.

14. Ibid.

15. Ibid.

16. Ibid.

17. Buschbacher, personal communication.

18. François Nectoux and Yoichi Kuroda, *Timber from the South Seas: An Analysis of Japan's Tropical Timber Trade and Its Environmental Impact* (Gland, Switzerland: WWF International, 1989).

19. Ibid.

20. Oldfield, *Report of a Feasibility Study for a Conservation Database on the Tropical Timber Trade.*

21. Food and Agriculture Organization, *Data Book on Endangered Tree and Shrub Species and Provenances* (Rome: U.N. Food and Agriculture Organization, 1986).

22. Sabina G. Knees and Martin F. Gardner, "Mahoganies: Candidates for the Red Data Book" *Oryx* 17, no. 2 (1983):88-92.

23. Oldfield, *Report of a Feasibility Study for a Conservation Database on the Tropical Timber Trade.*

24. Ibid.

References   435

25. Chris Rose, "Timber Organization Lays New Groundwork," *WWF News*, no. 46 (1987):8.
26. Ibid.; WWF International, *WWF Position Paper on Forest Conservation and the International Tropical Timber Agreement.*
27. Buschbacher, "Ecological Analysis of Natural Forest Management in the Humid Tropics."

Figures

29.1. François Nectoux and Nigel Dudley, *A Hard Wood Story: An Investigation into the European Influence on Tropical Forest Loss* (London: Friends of the Earth, 1987), p. 113.
29.2. Ibid.
29.3. Ibid, p. 114.

Conclusion

1. Michael J. Bean, "Reflections on the Tenth Anniversary of CITES," *Focus* 5, no. 5 (1983):2.
2. David Mack, personal communication.
3. "Biggest Ivory Seizures . . . outside Africa," *Traffic Bulletin* 8, no. 2 (1986):23.
4. "USA Seizes Rare Cacti," *Traffic Bulletin* 8, no. 2 (1986):32.

Appendix A. How CITES Works

1. Lee Durrell, *State of the Ark: An Atlas of Conservation in Action* (Garden City, N.Y.: Doubleday, 1986).
2. Michael J. Bean, *The Evolution of National Wildlife Law*, rev. ed. (New York: Praeger Publishers, 1983).
3. James C. Kilbourne, personal communication.
4. J. Barzdo, T. Goodwin, and R. Luxmoore, "The Implementation of CITES as Demonstrated by the Trade Statistics in the Annual Reports of 1984 and 1985 Submitted by the Parties," prepared for the Wildlife Trade Monitoring Unit, *Proceedings of the Sixth Meeting of the Conference of the Parties*, Ottawa, Canada, July 12-24, 1987 (Lausanne, Switzerland: CITES Secretariat, 1989), Doc. 6.17.
5. Manfred Niekisch, personal communication.
6. Barzdo, Goodwin, and Luxmoore, "The Implementation of CITES."
7. Ginette Hemley, personal communication.
8. "Financing and Budgeting of the Secretariat and of Meetings of the Conferences of the Parties," *Proceedings of the Sixth Meeting of the Conference of the Parties*, Doc. 6.11.
9. "Budgeting of the Secretariat," *Proceedings of the Fifth Meeting of the Conference of the Parties* (Lausanne, Switzerland: CITES Secretariat, 1986), Doc. 5.10.
10. Ginette Hemley, "International Wildlife Trade," in William J. Chandler, ed., *Audubon Wildlife Report 1988/1989* (San Diego: Academic Press, 1988), pp. 337-74.
11. Simon Lyster, "EEC Regulations on CITES Implementation," *Traffic Bulletin* 4, no. 6 (1983):69-70.
12. Jonathan Barzdo, personal communication.
13. Simon Lyster, *International Wildlife Law* (Cambridge: Grotius Publications, 1985).

14. Ibid.
15. World Wildlife Fund, "The EEC Annual CITES Report for 1984: A Preliminary Assessment of the Implementation of CITES in the European Economic Community," Washington, D.C., June 1986.
16. Lyster, *International Wildlife Law*.
17. Ibid.
18. Laura H. Kosloff and Mark C. Trexler, "The Convention on International Trade in Endangered Species: No Carrot, But Where's the Stick?" *Environmental Law Reporter* 17 (July 1987):10222-26.
19. Jonathan Barzdo, John Caldwell, and Richard Luxmoore, "CITES Conference in Canada," *Traffic Bulletin* 9, nos. 2&3 (1987):34-43.
20. Kosloff and Trexler, "The Convention on International Trade in Endangered Species."
21. Ibid.
22. Lyster, "EEC Regulations on CITES Implementation," *Traffic Bulletin* 4, no. 6 (1983):69-70.

INDEX

Italicized page numbers refer to figures.

A

Action. *See* Citizen action; Public opinion
Afghanistan
  CITES membership by, 337
  musk deer habitat in, 85
Africa
  cheetah population in, 40
  ivory smuggling from countries in, *65,* 66-71
  leopard population in, 43-45
  parrot trade in, 159, 160, 166
  primate trade in, 95
  python trade in, 217
  rhino trade in, 109-11
  songbird trade in, 175, 177
  See also individual countries in
African Elephant and Rhino Specialist Group (IUCN), 75
African Elephant Conservation Act, U.S. (1988), 74
Agriculture
  Chinese attempt to raise musk deer by using, 85
  conflict with leopards and, 43-44
Alaska
  bear hunting in, 32, 34, 35
  sea otter population near, 123
Algeria, 337
Alligators, 193-94
  See also Caimans; Crocodiles
American Association of Zoological Parks and Aquariums (AAZPA), 101
American ginseng, 300-2
Amstrup, Steve, 29
Anderson, Edward, 283
Andrews, Josephine, 212
Angola
  ivory trade in, 66
  rhino trade in, 109

439

Bharat Leather Corporation (BLC), India, 211-12
Bhutan, musk deer habitat in, 85
Birkinshaw, Chris, 212
Boas, 213-15
Bobcats, 54-55
Bolivia
    caiman poaching in, 195
    CITES membership by, 337
    primate trade in, 91-98
    small cat trade in, 53
    vicuña trade in, 115
Botswana, 337
Brack, Steven, 286
Brazaitis, Peter, 199-200
Brazil
    caiman trade in, 196
    CITES membership by, 337
    export bans on primates in, 91
    parrot trade in, 158, 164
    rhea trade in, 182
    small cat trade in, 52, 53, 54
    whaling by, 143
    wildlife protection laws in, 52, 53
Breeding, captive
    cactus plants, 280-81
    crocodiles, 190
    ostriches, 181
    parrots, 161
    primates, 93, 96, 97, 102-4
    raptors traded for, 172-73
    sea turtles, 233-35
    songbirds, 175, 176
    tarantulas, 274-75
    tomato frogs, 271
    See also Farming; Ranching
Bulb plants, 292-97
Burma
    big cats in, 38, 39
    musk deer habitat in, 85
    tiger trade in, 39
Burundi
    CITES membership by, 337
    ivory trade in, 67, 70
    primate trade in, 99
Buschbacher, Robert, 304, 311
Bush, George, 74
Butterflies, 243-48
    trade in live, 248-49

C

Cacti, 279-88
    See also Succulents
Caimans, Latin American, 195-202
Caldwell, John, 71
Cambodia. See Kampuchea
Campbell, Faith, 284, 287, 288

D

Deforestation
  habitat loss to, 121
  little spotted cat population and, 53
  timber extraction-caused, 303, 305, 309
Denmark
  CITES membership by, 337
  polar bear take and trade in, 30, 31
  primate trade in, 92
  raptor breeding in, 173
Department of Agriculture, U.S. (USDA), 159
Dodd, Kenneth, 209, 219, 237
Dominican Republic, 337
Douglas-Hamilton, Iain, 75
Durban Botanical Gardens, 298, 299
Drugs
  primates used in developing polio vaccine, 96
  rhino parts used as, 105-6
  See also Health
Dubai
  ivory carving in, 72
  See also United Arab Emirates

E

East Germany. *See* German Democratic Republic
Economics
  of bird trade, 179, 181-82
  of butterfly collecting, 243, 244, 246, 248
  of cactus trade, 287, 289
  of crocodilian species trade, 188, 194, 196, 200
  of elephant skin trade, 74-75
  of illegal rhino trade, 106, 111, 112
  of illegal trade in bears, 31, 33, 34, 35
  of illegal trade in large cats, 38, 39, 41, 42, 43
  of illegal trade in otters, 122-23, 124, 126
  of illegal trade in primates, 92
  on Japan of U.S. whaling sanctions, 142
  of live plant trade, 298-99, 302
  of lizard and snake trade, 203, 205, 206, 208, 209, 210, 214, 221
  of ornamental fish, 259, 262
  of parrot trade, 159-60, 162, 163-65
  of raptor trade, 171, 174
  of seal trade, 133, 134
  of songbird breeding, 176
  of tarantula collecting, 274
  of tortoise trade, 236, 237
  of trade in musk, 85, 86-87
  of traffic in ivory, 62-69, 71, 73-74
  of traffic in small cats, 51-52, 53, 54, 56, 57
  of tropical timber trade, 303, 306, 308, 311
  of whale meat smuggling, 144-45
Ecuador
  CITES membership by, 337
  hummingbird trade in, 181
Egypt, 337
Elephants, 61-77

El Salvador, 337
Endangered Species Act, U.S. (ESA), 49, 51, 91, 109, 147, 219, 240, 280, 299
  crocodilian controls under, 192-93
  ivory imports and, 73
  parrot smuggling and, 161
England. *See* United Kingdom
Environmental Defense Fund, 315
Equador, sea turtle trade in, 229
Equatorial Guinea, primate trade in, 102
Ethiopia, primate trade in, 93, 95
Eudey, Ardith, 97
Eurasian lynx, 57-58
Eurasian otter, 125
Europe
  bear trade in, 31, 40
  cat trade in, 37, 47, 50-51, 52
  hummingbird trade in, 181
  ivory trade in, 65
  macropod trade to, 82, 83, 84
  otter trade in, 126
  parrot trade in, 164
  raptor trade in, 170
  songbird trade in, 177
  See also individual countries in
European Economic Community (EEC)
  butterfly regulation by, 245
  macropod trade ban by, 82
  primates used by research, 91
  parrot trade in, 159, 160
  seal trade in, 130-34
  small cat trade in, 49, 54
  tortoise ban by, 236
  See also individual countries in
Exotic Newcastle disease, 159

F

Farming, crocodiles, 190-91
Falcons, in international trade, 171-72
Far East
  bear paws as delicacies in, 33
  center for precious coral processing in, 253-54
  ivory market in, 70
  macropod meat exports to, 84
  market for Asiatic black bear gall bladders in, 32, 33
  seal trade in, 133, 134
  See also individual countries in
Feathers, trade in wild bird, 182-83
Federal Republic of Germany (FRG)
  bird trade in, 173, 180, 181
  caiman trade in, 195-96
  captive breeding programs in, 103, 170, 173
  CITES membership by, 338
  marsupial trade in, 82
  otter trade in, 124, 125
  primate trade in, 92, 103
  raptor trade in, 171, 173
  small cat trade in, 49-50, 52, 53, 54, 56, 58

Finland
  CITES membership by, 338
  primate trade in, 92
Fish, ornamental, 259-65
Fish and Wildlife Service, U.S. (FWS), 29, 55
  cactus trade enforcement by, 287
  data on U.S. bobcat population, 54
  ivory quota system and, 74
  scientific authority, 54
  wildlife smuggling operations stopped by, 32, 216, 287
Florio, Pier-Lorenzo, 43
Food, wildlife hunted for human, 89
Food and Drug Administration, U.S. (FDA), 239
France
  alligator trade in, 194, 195
  caiman trade in, 196
  CITES membership by, 338
  marsupial trade in, 82
  musk used in expensive perfumes made by, 87
  polio vaccine from primates used in, 96
  primate trade in, 95
  small cat trade in, 49, 50, 52, 53, 54
French Guiana
  hummingbird trade in, 181
  wild bird feather trade in, 183
Freshwater turtles, 237-39
Frogs
  hides and skins in fashion trade, 271
  trade in legs of, 267
Fuller, Douglas, 287, 302

G

Gabon, 338
Gambia, 338
Geoffroy's cats, 53
German Democratic Republic (GDR)
  cat trade in, 58
  CITES membership by, 338
Ghana, 338
Giant otters, 123-24
Goodall, Jane, 98-99
Gorillas, 100-2
Green, Michael, 85, 87
Greenpeace, 135, 149
Guatemala, 338
Guinea
  CITES membership by, 338
  primate trade in, 99
Guyana
  CITES membership by, 338
  primate trade in, 95

H

Habitat
  fragmentation and wildlife population pressures, 33, 38, 42, 43-44, 53, 121, 183, 203
  loss for bears, 29, 33

loss for big cats, 38-39, 40, 41, 43-44, 45
loss for hummingbirds, 180
loss for lizards and snakes, 209
loss for musk deer population, 85
loss for parrots, 157, 162, 165
loss for primates, 89, 94
loss for raptors, 170
Hazardous waste. *See* Pollution
Health
care given primates, 93-94
concerns from pet turtles, 238-39
frogs legs and, 267-68
Hemley, Ginette, 49, 201, 260
Honduras, 338
Hong Kong
caiman trade in, 196
ivory carving in, 72
ivory trade in, 65, 67, 70, 76, 77
marsupial trade in, 84
musk deer trade in, 86
small cat trade in, 51
tiger trade in, 39
Hooker, Joseph, 290
Hummingbirds, 180-81
Hungary, 338
Hunting
legal "sport," 44, 121
monitor populations of wildlife and adjust regulations accordingly, 36
patterns for whales, 146-47
wildlife decline due to, 29, 31, 38, 41, 42, 44, 45, 53, 85, 90, 121, 122-24, 125, 132-38,
165, 183, 187-89, 193, 203
Huxley, Anthony, 290

I

Iceland, whaling by, 140, 143
Iguanas, 208-9
Immuno, Ag, 99
India
bear gall bladder trade in, 33
CITES membership by, 338
export bans on wildlife by, 91, 177
ivory carving in, 72
ivory trade in, 76
musk deer habitat in, 85
snake skin export controls in, 210, 211-12
tiger conservation in, 38, 39
Indonesia
CITES membership by, 338
crocodile trade in, 192
parrot trade in, 158-59, 162
primate trade in, 95
sea turtle trade in, 229
wild bird feather in, 183
International Convention for the Regulation of Whaling
lack of enforcement ability by, 139
native whaling allowed under, 150-51

Monitor lizards, 207-8
Morocco, 338
Morris, Michael, 243
Mozambique
  CITES membership by, 338
  rhino trade in, 109
Musk, trade uses for, 85, 86, 87
Musk deer, 85-88

N

Namibia, cheetah trade in, 40
National Institutes of Health (NIH), National Primate Plan of, 104
Natural Resources Defense Council (NRDC), 284, 287, 293
Nepal
  bear gall bladder trade in, 33
  CITES membership by, 338
  musk deer habitat in, 85
  tiger conservation in, 38, 39
Netherlands
  bird trade in, 180
  CITES membership by, 338
  primate trade in, 95
Nicaragua, 338
Niekisch, Manfred, 56, 267
Niger, 338
Nigeria
  CITES membership by, 338
  primate trade in, 93
North America
  small cats hunted and traded in, 47, 51, 54-56
  See also individual countries in
North American river otter, 125-26
North Yemen, rhino trade in, 111
Norway
  CITES membership by, 338
  polar bear take and trade in, 30
  seal trade in, 132, 133
  whaling by, 139, 143, 147

O

Ocelots, 51-53
Oldfield, Sara, 286, 287, 289, 296, 305
Operation Falcon, 173-74
Orchids, trade, enforcement, and economics concerning, 289-92
Ostriches, 181-82
Otters, 121-26

P

Packwood-Magnuson Amendment
  See U.S. Fishery Conservation and Management Act, Packwood-Magnuson
    Amendment to
Pakistan
  CITES membership by, 338
  musk deer habitat in, 85
Pallas's cat, 58
Pampas Galeras National Vicuña Reserve, 116

Index   451

S

St. Lucia, 338
St. Vincent and Grenadines, 338
Salm, Rodney, 230
Santa Cruz Predatory Bird Research Group, raptor breeding aid by, 172-73
Saudi Arabia, raptor breeding and trade in, 170, 173
Sea snakes, 217-18
Sea turtles, 225-26
Seals, 127-35
Sea otters, 122-23
Senegal
  bird exports by, 180
  CITES membership by, 338
  songbird trade in, 175, 177
Seychelles, 338
Sierra Leone, primate trade in, 99
Singapore
  CITES exemption on crocodiles by, 190
  CITES membership by, 338
  illegal wildlife trade conducted through, 39, 67, 68, 192
Snakes, 209-19
  See also invidual species of
Snow leopards, 41-42
Somalia
  CITES membership by, 338
  ivory trade in, 66
  primate trade in, 93, 95
  rhino trade in, 109
Songbirds, 175-77
South Africa
  CITES membership by, 339
  cheetah trade in, 40
  crocodile farms in, 190
  elephant management plan in, 75-76
  ivory trade in, 69, 74
  seal trade in, 133
South America
  habitat and wildlife population loss in, 29
  rheas trade in, 182
  See also Latin America; individual countries in
South American river otter, 125
South Korea
  demand for black bear gall bladders in, 32, 33
  whaling by, 140
Southern river otter, 124
Soviet Union. See Union of Soviet Socialist Republics
Spain
  CITES membership by, 339
  caiman trade in, 196
  primate trade in, 99, 102
  small cat trade in, 52
  whaling by, 143, 150
Spiders, 273-75
Sri Lanka, 339
Succulents
  trade in, 288-89
  See also Cacti

Wildlife Trade Monitoring Unit (WTMU), 293, 315, 316
Wood, Elizabeth, 262, 264
World Health Organization (WHO)—UN, primate research by, 103
World Wildlife Fund (WWF), 89, 304, 311, 316
    ivory trade data by, 74
    Operation Tiger involvement by, 38-39
    rhino medicinal study by, 106
    substainable tegu lizard harvest in Argentina aided by, 206
    vicuña population count by, 116
    wild collected bulb plants and, 293-94
    See also TRAFFIC(USA)

Z

Zaire
    CITES membership by, 339
    ivory trade in, 66, 69, 74
    leopard extinction in, 44
    primate trade in, 99
Zambia
    CITES membership by, 339
    ivory trade in, 66, 69
    primate trade in, 99
Zimbabwe
    CITES membership by, 339
    crocodile ranching in, 191
    elephant management plans in, 75-76
    ivory trade in, 69, 74
Zoos
    cetaceans traded to, 152-53
    primates obtained by, 92, 101

A lready worth at least $5 billion a year, international wildlife trade is growing rapidly. Properly managed, this trade can bring significant economic benefits to developing nations in desperate need of income from tourism, manufacturing, and exporting. Inadequately controlled, however, it can mean both economic and environmental devastation, not just in developing nations but in industrial countries as well.

In **International Wildlife Trade: Whose Business Is It?** author Sarah Fitzgerald carefully explores the many issues surrounding international trade in wildlife and wildlife products. In a straightforward, nontechnical style, she explains international and national laws governing this trade, problems with poaching and smuggling of endangered species of animals and plants, environmental and economic consequences of inadequate control of the trade, and innovative ventures to develop methods that manage the trade in ways that enhance the environment and help ensure individual species' long-term survival.

Sarah Fitzgerald is a consultant to World Wildlife Fund on public-policy issues. She served formerly as WWF's director of planning and evaluation. She is co-editor of *Conservation and Commerce of Cacti and Other Succulents,* also published by WWF.

WWF
World Wildlife Fund

ISBN 0-942635-10-8